Roots and Branches
THE STORY OF THE SISAM FAMILY

Roots and Branches
THE STORY OF THE SISAM FAMILY

PETER J. SISAM

Copyright © P.J. Sisam

ISBN 0-9521865-0-0

Published by Peter J. Sisam 1993
Marlow, Buckinghamshire.

British Library Cataloguing-in-Publication Data.
A catalogue record for this book is available from the British Library.

Produced by Alan Sutton Publishing,
Stroud, Gloucestershire.

Contents

	LIST OF ILLUSTRATIONS	vii
	PREFACE	xiii
1:	ORIGINS The Surname and 17th Century Ancestors	1
2:	VILLAGE YEOMEN Little Comberton, Hill, and Bidford-on-Avon 1743–1819	9
3:	FARMERS & MILLERS Arrow, Harvington, and Walton – The Bigamist	21
4:	THE ARROW FAMILY Henry the Miller and his Six Sons	36
5:	SEEDTIME & HARVEST Founders of the Canadian Branch 1875–1990	45
6:	TRIAL & TRIBULATION Transportation to Australia – Mormon Missionaries	56
7:	WAGONS WESTWARD Emigration to America 1866 and 1868	67
8:	A BRANCH DIVIDED Salt Lake City and Plural Marriage	78
9:	AT THE HOMESTEAD Joseph Henry the Utah Farmer	87
10:	AUTOMOBILES & ELECTRICITY The Utah Sons and their Descendants	93
11:	THE WESTERNERS The Idaho Sisiam Family	106
12:	TO THE ANTIPODES Emigration to New Zealand 1862 and the Maori War	113
13:	ALARMS & EXCURSIONS Armed Constabulary and Two Marriages	124
14:	THE WAITAKERE Walter's Farm in the Bush	135
15:	FOUNDING FAMILIES Opotiki and Whakatane – Waitakere Weddings	145

16:	TWO VALLEY FARMS Alfred Acquires Farmland – Death of Walter	157
17:	ACROSS THE RIVER Farm Expansion – 'Sisam & Sons'	170
18:	FOREST RANGER Walter's Grandson and Heart's Content	180
19:	OXFORD Kenneth the Scholar – The Oxford University Press	186
20:	KING STREET & OWHAKATORO The Next Generation in the Bay of Plenty	199
21:	THE BROAD ACRES Steady Progress at the Farm – 'Pete' O.B.E.	214
22:	ARROW & AFTER James Leonard, Patriarch of Arrow Mill, and his Heir	226
23:	SONS & DAUGHTERS Warwickshire Farming Hazards and World War II	238
24:	FRESH FIELDS Banking in the Cotsworlds – Adventures in Film-Making	250
25:	THE LOST BRANCH The Story of Thomas Marshall Sisam and his Family	261
26:	PHOENIX ARISING Cleeve Prior, Birmingham, and the Future	268
	SOURCES AND NOTES	279
	GENEALOGICAL TABLES	285
	BIOGRAPHICAL NOTES Who is Who in the Sisam Family	298
	INDEX Places, etc. and People other than Sisams	331

List of Illustrations

page

page		
1	Bidford-on-Avon from the Bridge	*(Peter J. Sisam)*
3	Syresham Post Office	*(Peter J. Sisam)*
4	Sisam's Meadow	*(Peter J. Sisam)*
5	Winchcombe View	*(Peter J. Sisam)*
6	Will of a John Sisam (Greet)	*(Diocese of Gloucester)*
8	Map of 'Sisam Country'	*(John Beadle)*
9	Little Comberton	*(Peter J. Sisam)*
11	Farmhouse at Hill	*(Peter J. Sisam)*
12	Will of John Sisam (1779)	*(Hereford and Worcester County Record Office)*
15	Strip-farming Map, Hill	*(from map owned by E. Righton)*
17	Welford-on-Avon	*(Sisam family collection, UK)*
18	Bidford-on-Avon	*(Alcester & District Local History Society)*
19	Maltster's house at Bidford	*(Peter J. Sisam)*
22	Arrow Mill from meadows	*(Peter J. Sisam)*
	Arrow millstream	*(Peter J. Sisam)*
	Copper Urn	*(Drawing by John Beadle)*
23	Arrow Mill	*(Peter J. Sisam)*
24	Bidford Bridge	*(Peter J. Sisam)*
26	The Mill at Harvington	*(Drawing by D.W. Showell)*
	Harvington Mill House	*(Peter J. Sisam)*
28	Mount Pleasant, Walton	*(Peter J. Sisam)*
30	River Isbourne at Winchcombe	*(Peter J. Sisam)*
	Postlip Lower Mill today	*(Peter J. Sisam)*
33	Frederick Sisam Marriage Certificate	*(Controller of HMSO)*
	Glossop in Derbyshire	*(Glossop Heritage Committee)*
37	Alcester Corn Exchange	*(Alcester & District Local History Society)*
38	River Arrow waters	*(Peter J. Sisam)*
	Diagram of mill turbines	*(by James Leonard Sisam Jnr.)*
40	Flint-lock gun	*(Drawing by John Beadle)*
	Powder flasks taken to New Zealand	*(Peter J. Sisam)*
42	The New family of Langley	*(Sisam family collection, UK)*
46	Radclive, Buckinghamshire	*(Peter J. Sisam)*
48	Map of Southern Burma	*(John Beadle)*
50	New Brunswick landscape	*(Canadian High Commission, London)*
54	William Bernard Sisam	*(St. George's Church, Moncton, N.B.)*
	John William Bernard Sisam	*(Peter N. Sisam collection)*

page

54	Peter Neill Sisam	*(Peter J. Sisam)*
57	Broom, Warwickshire	*(Alcester & District Local History Society)*
58	Painting of ploughman at work	*(Sisam family collection, UK)*
60	Worcester Trial Reports	*(Berrow's Worcester Journal)*
62	The Unicorn Inn, Warwick	*(Drawing by John Beadle)*
64	Alcester Warren Farm	*(Peter J. Sisam)*
	Arrow valley near Sambourne	*(Peter J. Sisam)*
65	Covered wagon from Arrow Mill	*(Sisam family collection, UK)*
70	American covered wagon	*(Peter J. Sisam)*
73	Fort Laramie	*(Yale University Library)*
74	Map of Emigrants' Trail	*(John Beadle)*
79	Statue of Indian Chief Massasoit	*(Peter J. Sisam)*
81	Salt Lake Valley	*(Peter J. Sisam)*
	Catherine Sisam	*(Mary Bateman collection)*
83	Joseph Henry and Hannah Sisam	*(Ruth Moulton collection)*
86	'City of Rocks'	*(Peter J. Sisam)*
89	West Jordan Homestead	*(Peter J. Sisam)*
	Old Meeting House	*(Peter J. Sisam)*
95	Drawing of the 1910 Model T Ford	*(Ford Motor Company)*
	Mormon Temple, Salt Lake City	*(Peter J. Sisam)*
	U.S. Smelting Company	*(Peter J. Sisam)*
98	Laverne Greathouse	*(Peter J. Sisam)*
	A horse and buggy	*(Drawing by John Beadle)*
103	Wilford Martin Sisam	*(Violet Seal Collection)*
	Alma Neils Sisam	*(Ruth Moulton collection)*
	Ukulele made by Wilford	*(Peter J. Sisam)*
105	Lorne Richard Sisam	*(Peter J. Sisam)*
106	Sawtooth Mountains, Idaho	*(Peter J. Sisam)*
108	Borax mule-train, Idaho	*(Sisam family collection, Idaho)*
110	Richard and Ruby Sisiam	*(Peter J. Sisam)*
	Nelse Sisiam	*(Peter J. Sisam)*
111	Wilford Sisiam	*(Peter J. Sisam)*
	Roy Sisiam	*(Peter J. Sisam)*
113	The 'Matilda Wattenbach'	*(Drawing by John Beadle)*
115	Auckland in the 1860s	*(from an old print)*
117	Uncleared bush-land (background)	*(Peter J. Sisam)*
119	Map of Waikato area	*(Whakatane & District Historical Society)*
126	Opotiki Garrison at St Stephen's Church	*(Sisam family collection, NZ)*
128	Alfred John Sisam as a Trooper	*(Fowler family collection, NZ)*
129	Official Kit List of Alfred John Sisam	*(Fowler family collection, NZ)*
130	Whakatane River Gorge	*(Peter J. Sisam)*
	Te Kooti, Maori War Leader	*(Hocken Library, Otago University, NZ)*

List of illustrations

page

130	Map of Bay of Plenty area	*(John Beadle)*
134	Olivia Marie 'Tottie'	*(Yvonne Lonsdale collection)*
	Drawing of Despatch Rider	*(Sisam family collection, UK)*
136	Waitakere Ranges	*(Peter J. Sisam)*
	Waitakere River	*(Peter J. Sisam)*
137	The Waitakere Forest Trail	*(Peter J. Sisam)*
	Walter Sisam's Grocery Bill	*(Benjamin Copedo collection)*
138	Caroline Sisam of Alcester	*(Sisam family collection, UK)*
142	Walter Henry Sisam's Diary page	*(Benjamin Copedo collection)*
	Washing Day, Waitakere	*(Benjamin Copedo collection)*
143	Walter Sisam and family by farmhouse	*(Benjamin Copedo collection)*
146	Opotiki Street Directory of 1880s	*(Opotiki County Council)*
148	Children of Alfred John and Maria Sisam	*(Joan Stewart collection)*
150	Whakatane Waterfront	*(Joan Stewart collection)*
	Alfred John Sisam	*(Sisam family collection, NZ)*
	Maria Sisam	*(Sisam family collection, NZ)*
152	Maria Sisam's Diary pages	*(Joan Stewart collection)*
153	Caroline Sisam, 'Carrie'	*(Benjamin Copedo collection)*
154	'Allie' and W.P. Browne's house	*(Peter J. Sisam)*
156	Walter and Nellie Sisam	*(Benjamin Copedo collection)*
158	John A.C. Lamont, 'Jack'	*(Yvonne Lonsdale collection)*
	Whakatane Cemetery	*(Peter J. Sisam)*
160	The Opouriao Valley	*(Peter J. Sallis)*
	Map of Opouriao Estate	*(Whakatane Historical Society)*
	Detailed map, Opouriao plots	*(Whakatane Historical Society)*
164	Whakatane Harbour	*(Joan Stewart collection)*
	Caroline Marshall Sisam, 'Lena'	*(Yvonne Lonsdale collection)*
165	Arrow Farm, Waitakere	*(Benajamin Copedo collection)*
166	Walter's new farmhouse	*(Benjamin Copedo collection)*
171	Commemorative plaque in Whakatane	*(Peter J. Sisam)*
172	Agricultural Show	*(Hazel Sisam collection)*
176	Clydesdale Horses at work	*(Celia Sisam collection)*
177	Alfred John Sisam in later years	*(Yvonne Lonsdale collection)*
179	Inscription on A.J.'s grave	*(Peter J. Sisam)*
	Alfred John Sisam's grave	*(Peter J. Sisam)*
182	Walter Leonard Sisam, Forest Ranger	*(Benjamin Copedo collection)*
	Walter L. Sisam with Sir Bernard Ferguson	*(Benjamin Copedo collection)*
184	Walter Leonard Sisam, 1985	*(Peter J. Sisam)*
187	Kenneth Sisam, Auckland graduate	*(Wynne Eccles collection)*
	View of Merton College, Oxford	*(Peter J. Sisam)*
189	Naomi Gibbons	*(Joan Stewart collection)*
192	The Clarendon Press building	*(Peter J. Sisam)*
195.	'Middle Carn', Isles of Scilly	*(Peter J. Sisam)*
	Kenneth Sisam in retirement	*(Celia Sisam collection)*
197	Hugh Sisam	*(Peter J. Sisam collection)*

page

197	Celia Sisam	*(Peter J. Sisam)*
201	Owhakatoro Farm entrance	*(Peter J. Sisam)*
202	Owhakatoro farmhouse	*(from a painting by Noeline Sisam)*
203	Walter Holtom Sisam	*(Joan Stewart collection)*
	Rose Stansfield Sisam	*(Joan Stewart collection)*
207	The Sisam home on King Street	*(The Whakatane Beacon)*
	'Sisam Place' road sign	*(Peter J. Sisam)*
208	Leonard Wilfred Sisam and his family	*(Wynne Eccles collection)*
210	Eileen and 'Buster' McCracken	*(Peter J. Sisam)*
212	Dulcie Ingley	*(Peter J. Sisam)*
	Walter John and Noeline Sisam	*(Peter J. Sisam)*
	Isabel and 'Andy' Quick	*(Peter J. Sisam)*
	Joan Stewart	*(Peter J. Sisam)*
216	Allen Leonard Sisam	*(Peter J. Sisam)*
	Hazel Sisam	*(Peter J. Sisam)*
	Adele Sisam	*(Jill Mcleod collection)*
	Harold Walter Sisam, 'Mannie'	*(Peter J. Sisam)*
219	Allen and 'Mannie' on horseback	*(The New Zealand Herald)*
	Sisam Valley	*(Peter J. Sisam)*
221	Owhakatoro farmland	*(Peter J. Sisam)*
	Branded Arab cross-bred horses	*(Peter J. Sisam)*
	'Sisam & Sons' farm truck	*(Peter J. Sisam)*
222	Leonard Alfred Sisam, 'Pete'	*(Edna Sisam collection)*
224	Peter Sisam – son of 'Pete'	*(Peter J. Sisam)*
	The Reunion crowd	*(Glenys Quick)*
	Reunion Cake is cut	*(Glenys Quick)*
227	Arrow Mill across the water	*(Sisam family collection)*
	Mill grindstone	*(Peter J. Sisam)*
228	Oversley Mill	*(G. Edward Saville)*
230	James Leonard Sisam	*(Peter J. Sisam collection)*
	The Alcester school	*(Alcester & District Local History Society)*
232	The Arrow Parish Council	*(Gloria Hudson collection)*
233	Henry Leonard Sisam	*(Gloria Hudson collection)*
	Mary Westlake Rouse	*(Gloria Hudson collection)*
236	Radbrook Manor	*(Strutt & Parker, Salisbury)*
239	Jim and Elsie Sisam 1946	*(Gloria Hudson collection)*
242	Gloria Hudson	*(Peter J. Sisam)*
	Jim Sisam in later years	*(Peter J. Sisam)*
243	Frank Marshall Sisam	*(Peter J. Sisam collection)*
244	Kingley Farm	*('Molly' Bunting collection)*
246	'Molly' Bunting, Len and Marion Sisam	*(Peter J. Sisam)*
247	Dorothy Clarke	*(Peter J. Sisam)*
248	'Harry' Sisam	*('Molly' Bunting (collection)*
253	Walter Sisam of Moreton-in-Marsh	*(Peter J. Sisam collection)*

page

254	Chastleton House	*(Peter J. Sisam)*
259	Peter James Sisam	*(Peter J. Sisam collection)*
263	Winchcombe Mill	*(The Times)*
266	Peacock House	*(Peter J. Sisam)*
269	Orphanage Appeal card	*(Richard J. Sisam collection)*
	Royal Hotel Slough, later a school	*(Royal Borough of Windsor Collection)*
276	Edmund Herbert Sisam	*(Marian J. Archer collection)*
	Edmund's great-grandchildren	*(Peter J. Sisam)*

Preface

This book tells the story of one family through several hundred years. It ranges from tallow candle to electric light, from horse to automobile, and from quill pen to computer. Its pages encompass the lives of ploughmen and farmers, soldiers, teachers, preachers, publicans, bankers and scholars, mothers and children, entrepreneurs and quiet family men. The founders laboured in the green fields of England through the years of the Land Enclosures and the Poor Law. Several were corn-millers. Some emigrated and settled in America, Canada and New Zealand. Their descendants include not only the pioneer and the achiever, the home-maker and the pillar of society, but also the bigamist, the polygamist and the convict.

The name of the family is Sisam. This is an unusual name but one which, by its rarity, was comparatively easy to research. Even so, the work of constructing a family tree from the often sparse historical records, and tracing therein the lives of individuals, has taken a long time; but the task has been none the less rewarding.

For convenience, this book takes the story as far as the early 1980s while the Family Tree does not include any of the ever increasing new generation of children. At the end of the volume will be found Tables showing the various sections of the Sisam Family Tree, and an alphabetical list of Who is Who in the Sisam family; together with a list of Sources and Notes.

It would not have been possible to piece together this story without the full co-operation of the family. I am grateful to all those who shared with me their personal memories and the fruits of their own researches, and who gave generous hospitality. Among them in New Zealand were: Walter and Noeline Sisam, Benjamin Copedo, Eileen McCracken, Wynne and Ian Eccles, Edna and Hazel Sisam, and Joan Stewart who made available the diary of Maria Sisam. In the U.S.A. there were many others: Mary Goff Bateman, the Sisiam families in Idaho, Ruth Moulton and Lorne Richard Sisam in Salt Lake City. There were also those in England: 'Molly' Bunting, Richard Sisam and his family in the Birmingham area, the late James L. Sisam, and Celia Sisam who read through the text of the book and gave many helpful comments, corrections and suggestions; and last but not least my ever-patient wife Margaret with her sense of accuracy and order in all things.

Peter J. Sisam
Marlow. 1993

1
Origins

THE SURNAME AND 17TH CENTURY ANCESTORS

On a late November day in 1834, beneath the western escarpment of the Cotswold Hills, a horse and rider were making their way along an ancient track through pastures and cultivated fields. This ancient way, sometimes known as Buckle Street,[1] had for two thousand years or more carried travellers across those high hills and down into this fertile valley of the River Avon. The rider was William Sisam, a farmer and miller, travelling homewards from his farmland at Sheen Hill to his corn mill at Arrow, four miles away on the far side of the Avon. The road would take him across the river at Bidford by a narrow 15th century pack-horse bridge.

This ancient trackway held memories for William, prompting him to reflect on the different stages of his life in which he had become first a family man and then a man of substance and of standing. As he breasted the summit of the hill sloping down to the river, the village of Bidford came slowly into his view. The family had once lived here and as he neared the bridge he could just discern on the opposite bank the tombstone of his second

'The road would take him across the river at Bidford by the narrow, 15th century pack-horse bridge.'

child, Ann, who had died at the age of three. It was a year and a half after this that the family moved away from Bidford and took the lease of Arrow Mill.

On this particular day, as he reached Bidford Bridge, William headed his horse as usual up the inclined approach and began to cross the river. Suddenly the horse took fright, reared up and threw him heavily. He never recovered from the fall, and died in his home a few days later. He was 53 and left a widow, four sons and three daughters; his eldest son being 20 years old.

This was a crucial time for the family. It was as if they stood upon the summit of a hill, looking back from whence they had come, while an unknown future lay before them. That future has now become history; but before exploring that history it is helpful to pause and look back at the family's origins and at the roots of their family tree.

The roots and branches of a living tree produce leaves and fruit that mature and fall to the ground and are replaced by new foliage and fruit. These in turn are nourished by the goodness put into the ground by what has already fallen. Most branches of the tree extend, bifurcate and continue to grow. A few die naturally and fall away. But the main tree may go on growing for hundreds of years. So it is with a family tree.

A family tree has much to teach. The lives of those who have gone before are often a store of wisdom and experience. As in many families, there are sterling qualities and facets of character inherited through generations of the Sisam line and through the wives who married into it. Some who laboured faithfully and selflessly seemed to have gained little in their own lifetime, yet their lives were full of good lessons for those who followed. Others were rewarded in ways beyond their imagining. Success and failure may not be true measures of a person's life; rather it is what is put into life that counts.

Seeking the roots of a family tree one is led to the origin of names. Surnames as we know them today did not come into use until the Middle Ages. Before that time in England everyone was known by their Christian name, followed perhaps by some word of description to differentiate them from others of the same name. This might be their father's name, i.e Johnson son of John. Names often derive from an occupation (Smith, Archer, or Marshall from the Old French *Mareschal* meaning 'one who tends horses'); or from physical appearance (Cole from the Old English meaning 'black or swarthy'); or from a dwelling place (Holtom from the Old English meaning 'a dweller at the enclosure in the wood'). They may also come from a quality of character (Hardy meaning 'bold, courageous'). Many of our present day surnames originate in this way. There are others which have their origins in places.

The name Sisam derives from the village of Syresham[2] on the Northamptonshire/Oxfordshire borders. The place probably began as a Viking settlement established in a clearing of the vast forest covering most of that part of Saxon England. The name is from the Anglo-Saxon 'sige-heres-ham' and means 'the home of the victorious raiding army'. The raiding army is likely to have been Viking, as the Vikings overran the North and East of England in the late ninth and tenth centuries, settling there and intermarrying with the Saxons. The spelling of the name became shortened during the centuries that followed, and by the sixteenth century it appeared on Saxton's 1574 map of the Oxfordshire area as Syrsam, and again with the spelling Sysam on John Blau's map of Northamptonshire of 1640. Later the village reverted to the original spelling of Syresham, which it retains today. If a man named John, in the 13th or 14th century, moved to live in another village he was known by the name of the village he had come from. So, if he came from Syresham, or Sysam as it may then have been spelt, he was called John of Sysam. With the passage of time this would become John Sysam.

Origins

The village Post Office at Syresham.

A study of parish records suggests that the name Sisam spread in a south westerly direction from Syresham. It appears in various forms – Sisham, Sysum, Sysom, Sysam, Seisam, Sysome, Sisam – dependent on how learned the local clerks were or whether the actual holders of the name knew how to spell it, as they may not have been able to read or write. More often than not it may have been written down phonetically, just as it sounded, being an unusual name; but it is also a fact that in the 16th century 'Y' and 'I' had in general become alternative spellings. Of course, although Sisams probably originated from Syresham, not all need be blood relations or come from the same line.

Interestingly enough, there is a legal document of 1786 in the Oxford County Records Office, referring to a piece of land containing a section known as Sisam's Meadow,[3] or Siseham's Meadow, and this is only about fifteen miles from present-day Syresham.

One of the earliest records comes from the Elizabethan Age and is of the marriage in 1588, the year of the Spanish Armada, of John Seisam and June Cila in Minchinhampton, in the Cotswold Hills of Gloucestershire. It is followed by that of Edward Sysam and Alice Finch in 1631, also in Minchinhampton and presumably of the same family. Further records show Sisams scattered along the western and north-western foothills of the Cotswolds, and latterly in the Vale of Evesham and the Vale of the Red Horse, which the hills overlook. There were Sisams living in the Winchcombe area from 1681 to 1794, in villages near Bristol from 1711 to 1763, and in the Fladbury–Bidford–Alcester area from 1786 until the present day. In this part of England, in the area where the counties of Warwickshire, Worcestershire and Gloucestershire adjoin, the detailed map is dotted with villages, towns, farms, malthouses, corn mills and dwelling houses that have Sisam connections. It is 'Sisam country'.

Sisam's Meadow beside the River Cherwell at Adderbury, Oxfordshire.

So far proven documentary evidence has traced the line of this Sisam family back to a John Sisam who was married to Ann Cole in 1743 in Little Comberton, Worcestershire, which lies roughly between Winchcombe and Fladbury. It is more than likely that he was a Sisam from the village of Greet, near Winchcombe, though the link has yet to be proved conclusively, and it is possible that the Winchcombe Sisams descend from the earliest known ones at Minchinhampton.

Since the village of Greet was too small to have a church of its own, it was to Winchcombe that people went for baptisms, marriages and burials. In the Parish Register of the church at Winchcombe the first record of any Sisam is the marriage of Nicholeus Sisome and Maria Didcoate on 30 June 1681. In the following years their children were baptised and listed as follows, written in Latin as was the custom in those days:

22 May 1682	Nicholeus filius Nicholei Sysome de Greet.
31 March 1684	Josephus filius Nicholei Sysome de Greet.
5 Sept. 1686	Margaretta fil. Nicholei & Maria Sysome de Greet.
15 Oct. 1688	Richard filius Nicholei et Maria Sysom de Greet.
23 Feb. 1689/90	Richard filius Nicholei et Maria Sysom de Greet.
8 March 1693/94	Johes filius Nicholei et Maria Sysom de Greet.

Winchcombe nestling in a fold of the Cotswold Hills, where Sisams lived for nearly 200 years.

> This is the Last Will and testament of Mr John Sysom of Greet in the parish of Winchcomb and County of Glowster Carpenter, Itam I Give to my Daughter Ann Smith Wife of Henry Smith all my Houses Lands and premisors free Hold and Lesshold Whatsoever Lying and being in Greet to Her and her Hayers for Ever subject to the Maintenance of My Wife In such a manner that she Have bine youse'd to Live In And all my Goods and personall Estate Whatsoever I Give to my said soninlaw Henry Smith and for his Use for Ever and I nomenet and make my said soninlaw Henry Smith hole and sole Executor of this my Last Will and testament In Witness hereof I have Set my Hand and Sale this 25th Day of November In the Year of our Lord 1762
>
> Sined Soled and Dellverd by the said John Sysom the Testator for his Last Will and testament In the presance of Us
>
> Ed Pigeon
> James Sysum
> Thos Freeman
>
> John ⊕ Sysom
> his — Mark
>
> 26th Day of November 1763
> The above named Henry Smith son in Law & sole Executor was Duely sworn before me
> Th: Bishop Sury

Will of a John Sysom, carpenter of Greet, with one of the witnesses being James Sysum.

The first Richard died an infant, less than one month after his baptism. Maria died when her last two boys were still quite young. She was buried on 1 January 1700/01. The entry in the Parish Register recording her burial also states that her husband, Nicholas Sysom, was a carpenter.

A will of this Nicholas, who died in 1728, exists. Joseph and Richard are mentioned in it, though they are not given very much. They had no doubt already received their portion. Most of the property is left to the eldest son, Nicholas, and the youngest son, John (Johes).

Of their four sons who grew to manhood and married, little can be found out about John, the youngest, except that his wife was probably Anna or Hannah and that he inherited some property under his father's will. Richard married Margaret Day in 1715 and moved out of the village of Greet. Their first children were baptised at Alstone, others at Winchcombe and at Newent.

We are more interested in the two older brothers and their families. Nicholas, the eldest, married Sara Day on 1 November 1711, and Joseph married Sarah Minett on 26 November 1709. Both these marriages took place in the church at Winchcombe, indicating that their wives were from local families. Nicholas had 11 children, including John, William and James.

Joseph had 8 children, including Joseph, John and William. These names are shown in their Latin form in the baptismal records, for example:

1 Feb. 1718/19	Johanis filius Nicholas & Sara Sisom Jr. de Greet.
17 Sept. 1731	Jacobus filius Nicholai & Sarae Seisom de Greet.
26 Dec. 1720	Johanis filius Josophus & Sara Sysom de Greet.

So here we have two Sisams named John (Johanis), either of whom might be the John Sisam who married Ann Cole in 1743 in Little Comberton, Worcestershire. There is John, son of Nicholas, and also John, son of Joseph, both in the village of Greet near Winchcombe.

Looking at the records of other parishes for any Sisams born at about the same date, we do not find any John amongst them. Of course there may have been other John Sisams, but no record of them has been found. Just as there are no records either of the birth or baptism of the first Nicholas Sisam, who married in Greet in 1681, so we do not know where he came from or who his forbears were.

It is interesting to note the Christian names of the boys in these families in Greet: Nicholas, Joseph, John and William. These are all names which recur later on through our Sisam family tree, which makes it the more likely that these are the ancestors we are looking for.

The question is, which of these two Johns was it who moved to Little Comberton and married Ann Cole? The answer may be deduced by a process of elimination. A will survives made by a John Sysom, also a carpenter of Greet like his grandfather. In this will he leaves everything to his daughter, Ann Smith the wife of Henry Smith, and one of the witnesses to the will is James Sysum. John, son of Nicholas, had a younger brother called James (Jacobus); but John, son of Joseph, did not. So here is John son of Nicholas seemingly having only one child, a daughter, to whom to leave his possessions. He therefore cannot be the John who married Ann Cole who had six children including a son who was alive and with a family of his own at the time this will was made.

So we conclude, though we cannot absolutely prove it, that John Sisam of Little Comberton descends from the Sisoms of Greet, near Winchcombe, and that his father was Joseph Sisom (b. 1684) and his grandfather was Nicholas, the carpenter, who married Maria Didcoate in 1681.

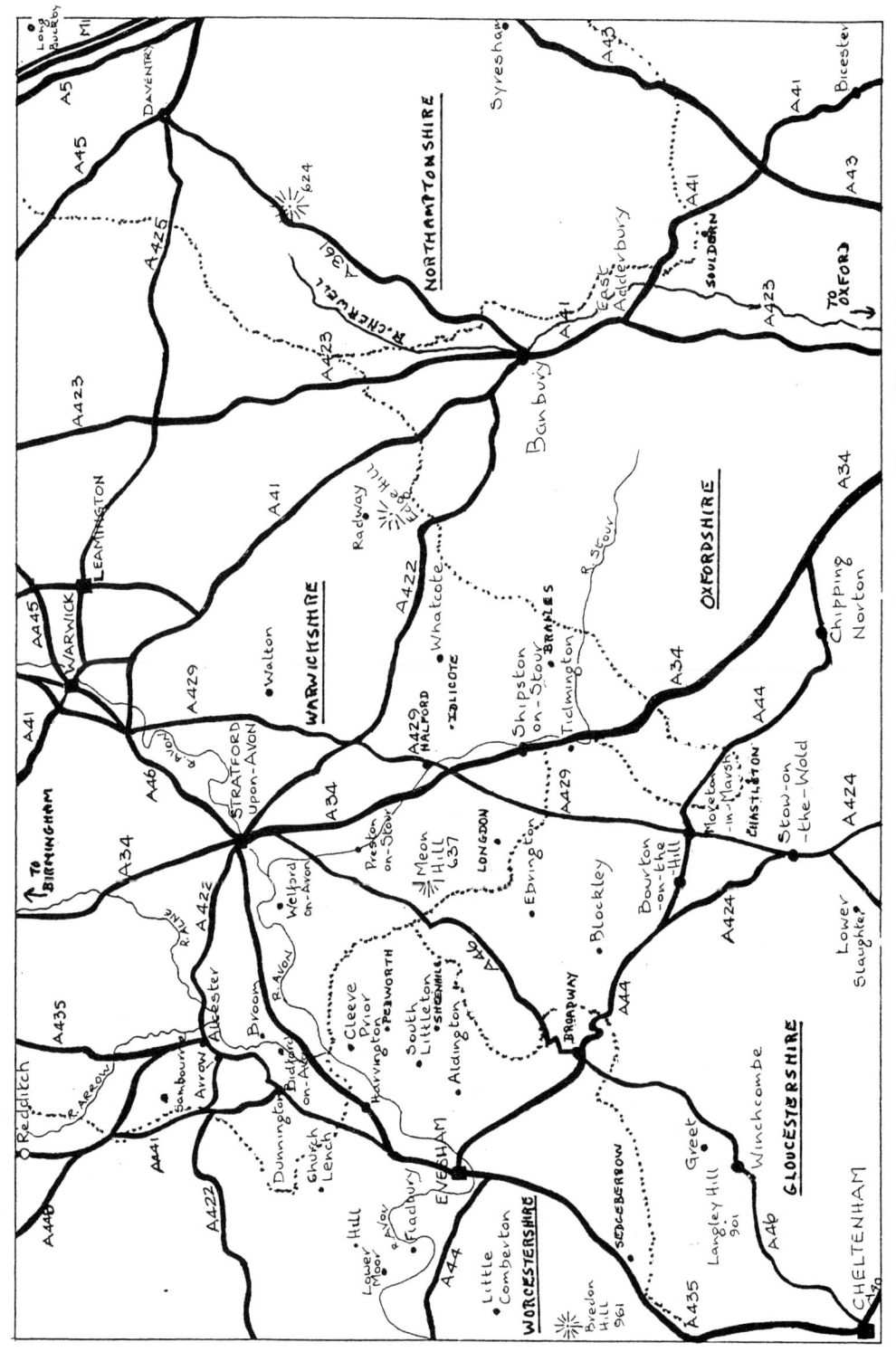

Map of 'Sisam Country' where the counties of Gloucestershire, Worcestershire and Warwickshire adjoin.

2
Village Yeomen

LITTLE COMBERTON, HILL, AND BIDFORD-ON-AVON 1743–1819

Little Comberton is a village lying beneath Bredon Hill. It is situated in the Vale of Evesham, famous for its fruit and vegetables. It is an old habitation and at its centre, near the parish church, there still remain some of the original medieval farm-houses and thatched cottages. These are distinguished by their black and white colouring, the walls being coated in white and the wooden beams in black. But this is not how they looked when first built. Their construction was of oak beams with walls made of wattle-and-daub, that is brushwood with clay-infilling. The black and white colouring was a decoration introduced in Victorian times. Until then the beams were their natural colour, as were the walls.

John Sisam would most likely have lived in a cottage of this kind, both before and after his marriage in Little Comberton on November 15, 1743, to Ann Cole. Very little is known about the couple other than that they both lived in the village. However, the parish records

Little Comberton, where John Sisam and Ann Cole were married in 1743.

show that their first child was baptised one month after the marriage, but only lived two days following the baptism. Cohabitation before marriage was an old custom in some parts of the countryside, as a means of determining whether a couple were able to bear children. Children were essential to a farm worker's family when wages were low. What the children earned was a vital part of the family income, and in later years they were expected to support their parents in old age. There were no pensions in the days of John and Ann Sisam. It was necessary to have a large family, on account of the high rate of infant mortality. In this respect life in England in the mid 1700s was similar to that of some underdeveloped countries today. John and Ann were reasonably fortunate. They had six more children, five daughters and another son, John II. This son was to become the founder of a flourishing and far-flung line of descendants. John and Ann lived very simply, he would first have rented his cottage and a small plot of land which he cultivated for his family's needs. He would probably have supplemented this by working for other farmers. He was what is known as a yeoman farmer, who had a certain independence and could progress to the point where he actually owned some land.

It was in fact only four years after his marriage to Ann Cole that John was able to buy the home where he was living in Little Comberton. It belonged to Robert Haines but had been lived in by two generations of Ann's family, first by John Cole the Elder and then by John Cole the Younger, both of whom were now dead. The property consisted of the cottage which had lately been pulled down and rebuilt, barn, stables, garden and orchard. All this he bought from Robert Haines for thirty seven pounds.

John II was born in 1748, just a year after his father had bought the property. He was not born to wealth. At Little Comberton he would have had to work on the land from an early age. But when he died at the age of 53 he was prosperous. A family legend, handed down orally from one generation to another, may explain how this came about. The story goes that sometime in the late 1700s a Sisam 'returned from India with a Captain Perrott', apparently having prospered, and on his return married and founded a family. Was this man John II?

When he married in 1778 at, for those days, the late age of 29 he was, according to the marriage register, living in the hamlet of Hill and Moor near Fladbury, a few miles across the River Avon from Little Comberton where he had been born. Hill and Moor, as the name suggests, is an area extending over a hill plateau and down its slopes on to lower ground where the village of Fladbury and the River Avon lie. Roughly speaking, Hill lies on the hill and Moor on the lower ground, but the two hamlets were grouped together for administrative purposes. He probably went to Hill and Moor quite early on when a young man, for farm workers often moved about the countryside to wherever there was work. He rented land and a house at Hill from Richard Bourne Charlett a local landowner.

Next to the hamlet of Hill was a sizeable country estate. The estate was Craycombe, and the owners were a family named Perrott. One of the members of this family, a nephew named George Perrott, spent most of his life in India working for the East India Company. When his uncle at Craycombe died without a direct descendant, George returned from India in 1782 and inherited the Craycombe property. He was not however a Captain and had never been in the army. Could John have been in India with this Perrott, perhaps as his servant? George Perrott probably went out to India when he completed his examinations for the Indian Civil Service in 1759, and John was only 11 years old then. He is unlikely to have gone to India later and returned with Perrott in 1782 because John had married in

The farmhouse at Hill, Fladbury, built in 1713, where John Sisam II and his family lived.

1778 and children were born to him in each of the following three years. In any case Perrott would have had Indian servants, and John was not an educated man able to serve as a clerk or minor administrator. All in all it sounds like a delightful, romantic myth. What is possible is that George Perrott, having returned from India as a wealthy man, may have helped John Sisam in some way; or John may have worked for him on land which Perrott owned at Hill.

When John Sisam II married in May 1778 his bride was Nancy George, daughter of John and Eleanor George who lived at Moor, Fladbury. The George family were, and still are, well known in the farming community of that area. Nancy's maternal grandfather was a ropemaker. Her father was probably a yeoman or tenant farmer, like John Sisam. Land Tax returns for the years following 1778, the year of his marriage, suggest that John Sisam was already a man of some substance. The returns have not survived for the years immediately after the marriage, but for 1787–1788 they show him as leasing a substantial acreage jointly with a Thomas Davis, and in 1792 leasing over 100 acres on his own account. At that time much of the land at Hill and Moor was still divided into small, individual strips, as it was in the middle ages, so that the 100 acres John now leased from Richard Bourne Charlett were scattered over the landscape. They included a homestead consisting of a pleasant house, built in 1713, and adjacent outbuildings, dating back to a

In the name of god amen I John Sisam being very sick and weak in body but in perfect memory and soundness of minde thanks be to god fast I do first by komanding my soul in to the hands of almity god that gave it and my body to be decently buryed in a Cristian burial at the decrition of my executios heass after named I giv and bequeath to my wife Debora Jon John Sisam in the parish of Bladuary in the County of dorsett: I giv and bequeath to my son John Sisam to whom I make hols executor of Hous garden and orchard to him and his ayers and assins for ever; and I giv to my son John Sisam on tabls and a bench and two stools on chist on ockplank _____

I giv and bequeath to my Daughter Hanah Sisam on Bed and Boster Being a flock Bed on pears of shoots and to Blancots and a quilts Baired _____

I giv and bequeath to my Daughter Elizabeth Sisam Hous all the komainder of my goods be longin to my Hous after my Decese _____

and my will is that my son John Sisam being my executor Shall pay in good Lawful money of great Brittan to my Daughter Sarah and ____ the Som of one pound ½ to my Daughter ann Hanton the Som of one pound _____

To my Daughter Mary parsons the Som of one pound _____

to be paid in on year after my Desese

— and I this my Present Revoke all other wills and Leacies ____ named by me and I Justius: this as my Last will and testament whear of have unto set my Hand and seale the the mark of John Sisam this instint Julay the twenty third in this years of our Lord one thousand seven Runderd Seventy nine and in the nineteenth year of the Reing of ours Sovring kingc: georg the third

Sealed sined
and delivered in the presence of
Beanse maifle

Thomas Hark s: M: Hooks
the mark + of Elizabeth Hooks

Will of John Sisam I (dated 1779). All his children are mentioned.

much earlier period. This was probably the house into which he and Nancy moved after their marriage. Today it is listed as a building of historic interest. Though no longer a farm, the house is occupied, and the old farm buildings are still there.

John II seems to have been a respected member of the community, and in 1788 was apppointed one of the two assessors responsible for making the Land Tax returns for the district. This tax was the main source of government revenue, there being as yet no income tax. John was a typical tenant farmer of the period, who lived on the land and worked it himself, helped probably by some hired labour, and later by his growing family. It was a time when great changes were taking place in the English countryside. The population of Britain was growing rapidly, not so much because of an increased birthrate but because medical care had improved and more children survived. Greater food supplies were needed, especially the staple cereals. At the same time, the invention of the steam engine, the spinning-jenny and a host of other devices was making the mass-production of goods possible in the newly established factories. Thousands migrated to these factories from the country areas nearest the manufacturing towns. They went for various reasons, low farm wages, more labourers available than farms could absorb, and some because it became uneconomic for them to continue working their small plots. These thousands of new town-dwellers were no longer food-producers, and they represented an ever growing market for the products of the countryside. In the years ahead, with the outbreak of the Napoleonic Wars in Europe, Britain's imports of food supplies were cut off and home agriculture became of even greater importance. The price of corn rose rapidly, to the advantage of the farmer; but to the farm worker, for whom bread was the basic nourishment and whose wage continued at a low level, this caused hardship. It is difficult to tell exactly how these upheavals affected John Sisam II. It seems that, on the whole, these were good years for him.

Meanwhile his father John I in Little Comberton was not at all well and in July 1779 he made his Will. His wife Ann had already died, four of his five daughters were now married and only Hannah remained single and was perhaps looking after him. In the event John I did not die until 1786, at which time the Little Comberton property passed to John II. He retained it but continued to live at Hill, Fladbury.

John and Nancy's first child, a girl, died in infancy. However in the first eight years of their marriage four more children were born, John, William, Mary and Joseph. Then sadly, in 1788, Nancy died after giving birth to twins, who also did not survive. In 1790 John married again. His second wife was Phoebe Russell from the village of Bishampton, about three miles from Hill and Moor. She and John had seven children, three boys and four girls, the first two of these children were again twins who died soon after their birth. Neither of their two remaining sons married or had male descendants.

When John Sisam II died in December 1801 he left considerable property in the form of leases, together with cash and a few plots of land that he had bought and now owned. The leases would have included the house, out-buildings and land at Hill. His will was carefully thought out and made provision for all his nine surviving children as well as for his second wife, Phoebe. He left sums of money and property to the sons of his first marriage. To his oldest son John III he left the house, outbuildings and orchard he owned in Little Comberton and £100. To William he left the sum of £140 and a house and garden at Moor; and to Joseph a house and land he had recently purchased in Hill and Moor, plus £100 to pay off the money still owing on the purchase. He also left £200 to Mary, the daughter of his first marriage. Everything else he left in trust for his wife, Phoebe, and her children; namely his personal estate and effects, stock in trade and implements, household goods, china and linen, etc. Any monies were to be invested in 'Government or real securities'. All this has the ring of a man with a good business sense. Phoebe was to educate her children 'in a manner suitable to their situation in life'. Clearly John Sisam was conscious of having attained a worthy 'situation in life'.

Phoebe Sisam remained at Hill after her husband's death. In several of the Worcestershire Directories of the time she is listed as a 'farmer', such directory listings usually indicating a person of some standing. The family lived in the same house as before, the household probably consisting of Phoebe herself, her daughter Phoebe aged 8, seven year old Daniel, five year old David, Ann aged 3, and Sarah 1; also perhaps, at least for a while, her stepsons, William aged 20, Joseph 15, and their sister Mary 18. John III, being already 21 when his father died, took possession of his inherited property in Little Comberton. About 1807 he leased this to William Cotton, and in 1811 sold it to John Field for one hundred and thirty pounds. Within a year or two of this transaction the owner is listed as Mrs. Dorothy Field. William sold his house and land at Moor shortly after he came of age. Joseph, on the other hand, remained and worked his land, finally selling it to Phoebe some ten years later.

The reasons for their disposing of their inherited properties are likely to have been the revolutionary changes taking place in English farming, which may not have affected their father, but which were certainly felt by his descendants. Small plots of land, though useful both productively and as a capital investment, would not support a man and his family. If he went to work for other farmers, the pay was meagre. There had been attempts to get farm wages increased, but instead a local Poor Rate Tax was imposed from which a dole was paid to those in need. This tax fell heavily on those who owned or rented a house or small plot of land, whereas the large-scale farmers who had opposed the raising of wages scarcely felt it. They had claimed that fluctuating corn prices made wage increases impossible. The Poor Rate system was also demoralising for the farm worker, as it tended to make him a pauper dependent on relief. As a result many lost the incentive to work.

In 1823 a survey was made of the Hill and Moor area on behalf of the major landowner, James Wakeman Newport (a successor of Richard Bourne Charlett, he later seems to have added Charlett to his own name); and a coloured map was prepared showing who owned or leased the various plots of land. This map has survived and the Sisam homestead is shown on it and the land farmed by Phoebe is marked in blue and with a letter 'S', and sometimes her name. The land thus marked is more or less what John Sisam II was farming when he died. There are other familiar names on the map such as Perrott, George, Wagstaff, all of whom rented plots alongside the Sisams. The Wagstaffs had the homestead opposite the Sisams on the other side of the lane, and later Phoebe's daughter, also named Phoebe, married Henry Wagstaff.

The survey was a warning of things to come. It had been prepared for the future enclosure of the land at Hill, under an Act of Parliament whereby scattered plots would be grouped together to create larger blocks. This was to facilitate more productive cultivation, and the adoption of new and better methods of agriculture, including the use of machines. This had been going on all over the country for many years. It was more than likely that when leases ran out some rented plots might disappear and become part of the landlord's large-scale land cultivation. Many tenants were bought out with a few pounds, soon spent.

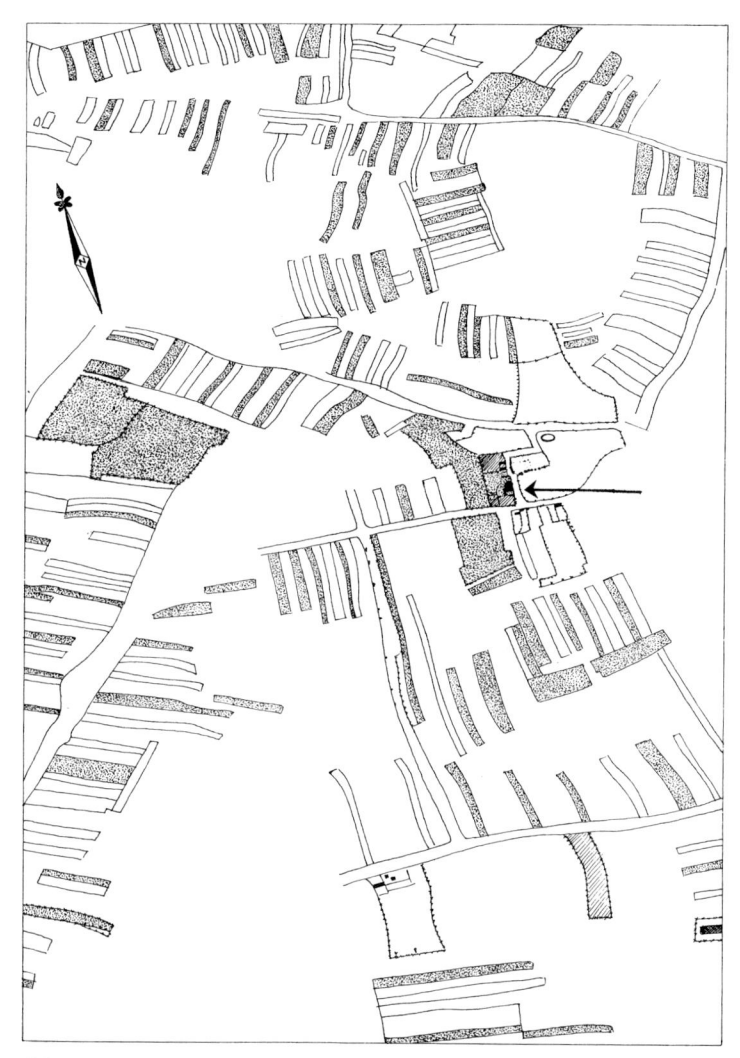

Copy of part of the Enclosure Award Map for Hill, Fladbury, 1823. The shaded areas, originally marked in blue, indicate plots of land farmed by the Sisams. (An arrow marks their farmhouse.)

Others were given alternative plots, but could not afford the now compulsory draining and fencing, and so were forced to sell.

Phoebe Sisam died in 1824 and was buried in Fladbury churchyard, Fladbury being the parish church for the hamlet of Hill. Her headstone is there, the inscription being just decipherable. Her husband John II's headstone and that of his first wife, Nancy, is probably one of the adjacent weather-beaten stones which can no longer be read. They lie next to the George family tombstones at the front of the churchyard, and are visible from the village street running alongside the low churchyard wall. Phoebe's son David Sisam, now 28 but unmarried, inherited the farm and continued there for the rest of his life. He became a leading member of the community and, like his father, he served as an assessor for Land Tax.

After John III leased his property in Little Comberton to William Cotton, he went to live in South Littleton, a village a few miles to the east of Fladbury. In 1807 we find him paying rent there for a cottage which was church property. He seems to have been respected because he was appointed Overseer of the Poor for that parish in the same year. Three years later there is no sign of John and it is his brother William who is in South Littleton paying rent to the church, of rather more than John had paid; and it is William who is the Overseer of the Poor for the year ending Easter 1810. He also agreed to serve for the following year, but did not in fact do so.

Little is known of the movements of John III. At the time when he sold his Little Comberton property in January 1811 he was living in Cheltenham and working as a gardener. But sooner or later he returned to Hill and worked with David on the farm. In December 1833, within ten years of David taking on the 100 acres at Hill, the long expected Enclosure of the land took place. There was some adjustment of the area farmed by David, but it is not known whether his total acreage was affected or not. By 1841 David and John were joined by Henry and Phoebe Wagstaff. Phoebe, who was David's sister, kept house for them all. In 1851 David had reduced his holding to 71 acres and was employing two labourers. For several years, his name appears in the Worcestershire directories as one of the main farmers of the district.

Both John III and Phoebe Wagstaff had died by 1851, but Henry Wagstaff was still with David. David's housekeeper now was his niece, Elizabeth (Betsy) Day, who was aged about 20. She stayed with him many years as in the next census of 1861 she is still listed as his housekeeper. However, she had become friends with the family next door, named Firkins, and in 1864 she married William Firkins. At some point David must have bought the family homestead, because in David's will, made in February 1865, he left 'my Freehold House Garden Orchard Land and Premises' to his nephew Charles Day Jnr. He left 'all my other personal estate chattels and effects . . . unto my late housekeeper Betsy Firkins'. He died in 1869. His tombstone is in Fladbury to the left or west side of the church in the large, open portion of the churchyard. He never married and having left the land he owned to Charles Day, son of his married sister Ann Day, the house and land at Hill went out of the Sisam family. Phoebe had no Sisam grandsons. Thus it was through the children of John Sisam II's first wife, Nancy, that the Sisam line continued; that is through her son William and his younger brother Joseph, for John III the eldest brother never married.

❖ ❖ ❖

William had been given a modest start in life by the inheritance from his father of property at Moor, which was leased to a Thomas Turner and which William soon sold. He probably did not stay in South Littleton for very long. The next we hear of him is his marriage in December 1813. His bride was Lydia Marshall, daughter of Thomas and Mary Marshall of Whatcote, a village near Shipston-on-Stour, in Warwickshire, not all that far away from his home ground, about twenty miles as the crow flies. Surprisingly, and contrary to the usual custom, the wedding did not take place in the bride's village, but in the heart of the city of Birmingham at St. Martin's Church. The reason for this is not known. Marriages outside a bride's parish were usually those arranged by licence in order to avoid the delay and publicity that banns involved. But this marriage was by banns and not by licence. It

William Sisam's house and malthouse to the left of the church at Welford-on-Avon. The carter wears a smock, the standard work garment of European farm labourers.

proved to be a good union. The Marshalls were an old farming family and the marriage of this couple was the beginning of a close association of the two families that lasted several generations. Lydia seems to have been a remarkably able young woman and brought many enduring qualities with her into the Sisam family.

That William and his brothers should have sold their inherited property may seem on the face of it surprising. On the other hand, as we have seen, prospects for the small property owner were not encouraging. Many younger men looked for other ways of making a living. Some left the land and went to work in the towns, and some remained in the countryside and took up trades related to farming. They became millers, malsters, builders, carpenters and the like. Some diversified their work, and this is the road William decided to take. As well as farming he became a maltster. He and Lydia settled in the village of Welford-on-Avon, about six miles from Stratford-upon-Avon, and here he leased a dwelling, a malt house and an orchard.

The heart of the present-day village of Welford is picturesque, has many old thatched cottages and has a maypole on the village green. Around this on the first day of May the coming of spring is celebrated in music and dance. Beyond the wall on the far side of the churchyard is a medium-size building, like a small barn. This is the back of what was the malthouse and maltster's dwelling house, which William Sisam leased. This is where

William and Lydia's first child, Henry, was born, the first of nine children. His birth deserves special note as Henry was later to become the father of the Sisams who founded the New Zealand branch of the family.

William seems to have been something of an entrepreneur. Soon after he began malting at Welford he took the lease of Sheenhill Farm near South Littleton; the village where he had lived before he married. This was probably in order to grow barley for malting, the distance to Welford being about nine miles. Lydia may have played a part in this enterprise with a marriage dowry. She certainly brought with her a sound business sense, which revealed itself in the years to come. The farm consisted of a dwelling house, barns, stables, rickyard, foldyard and a garden, together with arable and pasture land, the whole totalling 146 acres. It lay in the fertile Vale of Evesham and was named from a small hill nearby, Sheen Hill or Shine Hill, which was reckoned to reflect the sunlight in a particular way at certain times of the day. At Sheenhill their second child was born, a daughter Ann. She was christened in the parish church of North Littleton in 1815, the year of the battle of Waterloo.

William by now was well established in both farming and malting. By 1817 he and his family had moved to Bidford-on-Avon, where he took the lease of a second farm, with barns, a dwelling house and a malthouse. These buildings can be seen in Bidford today and are still occupied. The house, now known as Icknield House, was built about 1800. Here three more sons were born, William, John and Frederick. Bidford itself was a pleasant village by the River Avon. As it's name implies there was originally a ford across the river. In the 15th century a narrow eight-arch, pack-horse bridge was built. It is still used today, with its ancient niches into which pedestrian stood to let the pack-horses and wagons pass. Today modern traffic which uses the bridge is single-line, controlled by

The village of Bidford-on-Avon.

Icknield House, Bidford-on-Avon, where William Sisam lived. His malthouse lay behind it.

traffic lights, but pedestrians still have to squeeze into the niches to let it pass. The village has narrow streets opening into a square; at one end is the parish church overlooking the river. Also in the square is the old Falcon Inn, where Shakespeare is said to have caroused with Francis Bacon. Perhaps this is reflected in the last line of a much quoted Elizabethan jingle about these villages which runs:

> 'Piping Pebworth, dancing Marston,
> Haunted Hillborough, and hungry Grafton;
> With dodging Exhall, Papist Wixford,
> Beggarly Broom and drunken Bidford.'

Sisams have had close connections with at least five of these villages. Bidford, in Shakespeare's time, seems to have had a reputation for conviviality. Three hundred years later, William Sisam probably found that there was a good living to be made from supplying dwelling houses and inns with malt for brewing, for in the early nineteenth century beer was still the staple drink at meals. Most housewives brewed their own beer for their families, whilst the inns catered for travellers.

In the churchyard at Bidford, looking out over the river towards the old arched bridge, there is a tall tombstone. The inscription reads:

> Sacred to the
> memory of
> ANN
> daughter of
> William and Lydia Sisam
> who departed this life
> the 30th June 1819
> aged 3 years
> and six months

About that time there was a smallpox epidemic which carried off many children in the district. The child was probably one of the unfortunate victims. William and Lydia, who soon had a sizeable family, were more fortunate than many. Seven of their children reached adulthood. Only little Ann was lost and, later, David who died when aged eleven.

3
Farmers & Millers

ARROW, HARVINGTON, AND WALTON – THE BIGAMIST

In the year 1821 William Sisam made a decisive step. He moved from malting to corn milling, and took the lease of Arrow Mill, about two miles from Bidford. The mill was on the River Arrow, a tributary of the Avon, and formed part of the Marquis of Hertford's Ragley Estate. A mile or so beyond the village of Arrow was the thriving market town of Alcester, once an important Roman settlement. There had been a mill at Arrow since Roman times. In about 1800 the old mill with dwelling-house attached was rebuilt. William and his family therefore moved into what was a comparatively new house.

In its tranquil rural setting Arrow Mill looked then very much as it does today. It stood amongst green meadows, a single brick building with a dwelling house at the front and the mill immediately behind. A mill stream diverted from the river flowed through the meadows towards the house, forming a small mill pond, and then disappearing beneath it to drive the mill wheel and emerging into a pool beyond, to rejoin the river further downstream. Thus the river and mill stream together formed an oval island of green meadowland, at one end of which stood a walnut tree. Beyond lay the long slope of Primrose Hill providing a pleasing backdrop to the scene. In springtime the hill, as its name suggests, was covered with pale yellow primroses. On the near side of the house a footpath led across another meadow to the village and the parish church. The upper floor windows of the house commanded a vista of the curving mill stream and the village in the distance. It was a home of ample proportions and seems to have been well appointed.

Fifty years after William and Lydia's time another Sisam miller's wife, Letitia Sisam, found a fine copper tea-urn in the attic covered with cobwebs; which she brought out, polished and put to use. It was made round about 1805 and probably had belonged to William and Lydia. It was decorated with Egyptian emblems such as a sphinx and serpents reminiscent of Cleopatra, and of course with the British lion; these being popular motifs of the period commemorating Admiral Nelson's victory over Napoleon at the battle of the Nile in 1798. It was also a sign that tea, brought to England by merchants of the East India Company, was beginning to rival ale as the main family beverage. Perhaps this is one of the reasons that prompted William to leave malting for corn milling, since there was always likely to be a demand for bread, and the flour from which it was made. Whatever the reasons the decision proved a sound one, for Arrow Mill was to remain in the family's hands for a hundred years or so and provide the base for a growing Sisam dynasty. William, it seems, had inherited his father John Sisam's good business sense, for not only did he move to Arrow Mill but he also retained the lease of Sheenhill Farm at South Littleton as a continuing investment.

William's farming and corn-milling operations brought him in touch with a great many

Arrow Mill from the meadows, with the winding River Arrow in the foreground.

'A mill stream diverted from the river flowed through the meadows towards the house, disappearing beneath it to drive the mill wheel.'

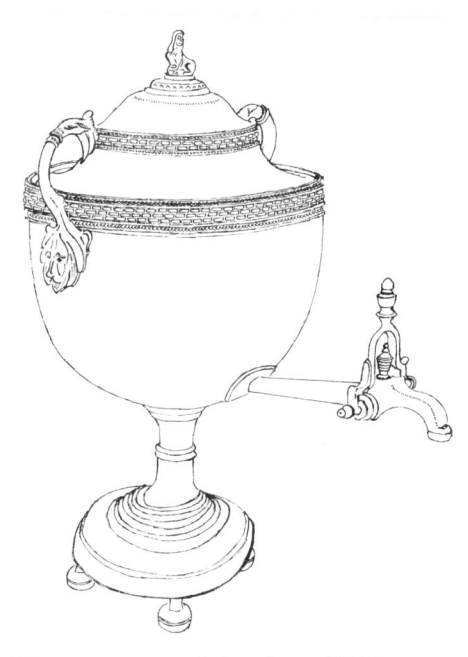

The copper tea-urn belonging to William Sisam, which was found in the attic of Arrow Mill many years after his day.

Arrow Mill and its mill pool.

people in Arrow, Alcester and the surrounding countryside. He made some good friends, especially amongst the farmers. Alcester was at that time a market town with a population of about 2,200. In that pre-railway age it had become a communications hub with long-distance, horse-drawn coaches running several times a week from the Swan Inn in Huckerhurst Street (now Swan Street) to London, Birmingham, Bristol, Leicester and Kidderminster. Its inhabitants practiced many skills and trades. There were wheelwrights, blacksmiths, needlemakers, clockmakers, brickmakers, butchers, grocers and the like. Amongst other amenities the town boasted a large number of bakeries, which in later years proliferated to such an extent that Alcester became known locally as 'Caketown'.

When the family first moved into Arrow Mill, William and Lydia had four young sons; their first daughter having died in Bidford. During the next six years there were added another son, David, and three daughters, Mary Ann, Harriet and Caroline. These early years no doubt saw much happiness, with a houseful of lively children delighting in the meadows and woods, the rumble and clatter of the mill and the ever-flowing river. But there were sorrows as well, for on a spring day in May 1833 young David was drowned in the river. He was 11 years old. Then, in November of the following year, William was thrown from his horse whilst crossing Bidford Bridge. He was carried home to Arrow where he was just able to make his will, appointing two friends as executors. He died a few days later, aged 53, and was buried in Arrow churchyard, where his headstone stands together with those of his descendants.

The two friends to whom William entrusted the care of his family were local farmers, Thomas Shayler of Arrow and Samuel Jackson of Bevington. Their brief was to act as

Bidford Bridge where William Sisam's horse reared and threw him in November 1834.

trustees for Lydia and her eight children until the youngest reached the age of twenty-one. They were to continue the business of Arrow Mill and of Sheenhill Farm for as long as was deemed appropriate, and from these to provide for the maintenance and education of the children. An annuity of £40 a year for life was to be paid to Lydia.

The eldest son Henry, aged 20, now assumed responsibility for the day-to-day running of the mill. William Jnr. aged 17 and John aged 16 supported him. There was also Frederick aged 14. Between them there was the work to be done at the mill and at Sheenhill Farm, under the guidance and advice of the two trustees, Farmers Shayler and Jackson, and of Lydia herself. Sheenhill Farm comprised 200 acres carrying sheep, cows, horses, and pigs, as wall as crops. There were probably several employed men living on the farm with their families. The lease of the farm remained in the Sisam family for some time, certainly until 1842 and perhaps later.

Henry soon got into his stride, for he was not a man to let the grass grow under his feet. He married within a year of taking on the mill, after reaching his 22nd birthday. The wedding was on December 31, 1836, at Whatcote, just in time to celebrate the New Year. His bride was his first cousin Caroline Marshall, of the Marshall family of Whatcote, Lydia's family. A few eyebrows may have been raised at this union, but at that time the marriage of first cousins was not considered unusual. Caroline joined the large family at Arrow. Unhappily for the young couple they lost their first child, Thomas Henry, who did not survive much more than a year. But during the next two years William Henry and Ann Emily were born, both of whom flourished. With these additions to the household it was time to reconsider the menage at Arrow and to think of the future. Lydia and the family trustees no doubt gave much thought to this, especially as to the prospects for the three younger sons.

The solution arrived at was a bold one. In about 1838 a lease was taken of an additional corn mill in Lydia's name, at Harvington, a few miles downstream from Bidford on the River Avon. It consisted of a mill and a separate dwelling house and malthouse. The landowner was William Marshall, a farmer whose family had lived in Harvington for several generations. It is possible that these Marshalls were related to Lydia's family, the Marshalls of Whatcote. Lydia moved from Arrow with two of her sons, William now aged 21, Frederick aged 20, and the three girls, Harriet 15, Mary Ann 14, and Caroline 12. This left Henry to run Arrow with the help of his brother John, a labourer who worked in the mill and a maid-servant to be with Caroline in the house. At Harvington the property, by its diversity, needed a good deal of manpower for it included not only a mill and a malthouse but also farmland. Frederick took charge of the mill and William the farmland. As at Arrow the family had living on the premises a labourer and a maid-servant.

The move to Harvington was an historic step. For the next fifty years or so Harvington Mill and Arrow Mill were to be the two main Sisam homesteads and were run as a joint family enterprise. Harvington proved a useful adjunct to Arrow in that it provided a living for sons and grandsons over the years. Arrow Mill was occupied by Sisams up until 1921, a span of nearly a hundred years. Occasionally Harvington – the Mill or the Mill House or both – had a tenporary occupant from outside the family, but most of the time it was a Sisam base with various members of the family moving in or out according to circumstances. This continued until the late 1880s when the lease was relinquished.

The property at Harvington was half a mile or so from the village. It was on the banks of the River Avon, some thirteen miles downstream from Stratford-upon-Avon. The

Harvington mill building, showing its two broad mill-wheels.

The Miller's House at Harvington and the adjoining malthouse and bakery. It is now a pleasant, family-run riverside hotel.

Harvington Mill House, where Lydia and her family lived, stands today as it did then looking out across the water to the hills beyond. It is a Georgian period building with lawns running down to the water's edge, and is now an attractive hotel run by a family. The exterior has been preserved together with that of the old malthouse adjoining the main house. A track leads from the house along the river and across a bridge to the island on which the mill stands. Like most country corn mills in England it is no longer working. The great frost of 1897, when rivers were frozen over, damaged the machinery beyond repair and, as imports of foreign wheat increased and were milled at the ports of entry, there was less and less work for such country mills. The building stood empty for many years. The roof decayed and it became a picturesque relic. It was however solidly built. Today the main structure is unimpaired, the magnificent oak beams are intact and much of the old machinery remains. Fortunately the building has come into good hands with a view to its eventual restoration as a dwelling house.

On the hill overlooking the mill there was Harvington village. In the late 1840s Frederick attended the parish meetings at which affairs of the village were conducted and decisions made, such as to build a local school. These meetings were held in the church, after which the village councillors repaired to the Coach and Horses Inn across the road. They went through the churchyard past the tombstones of generations of local farming families; among them the Bullocks who kept the farm next to the Sisams. In the years to come the Bullock and the Sisam families were to be drawn closer through the marriage of Frederick's niece, Ann Emily of Arrow, to William Bullock.

Lydia stayed on at Harvington for ten years or so, until she was 63. Of her family, Henry was well established at Arrow Mill, John had left Arrow, was married and had his own mill at Winchcombe, whilst William and Frederick remained with her at Harvington. William was aged 32 and still single. Frederick, on the other hand, early in 1849 had married Elizabeth Hoare, a farmer's daughter from Radway near Kineton in Warwickshire. This added to the family at Harvington. Lydia may have felt that it was the moment to make a second move. At any rate, in the same year as Frederick's marriage, William took the lease of a 200 acre farm at Walton, near Wellesbourne, a few miles east of Stratford-upon-Avon. Lydia and his three sisters moved there with him, leaving Frederick in charge of Harvington Mill with its farmland, dwelling house and malthouse.

The farm at Walton was aptly called Mount Pleasant. It was in the Vale of the Red Horse, so named from an ancient figure cut out of the turf on a red-earthed hillside.[4] The house, like the Harvington Mill House, was in the Georgian style, well furnished with barns and garden and an orchard in front. It stood on a hill-top, approached by a long drive. Below it was a mansion, Walton House, the farm being part of that estate. The owners were the Mordaunt family the head of which, Sir John Mordaunt, had recently been killed in a shooting accident. His son Charles, aged nine, had inherited the property and was William's titular landlord.

William now had a fair-sized farm to run and one that was in good shape. Immediately prior to his occupancy the Mordaunt estate had done extensive work on the house and farm buildings. One of the last items to be tackled was listed in the estate accounts as a new set of posts and rails 'to divide Mr. Sisam's yard.' It was a valuable property. The rent paid by William for the year 1851 was over £300. In addition there was a tithe rent charge of £23.6.9 and parish rates of about £34. The farm prospered in William's hands; it was employing ten men. As well as the family, a staff of five lived on the premises: a

Mount Pleasant, Walton, the farm to which William Sisam Jnr., his mother Lydia and his three sisters moved in about 1848.

laundress, a housemaid and three young farmhands. In 1853 William served as a land assessor in connection with the levying of the Land Tax for the district. Eight years later, the farm employed five boys in addition to the ten men. The men included a shepherd, a carter and a groom. The chief crops were wheat and beans.

William's three sisters, Mary Ann, Harriet and Caroline, together with their mother Lydia, were all receiving annuities from the estate of their father, William senior. The girls never married, nor did William. It is sad to think of those young women, hidden away in the isolated farmhouse on the hill, with very little social life or opportunity to mix with people, and only a bachelor brother for male company. When their mother died in 1865 they faithfully remained at Mount Pleasant and looked after their brother, until one by one they died and only William was left. That was in 1883. Two of the sisters are buried side by side in Arrow churchyard.

After their death William left Walton and spent his last days with his younger brother John Sisam; both having retired, William from farming and John from milling.

This younger brother John was the one who, after the death of their father William senior, had remained at Arrow Mill to help his older brother Henry. John stayed there until he married in 1847, at the age of 29. His bride was Sarah Hannah Potter the daughter of William and Elizabeth Potter, a prosperous farming family of Lark Stoke near Ilmington and not far from Shipston-on-Stour. The marriage took place in the nearby parish church of Stretton-on-Fosse.

The Potters were a well known family in that part of South Warwickshire. William Potter's ancestors had lived in the Shipston area since the year 1700. For many years he and his family were at Lark Stoke, a fine house with garden terraces and fishponds. Its setting was romantic, with a winding stream flowing through copses which in springtime were 'sheeted with primroses'. This was where Sarah and her brothers and sisters grew up. They were a cultured family. Sarah's young brother, Frederick Scarlett Potter, studied art at the Royal Academy in London where, in 1863, he won the Royal Academy Gold Medal for sculpture. He is remembered locally for the fountain he designed, which stands at the cross-roads in the middle of the village of Mickleton. He was also a distinguished writer of history and folklore, and the author of numerous children's books.

After their marriage John and Sarah Sisam made their home at Winchcombe, an old market town lying at the foot of the Cotswold hills, about 25 miles from Arrow. John took the lease of Postlip Lower Mill, a grist or corn mill with a bakery on the River Isbourne, at the western end of the town. Winchcombe had a long history going back to very distant times. A steep lane leads from the town to the summit of the hills where, in a commanding position dominating the valley below in one direction and the upland heights in the other, there is Belas Knap, the magnificent four thousand year-old burial mound of a people who lived in these parts before the Romans occupied Britain. In the ninth century Offa, the Saxon King of Mercia, had a palace at Winchcombe; and in the middle ages thousands of pilgrims came here each year to the shrine of St. Kenelm at Winchcombe Abbey.

In the Sisams' day the population was about 2,500, most of whom worked on the land or in the town's four corn mills. Some of the families had lived in Winchcombe for several hundred years. The Oakey family was one of them. John Oakey, who started life as a farmworker, had been born in the year that John and Sarah Sisam came to Winchcombe. He later wrote his childhood memories in *Reminiscences of Winchcombe*, which gives a detailed picture of how people lived in those times. He describes the various buildings and who lived where, and when he comes to the bottom of Corndean Lane he notes 'the grist mill and bakery of Mr. John Sisam'. He tells of the life of the farmworkers, rising sometimes at four in the morning, walking to work for a 6 a.m. start and returning home at 7.30 in the evening. He tells of the meagre wages and of how, when the harvest was done, whole families would glean the stubble fields for the left-over ears of corn, which they would thresh, grind and make into dough. Certain bakers would lend their ovens one afternoon a week and bake the people's loaves without charge. In those days the fields on the hills and in the valleys for miles around were golden with corn, which when harvested was brought to the Winchcombe corn mills to be ground.

Some Winchcombe millers sent their bread to Cheltenham to be sold, loading it onto flat carts, or onto donkeys carrying two large baskets on each side of them. The aim was to be first at Cheltenham with the bread. One man had a 'strong and cunning' donkey which would not move over to let anyone pass him in the race to scoop the market. Winchcombe was a lively town. Life there had its pleasures as well as its hardships. There were boxing matches on Saturday nights. There was much poaching and hard drinking. There were shin-kicking contests, twice-yearly horse fairs, a pig sale on Sunday mornings, hiring fairs, travelling players, visiting circuses and harvest suppers on the farms.

The John Sisams lived in Winchcombe about 20 years, during which time their four children were born, two sons and two daughters. The sons were Edward Godfrey, who died at the age of four, and William Bernard. The daughters were Elizabeth Lydia and Mary Catherine. Their mother, Sarah, kept in close touch with her parents, who had now moved from Lark Stoke to Longdon, a 180 acre farm to the east of Ilmington. Her father was still farming at the age of 75 and had four men and three boys working for him. There

The River Isbourne at Winchcombe, on the banks of which was Postlip Lower Mill occupied by John and Sarah Sisam.

The present day house that was formerly the miller's home at Postlip Lower Mill.

seems to have been frequent coming and going between the two families. Sarah was not very strong and had her hands full with the two youngest children. Because of this the eldest daughter, Elizabeth Lydia, known as Lily, lived much of the time with her Potter grandparents at Longdon Farm. They more or less brought her up and saw to it that she had a good education. She is said to have gone to the well-known boarding school Cheltenham Ladies College, conveniently located six or seven miles from Winchcombe.

John and his family left Winchcombe in about 1869 to take charge of Harvington Mill where there was a vacancy. John was 52 when he went to Harvington. He and Sarah had with them their son William Bernard who was about 15, and Mary Catherine who was 13. It is possible that the older daughter, Lily, may also have been there for a time. After completing her education, she had developed into something of a teacher and in this period she taught her brother William Bernard. This may have been at Harvington or with the Potters at Longdon Farm. Her tutoring was so successful that William Bernard won an exhibition to Oriel College, Oxford, to which he went in April 1875. Altogether she seems to have been a rather remarkable person, inheriting many of her mother's qualities.

John retired from milling sometime in the early 1870s, and he and Sarah went with their daughter Mary to Shipston-on-Stour to live with Lily. Lily had taken over a Ladies' Boarding School there which she was now running. It was a large private dwelling known as Fairview House, in a quiet street quaintly named Back Road. Both Sarah and her daughter Mary became governesses and helped Lily with her teaching. There were seven of her pupils living in as boarders, their ages ranging from 7 to 19. Having helped Lily to become fully established in her school, John and Sarah moved for a while to the village of Burmington; they then retired to the seaside resort of Weston-super-Mare in Somerset, taking Mary with them. There they were joined by John's brother William from Walton. They lived in Severn Road which leads down to the sea. All four spent the rest of their days in Weston. Sarah was the first to die, in 1887, followed within a few years by John and then William, aged 72 and 75 respectively. Lily visited them from time to time and was there when her father died. Mary lived for just two years after her uncle William's death, dying in 1895 at only 37 years of age. They were buried in a pleasant municipal cemetery which occupies a large area on two hillside slopes that form the sides of a small valley. Although the sites of the graves are listed and numbered in the cemetery records, no gravestones remain bearing their names since, with the passage of time, as is customary in such municipal cemeteries the ground has been assigned to other burials.

When Lily retired from her school in Shipston she went to live with her uncle Frederick Scarlett Potter, the sculptor and author, and his sister Rebecca (Bessie). They lived in Halford, a village near Shipston, at Rivat House, an interesting building known locally as 'The Folly'. Lily made many friends there and in the surrounding district and was held in great affection. In her later years she was presented with an easy chair by the people of Halford, and when she died in 1935 she left most of her few possessions to them.

❖ ❖ ❖

So far we have followed the fortunes of two of Lydia's sons, William and John Sisam, through the years since she moved with William from Harvington in 1847, leaving Frederick Sisam and his new bride Elizabeth in charge. Frederick prospered at Harvington and by 1851 he was raising crops, milling flour, producing malt, as well as baking and selling bread. He employed nine men, three of whom lived on the premises; namely Arthur Egg a baker, George Batchelor a carter, and George Ellis a maltster. The family household consisted of Frederick and Elizabeth, their baby daughter, Henrietta, aged one year, and Marty Harris, a seventeen-year old servant girl. Very soon there were added to the family two more daughters, Elizabeth and Marian.

On the surface all seemed to be well but, in the light of subsequent events, it seems as if something began to go awry during that time. For some unknown reason the family moved from Harvington to Sedgeberrow a few miles to the south of Evesham. There was a mill there on the River Isbourne where Frederick may have continued as a miller. At Sedgeberrow in 1854 a fourth daughter, Harriet, was born. At some point in the next few years Frederick disappeared and the family became scattered. Their names appeared without Frederick's in the Warwickshire section of the census returns of 1861. Elizabeth was listed as keeping house for a Marshall relative of Lydia's at Foss Farm, Compton Verney. The oldest daughter Henrietta was with her grandmother Lydia Sisam not far away at the Walton farm. Elizabeth the second child was boarding with the Winnett family at Inkberrow near Arrow, and Harriet was with her Hoare grandfather and aunts at Radway. It is not known where the other child Marian was. She would have been about eight years old.

No letters have survived to throw light on the reasons for Frederick's sudden disappearance. It may have been due to some quirk of character, or it may have had something to do with the circumstances under which he grew to manhood. He was the youngest of four brothers and lost his father when he was 14. His life during the next formative years was very much under his mother's influence. Then suddenly he took the initiative and married. After his marriage, when he was in full charge of Harvington, he had plenty with which to occupy himself, but he may have been restless in spirit. The fact that he and Elizabeth had daughters but no sons could have been a disappointment to him. It was shortly after the birth of his fourth daughter that he vanished. Where he went may well have remained a mystery as far as the family were concerned. His eventual whereabouts were nevertheless recorded in official government archives in London, to be discovered by future generations.

The first indication of where he went was found in the list of marriages that took place in England in 1864. In that year a marriage was recorded in Yorkshire between a Frederick Francis Sisam and a Martha Hargit. Although he was christened simply Frederick, by the time of this second marriage he had added Francis as a middle name. The marriage certificate showed that the wedding took place in the parish church of Penistone and that both bride and groom lived in the neighbouring village of Oxspring, which was a few miles north-west of Sheffield. Frederick was described as a miller and a 'widower', son of William Sisam, miller. The bride's age was given as 25 and Frederick's as 39 – five years younger than he really was. Earlier census records of 1861 for that part of Yorkshire do not list Frederick, but they show Martha Hargit working in the household of a miller, Henry Rolling and his wife, in Oxspring; which suggests that Frederick may have met Martha through working at the same mill. Frederick Francis is listed in a census ten years later, again he did not give his true age and he gave his birthplace as Faversham, Kent, instead of Arrow, Warwickshire. As to his being a 'widower' that cannot be so, for official records show that his first wife, Elizabeth, lived until 1903. It is unlikely that there had been a divorce; for although the process had become available about that time, the records

Certificate of Frederick Sisam's bigamous marriage. He added the name Francis, altered his age and described himself as a widower – though his first wife Elizabeth was still living. However he gave his father's name correctly as William Sisam, miller. (Reproduction permission: page 279)

The cotton-mill town of Glossop in Derbyshire where Frederick Sisam raised a second family.

show no proceedings on behalf of either Frederick or Elizabeth Sisam. There are no others by the unusual name of Frederick Sisam in the Public Records of births, deaths and marriages for any year. This is therefore clearly the same man.

Frederick Francis and Martha settled in Oxspring, where two children were born to them, both sons. They were named Hector Marshall and George Hargit, their second names commemorating in one case their grandmother Lydia's family, and in the other their mother's Hargit family. Soon after the birth of the second child in 1867 the family left Oxspring, travelling across the magnificent moorland area of the High Peak district into Derbyshire; to Glossop, a cotton-spinning town in a valley. Here they set up their second home at 5 Jordan Street, just off the High Street. Frederick continued his profession as a miller, probably at the corn-mill on a small river near their home. Further children were born here, Herbert in 1869, Mary Ann in 1872 and Harriet in 1874. Harriet it will be remembered was also the name of Frederick and Elizabeth's fourth daughter. This second Harriet only lived until she was twelve years old. Mary Ann grew up and married Dick Laycock, a draper from a neighbouring village, in 1903.

Glossop was originally a quiet market town in a predominantly sheep-rearing area. It was only a few miles from Manchester, where the manufacture of cotton was becoming established. Because of its plentiful water-power from the streams draining off the high moorland, Glossop attracted the building of water-driven cotton mills. The humidity of its atmosphere made it highly suitable for cotton-spinning. Through the development of the steam engine, waterpower was replaced by steam power and Glossop became a major cotton town providing employment for large numbers of people. It is not surprising that by 1881 Frederick Francis' three sons, Hector, George and Herbert, aged 15,14 and 12, were all working as twisters in the cotton mills.

Hector, who went on to become a cotton-weaver, married Mary Ellen FitzGerald in 1890. They lived at 9 Manor Street, Glossop. They had two sons: Frederick Francis, named after his grandfather, and George. Mary Ellen was a Roman Catholic. There had always been a flourishing Catholic community in Glossop, due to the influence of the Howard family who owned a large estate in the area. For several hundred years they had been the premier Roman Catholic family in England. The head of the family was the Duke of Norfolk. It was the Howards who built Glossop's magnificent Catholic church. The young Frederick Francis, Mary Ellen's elder son was almost certain to have been brought up in his mother's faith. He became a member of a Franciscan Order and took the name 'Father Gilbert'. He served many years in Italy at Bordighera, close to the French border and a few miles from Nice. He was also at Franciscan establishments at Forest Gate in London, at Clevedon in Somerset, at Cambridge, and finally at Gorton, Manchester where he died.

His brother George married Annie Beeley of a Derbyshire family, whose name probably originally derived from the village of Beeley near present-day Chatsworth. They lived at Altrincham, Cheshire, where their only child John was born in 1934. Later they moved to Ipswich and then to Tavistock in Devonshire, where George was a political party agent. John did well in mathematics at school and from there went to Exeter College, Oxford in 1954, where he took a B.A. degree in the subject. His speciality was computer programming. He worked for some years for Powers-Samas (which became I.C.T.) and for British Aluminium. He was in Ghana and Nigeria for three years, under the aegis of Cambridge University, working for the West African Examinations Council. He then settled in Cambridge, working for the University's Local Examinations Syndicate.

George Hargit the second son of Frederick Francis and Martha, who started life as a cotton twister, never married. The youngest son, Herbert, married Sarah Ann Jones in 1900. Their children were Harriet, Evelyn, Lilian, and Clifford. Clifford married Kathleen Dolan in 1943. They had two daughters, one of whom died in infancy.

As far as is known, none of the descendants of Martha and the first Frederick Francis were aware of his background or of the bigamous nature of his marriage, nor of the existence of his first family. Little is known about the lives of the daughters of his marriage to Elizabeth. The eldest, Henrietta Phoebe, went to live at Leamington Priors close to Warwick and became a dress-maker. Elizabeth, the second girl, lived to a great age and died in 1935 in the Alcester district. Marian probably went into service in London, as she married Charles Hugh Lewin at St. Peters, Pimlico in the district of St. George's, Hanover Square, London, in February 1890. He was a carpenter, the son of a cabinet maker and lived near Regents Park. Before the marriage Marian had been living and working at an elegant address in Grosvenor Place, behind Buckingham Palace. Of Harriet there is no trace after the mention of her in the 1861 census, aged 6 and living with her grandfather at Radway. Their mother Elizabeth went to live with Henrietta Phoebe at 2 Holly Street in a quiet part of Leamington Priors. Frederick Francis died in Derbyshire in 1898 at the age of 78. Elizabeth lived to be 81, dying at Leamington in 1903. At her death she was described as the 'wife of Frederick Sisam'.

4
The Arrow Family

Henry the Miller and his Six Sons

Throughout the years that saw the family's acquisition of Harvington Mill and the launching of the other enterprises at Mount Pleasant Farm, Walton, and at Postlip Lower Mill, Winchcombe, it was Henry and Caroline who had nurtured and maintained the family base at Arrow. Henry carried the responsibility of running Arrow Mill and of seeing that Harvington was adequately manned and functioning efficiently. The vacancy at Harvington caused by his brother Frederick's departure to Sedgeberrow and subsequent disappearance from the family scene, had presented a problem; for there was no one available in the family who could take Frederick's place. Henry had six sons, but they were all young boys except for William Henry, who was about 16. What immediate steps Henry took is not known. He probably employed a miller until one of his own sons could take charge, meanwhile exercising supervision himself whenever the work at Arrow permitted. The boys at Arrow were given a good education at Newport's School in Alcester (later to become Alcester Grammar School). They naturally became familiar with milling and helped in the mill, whatever might be their eventual occupation. As soon as William Henry was old enough his father sent him to take over Harvington Mill and, since he was as yet unmarried, his sister Ann Emily went with him as his housekeeper.

Fortunately for all those family undertakings, agriculture in England had recovered from the economic depression following the Napoleonic Wars. The general spirit of the time now seemed to be one of optimism. The streets of Alcester were already being lit by gaslight from sundown until two in the morning (except when there was a full moon), the railway had reached nearby Evesham, and Alcester itself was soon to be linked with the main railway networks. In 1857 a large and impressive Corn Exchange was built in Alcester's High Street. Henry became a shareholder in December of that year (Share number 239, £5) and the following year his name appeared in a list of annual subscribers together with those of Sir Richard Throckmorton a prominent local landowner, Richard Fisher a farmer, and members of the Bomford family. Arrow Mill was operating successfully, and the Sisams' lease from the Marquis of Hertford continued to run year after year.

Situated in a fertile river valley, Arrow Mill was in the heart of good farming country. There were close relationships between millers and farmers. Of the Bomford farming family, three were fellow members of the Alcester Corn Exchange with Henry Sisam and there developed a close connection between the Sisams and Bomfords, both in the older and younger generations. Henry's third son, Walter Sisam, struck up a friendship with Fred Bomford, whose parents farmed at Atch Lench near Harvington. The Bomfords were

The old Corn Exchange in Alcester High Street.

sincere Baptists and there was a large and well attended chapel near Atch Lench which they loyally supported. Fred Bomford was an ardent believer and he and Walter had many talks about faith. Walter had been brought up in the faith of his parents and would probably have attended the Anglican church at Arrow, just across the meadows from Arrow Mill, which was the church where he and all the family had been baptised. Then he began attending Baptist services and responded to the message he heard. He seems to have experienced a deepening of faith at that time, because after a while he began to preach occasionally at the recently built Baptist Chapel at Dunnington, near Arrow. The land for this chapel had been given by the Bomford family.

Oral tradition has it that Walter had thought seriously of becoming a minister of the Anglican Church and made some preparations for this in the course of which he learned Greek. He did apparently attend an interview and had to answer some theological questions. But, being of an independent mind, he sometimes gave his own answers rather than the answers expected, and he disagreed on some basic question of doctrine. He was not therefore considered a suitable candidate. However, he continued participating in the Baptist chapel gatherings. At some point, perhaps about this time, Henry sent him to Harvington to work at the mill with his eldest brother William Henry.

Henry and Caroline at Arrow had many things to ponder during these days, apart from the well-being of the two mills. There was the question of their sons' futures, including that of their youngest, Marshall, now in his early teens, who was delicate and would be unable to undertake physical work. William Henry was enjoying the responsibility of

The swiftly flowing waters of the River Arrow.

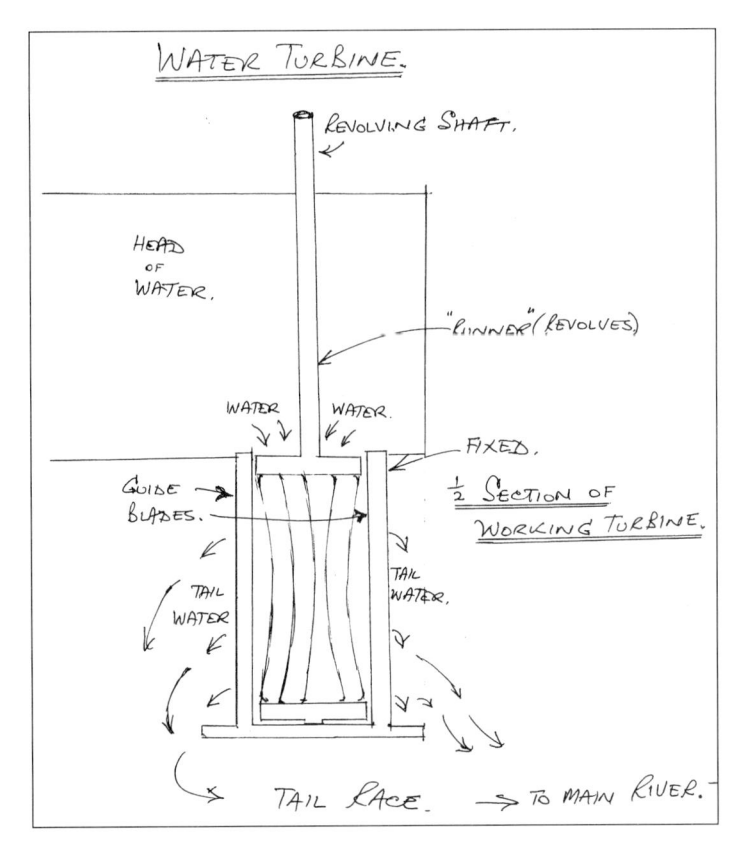

Diagram of the steel turbines with which Henry Sisam replaced the water-wheel at Arrow Mill.

Harvington Mill. As for the rest, Thomas Marshall (Tom) was of a happy disposition and full of humour. Walter had a good mind with a scholarly bent and a strong religious inclination. Alfred John proved to be reliable, able and adventurous. James Leonard showed promise, but being young was still an unknown quantity. All had a certain independance of spirit. At Arrow there would only be room for one son and his family when their father retired. The others would have to seek a living elsewhere.

It was now the year 1861 when there was much talk of emigration in Britain. In August there appeared in one of the Birmingham newspapers an announcement offering free grants of land in New Zealand to anyone who could pay his sea passage. Thirty thousand acres were on offer, each man to be given 40 acres, which he must hold for at least five years. The sea passage cost about £16 and the settlers had to be of good character and recommended by a magistrate. This bold scheme was the idea of William Rawson Brame, editor of *The Birmingham Mercury*, and son of a Birmingham Baptist minister. Very soon a settlers' organisation was formed with an office in Waterloo Street, Birmingham, and meetings were held throughout the Midlands. There was strong non-conformist and Anglican support. The project was based on idealistic and religious principles, and was imbued with the vision of a Promised Land. The settlement was to be known as Albertland, named after Prince Albert, Queen Victoria's late husband.

The fact of the matter was that the Government of New Zealand needed settlers, which was why free plots of land were being offered. The announcement attracted much attention, particularly as the war in America between North and South was deterring many would-be emigrants to that country. The scheme caught the imaginations of many young men in the area. Arrow was only 25 miles from Birmingham and three of the Sisam brothers, Tom, Walter and Alfred John, showed interest in the scheme. The opportunities it offered appealed to them, as did its idealistic concepts.

The latter appealed especially to Walter. The time was ripe for enterprise and adventure. Who amongst the three was the leading spirit is a matter of conjecture. Each would have had his reasons and motivations but, being young, they were of one mind in wanting to seek opportunity and fulfillment, and all three decided to emigrate.

It is said that Henry their father was against their going. Both he and Caroline must have experienced much heart searching. Nevertheless, Henry gave all three his blessing and sent them off with £100 and a zinc-lined wooden chest full of clothes each, plus the muzzle-loading gun used at Arrow to shoot sparrows in the ripening corn. They left England on May 29, 1862, from London's East India Dock. Before they boarded a band played *Auld Lang Syne* and the National Anthem, cannon were fired and a crowd of 15,000 sang a hymn as they waved good-bye. The emigrants departed on the sailing ship *Matilda Wattenbach*. Their destination was Auckland.

At Arrow now Henry and Caroline were left with their two youngest sons, James Leonard and the semi-invalid Marshall, and their youngest daughter Alice Jane, aged 14. Also living on the premises were George Knight a sixteen year-old miller, a cook Clare Partridge and a maidservant Hannah Molesworth. There was a wagoner who came in each day and this may have been Henry's cousin Joseph Sisam, now living in Alcester with his family. Under Henry's care the business at Arrow Mill prospered and expanded. In 1865 he took the lease of Oversley Mill, a mile upstream on the river, and used it to produce animal feed. Life at Arrow itself proceeded in a steady and tranquil

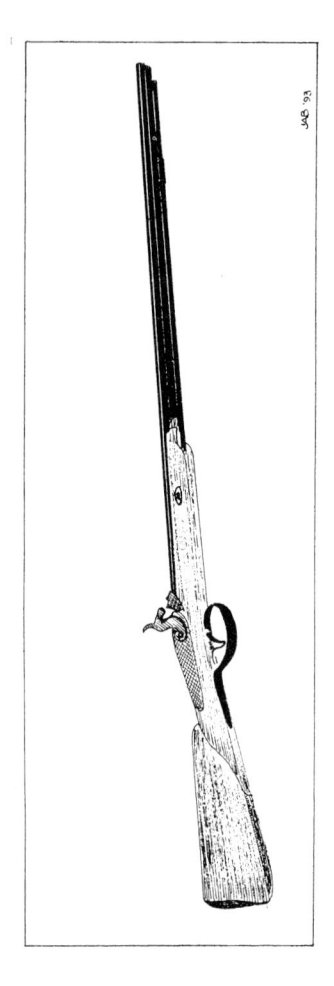

Flint-lock gun and powder flasks used at Arrow Mill to keep sparrows off the corn, and taken by Walter Sisam to New Zealand in 1862.

manner, and the neighbourhood went about its affairs as usual. The Alcester Corn Exchange reported on the fluctuating price of wheat and beans, the town saw the launching of its two newspapers, while in 1868 there was a very hot summer with a good wheat harvest.

With the rapid growth of railway construction in Britain, Alcester now had its railway link with the rest of the country. Coal was much in demand for domestic and other purposes, and it could now be brought to Alcester from the coalfields rapidly and cheaply, particulary from Cannock Chase in nearby Staffordshire. Although he was running Harvington Mill, William Henry saw this as an opportunity. He opened a coal business in Alcester, and at the same time set up as a dealer in agricultural commodities. He had his office in Alcester High Street and depots at railway stations in the locality, including Harvington. He had gone about it in a forthright fashion. On the front page of *The Alcester Chronicle* for November 7, 1868, there appeared two advertisements aimed at different types of customers. They were written in the polite yet business-like style of the time. The first one read as follows:

CANNOCK CHASE COALS

W. H. Sisam begs to inform the public that in consequence of the increased demand for the above Coals he will (from this date) have men in constant attention at Alcester, Wixford and Harvington Stations, where all orders will be promptly attended to. Orders will also be thankfully received at the OFFICE, HIGH STREET, ALCESTER, where a list of prices (much reduced from last year) may be had. Truckloads delivered to any station. August 27, 1868.

The other read:

W. H. SISAM
Wholesale and Retail Dealer in Corn, Flour, Meals,
Horse Corn, Stuffs, Bran, etc.
Dealer in Hay, Straw, and Salts of all descriptions.
High Street, Alcester. August 27, 1868.

Other advertisements in the same paper give a picture of the thriving social life of the town. The stationer and bookseller E.W.Wright, was offering cartes-de-visite, crests, monograms, Morocco-bound postage-stamp books, stereoscopes and collections of photographic views, as well as the latest novels. The annual hiring fair to be held in October was advertised, at which 'a fat ox' and 'a fat pig' would be roasted outside the Talbot Inn, and a travelling theatre company was reported as being in the town.

Harvington also had its cultural events. *The Evesham Journal* of February 3, 1866, had carried a glowing description of a musical evening held in a capacious room lent by G. Malin Esq., when the Harvington Choir gave their annual concert. There was a large audience and the room was decorated with flowers and Chinese lamps. The programme included such favourites as, *Autumn Winds, Lordly Gallant, The Sleep of Flowers,* and *The Soldier's Farewell.* Ann Emily Sisam the sister of William Henry, then living at Harvington Mill, took part as did four of the Bullock family, the Sisams' nearest neighbours. Amongst the Bullock party was William Bullock, Ann Emily's future husband.

The following year there was the first wedding in Henry and Caroline's family; not Ann Emily's wedding but that of her brother William Henry, for whom she had keen keeping house at Harvington. The bride was Helen New from Langley Farm, a 16th century homestead on the hills above Winchcombe. The name New, like that of Bomford, was well-known in the district. News had lived in Evesham for over three hundred years. In the 1860s there were several branches of the family farming among the valleys and hills between Evesham and Cheltenham, particularly at Ashchurch and Beckford under Bredon Hill, and at Winchcombe and Bishop's Cleeve. Charles Morris Marshall New, Helen's father, was a prosperous farmer who had died in 1862 at the age of 59. The elder New girls had many friends in the neighbourhood and enjoyed a lively social life. They did not lack suitors.

Helen New's marriage to William Henry Sisam took place on June 24, 1869, at Winchcombe. He was 30 and she was 20 years old. It was held in the medieval church with its golden weather vane and grotesque gargoyles designed to ward off evil spirits. It was a grand occasion at which the two families met, the News from Langley and

The New family of Langley Farm, Winchcombe, c. 1872. Front row seated: Mary, Mary Ann (widow), Ellen. Second row: George, Letitia (married James Leonard Sisam), Helen, (married William Henry Sisam), Nora, Bessie, Fanny, Maria, Frank, Joseph. Back row: William, John, Charles.

elsewhere and the Sisams from Harvington, Arrow and Winchcombe. The joining of the families proved to be a happy event for more reasons than one, for it was followed later by another marriage between the Sisams and the News. In Helen's bridal party was her younger sister Letitia, one of the two witnesses to sign the marriage register. A few years later Letitia was to marry James Leonard Sisam, William Henry's younger brother.

There is an old photograph, taken shortly after Helen's wedding, which gives an interesting glimpse of the life-style of the New family. It is a picture of the family posed in a formal group on the front lawn at Langley, showing Mary New surrounded by her five sons and eight daughters. All are immaculately dressed. The men are in perfectly tailored suits and bow-ties. The youngest boy, aged about ten, is in a dark jacket, striped trousers, and what appears to be a spotted neck-tie. The older daughters are in fashionable, wasp-waisted dresses, flounced and frilled, and surmounted by chokers with oval brooches. The oldest daughter Mary who married George Harvey, son the the Vicar of Winchcombe, sits next to her mother, who in contrast to her daughters is dressed in widow's black. Behind them stands the very handsome Helen, who dominates the scene with an impressive bouffant hair-style.

After their marriage in 1869, William Henry and Helen, instead of going to Harvington, went to live in the High Street at Alcester, where William Henry had his corn and coal-dealing business. This was part of a somewhat complicated family re-shuffle to ensure the effective operation of the three main branches of the family enterprise of which Arrow Mill was the cornerstone. These branches were now Arrow Mill itself with Oversley, Harvington Mill, and the flourishing corn and coal business in Alcester. Henry had now retired from milling at Arrow, leaving one of his younger sons, James Leonard aged 24, in charge of the day-to-day running of the mill. In this James Leonard worked in close consultation with William Henry who, as the eldest son, bore the ultimate responsibility for the family undertakings. The whole operation was greatly facilitated by William Henry's move to Alcester. He and James Leonard also worked closely together in the operation of the Alcester corn and coal business. It was at this point that their uncle John Sisam, who had been corn-miling at Winchcombe, moved to Harvington to take on the mill there.

William Henry must have carried a heavy load since these events all took place within a few years of his marriage, and in the midst of them were other events affecting the inner life of the family. The home where he and Helen lived was pleasantly situated in the High Street. This street was comprised of dwelling houses and shops on either side, the Corn Exchange, various hostelries and the church standing foursquare at the top. Here the road curved round the church and the adjacent medieval houses to the old market hall, and thence into the open countryside beyond. William Henry and Helen had been settled less than a year in their new home when Henry Sisam died at Arrow Mill in May 1870. Only two months later his first grandson was born, William Henry and Helen's son Henry Charles. The child was named after his two grandfathers, but only lived until he was two years old. William Henry was now employing seven men in the corn and coal business. His semi-invalid youngest brother Marshall, aged 23, had joined the family household in the High Street, and was acting as clerk responsible for the accounts. The following year a daughter, Emily Mary, was born to William Henry and Helen, and earlier in that year there had been a family wedding at Arrow. The loyal and faithful, Ann Emily, William Henry's sister, was married to William Bullock from the farm next to Harvington Mill.

John and Sarah Sisam were soon well established at Harvington. He had three men working for him, plus a carter, and a maid-servant in the house. John took part in local affairs, as his predecessors had done and, being what was known as a 'substantial householder', he was appointed as one of the Overseers of the Poor for the village. He was however getting on in years and, as we have already seen, it was not long before he retired from milling. When that time came William Henry and Helen moved from Alcester to live at Harvington, taking charge of the mill; at the same time they continued the Alcester business with the help of James Leonard and Marshall.

William Henry and Helen had nearly five happy years together at Harvington. Three more children were born to them, Caroline Helen, William, and Alfred John Marshall. In the wider family the year 1876 was long remembered for two weddings that took place on two successive days. On Tuesday, April 19, in Arrow Church, James Leonard took part in the marriage of his younger sister, Alice Jane, to John Fisher, a farmer's son of Arrow. The next day James Leonard hurried over to Winchcombe where he himself was married to Helen Sisam's younger sister, Letitia New, in Winchcombe Church; and thereby the household at Arrow Mill gained a new mistress, who was to preside over it for nearly 35 years. The following year, 1877, began with rejoicing but then brought sadness and change. In January there was the birth of William Henry and Helen's youngest child,

Alfred John Marshall Sisam. In March, William Henry's youngest brother, the ailing Marshall who had been his clerk in the Alcester business, died; and in December, in the last days of the year, William Henry himself died at the age of 39. The mantle of the family enterprises then fell upon the shoulders of James Leonard, who was then 32.

For some years Helen continued to run the corn and coal business in Alcester, supported and encouraged by her sister Letitia Sisam, at Arrow, and Letitia's husband James Leonard. The two sisters had always been close to one another and in Alcester visited each other once a week. Helen's mother-in-law, Caroline Sisam, was also living in Alcester, in a street quite near to her known as the Priory. Caroline's home was a detached white house standing on the corner of School Lane. When in 1881 she went to Park Cottage in Arrow, Helen and her children moved into the Priory house. A few years later Helen remarried. Her husband was William Hunt, an Alcester builder. They made their home in Henley Street, where their two children were born: a son, Ernest (Josh), and a daughter, Emily (Peggy), and these children grew up together with Helen's older Sisam children. By nature Helen was a quiet, capable person with a sincere religious faith, which she did her best to encourage in her children. Ironically Josh, her son by her second marriage, grew up an agnostic and was keen on horse-racing and became a book-maker. Josh had a daughter Helen Diana who, on the other hand, graduated in sociology at London University and while there felt called to spiritual work. She spent most of her life in India working in Bombay at a university hostel. Josh's sister Peggy married a naval officer, Thomas Fox, and later married Clive Rattigan, thus finding herself aunt to Terence Rattigan, the West End playwright. Of Helen's Sisam children: Emily Mary, following her mother's spiritual inclinations, became a Salvation Army officer. Caroline married John Hook. William qualified as a doctor, married Florence Louise Hall, but had no children. He became Medical Officer of Health in Reading. Alfred John Marshall never married.

The passing of these years had seen a steady progression of marriages, births and deaths in the family, and the upheavals that sometimes accompanied them. Throughout it all Arrow Mill and Harvington Mill had remained islands of stability in a changing world; and in the next years under James Leonard's care they would continue to fulfill this role.

❖ 5 ❖
Seedtime & Harvest

FOUNDERS OF THE CANADIAN BRANCH 1875–1990

One of the most important family events during John and Sarah Sisam's years at Harvington Mill was their son William Bernard's departure for Oxford University. He went from Harvington to Oriel College in April 1875 to study for the degree of Bachelor of Arts in Modern History. His ultimate calling was to be a minister of religion. This may have been in his mind at the outset, or it may have come to him during his years of study. He arrived in Oxford at a time of great change when in 1875, following a Royal Commission, the whole system of teaching and the curriculum had been transformed. Up until this point it had been possible to get a degree after three years of study without taking an examination. Now a degree was only given after successful examinations. Having first satisfied the Oxford examiners as to his proficiency in Latin Prose and Mathematics, William Bernard spent his first two years on ancient classical subjects, this being the normal foundation on which any main study was based. He read the Greek orator Demosthenes and the Latin philosopher Cicero. He studied Logic and the Gospels of the Bible. Then came a final year's study of Modern History itself. He received his degree in the summer of 1878. The following year in Worcester Cathedral he was ordained a priest in the Church of England, and was appointed to work as a curate at the parish church of Shipston-on-Stour under the rector the Rev. William Briscoe. Shipston was in Worcestershire then, but was later incorporated into Warwickshire. It was the home country of his mother's family, the Potters, who lived at Longdon Farm about three miles away. William may have applied for the appointment for this reason, and also because his sister Lily was now running a private school in Shipston. Their parents, who had by now retired from Harvington Mill, moved into the area at about that time.

Shipston-on-Stour, which lies about eight miles from Stratford-upon-Avon, was originally a Saxon settlement on the banks of the River Stour. It's name meant 'a dwelling place near the ford over the river, where sheep are washed'. The first church was built there in the 11th century beside the river, with the churchyard reaching down towards the water's edge. When William Bernard came there it had recently been rebuilt but retained it's Norman porch and tower. A little way upstream was a flour mill, and opposite the church narrow streets led to the market square. The town had spacious inns and had long been a centre for passing travellers and the local farming community. The extensive parish boundaries included farmland, homesteads and hamlets, and a small 12th century subsidiary church in the village of Tidmington.

The name curate, from the latin word 'cura' (care), means a man with the care of souls, and William Bernard's work was to assist the rector in ministering to the spiritual needs of the people of the town and district. Much of this was concerned with the various church services and the conducting of marriages, baptisms and burials. The rector, being the priest in charge of the parish, would naturally carry out the more important duties, but William played a full part. It brought him in touch with families in the town and in the surrounding countryside. Within a short time of his arrival he was announcing in church the Marriage Banns of various couples declaring their intention to marry, and from time to time he performed marriage ceremonies. One such was for Charles Hopes, a farmworker, and his bride Hannah Martha Carter; another was for Thomas Marshall, son of an innkeeper and a carrier by trade, to Sarah Ann Cooper. In the three months from July to October 1880, when the rector was abroad, William Bernard baptised no less than twenty-two children. They were from a cross-section of the community. The proud fathers included two carpenters, a farmer, a butcher, a tanner, a hay-trusser, a shoe-maker, an ostler, a blacksmith, an auctioneer, a grocer, a lawyer, a sawyer, a tailor and a road-mender. For him the personal contact with people was as important as the conducting of services.

As he went about the countryside in the seedtime of early spring, William Bernard would have seen the sowers at work in the fields scattering the seed by hand in anticipation of the harvest to come; and no doubt he was reminded of the biblical story of the sower. William's work of sowing the good seed of the gospel was just beginning, but he had no means of knowing what harvest there might be, or whether he would see it. As it happened he was only in Shipston for two years. In 1881 he was appointed to Newton-le-Willows in Lancashire. This was a complete change of scene. Newton-le-Willows was once a country village, but when he went there it was fast becoming part of the great manufacturing area centred on Manchester. At that time it had a population of about

Radclive, Buckinghamshire, where William Bernard Sisam was curate and from where he left to go to Burma in 1887.

12,800 and contained foundries, paper-mills, glass-works and sugar refineries. Nearby were the highly productive mines of the Lancashire coalfield, which provided it with fuel.

Owing to the nature of his work, a constant change of scene was to be a feature of William's life for many years to come. Though in some ways a restless life, it was to afford him wide experience. Within two years he was transferred from Newton-le-Willows to the church of St. Paul, Camden Square; in Camden Town, a large residential area in north-west London. The Square and its surroundings were part of the building development that followed the opening of the great London railway termini: Euston, Kings Cross and St. Pancras stations. Camden Town was part of the borough of St. Pancras, a thickly populated area of 236,000 people. William worked as a curate here for two years.

After Camden Town he returned to the countryside. He was appointed to the village of Radclive in Buckinghamshire, a few miles from the town of Buckingham. Radclive, with its tiny Norman church, lay on a peninsular of land formed by a loop of the river known as the Greater Ouse. About eleven miles upstream from Radclive on this winding river was Syresham, from which the Anglo-Saxon name Sisam had originated. After two years at Radclive an opportunity came to serve overseas. He was posted to Burma, to the Dioscese of Rangoon, where there was a shortage of trained men. The year was 1887. This was an eventful year in England. The novelist and poet Thomas Hardy published his rural idyll, *The Woodlanders*; Mr. W.H. Smith, whose family founded a chain of stationers and booksellers, became leader of the House of Commons; and Queen Victoria celebrated her Golden Jubilee of 50 years reign, with rejoicings in every city, town and village. Zululand was annexed and Baluchistan, lying between India and Persia, was incorporated into British-ruled India. The boundaries of the British Empire were spreading wider and wider.

The Burma to which William Bernard's duties took him had by this time become a province of British India. It had been ruled hitherto by a succession of Burmese kings, many of them able men and some of them notable warriors, as eager to extend their territory as the British were to defend what they held. Trade was a dominant factor. The British were anxious to obtain control of the coastline from Calcutta to Singapore, including the coast of southern Burma, in order to protect their trade. It had been only a matter of time before the Burmese and British clashed. In the event three wars occurred at intervals, the final and decisive one ending in 1886. When William Bernard arrived in Rangoon units of the British Army of India, now stationed in the city, had only recently subdued the last of Burmese guerilla bands operating in the upper reaches of the Irrawaddy Valley.

British rule brought a certain stability and prosperity to the country. Travel and communication were greatly improved. A railway was built northward from Rangoon to Prome, and later to Mandalay and Lashio towards the Chinese frontier. The Irrawaddy delta became one of the most productive rice-growing areas in the world. The timber trade also developed. The people's standard of living rose, but at the same time the greater part of the wealth created was taken out of the country. Many of the population remained sad at heart. They were a people of ancient traditions and resented having to live in a mere province of India. They felt a cultural loss, especially as their indigenous schools, nurtured for centuries by the Buddhist monasteries, seemed threatened by Christian missions.

Rangoon lay some seventy miles east of Burma's largest river, the Irrawaddy. It was situated on the banks of the Hlaing, a shorter river running roughly parallel to the Irrawaddy. At Rangoon itself the Hlaing was over a mile wide and provided a huge natural

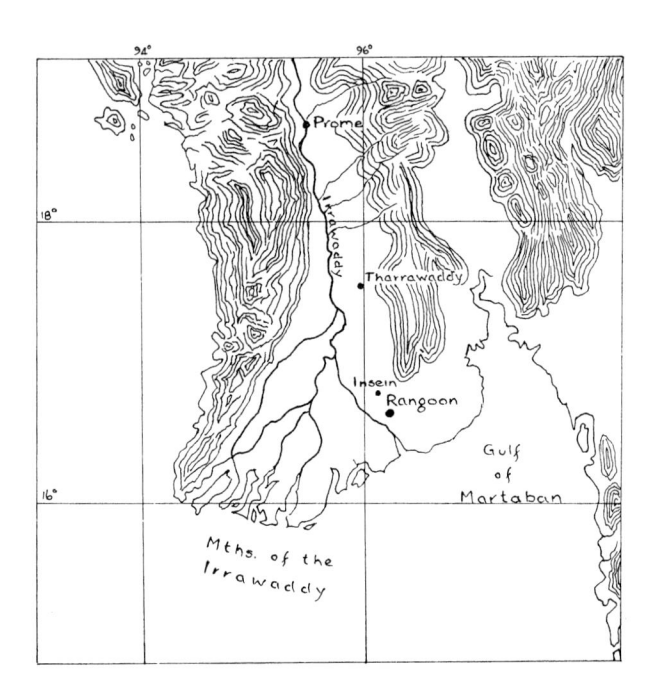

An area of Southern Burma showing the Irrawaddy River valley where William Bernard Sisam worked.

harbour, the shores of which were lined with innumerable warehouses, rice-mills and teak wharves. Taller than London's St.Paul's cathedral and dominating the scene, stood the gold-coated stupa of the great Buddhist Shwe Dagon Pagoda. It was surrounded by a population of over 200,000 people, mainly Buddhist and Hindu. As a trading port Rangoon was, after Calcutta and Bombay, the third busiest in that part of the world.

William Bernard Sisam was posted to Burma as chaplain in charge of the parish of St. Philip in East Rangoon. His duties were not primarily those of a missionary to the Burmese but of a minister to the English population who lived and worked in the city. His congregations would have been mainly drawn from the shipping and commercial community, and would have included Anglo-Burmans. His outlook was probably that of most Europeans of that time; for it took a great many years for the concepts of de-colonization, self-rule and international cooperation to emerge and become widely accepted. Nevertheless, one of the duties of a chaplain in Rangoon would have been to encourage his parishioners to live their faith in practical terms in their dealings with others, regardless of race or status. If he succeeded, then this might eventually lead to new attitudes and enlightened thinking.

After two years in East Rangoon he was moved ten miles north-west of the city to Insein. It lay in the lower part of the Irrawaddy Valley, and was a centre of the Burmese railway. The main workshops were here, also a government engineering school and the largest gaol in the area. Personnel of these and other establishments would have been amongst his congregations. The valley became familiar to William as his duties at Insein also included responsibility for the parish of St. Mark at Prome, and the settlement of Tharrawaddy, both of which were on the banks of the Irrawaddy to the north of Insein.

Prome was known for its pagaoda-topped hills, silk cloth, lacquer-ware, and custard apples; also for a temperature reaching 100 degrees Fahrenheit in June.

Unfortunately the damp, hot climate of Burma took its toll. William suffered severe attacks of malaria and was finally advised by doctors to leave Burma and to go and live in a more favourable climate. He left in 1890 for the dry warmth of Australia, where he hoped to recover his health. Two years later he was fit enough to resume work. He was sent as curate to the small town of Bourke in northern New South Wales, located on the upper waters of the Darling River, where the winter navigation reached its limit. It was a sheep-farming community of 2,500 souls, and boasted one of the best annual agricultural shows. The surrounding country, although it had narrow strips of pasture along the river banks, was mainly arid plain. It contained plentiful deposits of rich copper ore. He served two years at Bourke and was then moved to Wentworth to take charge of the parish. This was a township over a thousand miles downstream from Bourke, at the point where the Darling River joined the Murray on its way to the sea. His next move was in 1899 to New Zealand, first to Leeston, south-west of Christchurch, and then to the Banks Peninsular where he was appointed Vicar of Little River.

He had now served overseas for twelve years, and was as yet unmarried. His thoughts had been turning to his family in England. His parents had died and there was only one close relation left, his eldest sister Lily, to whom he owed his early education. Determined to visit her, he set off from New Zealand in 1903. The route he took was a circuitous one across the Pacific Ocean to the North American continent, for he had friends he wished to visit first in eastern Canada. After a short stay in the West at Brandon in Manitoba he crossed the country to Halifax, Nova Scotia, where he expected to stay two weeks before resuming his journey. Here he met Emma Annie Ancient, the eldest of five children of an Anglican minister. Her father was best remembered for rescuing shipwrecked passengers from the *S.S. Atlantic* off the stormy Nova Scotian coast in 1871. Annie and William fell in love. He was 47 and she was 38. As one of the family later wrote, 'That must have been love at first sight for instead of going to England in two weeks it was some years before he saw his sister'.

William and Annie were married in September 1904. Meanwhile he had become temporary curate of St. Luke's church, Halifax. Shortly afterwards in the same year the couple moved to Summerside on Prince Edward Island, where they set up their own home. He held the post of Rector of Summerside. After a year they moved to Springhill on the mainland, where they remained two years. Here in May 1906 a son was born to them, John William Bernard. The following year William was appointed Rector of St. George's Church, Moncton, in the neighbouring province of New Brunswick; the western border of which, together with that of the New England State of Maine, forms the Canadian–American frontier.

Moncton was a town of 9,000 people and a railroad centre, where the Intercolonial Railway had its headquarters. This railway played an important part in the development of eastern Canada as it united the Maritime Provinces with the Great Lakes region, and later linked up with the transcontinental Grand Trunk Railway. As well as being the Intercolonial's operating headquarters, Moncton was the location of the railway's engineering workshops. When the Sisams moved to Moncton in 1907 it was recovering from a major disaster. The previous year a fire had broken out in the railway workshops destroying not only them but most of the town as well. A vigorous rebuilding programme was in progress. The population was mixed, a third being of Irish and French Catholic descent, and two thirds English. The latter were largely descendents of New England settlers from across the American border, who lost their lands during or after the 1775–1781 American War of Independence.

It was probably soon after they came to Moncton that William made his long delayed journey to England. It is unlikely that Annie would have accompanied him, since she had an infant son to look after and a new home to care for. Lily Sisam in England had now retired from teaching and was with her Potter uncle and aunt at Halford near Shipston-on-Stour. The date of the trip may have been 1912, for in that year he was in Oxford to receive his M.A. degree. Perhaps his sister Lily accompanied him and watched her erstwhile pupil take part in the ancient and colourful degree ceremony in the Sheldonian Theatre, in Oxford's wide street known as The Broad.

When William returned to New Brunswick he settled into what proved to be a permanent sphere of work and a permanent family home. Being now a family man he was no longer likely to be moved from parish to parish, or to be called on to fill vacancies wherever they occurred. New Brunswick was now his homeland and he would have time to come to know and appreciate it. It was a comparatively small province but rich in natural resources and scenery. It had fertile valleys supporting prosperous farms, and a network of rivers and lakes. There were dense forests where moose, caribou and deer were plentiful, and where the native black spruce fed a major pulp and papermaking industry. It was a province of great beauty where, after the first frosts of autumn, 'Indian summers' of magical light and colour occurred. It's coasts abounded in herring, salmon, lobster,

Landscape of river and forest in New Brunswick, Canada.

sardines and ocean perch. The climate was invigorating and productive, with an average yearly rainfall of 32 inches and snowfall of 97 inches. This was the setting in which the young John Bernard was to grow from childhood to maturity.

St. George's Church in Moncton was under the jurisdiction of the Bishop of Fredericton, the capital city of New Brunswick, where the cathedral and headquarters of the diocese were situated. William very soon became active in diocesan affairs, and was appointed Examining Chaplain to the Bishop the year after he came to Moncton. Four years later, in 1912, he was made a Canon of Fredericton Cathedral, which title he held for life. He worked assiduously in Moncton for twenty-five years, during which time the spiritual life of the parish developed and flourished, culminating in the building of a new and larger church. To describe his work in these years as that of a sucessful minister of religion would be superficial. His colleagues and contemporaries in New Brunswick knew the secret of those years. They saw him not only as a man of wide experience dedicated to his calling, but as a man of great sincerity with a deep love and understanding of individuals. In recalling his years at Moncton they remembered how he helped people personally in their lives and was a guide to many. He was, they said, 'courteous, humble and kindly' and, in the words of their day, 'a Christian gentleman'.

During this time young John Bernard was receiving his schooling. He went first to Aberdeen High school in Moncton. As a young boy growing up in a region of magnificent scenery, richly forested and with a flourishing lumber industry, he set his heart on a career in forestry. His father disapproved on the grounds that forestry was a new profession as yet unproved. So John was sent to a teachers's training college in Fredericton, the provincial capital, for a two-year course. From there he went to teach in a single-room country schoolhouse. After a year there he convinced his father that forestry was his calling, and went to the University of New Brunswick in Fredericton. He graduated as a Bachelor of Science with First Class Honours in 1931 and was awarded the Lt. Governor's medal at the age of 26. He was now stepping into an era of scientific progress in which world forestry would make significant advances in the management and conservation of woodland areas. When he was a child Canada was already the fourth largest exporter of timber in the world and demand was increasing. To meet that demand and yet conserve resources, trained men were now needed.

John Bernard joined the Dominion Government Forestry Service on leaving the University of New Brunswick, and in the following year he married Elizabeth (Betty) Stewart Neill on October 15, 1932. She was from an old and distinguished Fredericton family. Theirs proved to be a truly happy marriage for they had many things in common. For the next five years John conducted forestry research in the provinces of Nova Scotia, New Brunswick, Quebec, Ontario and Manitoba. Towards the end of this period he studied for his master's degree. Since New Brunswick did not offer a master's degree in forestry, graduates usually went to the United States to take the further, two-year advanced course. John Bernard went to Yale University at New Haven, Connecticut, the southernmost of the New England States. As distances go in that part of the world, Yale was not all that far from New Brunswick, being about 300 miles south of the New Brunswick-United States border. He and Betty made a temporary home at New Haven for the duration of the university course.

His father, the long-serving Canon of Fredericton Cathedral, was now in his seventies and nearing the end of his eventful and fruitful life. He had lived through 'seedtime' and he had begun to see the 'harvest'. He died in 1937, the year that John Bernard gained his master's degree. In that same year a first grandson was born in New Haven, Peter Neill Sisam.

Like his father, John Bernard was a tall and well-built man. In him would also be seen many of his father's rare human qualities. In 1936 the Dominion Forestry Service had appointed John to head the tree-cultivation research at the Petawawa Forest Experimental Station in Ontario. It was situated on the Ottawa River, about 100 miles north-west of Ottawa, near the Algonquin Provincial Park, one of the first forest areas in Canada to be set aside for conservation and research. This was a time when the Canadian pulp and paper industry was expanding to meet growing world demand. Research into the growth of trees, by controlled seeding and planting, was therefore of prime importance, not only to the pulp and paper industry but to all users of timber. At the same time, forestry research was enlarging its scope to include wider issues, such as the effects of tree cropping on soil fertility, rainfall, soil erosion, flooding, and water supplies. These issues were now coming under scrutiny at government level in an increasing number of countries. There was also need for a greater interchange of information on forestry techniques and on these wider issues. In 1938, in England, the Department of Forestry at Oxford University established a Bureau for the collection and dissemination of forestry information on a world-wide basis. This was the Imperial Forestry Bureau, later known as the Commonwealth Forestry Bureau. John William Bernard Sisam transferred to Oxford from the Canadian Forestry Service that same year, and as assistant director took part in establishing the Bureau. In July 1939, when its initiator left for Nigeria, he was appointed Director.

He planned to bring his family over from Canada and make a home in Oxford, and accordingly rented a house. But the international situation in Europe was deteriorating rapidly. Events were leading to the outbreak of war, and the house in Oxford was soon commandeered for war purposes. The family furniture that had come from Canada was stored in London and John Bernard took lodgings in Oxford, in Crick Road. Betty and young Peter were marooned in Canada as, owing to wartime shipping restrictions, they could not join him.

The work of the Department of Forestry in Oxford, and of the Forestry Bureau which was a part of it, was regarded as important in time of war and continued without interruption. John Bernard, in addition to his responsibilty for collecting, co-ordinating and distributing technical information, made a number of special studies which in due course were published. A book on *The Use of Aerial Survey in Forestry and Agriculture*, was one of these. In between his administrative work and military service in the British Home Guard, he also travelled extensively in Britain collecting scientific information and advising on woodland planting and cropping. Timber imports, on which Britain normally depended, had been severely reduced by enemy attacks on shipping, so that home-grown timber became a priority need, as was the planting of new trees to replace those being felled. On these expeditions he often worked with a colleague from the Agricultural Bureau, R.O. Whyte. Amongst other undertakings they jointly researched and wrote a study on land reclamation, published under the title, *The Establishment of Vegetation on Industrial Waste Land*.

John Bernard's association and friendship with R.O. Whyte was instrumental in re-establishing the contact between the Canadian and English Sisams. William Bernard, the father of John Bernard, was a first cousin of the Sisams who were at Arrow Mill in the

1870s and 1880s, but, through his subsequent peripatetic life overseas and eventual settlement in New Brunswick, he had lost touch with most of the family in England, and by John Bernard's generation the link was non-existent. The latter's friend, R.O. Whyte, had a sister working in the Radcliffe Infirmary, a large hospital near the centre of Oxford. On the staff there was a Letty Sisam, whose father had been born at Arrow Mill. Her family knew of the Sisams in Canada but had no idea that John Bernard was in Oxford. Now the two branches of the family were able to link-up again.

In late April 1944, John Bernard was about to visit these Sisams at their home at Moreton-in-Marsh in the Cotswolds, when, out of the blue, he received a message saying that Betty and the boy Peter were en route for England by sea. He had to cancel his Cotswold visit and search Oxford for somewhere for his family to live. Betty and Peter arrived in early June. This was at a time of high drama. On June 6 the Allied Invasion of Europe began with the landings on the Normandy Coast of France. Within 24 hours ambulance trains of wounded men were passing through Moreton-in-Marsh. At the Radcliffe Infirmary in Oxford, Letty Sisam had been called out at midnight to run a canteen for army stretcher bearers, who had suddenly and without warning arrived with casualties. On June 13 the first of many German jet-propelled flying bombs landed on London.

John Bernard and Betty settled into a furnished house in Hernes Road, Oxford, belonging to a London newspaper cartoonist named Burrows, 'Our Obstinate Artist' of the *Daily Sketch*. Here in Hernes Road they were able to make a home together, after five years of unforeseen separation. John Bernard could now devote himself to his family, and begin to think about the future. He and Betty were a couple of great charm and made a deep impression on the English Sisams, who met them in Oxford. To Letty's mother, Betty appeared 'a fascinating creature, dark and rather lovely and so friendly', and as relatives they were 'a family to be proud of'. Six and a half year-old Peter was tickled to see two Mrs. Sisams in their home at the same time. He was attending New College School from 9 to 4 daily, a tough little boy who took himself to school and back each day on the bus, and thought nothing of it. Soon he had a new baby brother, John David, born in Oxford in 1945.

Strangely enough three years earlier, in 1942 while John Bernard was in Oxford, one of his English cousins, Harry (Francis Henry) Sisam of the Arrow Mill family, visited Toronto, Canada, on leave from the British Royal Navy, while awaiting posting to a new ship. Hospitable Canadians entertained such birds of passage. Harry found himself dining with the Bishop of Toronto. The Bishop, noting Harry's surname, said to him, 'Ah, Sisam – are you any relation of my old friend Canon William Bernard Sisam of Moncton, New Brunswick?', and was delighted to find that this was so. When peace came Harry settled in Canada.

The Canadian Sisams in Oxford returned to their home country in November 1945. John Bernard had relinquished his post in England, and joined the University of Toronto as an Associate Professor, becoming Dean of Forestry there in 1947, where he was able to fulfil his basic desire to teach forestry. He held the post for nearly thirty years and after retirement retained the honorary title, Dean Emeritus, for his remaining life-time.

He always worked extremely hard but at the same time he had wide-ranging interests and made the most of his leisure. At home he produced the breakfast each morning – usually bacon and eggs; after which he would read the paper and play a few records, some

Canon William Bernard Sisam of Monckton, New Brunswick.

John William Bernard Sisam, Dean of the Faculty of Forestry at the University of Toronto.

Peter Neill Sisam, television executive, a grandson of William Bernard Sisam.

piano concertos sprinkled with the odd Broadway musical such as *South Pacific* or *Oklohoma*. He loved the ocean and spent many holidays on the coast of New Brunswick or over the border in Maine.

His years at the University of Toronto were years of intense activity in the promotion of the principles and practice of sound forestry, not only within the university but throughout the province of Ontario and beyond. He served as President of the Conservation Council of Ontario, he was chairman of forestry committees advising the Government of Ontario, and the Food and Agricultural Organisation of the United Nations. In 1971 in Stockholm he acted as Chairman of the World Consultation on Forestry Education and Training. In his later years, he and Betty travelled widely abroad on FAO(UN) work on behalf of the Canadian Government. This was a great bonus to them, for travel was one of the many loves they had in common. The full programme of work was relieved in later life by welcome, annual breaks in the sunshine of the Barbados when the Canadian winter was at its severest. His last publication, issued in 1983 by the Toronto University Press, was *Forestry and Forestry Education in a Developing Country – a Canadian Dilemma*.

John William Bernard Sisam died in 1990 at the age of 86. Whilst in England he had always been called John, but latterly in Canada he was affectionately known as Bernie. When in 1956 his old university, New Brunswick, honoured him with a doctorate, in addition to his various achievements the citation referred to his 'work ably done and yet to do' and to his 'engaging personality'. Of his work since then the Toronto University publication *The Forestry Chronicle* wrote of him, 'most Canadians will never realise what gratitude they owe to Dean Sisam for what he has done to help place Canadian forestry on a solid foundation'; and referred to him as 'a gracious gentleman'. John William Bernard and William Bernard, his father, were outstanding men, both in their ability and their humanity.

John Bernard's sons remained in Toronto. Peter Neill became a Vice-President of Canada's leading television network (CTV), and later joined Baton Broadcasting as Director of Marketing. Peter married Mary Susan Hamilton in 1959 in Toronto. They have two sons, Christopher Neill and Patrick Hamilton, and one daughter Joanne Mary. John David became an architect and in 1977 he married Elizabeth Szubski, whose family came from Poland. They have two girls, Kate and Amy, and a son Matthew. Since both Peter and David have flourishing families, the future of this branch of the Sisam family seems assured and full of promise.

6
Trial & Tribulation

TRANSPORTATION TO AUSTRALIA – MORMON MISSIONARIES

The founder of the Canadian branch of the family, William Bernard Sisam, was named after his grandfather, William Sisam of Arrow Mill, who had begun as a farmer and then moved into malting and corn milling. William's descendants in England were mostly corn millers and continued as such for a hundred years. William's younger brother Joseph did not turn to milling but remained a farmer, thus following earlier Sisams who had worked the soil of this area since the early 1700s.

Joseph Sisam was aged 15 when his father died in 1801 and left him a plot of land and a dwelling house in the hamlet of Hill and Moor, Fladbury. The plot was probably two or three acres and the house a thatched cottage. He would already have been familiar with it, and may have worked on the plot as part of the acreage the family had farmed over the years. In 1808, when he was 21, he married Elizabeth Wells from the village of Broad Marston, near Pebworth, just over the border in the neighbouring county of Gloucestershire. The wedding was held, not in Pebworth, but in Worcester, at St. Clement's Church, near the south bank of the River Severn. Their first daughter, Sarah, was born a year later at the home of Elizabeth's mother who was now living in the village of Long Marston.

In 1811 Joseph moved with his family to the Bidford-on-Avon area, living most of the time at Marlcliff. This was close to the river Avon, it's name 'marl cliff' deriving from the fertile, local soil or 'marl' of clay and lime, and the cliff or hill above the village. In the same year, Joseph's first son, William George was baptised, and two years later a second daughter, Ann.

Joseph rented a small plot of land at Marlcliff, insufficient in itself to support a family, so that he would have had to work, either part-time or wholetime elsewhere, in order to make ends meet. In the official records of the time, he is described as a 'labourer'. This was a general term used for those working on the land and does not necessarily mean an unskilled labourer, as it often does today. Most farm workers in the early 1800s were skilled men, knowledgeable in raising crops; the care of animals; and usually in the time-honoured crafts such as ditching, hedging, ploughing and thatching. Such men often worked two or three days a week on their own plot and the rest on other men's land. Doubtless many would have welcomed an opportunity to own more land, but land was not often for sale, and the farm worker had few resources. Wages were low and the Napoleonic Wars had sent up the price of bread, which was their staple diet. It was during this time between 1812 and 1815 that Joseph sold his Hill and Moor property to his stepmother, Phoebe Sisam. It was added to the land she was already farming there.

In these years Joseph and his older brother William were never very far from one another, and there are indications that the two kept in close touch. Both were recently married and both had young families. When in 1813 Joseph and Elizabeth were living at Marlcliff near Bidford-on-Avon, William and Lydia settled a few miles distant at Welford-on-Avon. When later William and Lydia went to live at Sheenhill Farm, Joseph and his family themselves moved to Welford and remained there about three years. The parish registers there show that their son, John, and daughter, Phoebe, were christened in Welford church in 1816 and 1819. However, when John was born early in February 1816 the family had been living in Hill and Moor for a while. They were in great poverty and receiving Poor Relief from the Overseers of the Poor in the hamlet of Hill and Moor; but as Joseph no longer owned property there this parish saw no reason why they should support them. They were ordered to move out of Hill and Moor, and into the parish of Long Marston where Elizabeth's family lived. This Order of Removal was delayed since Elizabeth's fourth child was due any day, and she was not well. On March 19, 1816, the Order of Removal was renewed, as the baby had now been born and Elizabeth was deemed fit to travel. If they went to Long Marston it was not for long as by July of that year they were living in Welford, as we have seen, Joseph having presumably found work there. William and Lydia meanwhile had moved to Bidford-on-Avon, where they occupied the malthouse. In about 1820 the Joseph Sisams moved to Broom, a small hamlet in the Bidford area. Here they lived in a part known as Tinker's Close. While they were there a third son, Joseph, was born; but in the same year their second son John died aged five. By December of that year they had left Broom and returned to Marlcliff, which was but a mile or two from William at Bidford. What prompted Joseph's frequent moves is not known.

Broom, Warwickshire. One of the villages where Joseph Sisam went to seek work.

Ploughmen at work in England in the early 19th century.

Most likely it was the continuing agricultural depression when a man had to move to wherever there were opportunities of work.

Those particular years continued to be difficult for the smallholder, tenant farmer, and farm worker alike; and farm workers' wages were particularly low. The Poor Rate tax was levied on landowners and tenants in each parish to supplement the wages of impoverished farm workers. This tax was especially hard on a small tenant like Joseph, who was renting a cottage and garden in Marlcliff. But he seems to have kept his head above water. Records show that he worked this small plot until at least 1837. However there were difficult periods; for, in May 1829, we find that William paid Joseph's Poor Rate of 2/- for him. Meanwhile, Joseph and Elizabeth's family continued to grow in size. While living at Marlcliff, three more daughters, Mary, Susannah, and Harriet Elizabeth were born to them.

By now their eldest son, William George, had begun his working life. Like that of most village boys it was on the land. His uncle David Sisam, who farmed at Hill, Fladbury about ten miles away, took him into his household and gave him a job on the farm. It was a pleasant home and a much larger house than any to which the young man had been accustomed. He spent some time here, though it is not known whether, when he eventually left the farm, he did so amicably or not. What is known is that he returned there on the night of November 11, 1830, together with a youth of 16, named George Wincott, and broke into the farmhouse. They stole a gun, two neckerchiefs, one book, three pairs of stockings, one tea kettle, four shirts, one pair of steelyards, and a pestle and mortar, plus a watch and a pair of shoes. They were arrested on a charge brought by David Sisam, appeared before a magistrate in Worcester, and were committed to gaol on November 18. The offence was considered a serious one and the two prisoners were to remain there until the next County Assizes. William George was then about 20. Neither of them could read or write. Very few country folk could in those days so that involvement with the law, or educated officialdom, invoked fear and a sense of being disadvantaged.

On the face of it, this burglary seems a rash and senseless act. However, these were violent and unsettled times particularly in certain country districts. A Worcestershire historian describing events in this very year of 1830, noted 'distress amongst agricultural labourers', and the burning of ricks and farm buldings. Farm workers had endured low wages for a long period and there seemed no redress under the existing parliamentary electoral system. The politically educated were working for parliamentary reform, but the farm worker knew no politics and his frustration was often vented in violence.

On the same day that William George Sisam was charged before the Worcester magistrate there were other cases heard. A Bredon man had cut off the manes and tails of two horses, two men had stolen children's caps from a Stourbridge shop. Another had stolen three tame rabbits, and a woman stole four geese at Welland. In Worcester itself at that time there was real hunger. So much so that a public subscription of £1,108 was raised to distribute bread and soup. In nearby Kidderminster there were riots of carpet-weavers and a troop of the 14th Dragoons was called in. In a number of places in the countryside threshing machines were broken up.

How much William George Sisam was influenced by the events of the day is hard to estimate. At least we know he was living in troublous times when desperate measures were adopted and there was an atmosphere of violence. Prior to this he had already been imprisoned for a month for stealing a donkey. William George may have had a grudge against his uncle David. His childhood had been an unsettled one with the family making frequent moves. He would have been well aware of his father's struggle to make a living, and also of the comparative prosperity of his two uncles, William and David Sisam. There were a number of possible factors making for unhappiness in his life. Gaol at any rate was unikely to have healed that. This proved to be so, for it was noted by the authorities, during the 3½ months awaiting trial, that 'Sisam's conduct in gaol has, at times, been very violent'. It is not known whether Joseph Sisam, William George's father, went to see his son in Worcester Gaol or not, either at this time or later.

William George's case was one of 43 to be heard at the Lent Assizes in Worcester, presided over by Sir John Bernard Bosanquet, a Justice of the Court of Common Pleas at Westminster, and other Justices, which began on Saturday, March 5, 1831. There were 63 prisoners, most of whom had committed theft. A Grand Jury of twenty-three men of the county of Worcestershire decided that there was a case against Sisam and his accomplice. At the end of the first day, the court adjourned until after the weekend. On Monday William George Sisam and George Wincott were called for trial. Evidence was given by David Sisam, his sister Ann, and others. Both men were found guilty and, according to the law of the time, were sentenced to death by hanging. They were returned to gaol to await the implementation of their sentence.

By the year 1831, the death penalty for theft was becoming less and less frequently applied, and most cases were automatically referred to a higher authority for review and possible commutation. The higher authority was the new king, William IV. What happened to the young George Wincott is not known, but William George Sisam's sentence was

> **GRAND JURY.**
> Viscount Deerhurst, Foreman.
>
> | | |
> |---|---|
> | Hon. Wm. Jas. Coventry. | R. Hudson, Esq. |
> | Sir T. E. Winnington, Bart. | T. Pargeter, Esq. |
> | Sir Edward Blount, Bart. | W. C. Russell, Esq. |
> | Sir C. S. Smith, Bart. | T. Marriott, Esq. |
> | Sir A. Lechmere, Bart. | T. B. Cooper, M. D. |
> | W. Wall, Esq. | E. H. Lechmere, Esq |
> | J. J. Martin, Esq. | T. Hawkes, Esq. |
> | J. Brown, Esq. | J. Williams, Esq. |
> | C. E. Hanford, Esq. | J. Patrick, Esq. |
> | T. H. Bund, Esq. | J. H. Hallen, Esq. |
> | A. Skey, Esq. | R. E. E. Mynors, Esq. |
>
> *William George Sisam,* aged 22, and *George Winnitt,* 16, were charged with stealing, in the night of Nov. 11, a gun and other articles, from the dwelling of David Sisam, of Hill, in the parish of Fladbury. The prisoner Sisam was related to, and had formerly lived with, the prosecutor.—*Sentence of death recorded.* [Sisam's conduct in gaol has, at times, been very violent.]
>
> REMOVAL OF CONVICTS.—Last week, the following convicts were removed from Worcester County Gaol to Chatham:—Charles Heath, Thomas Hodgkins, Henry Reever, Wm. Crumpton, Thos. Brooke, Wm. Hooth, James Drew, Wm. Sparkes, Wm. George Sisam, John Boulton, Wm. Griffiths, Wm. Mason, Thomas Tomlins, and Richard Robinson, *to be transported for life;* and Jas. Gibbs *for fourteen years.* To Portsmouth:—Frederick Garrett, Benjamin Cox, George Webb, Wm. Hodges, Geo. Tonsell, Wm. Cox, Joseph Willetts, and Thos. Mathon, *to be transported for life.*

Newspaper reports in Berrow's Worcester Journal of the trial of William George Sisam, 1831

commuted. In due course a general directive concerning a specific group of the prisoners, with a list of their names attached, was received at Worcester, worded as follows:

'Whereas . . . William George Sisam . . . hath been at the Assizes and general gaol delivery CONVICTED of Housebreaking and judgement of Death was recorded against him for the same, But his Majesty being graciously pleased to extend the royal mercy to him on condition of his being Transported to parts beyond the seas for the Term hereinafter specified and such intention of Mercy having been signified in writing to the Court by Viscount Melbourne one of his Majesty's principal secretaries of State, the Court hath allowed to this said offender the benefit of a conditional pardon and it is thereupon ordered by this Court that the said . . . William George Sisam . . . be immediately transported to such parts beyond the seas . . . as his Majesty's . . . Privy Council think fit . . . for his Natural Life.'

Escaping the death penalty no doubt brought a sense of relief to the convicted men, but was transportation and imprisonment for life any better? For some perhaps it was, but for others not. The course of events up to and after their trial does not seem to have broken their spirits. During the waiting period in gaol they received regular food to the value of 2/6 a day, and they had not been idle. Within a month of their conviction they had 'formed a plan and commenced preparations for attempting to break out of the Prison', according to an official report. But the prison governor had discovered what was afoot and the convicts were put into solitary confinement. Finally, in the third week in April, the *Berrow's Worcester Journal* reported that 24 prisoners, including William George Sisam, had been sent to the prison hulks in Chatham, the first stage of their transportation overseas. These hulks were old, dismantled ships, used as convict prisons, such as Charles Dickens described in the opening chapters of *Great Expectations*.

In the same newspaper it was stated that Tetbury races would take place on June 9; in Warwickshire G. Dyke was killed while fighting with Wm. Bertram, a plasterer; the Earl of Clarendon had allowed his tenants in Wiltshire 20 per cent off their last half-year's rents; the Corn Laws were likely to be repealed soon; and the 'the Pear and Apple Trees promise very well for fruit' as the easterly winds had checked the blossom at the right moment. And so life went on.

It was indeed fruit blossom time in the gardens and orchards of Marlcliff, and time of rejoicing and hope in the countryside, but as Joseph Sisam walked to his work amidst the blossoming trees it must have been with a heavy heart; and likewise for Elizabeth busy with the care of four young children, the youngest but one year old. She also had her daughter's wedding to think about, due in a month or two. For Sarah was marrying William Fairfield, a housepainter of Warwick. She was the oldest daughter of the family, and closest in age to her ill-fated brother, William George.

Sarah's wedding was on June 5. While it was taking place William George was on the prison hulk *Cumberland* at Chatham, waiting for his transportation to the Antipodes. Two days later he was transferred to the ship *Larkins*, which sailed on June 11, carrying him to faraway Van Diemen's Land (Tasmania). Three other men who had been tried at Worcester Assizes, and sentenced on the same day as William George, were also transported in the ship *Larkins*. From the official records William was described as five foot four and three-quarter inches tall, with brown hair, round head and face, large nose and mouth, small chin, and a scar on the right side of his head. His trade was shown as a ploughman who could also reap and milk. On board the ship *Larkins* his behaviour was orderly.

On arrival in Van Diemen's Land in October 1831, 'Convict No. 1394 SISAM, William George' was put to work for a Mr. Boucher, a civilian settler, probably on his farm. Just one year later William George was given twenty-five lashes as punishment for 'neglect of duty and gross insolence'. By December 1833 he had been moved from Mr. Boucher to the Public Works, which meant road-mending or other such work, and was again in trouble. For threatening his overseer he was given fourteen days 'in Solitary Confinement on Bread and Water'. A few weeks later, still on Public Works, he tried to abscond and it was recommended that he be moved to another part of the island. In July 1836 he was in more trouble, for 'neglect of duty and with working for his own benefit during Government hours of Labour'. For this he was given three months hard labour. This behaviour went on for a number of years. But it must be remembered that convicts were often very cruelly treated. At one time he was sent to the Penitentiary at Hobart and at another was recommended to be removed to the lunatic asylum.

Eventually he was listed for conditional pardon along with 125 other convicts, on October 18, 1850, and these names were sent to London for approval to be agreed. Nothing more is known of the unfortunate William George. No record has so far been found that he ever married. No death was recorded under the spelling SISAM. However, a George SANSUN, who had been born in England, is recorded as having died on 22 June, 1874, aged 63, in Hobart General Hospital. This is very likely to have been William George Sisam with the name misspelt. Or he may have changed his surname as did many convicts on being released. The prison records show that he was known as George William Sisam, rather than William George Sisam, when he was given his Conditional Pardon. He was born about 1811 so the age of 63 at death in 1874 would tally.

❖ ❖ ❖

For William George's father, Joseph, the wedding of his daughter Sarah in 1831 may have brought him some consolation at a time of great unhappiness; as may the birth of his son, Daniel, at the New Year of 1833. But this consolation was shortlived, as Daniel died at the age of two. Joseph and Elizabth had now, for all intents and purposes, lost three of their sons. John and Daniel had died in childhood, and William George had been transported for life. Only one son Joseph Jnr. remained. He was now about 14 years old.

The family continued to live at Marlcliff where in December 1837 Phoebe, the third daughter, married a farmworker, Henry Cowper, living in the same village. A few years later, the family made a final move. It was to Warwick, the county town, where their daughter, Sarah, was living with her husband, William Fairfield. For Joseph and Elizabeth the move to Warwick was a complete change, and the surroundings in this old town were quite different from the village of Marlcliff. It may have been a relief for them to leave behind them old and unhappy associations, for they had suffered many hard blows in the preceding years.

Joseph was now about 52, and his farmworking days were drawing to a close. In Warwick he was able to afford the lease of a fair-sized house in West Street. It was near the ancient West Gate and a few doors away from where Sarah and her husband lived. Warwick had a long history and was famous for its fine castle above the River Avon, its old buildings, and the medieval church of St Mary, the graceful tower of which looks out from its hilltop position over the surrounding landscape. It was in this church that two more of Joseph's daughters were to be married.

The Sisam's house was quite commodious and, as in the course of time members of the family left home to marry or to earn their living, there was space to spare and room for lodgers. In 1841 the census returns record that Nathan Cooper, a shoemaker, aged 60, was

The old Unicorn Inn (foreground right) in Westgate, Warwick, kept by Joseph Sisam and his wife Elizabeth in their later years.

staying in the house. By 1846, when only one daughter remained at home, Joseph had made the house into an inn, providing victuals and living accommodation. It was known as the Unicorn.

As the years went by Joseph's health deteriorated. In 1858 he died at the age of 70. Elizabeth, his widow, continued at the Unicorn Inn as best she could. In her last few years she was helped by her grand-daughter, Harriet, the eldest child of Joseph Jnr. and Catherine. Elizabeth also had the comfort and companionship of her daughter Sarah, who with her husband, William Fairfield, lived a few doors away. These two and their family had lived alongside Joseph and Elizabeth very faithfully over the years. This they had done through thick and thin, particularly during the difficult time of Joseph's last illness.

Elizabeth died in 1862. William Fairfield Jnr., Sarah's son, was present at her death and it was he who took charge of things and notified the authorities. Elizabeth's remaining son, Joseph Jnr., had left Warwick many years before to find work in the Alcester area.

In his early years, Joseph Jnr. had learnt the rudiments of farming from his father. By 1843 he was working at Alcester Warren, a farming hamlet not far from Arrow Mill, which was now operated by his cousin Henry Sisam. Joseph was most likely employed on the large farm known as Alcester Warren Farm and, as was the custom of the time, may well have lived with the farmer's family in the farmhouse. The house was built in the early part of the 18th century and stands in a good position on rising ground. Beside it runs a lane leading to Sambourne village. Across the lane from the house the undulating farmland slopes down to the valley of the River Arrow. Adjoining the house is a sizeable farm yard of barns and outbuildings. The barns are much older than the house. They are half-timbered, built of oak beams and brick, and date from the Middle Ages.

It was here at Alcester Warren that Joseph met his future bride, Catherine Payne. They were married in 1843 in Alcester parish church. As the couple walked from the church, on that summer day of July 30, down the churchyard path and into the High Street, there was with them in the wedding party a friend from Arrow named Joseph Locke. He was married to Catherine Payne's sister, Elizabeth, and had acted as a witness at this wedding.

Joseph and Catherine may have continued to live at Alcester Warren Farm for a while or else in the neighbouring village of Sambourne. Their first child, Harriet, was certainly born in the neighbourhood in 1844. By 1847 they had moved to Cladswell Lane, Cookhill, a few miles away near the village of Inkberrow, where Catherine had grown up; and in the same year that they moved their second child, Ann, was born. In 1849 there was another daughter, Emma.

Cladswell Lane was a quiet country road winding through fields, with farms and thatched cottages here and there. Joseph farmed land here. The soil was fertile but economic conditions were such that most families sought ways of supplementing their income. Some women took up glovemaking, for it was a local industry centred in the county capital, Worcester, from which factories would supply materials to rural villages and collect the work when completed. In one of the census returns for this period, Catherine Sisam of Cladswell Lane is listed as a 'glover'.

In 1845, two years after Joseph and Catherine's wedding, a remarkable change occurred in the lives of Catherine's sister, Elizabeth (Eliza), and of her husband, Joseph Locke. It appears to have been an inner and spiritual change which transformed their lives outwardly and gave them a living faith. They had come into contact with Mormon missionaries from America who were at work in the Midlands. Meetings had been held in

Alcester Warren Farm near Sambourne, where Joseph's son Joseph Jnr. met his future wife.

The fertile valley of the River Arrow, near Sambourne.

Birmingham and Alcester where a branch of the Mormon Church, or Church of Jesus Christ of Latter Day Saints, had been established. In 1851, through the influence of Joseph Locke, Joseph and Catherine Sisam were both baptised into the Mormon Church. They were confirmed as members a few days later by a William Timms, an elder of the church. William Timms' son, also called William, was later to marry Joseph and Catherine's daughter, Harriet.

The Mormons were a God-fearing Christian people who applied their faith. Central to it was obedience to God, belief in Jesus Christ and the power of the Holy Spirit, and the Bible; together with their Book of Mormon. This book, which is regarded as a revealed addition to the scriptures, tells of Israelites who fled from Jerusalem in about 600 B.C. and settled on the American continent. It narrates how, many generations later, Christ appeared to these peoples, after his death and resurrection, and repeated to them his basic teaching.

The Mormons regarded the family as sacred and everyone was expected to care for his neighbour. It was considered natural that God should speak to ordinary men and women today as in centuries past; for religion was meant to be practised amidst the realities of everyday life. Contrary to rumours, the acceptance of the Mormon way of life meant for each individual a radical change in attitudes and behaviour – not merely formal membership of an organisation. Morality was strict, and the consumption of alcohol and other stimulants was forbidden. It made a strong appeal to many of the country people of Warwickshire; but, like any independent religious movement, it was attacked by those whose mode of life it challenged.

For Joseph it was no flash-in-the-pan experience. He maintained his beliefs and practised its tenets through the years. His family, meanwhile, increased and they too were

A covered wagon from Arrow Mill, drawn by shire horses, delivering flour to local bakeries.

brought up in the same faith. A son, Joseph Henry, was born in 1853. He was named Henry after Joseph's cousin, Henry Sisam of Arrow Mill. A fourth daughter Rebecca, born in 1855, died in childhood. By 1861 the family moved into Alcester where their daughter, Ann, at the age of 13 went to work as a 'house servant' with another Alcester family. Joseph now became a miller's wagoner and it is most likely he worked for his cousin Henry Sisam at Arrow Mill.

The wagon was the main means of bulk transport in those days. Arrow Mill had its wagons, equipped with canvas hoods or covers (covered wagons in fact), each drawn by four powerful shire horses, for which the meadows surrounding the mill provided hay and oats. The wagons delivered flour to bakeries in the district. A wagoner took a great pride in his turnout: the brasswork on the harness brightly polished and jingling with the movement of the horses. The whole would make a brave show and was a sight familiar to the village boys and girls of the district. Many is the time young Joseph Henry must have thrilled to see his father drive by, or perhaps he sometimes rode with him and was allowed to take the reins.

❖❖❖ 7 ❖❖❖
Wagons Westward

EMIGRATION TO AMERICA 1866 AND 1868

Living not far from Arrow Mill, Joseph Sisam the wagoner would have been well aware of the emigration of Henry Sisam's three sons to New Zealand in July 1862. Emigration was much in people's minds at that time. Settlers were being sought for the new countries, and there were many in England who saw little future prospect for themselves in their own country and were attracted by the opportunities offered abroad. There were also those who saw in emigration the chance to live in a more tolerant religious atmosphere where a better society might be established. The departure of Joseph's three cousins to New Zealand would certainly have made an impression, and it was not long afterwards that the Joseph Sisams' thoughts also began to turn towards emigration; not to New Zealand, but to America and the recently founded Salt Lake City in Utah, the Mormon settlement in the Rocky Mountain area.

Throughout history dissidents and minorities, especially religious groups, suffered persecution. The Mormon people in America were no exception and deaths had resulted. They were finally forced to leave farms and homes and move inland, where they took refuge by the Missouri River. Here they continued to face dangers, both external and internal, for there were deep divisions in their midst. They also faced the problem of protecting their unmarried women in times of persecution and violence. For this reason married men were encouraged, with their wives' consent, to take additional wives into their homes. This was a practical and basically charitable measure, which may have stemmed from a literal reading of the Old Testament in the Bible; but it gave rise to charges of immorality and polygamy. In the spring of 1845, Brigham Young led a mass migration by wagon train westward from the Missouri River across the Great Plains, to seek a spot where they might live in peace. The travellers endured all kinds of hardships and dangers. The story of this migration and the founding of the State of Utah is one of the pioneering epics of American history. The Mormons were a people of faith and firmly believed they would be led to the Promised Land. This they found in a great desert valley on the edge of the Wasatch Range, beneath the south western slopes of the Rocky Mountains. Here they built Salt Lake City, named after the huge landlocked expanse of salt water that lay there. Although it was arid, desert country it suited them since other migrants were less likely to settle there. Besides, they believed they could irrigate it. From the arid valley they created a flourishing settlement, which became the admiration of generations of Americans. This was the place to which Joseph and Catherine Sisam were thinking of emigrating with their family, and they were encouraged in their intent by the fact that the Mormon Church was seeking settlers amongst their overseas adherents, particularly from England .

Already in 1864 Catherine's sister, Eliza Locke, had travelled to Salt Lake City with her two younger daughters; ahead of her husband Joseph Locke and their eldest girl who, being gifted with a fine singing voice, was helping her father on a mission in England. Joseph Locke knew that his family would be well cared for by Mormon folk on the journey to America and on arrival in Utah. The Joseph Sisams, meanwhile, began to save for the day when they too could emigrate as a whole family. They decided to send an advance party consisting of the two daughters, Harriet and Ann, under the care of their uncle, Joseph Locke. He and his eldest daughter were now ready to join the rest of their own family already in Utah. Harriet and Ann had saved enough money to buy passages. Harriet was by now betrothed to William Timms Jnr., son of the man who had confirmed her father, Joseph Sisam, into the church. The young couple were planning to make their home in Utah.

The party left England on April 30, 1866, by the sailing ship *John Bright*, out of the port of Liverpool bound for New York, under the command of Captain C.M. Gillett. It was a crowded ship carrying 747 passengers, the majority seeking a new life in a strange land. For much of the voyage the weather was rough and it took more than a month to reach the shores of America. For the two young women, Harriet and Ann, it was an astonishing yet frightening experience, for neither had been away from home before. Yet this was only a beginning. In New York they found themselves faced with an overland journey of over two thousand miles, before they would reach Salt Lake Valley in the far west of the continent.

This next stage of their journey was by railroad across eastern America to the riverport town of St. Joseph on the bank of the Missouri River. This river, so familiar to the early explorers and adventurers, formed the natural boundary between the state of Missouri on the east bank and the as yet unorganised territories of Kansas and Nebraska on the other. West of the river lay what remained of the vast, undeveloped prairie grasslands that had originally stretched from the Mississippi River to beyond the Missouri as far as the foothills of the Rocky Mountains. These grasslands, known as the Great Plains, had for generations been the home and hunting ground of the indigenous American Indians, the Sioux and Pawnee particularly, and various sub-tribes such as the Oglala, Arapaho, Cheyennne, Crow, Kiowa, Apache and Commanche.

But it was disputed land. Although acquired by the United States Government in 1803 from France, through the Louisiana Purchase, to the Indians it was a homeland owned by them communally, which had always supplied their means of existence. The vast herds of wild buffalo fed them, the watercourses dotted with cottonwood trees provided shelter for their encampments, and the foothills and valleys of the adjacent mountains their winter quarters. They therefore resisted the ever growing incursion by traders and explorers, and by the settlers who followed them.

The Great Plains of the West and the mountains that bordered them had become the last refuge of these nomadic Indians. Originally occupying the whole North American continent they had gradually been pushed westward by the tide of emigrant settlers, or had been confined to designated reservations within the already settled regions. The first Europeans landing on the eastern seaboard had acquired land, some by treaties, others by direct seizure. The treaties attempted to lay down demarcation lines as to which should be European land and which Indian. But it presupposed an understanding of property that was entirely alien to Indian thought and custom. There were breaches of the agreements on both sides. The pressure to acquire more and more land increased as more and more settlers arrived. Not all Europeans were motivated by goodwill and fair play, any more than were all Indians. There were bad eggs in both baskets, and commercial greed was always a strong factor.

At one time the Government had visualised the whole of America west of the Mississippi as a huge reservation to which all Indians in the east could be removed. But the tide of European settlement swept beyond the Mississippi to the next natural frontier the Missouri River, which in turn became a launching site for expeditions across the western prairies. Fur-trappers, explorers, traders, gold-miners and settlers, together with the stage coaches and Pony Express mailriders, penetrated the Great Plains and beyond, marking out permanent trails. The ending in 1865 of the Civil War between the Northern and Southern States of America increased the flow of imigrants from other countries, and also released large numbers of gun-carrying adventurers into the wilderness. Some of these set about slaughtering the buffalo for their valuable hides in direct competition with Indians who also traded in hides, as well as depending on the buffalo for meat. As a result the herds were rapidly diminished. The Plains Indians became anxious for their own survival and regarded the future with growing alarm. There were massacres and reprisals, and the United States Army became increasingly involved in attempts to keep the peace. Forts manned by troops of cavalry were established to guard the trails. Meanwhile the pressure of settlement increased. In 1863 President Abraham Lincoln signed a Congressional bill authorising the building of a railroad across the Great Plains to the Pacific Ocean. By the early 1860s the ever-expanding eastern railroad system, advancing westward, had already reached the Missouri River, the last frontier. Here it paused, while railroad-builders eagerly eyed the prospects beyond and manoeuvred to be the first across.

It is unlikely that the Lockes and Sisams landing in New York in June 1866, or for that matter the Sisam parents waiting in England, would have had much, if any, inkling of these issues; or even of the hazards of a journey to the far west of America, other than from scraps of information gleaned from earlier travellers. But they may well have been acquainted with the Mormon teaching regarding the American Indians, namely that they were descendants of the Lamanites, one of the lost tribes of Israel, and that their dark skins were a punishment for early wrongdoing. However, the Mormon attitude to Indians was humane and friendly, and Mormons sought to live in peace with them and to share with them, as they did with everyone, their Mormon faith. Whatever thoughts the Sisam parents and the party newly arrived in New York may have had about the Indian question, from the moment the travellers took the railroad from New York to the banks of the Missouri River, the whole family had became a part, albeit unwittingly, of one of the most significant eras in American history, the opening up of the American West; and the story of it would be perused and studied until the end of time.

It was the summer of 1866 when the Lockes and Sisams reached the Missouri River at St. Joseph, and boarded a wood-burning paddle-steamer heading upstream for Florence, Nebraska. Florence was a small town a few miles north of the then recently-founded city of Omaha, and served as a fitting-out station for wagon trains leaving for the journey westward. It was near the spot where in 1846 the Mormon leader Brigham Young had set up the original Winter Quarters amongst the Omaha Indians, before leading the great Mormon migration westward to the Salt Lake valley in the following spring. In the subsequent years Florence continued to serve as a fitting-out station for Mormon emigrants travelling the same trail.

Typical American covered wagon of the 1860s.

There were several such fitting-out points on the banks of the Missouri. Here families and parties of emigrants could join organised wagon trains led by experienced men, many of whom had had military training. Such an arrangement had proved the safest and most efficient method of travel across wild, undeveloped territory. The wagon trains usually consisted of separate groups of three or four wagons, each with passengers and baggage. These units or 'messes' would eat together and stay together within the wagon train throughout the journey. At night tents were erected for the evening meal, each group being responsible for their own cooking, and the tents served as sleeping quarters in additon to the wagons. Every party provided its own wagons, each drawn by four to six mules or oxen. The wagons were standard farm wagons used throughout the eastern part of America and were readily available. Sturdily built, they were equipped with iron-shod wheels, a brake, chains to deadlock the wheels down steep inclines, a bench for the driver, and a tall arched covering made from heavy, close-woven cotton. This latter the travellers made waterproof with a mixture of linseed oil and melted beeswax. The wagons offered little comfort to passengers, there being no suspension springs to soften the shock of lurch and jolt. During the weeks of preparation at the fitting-out station travellers had time to come to terms, at least in their minds, with the hardships they might have to endure for the next two months of rough travel. At the same time, while the wagon train was being assembled, they could purchase necessities for the journey. These ranged from bacon, beans, coffee, dried fruit, flour, kerosene lanterns, salertus (bicarbonate of soda), rope, tin stoves and cooking pots to India-rubber blankets, medicines, wide-brimmed hats and striped woollen shirts for men, and sun-bonnets for women. At last, when the preparations were complete, the long line of wagons moved out in the month of July amidst the crack of whips, the shouts of teamsters, the barking of dogs, and the never-ceasing creak of the heavily laden wagons.

The route followed was known as the Mormon Trail and like all western trails of that time was but a mass of rough tracks, mostly not made-up and deeply rutted from the thousands of wheels that had already passed over them. Beginning in the south east of Nebraska, where rainfall was plentiful, it led at first through a well-forested area which, as the rainfall decreased, gradually gave way to the waving grasses of the boundless prairie. Chief among these native grasses were the blue Grama, the tall Bluestem and the grey-green Buffalo grass that nourished the wandering herds of an unfenced territory stretching as far as the eye could see. Across this landscape of open skies and a sea of grass the column of 50 to 80 lumbering vehicles slowly snaked its way, averaging about twenty miles a day. At nightfall an encampment would be set up. Wagons were grouped together, mess tents pitched, stoves and campfires lit and the evening meal prepared. Afterwards fiddles and flutes appeared and likely as not there would be dancing.

After about a day and a half the trail reached the north bank of the Platte River, the course of which it would follow upstream for some 200 miles, most of it through the vast grassland prairie. The waters of the river were heavily silted with topsoil. The name Platte had been given to it by French traders on account of its smooth muddy surface. Like the word prairie, meaning grassland, Platte was but one of the many French names dating back to the years when France laid claim to this and the greater part of the then known America.

Magnificent though the vistas were in this broad valley, sometimes fifteen miles wide, the trail's close proximity to the river had its disadvantages. Mosquitos abounded and the ever present silt prevented the river water from being used for drinking purposes.

Fortunately there were usually freshwater streams within easy reach, and the terrain was such that the going was good. This was also buffalo country where the great herds had hitherto roamed at will. After a week moving through this continuous expanse of grassland Fort Kearney came into sight. This was one of the series of military forts built in the 1840s to protect travellers and keep the peace between the two dominant Indian tribes, the Sioux and the Pawnees. The building of these forts had made these trails much safer from Indian attacks, so much so that wagon trains often made the whole journey and scarcely ever saw an Indian. This was particularly true in midsummer because the buffalo had moved north in June to fresher pastures and the Indians followed them. Although there was always the latent danger of attack and a sharp lookout had to be kept by day and night, this particular wagon train was not molested.

Fort Kearney, built on an island in the river, was a convenient spot for wagon trains coming up from the southeast, or from the Mormon Trail from the east, to pause and take stock before tackling the longer and more arduous part of the journey through the mountains ahead. As well as its garrison of U.S. Cavalry, Fort Kearney had a sutler's shop, repair facilities, and mail could be left here for carriage back to the east. Forts like Kearney, and Laramie further along the trail, in a hundred years time would be featured again and again in novels, magazine articles and motion pictures. Locke and Sisam descendants and millions of others would avidly devour these, with fascination and perhaps awe.

From Fort Kearney onwards the trail began to ascend imperceptibly yet steadily as it approached nearer and nearer the distant mountain region. The grasslands came to an end giving way to dry soil. The temperature increased and clouds of dust rose up from the movement of the wagons, forcing drivers to cover their faces with kerchiefs. After four days the wagon train reached the spot where the river forked into two separate channels, the North and the South Platte. The trail followed the North Platte and proceeded along the level plain through which the river, now about two miles wide, flowed. The altitude had increased since leaving Fort Kearney to about about 5,000 feet above sea-level. The ground had become sandy and the temperature was now far above that of the summer heat to which most of the emigrants were accustomed. Strange rock formations and tall bluffs appeared on the horizon, some of which the more adventurous explored when the wagon train made camp.

The landscape was also changing. For much of the way tall bluffs lined both sides of the river, from the tops of which, notably at Scott's Bluff, magnificent views could be had ranging for mile upon mile to the distant horizon. At other times there were rolling hills along the river, from which the ground sloped gently down to the river flats, which were sometimes broad and smooth enough for wagons to run abreast. From here onwards the hills became steeper and the streams ran swift and clear, while along the trail wild sage and artemesia grew plentifully. This was the beginning of the mountain country.

At the junction of the North Platte and the Laramie River, the wagon train crossed the water to join the Oregon Trail on the south bank and reached Fort Laramie itself, over five hundred miles from the starting point in Nebraska. Fort Laramie was the gateway to the Rocky Mountains, the lower reaches of which rimmed the skyline and formed a background to the fort. The broad plains were now behind the travellers. Ahead lay the mountains.

Fort Laramie, and the area that surrounded it, in later years became one of the famous historical sites of the West; first as a trading post on the long trail to California and

Fort Laramie in Wyoming Territory. A famous stop-over for the wagon trains.

Oregon, and then, as hostilities between the Indians and white emigrants increased, as a fortified military post. Within a few hundred miles of Fort Laramie, where the Great Plains and the Rocky Mountains begin to merge, are place names familiar to millions across the world who have never been to America; names that conjure up historic events and associations in a mixture of reality and romance; names such as Little Bighorn and Custer, Buffalo, Wounded Knee, Cheyenne and Medicine Bow, Rawhide and Sundance, Yellowstone, Grand Teton, South Pass and the Great Divide.

It is worth pausing at this point of the journey westward to consider certain ominous events that had occurred recently in the area through which the travellers were now passing, and also what these events led to. On June 5 that year, about a month before Harriet and Ann Sisam and their party reached Fort Laramie, Red Cloud the Sioux leader had come to the fort with his chiefs and two thousand of the tribe, to meet with Government Peace Commissioners. The Sioux were concerned that a recently established branch of the Oregon Trail, leading to the gold diggings at Alder Creek (later known as Virginia City), had been made through the best of the tribe's hunting grounds. Agreements about this had been made previously, but the interpretation of them was in dispute. At Fort Laramie the negotiations ran into trouble when a newly arrived cavalry officer from another fort announced, without consultation, the building of a new series of forts along the trail through the Indian hunting grounds. The Sioux replied with war on the forts and their occupants.

Six months later in December 1866 occurred the Fetterman Massacre, when the Sioux under Crazy Horse out-manoeuvred, defeated and killed Captain Fetterman of the U.S. Cavalry and all of his 80 men, – the same Captain Fetterman who had once boasted, 'Give me 80 men and I would ride through the whole Sioux nation'. The Sioux nation continued their struggle for survival, but the ensuing events had terrible consequences. Red Cloud once again sought peace and later went to Washington to confirm it. But there were further tragedies. The Sioux resumed their war in protest at the exploitation of gold in their last homeland, the sacred Black Hills of what later became known as the State of Dakota. At the battle of Little Bighorn, some 250 miles north-west of Laramie, they annihilated General Custer and his Seventh Cavalry. It was, incidentally, Custer's scientific survey of the Black Hills that had brought the gold prospectors flooding in.

In the end the Sioux were crushed. Driven from their last refuge in the Black Hills, which became settler farmland, they were forced to live in small, confined reservations near the upper reaches of the Missouri River. In one of these reservations, in December 1890 four days after Christmas, a tragic massacre took place at Wounded Knee. It was carried out by the re-constituted Seventh Cavalry. In the reservations in the years that followed the Sioux people, unable to adapt to a settled form of existence or maintain their traditional culture, sank into inevitable decline.

In the 1860s, when English families, such as the Sisams living in Warwickshire, had thought of emigrating to New Zealand and North America, most Europeans regarded the indigenous peoples of America, Africa, Asia, and Australia and New Zealand, as savage and uncultured. To some extent they felt in duty bound to bring the advantages of western civilisation to these parts of the world, while seeking economic opportunities for themselves. The political leaders of the day naturally thought in terms of the acquisition of territory to safeguard trade, and saw nothing wrong in that. Amongst them were many idealists and men and women of spiritual perception, who did much good, but they were in a minority. The full concept of human rights had not yet entered public consciousness, nor had there been sufficient awareness of the need to understand and respect other cultures.

In the summer of 1866 when the Lockes and Sisams left Fort Laramie, they continued by the Oregon Trail along the south bank of the Platte. They were now entering the foothills of the Rocky Mountains, where there were dark stands of juniper and pine which clothed the mountain sides. It was a desolate area, though its sombre atmosphere was relieved a little by the abundance of prickly pear and wild aster that lined the tracks. The days were hot, the temperature reaching 100 degrees Fahrenheit, and the nights cold. Thirteen miles from Laramie they came to Warm Springs where there was good clear water flowing from the rocks. The way beyond was strewn with boulders and there were many ravines and creeks to cross and knolls to negotiate. The river was now but a

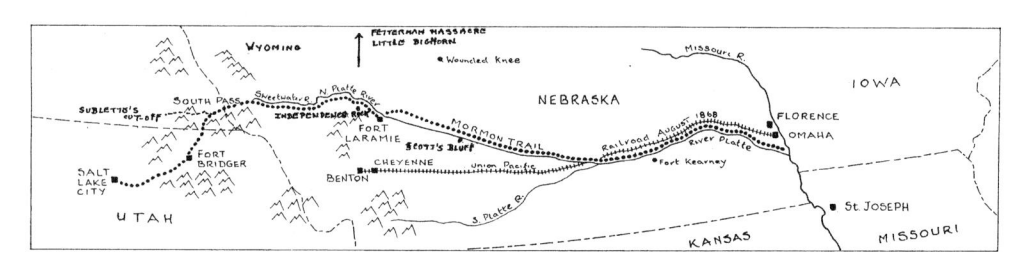

The overland trail to the American West followed by the Sisam emigrants.

mountain stream. The surroundings were very dry, with sagebrush abounding. Later they came to areas permeated by mineral salts, making the water unpalatable and even dangerous, especially to the mules. Encrusted saline pools were everywhere, some white with salertus (bicarbonate of soda), very similar to that which the emigrants had purchased in Nebraska before setting out.

A day or so later, near Independence Rock, they descended to the 'winding and silvery Sweetwater' as an earlier traveller William Swain described this river, rejoicing no doubt at its fresh, uncontaminated waters. They now followed the Sweetwater River, leaving it from time to time to avoid its broad and winding curves, sometimes crossing it again and again. This took them through Devil's Gate, an extremely narrow canyon, a mile and three-quarters long, shut in by 'perpendicular rock walls from 400 to 600 feet high.' When they emerged the trail led through a sixteen mile desert of more alkaline ponds and sagebrush. Again the trail rejoined the Sweetwater and travelled through groves of fresh, grey-leaved willow trees. A few days later they came to the Continental Divide at South Pass nearly 7000 feet above sealevel; the Divide being a line on the map marking the watershed of the Rocky Mountains, from whose opposite slopes the water streams flowed either eastward or westward. The Pass was formed by the passage of the trail between two hills beyond which lay the Far West and the distant Pacific Ocean.

Descending steeply from South Pass they came to narrow flats of further strongly alkaline soil, covered with tufts of sagebrush. The intense heat continued. The trail divided at Sublette's Cut-off, where the Oregon Trail turned westwards and the Mormon Trail continued southwards. After two days of travelling through a hot and arid terrain they came once more to signs of civilisation, to the trading post of Fort Bridger which lay beside Black's Fork of the Green River. Two days later, after descending Echo Canyon into the Valley of the Great Salt Lake, they reached Salt Lake City in late September 1866.

All had come safely through the ordeal of the journey; the two Sisam sisters, Harriet and Ann, and Joseph Locke and his daughter. The following year Harriet married her fiancé, William Timms, who had been waiting for her in Salt Lake City. Ann went to work for a while as a pastry cook in the household of Brigham Young, the Mormon leader. Ann herself married in 1867. Her husband was an English settler from Leicester, Isaac Goff Jnr., also a Mormon. His family played a leading role in the community in which the Sisams eventually settled and became their good friends. Ann and Isaac Goff had four children: Catherine Rebecca, Isaac Francis, Joseph Henry Willard, and Mary Ann who died in childhood.

In England, meanwhile, Harriet and Ann's parents Joseph and Catherine Sisam, their younger sister Emma and their brother Joseph Henry had been getting ready to leave for America. They eventually left England on June 4, 1868. Joseph was 46 and his son Joseph Henry was nearly 16. They sailed on the same vessel as the earlier party, the *John Bright* from Liverpool, under Captain James McGraw, together with 743 other passengers. The total cost to the family was $700, which they raised from their savings and the sale of their property. Joseph also had with him a draft for $1100. They arrived in New York on July 13 and, like Harriet, Ann and the Lockes before them, they boarded a train. By now the railroad had reached beyond the Missouri River and had crossed it to Omaha only the previous year. From Omaha the Union Pacific track was now forging ahead at a great pace, laid by Irish navvies. It had already reached the Platte River valley. The Cheyenne and

Sioux Indians, knowing it would bring in more and more settlers, fought against it. At Fort Kearney they had already wrecked a freight train and killed the crew. Telegraph poles had been torn down, and in the Wyoming stretch the Sioux had attacked work gangs and killed surveyors, so that diggers had to work with rifles stacked beside them.

Joseph Sisam and his family were indeed living through historic days, for their journey overland to Salt Lake in 1868 was taking place during the most crucial stage of the construction of America's first transcontinental railroad. They were in the thick of it. For as they rode westwards from Omaha day after day the construction gangs were labouring ahead of them, laying ties and rails at the astonshing rate of a mile of track per working day. These were already known as the 'hell-on-wheels' gangs. When the train carrying the Sisams eventually caught up with them it was at a temporary construction camp named Benton, some 150 miles west of the newly founded township of Cheyenne and 698 miles from where they had boarded the train on the west bank of the Missouri. Benton, which lay somewhere between present-day Walcot and Sinclair, was a rip-roaring settlement, raucus and short-lived, for when the construction men moved on this settlement faded away. It was scarcely an encouraging place for newly-arrived travellers. It was situated in a grey flat of alkali desert, with the streets ankle-deep in sand. Within a few weeks a township of 3,000 people had sprung up there with no form of government or policing, for Cheyenne was too far away for the sheriff to take any action. It offered evey kind of indulgence to men whose pockets were bulging with construction workers' pay. Because it was beyond the reach of the law the settlement had attracted ne'er-do-wells. There were daily robberies, holdups, shootings and killings. Gambling was rife and the dance-halls were crowded day and night. Here Joseph and Catherine Sisam and their children, Emma aged 18, who was crippled, and Joseph Henry aged 16, had to wait while the wagon train for Salt Lake was being assembled.

They left eventually on August 24, 1868, in a train of 50 wagons, 500 people in all, under the command of Captain John Gillespie. Amongst the company was a family who were short of a driver. Hired by Captain Gillespie, young Joseph Henry stepped in and filled the gap, putting to good use what he had learned from his father in England about the handling of millers' wagons, though there was a good deal of difference between handling English draft horses and American mules. The journey was a rigorous one for Emma who, unable to walk, sat on a hard wooden bench at the front of the wagon. She would have to endure this for twenty-three days on end as the wagon jolted its way to their final destination.

Fortunately the emigrants had only physical hazards with which to contend. After the earlier spate of Indian attacks on the railroad builders, a treaty had been signed at Fort Laramie in April of 1868 by which the Indians undertook to cease their attacks, and in exchange were granted the exclusive use of land north of the Platte River. It was an uneasy peace and difficult to maintain. As the Sisam party made their way slowly forward, the wagon convoy was shadowed night and day by a band of restless Indians, but no attacks were attempted. By now autumn was approaching, the weather was becoming cold and damp and the trails rocky and muddy, as the wagons climbed higher and higher towards the mountains. Six deaths took place on the way. Nevertheless, the journey from England and across America was well organised, and although there was hardship, everything possible was done for the emigrants. The final stage led them into the haven of the Salt Lake Valley, where the last lingerings of summer warmth greeted them. It was the first week in September and they had trekked 400 miles by wagon, and four times that distance by railroad. By the time the next spring came round the Union Pacific had reached Promontory Point, Utah, north of Salt Lake. Here in the Rocky Mountains on May 10, 1869, history was made; when the Union Pacific coming from the east and the Central Pacific working its way from San Francisco in the west met and joined, to form the first coast-to-coast rail link. The last 200-mile section of the Central Pacific track advancing from the west, from Humboldt Wells to Promontory Point where the joining ceremony took place, was built by Mormon engineers. Their men were such good workers, and so expert at handling the nitro-glycerine required for tunneling and blasting, that they had been awarded the contract by Leland Stanford, the president of the Central Pacific.

8

A Branch Divided

SALT LAKE CITY AND PLURAL MARRIAGE

When the settlement of the Salt Lake Valley was first begun in the 1840s, the city itself was laid out in planned blocks. In the centre there were ten acre blocks, each divided into one-and-a-quarter acre lots, assigned to business and professional men. Beyond these were 5-acre lots for mechanics, and beyond them again were 10 to 20-acre lots for farmers, varying in area according to the size of their families. When Joseph Sisam arrived in 1868 he is said to have gone to see Brigham Young and received a grant of land. He was allocated 10.25 acres in the West Jordan area, about 12 miles south of the city centre. It lay in a broad valley between the Wasatch and Oquirrh Mountains, through which flowed what was originally known as the Utah River, and later renamed the Jordan River.

The first Mormon settlers had arrived here in the late summer of 1847, when Brigham Young made a preliminary exploration and declared the Salt Lake Valley, rather than California, to be the Promised Land. Legally it was Spanish-Mexican and had not been settled, but in February 1848, at the end of the war with Mexico, it was ceded to the United States. It was mostly semi-desert and uninhabited, except for the annual migration of groups of Paiute, Shoshone and Bannock Indians moving south from Bear Lake, in the northern mountains. They followed the Utah River to where it flowed into Lake Utah, for the waters of Lake Utah were their winter fishing grounds. They were primarily hunters rather than agriculturalists, and had little interest in the semi-desert of the Salt Lake Valley. On their journeys they would camp by the river and were apt to steal cattle whenever opportunity afforded. If modern historians are correct these, like the other American Indian tribes, were probably descendants of the ancient peoples who, during the ice age, had crossed the Bering Straits from Mongolia and colonised the American continent, displacing whatever peoples were there before them.

To the Mormon pioneers of the 1840s these apparently unpopulated areas in Utah were available for settlement. With regard to the Indian people, Brigham Young's advice to his early settlers was to make friends with them and, if they were in need, to share food with them. This was a genuine, humanitarian sentiment. He also urged settlers to trade. He had learned earlier in Nebraska to make friends with the neigbouring Omaha Indians, when the Mormon emigrants paused to winter in Nebraska before moving westward. Young had sought permission from the Omaha Chief, Big Elk, to sojourn there and plant crops for the following spring. This was granted and trust was established to the extent that Indians looked after the Mormons' cattle during the winter.

Brigham Young was a man of faith but he was also practical. He understood human nature. At Salt Lake he not only told his people to make friends and to trade but also to keep their gates locked, and only to trade in the Indian camps and not within the Mormon

Statue of Massasoit in front of the State Capitol of Utah. This Indian Chief befriended the early New England settlers in what is now Massachusetts.

settlements. The situation at Salt Lake was somewhat different from Nebraska. The Mormons were no longer transients, but were making their own permanent settlements in an area in which no one else seemed interested, and it was the Indians who were the migrants. The settlers therefore set about clearing the land of sagebrush, digging a canal from the Jordan River, and making irrigation ditches. By the first winter there were 3,000 souls in the Salt Lake Valley living in shacks and tents.

The main group of Indians in Utah were the Utes, after whom the territory was later named. Mormon settlers sought to build friendly relations with them, but with varying success. In 1850 the United States Government declared Utah a territory and established its legal authority there, installing its own officials in what was an otherwise mainly Mormon government. Conflict arose with the Utes when the Utah state government forbade them to sell captured Indian children to slave traders from New Mexico. The Utes response was scalping, cattle stealing and the destruction of property. Brigham Young's aim remained constant, to build friendship. He sent gifts to the Ute chief, Wakara, and told him, 'You are a fool fighting your best friends.' There was intermittent warfare, in which United States Government troops were involved, until 1865, when treaties were made between Washington and most of the Indian tribes in the region, whereby Indian reservations were established in the Uinta Mountains and elsewhere. Brigham Young's concept of friendship with the Indian people, which was also held by the Pilgrim Fathers before him, did not become universally accepted in America; nor did it result ultimately in the effective participation by Indians in the government of the nation. But at least the concept of friendship and respect was preserved in Utah when Utah's first State Capitol building was completed in 1916 and remains there today in visible form. For standing in front of the Capitol buildings, and dominating the approach, is a magnificent bronze statue of Massasoit, the Indian Chief, who was a good friend to the early settlers in what is now Massachusetts. It stands there as a salutary reminder, and a prod to the conscience.

When Joseph Sisam settled his family in the West Jordan Valley in 1868 the situation was peaceful. A thriving community of farmers, tradesmen and shopkeepers was already established. At the heart of these communities were the Mormon gatherings, held in homes or halls. These welcomed newcomers and provided a social nucleus where they could make friends and find the help, advice and encouragement they needed. By and large there was a good atmosphere in this very mixed population. Scandinavian names were much in evidence – Olson, Nilson, Christensen, Jorgensen, Larson, Jenson, Lind and Stenquist, to name a few. There were also many English and Welsh – Glover, Borlease, Wilcox, Barnes, Turner, Naylor, Clark, Phillips, Lloyd, Powell and Rees Jones. Folk had come from many parts of Britain: from Northampton, Yeovil, Leicester, Nottingham, Worcester, Greenwich and districts of Somerset, Lancashire, Glamorgan and Kent. Many of these people became church elders and some became close friends of the Sisams through officiating at family baptisms and similar occasions.

Almost from the moment of arrival Joseph's wife, Catherine, had sought out the spiritual heart of the community and made contact with the folk in the local church. The records at West Jordan show that on September 7, 1868, about four days after the family arrived, she was re-baptised into the church, this being the custom for newcomers from overseas. To her this was all part of seeing to the needs of her family, whether material or spiritual. The faith she had discovered through her sister, Eliza, in England thirteen years previously had remained with her; and she was anxious that her own children should have

The rich ore-bearing Oquirrh Mountains overlooking the Salt Lake Valley where Joseph and Catherine Sisam settled with their family.

'Almost from the moment of arrival Joseph's wife, Catherine, had sought out the spiritual heart of the community.

a firm foundation for their lives, not least her only son, Joseph Henry, on whom the continuation of the family would depend. Perhaps the tragedy of what had happened in England to her husband's brother, William George Sisam who was transported to Australia as a convict, still lingered in her mind. The next year, in September 1869, the rest of her family followed her example and were re-baptised; they were her husband Joseph, young Joseph Henry, and the youngest daughter Emma. Catherine did her best for her children's spiritual upbringing. Time would show how they responded. As the country saying goes: 'You can lead a horse to the water but you cannot make it drink.'

By irrigation of the 10.25 acre plot, coupled with hard manual work, Joseph laid the foundations of a small farm that could feed his family. They all shared the work, with Joseph and Joseph Henry bearing the brunt of the heavy labour of digging, ploughing, planting and harvesting. The main crops were wheat and lucerne, plus fruit and vegetables. Both Joseph and Joseph Henry sought other work from time to time. By the end of the first eight years the farm was prospering. The family were also able to increase their acreage as plots came up for sale. In March 1874, Joseph bought 3.72 acres from a Charles Jenson, and in January 1876 there was a major purchase by Joseph Henry of 23 acres from a Francis Cundic.

Joseph Henry was now a grown man of 23 and beginning to strike out on is own. On February 4, 1877, at a civil ceremony he was married to the 18-year old daughter of one of the many Swedish settlers in the neighbourhood. She was Hannah Poulson, who had been brought up on a farm at Skarby, in the Malmohus district of southern Sweden. The family, which consisted of parents and seven children, were Mormons and had emigrated to Salt Lake City in 1875 when Hannah was sixteen. The year after he married Hannah, Joseph Henry was elected an elder in the church, a normal custom when young men, brought up in the church, reached manhood and were considered suitable to hold office. On the same day, his father, Joseph, was also appointed an elder in the church. A month later on March 1, 1878, a church marriage was performed for Hannah and Joseph Henry. The couple made their home on the plot of land that Joseph Henry had bought earlier in West Jordan. On it he built a typical, single-story wooden house, with gables either end and a long porch between. In due course this became the main, combined family homestead because Joseph and Catherine, Joseph Henry's parents, also came to live there together with Joseph Henry's invalid sister Emma, now in her late twenties. The farmhouse still stands, (number 7350 State Street), and the farm is still operating, though it has long since passed out of the Sisam family.

Although the Mormons of Salt Lake City were free of the physical dangers they faced before and during the great migration westward, many continued the custom of plural marriage. Joseph Henry was one who did so. Whether it was a carefully premeditated step or not is uncertain. On July 25, 1878, he took a second wife. She was Hannah's older sister, Ingrid. It was a church marriage, without a corresponding civil ceremony, since United States law did not recognise plural marriage. Ingrid, who had not been re-baptised on arriving from Sweden, was re-baptised a few days before the wedding. After the wedding, Ingrid joined the family household. Hannah, like most Mormon wives faced with this situation, loyally supported her husband, but it pained her deeply. She would never talk about it. In December, the same year as the second marriage, both Hannah and Ingrid gave birth to their first children, and later there were further children from both marriages. The two sisters seem at first to have moved to and fro between the Poulson home and

Joseph Henry Sisam and Hannah Poulson at the time of their marriage.

Joseph Henry's. Ingrid's first child, Joseph Willard, was, for instance, born not at the Sisam home but at Sandy, where the Poulsons lived. On the other hand, the census taken in June 1880 shows that Ingrid and her baby were at State Street with Joseph Henry, but not Hannah and her baby. The combined family was not to continue for very long.

Disaster very soon struck Joseph Henry. Ingrid's first child by him was born five months after the marriage. Since Joseph Henry was then an elder of the church, this inevitably caused comment. Bound by the strict moral code of the Mormon Church, the local church officials had to take notice and consider what should be done. The penalty for drunkeness, apostasy, unresolved disputes or immorality could be excommunication. The imposition of such a penalty was not a hasty process or based on immediate reactions. The question of bringing charges, which was the responsibility of the local church officials, involved careful investigation and deliberation. This went on for five years, during which time Joseph Henry lived under the shadow of uncertainty and threat.

Meanwhile a more tangible shadow fell across the homestead. It also was a threat, but a physical one. A mile and half away from the farm a smelter had been built to process ores mined in the nearby Oquirrh Mountains, where copper, silver and gold had been discovered; the site of what later became the largest open-cast copper mine in the world. The shadow that the smelter cast over the landscape was both visible and invisible, because its chimneys emitted both smoke and invisible fumes. Probably few were aware of its long-term effects on crops and human beings. Yet the smelter provided useful employment, especially for those who needed to augment their income. Both Joseph Henry and his father worked there from time to time when the farm did not require their total attention or when the market for produce was slack.

By now the deliberations of the church had finally reached their conclusion, and the blow fell upon Joseph Henry. On July 15, 1883, the Bishops' Court of West Jordan made a recommendation to the High Council of the Church that Joseph Henry be penalised. The recommendation was confirmed and, on July 27, Joseph Henry was 'cut off' from the church by the High Council – that is he was ex-communicated, for his cohabitation with Ingrid Poulson before marriage.[5]

But there was more to come. The second blow came from the United States Federal law officers. For some time the Department of Justice in Washington had been determined to outlaw polygamy, and legislation was being sought on the issue. Joseph Henry could see which way the wind was blowing. But, unlike many other Mormons who had made polygamous marriages, he decided it would be wiser to separate from one or other of his two wives and so avoid future harassment by the law. But he was in a dilemma. He genuinely loved both Hannah and Ingrid, and did not want to be parted from either. However, after consultation together, it was decided that Ingrid should leave the household with her children. She went at the end of June 1885, and shortly afterwards married again. Her second husband was a Swedish settler named Christian Lilya. She had by now had three children by Joseph Henry, Joseph Willard born 1878, Miranda born 1881 and Alice Ellen born in 1884. Miranda died in 1882.

In the meantime the legislation making polygamy illegal had been passed by the Federal Government in Washington. The enforcement of this law was placed in the hands of the Governor in each state and territory, and of the local judges appointed by Washington. This was due to be implemented in Utah from 1884. Although he had already complied with the law, Joseph Henry was nevertheless arrested in October 1885, brought to court and charged with unlawful cohabitation. The actual trial took place in February 1886, when the jury found him guilty. Since Joseph Henry had already been separated from his second wife for eight months and now undertook to abide by the law in future, the judge only fined him $200 and costs. This judge was well-known for his leniency, and was in fact removed from office later after pressure from the Federal Government. Joseph Henry pleaded unable to pay the fine and was sent to prison for a month for non-payment.

He was lodged in the State Penitentiary in Salt Lake City. This had been set up in 1855 with a 20 foot adobe wall surrounding it, four feet thick. The main prison buildings were at the entrance and there was an acre of prison yard. The entrance gate was heavily built of wood and iron. There was a sentry box and a reception room. For the prisoners there was a wooden bunkhouse, known for its proliferation of bed bugs. Armed sentries patrolled the catwalks surrounding the upper yard where the prisoners exercised. At the corners there were watchtowers. Inmates were allowed fifteen minutes to eat a meal. For many Mormons it was considered an honour to have been imprisoned for their beliefs, but this was hardly true of Josph Henry. He was in prison from February 18, 1886 until March 20, 1886.

With regard to Joseph Henry's plea of poverty, his financial position was not all that it appeared to be. Well before the trial he realised he might face a heavy fine, and had deeded his property temporarily to his father. Strictly speaking, therefore, he was by no means impecunious and, in fact, the property was deeded back to him a few years later.

The trial was a painful experience, nevertheless, as were the humiliating comments in the press. There were reports in the *Deseret News*, a leading daily paper in Salt Lake City, in 1885 and 1886. They stated that in court Joseph Henry was of a 'hang-dog' appearance, that he was a 'non-Mormon', and a thoroughly undesirable character. The two main witnesses, no doubt under legal compulsion, were the father and brother respectively of Hannah and Ingrid. Ingrid also was called to give evidence. Strangely enough the *Deseret News* was, and still is, a Mormon church-owned newspaper. It's attitude to Joseph Henry probably reflected conservative elements in the church, which regarded Joseph Henry's promise to obey the law as a betrayal of principle.

Another Salt Lake newspaper, the *Salt Lake Tribune*, threw further light on the situation. On May 3, 1885 it wrote of the hounding of Mormons in the courts of law:

'Families are dragged before commissioners and grand juries, and on pain of punishment are compelled to testify against their fathers and husbands. . . . Attempts are made to bribe men to work up cases against their neighbours. Notoriously disreputable characters are employed to spy into men's family relations. . . . Those accused of crime were considered guilty until proven otherwise. Trial by jury in the Territories is no longer a safeguard against injustice to a Mormon accused of crime. . . . Juries are packed to convict.'

There is no question that some in authority were determined to get convictions at all costs, and no doubt the new law opened the way for the venting of long-held prejudices and animosities. Altogether the situation was a complicated and confusing one in which many different factors and motives were operating.

Within a year or so of the trial Ingrid and her two surviving children, Joseph Willard and little Alice Ellen, left Salt Lake with her second husband, Christian Lilya, to settle in the territory of Idaho, north of Utah. To differentiate her children from Hannah's, Ingrid added an 'i' to the Sisam name, spelling it 'Sisiam', but the second 'i' was not pronounced, and it is still spelt in this way by her son's descendants.

After the heartaches and stresses that the family endured during the time of Joseph Henry's trial, one can understand Ingrid and her new husband wanting to move away from Salt Lake City. Their chosen destination was the southern part of Idaho, a very sparsely settled area where settlement had been stimulated by the discovery of gold and silver around 1860. By today's standards it is not an overlong journey from Salt Lake City, but in the 1880s it was a considerable trek if attempted by wagon.

Christian and Ingrid and the two children probably travelled north from Salt Lake City to join the Oregon Trail. After that the route was due west as far as the Raft River, in southern Idaho, where they would follow the north fork of the river and then cross it by raft. This would lead them through the 'City of Rocks' landscape, a much used emigrant trail to the Far West. Thirty years previously this area had been the scene of a terrible massacre of emigrants, by a combined band of Indians comprised of Shoshones, Arapahos, Cheyennes, Utes, Bannocks, Pimentos, Cazuns and Orozhios. The massacre was provoked by indiscriminate shooting of Indians by some of the emigrants.

In the 'City of Rocks' the trail divided, one branch going south-west to California, the

'City of Rocks' terrain through which Christian and Ingrid Lilya may have passed on their way to Idaho.

other north-west to Oregon. Here, beside the spring, wagon trains would pause and travellers used to leave messages for friends and relations following them, scratched on the rough surfaces of the rocks or written in axle grease, some of which can still just be deciphered. The Lilya party travelling by this route would have taken the Oregon branch and a little distance along this left the trail, turning north towards the Snake River which could be crossed just east of present day Burley by a horse-operated ferry at Starr's Crossing. Their route then lay northwest through volcanic, desert country to the fertile valleys of the Big and Little Wood Rivers, and the township of Gannett. It was here that they settled, in an area of great scenic beauty lying in the foothills of the mighty Sawtooth Mountains.

The Lilya household consisted of Christian and Ingrid Lilya and her two Sisiam children, Joseph Willard, who was about eight, and Alice Ellen aged three. Joseph Henry made provision for these two children and sent regular sums of money to Ingrid for their upkeep. Although they were living in a remote part, Ingrid saw to it that they received what schooling she could give them. Christian Lilya does not seem to have been a Mormon. Nevertheless, Ingrid encouraged Joseph Willard and Alice to become members of the Mormon congregation at the nearest church. At their birth in West Jordan they had been blessed in a church ceremony. When later at Silver Creek they came of age, they were baptised on August 27, 1899, according to the church records. There is no mention of any Lilya children in the church records. It was very soon after the family arrived in Idaho that Lilya step-brothers and sisters began to appear on the family scene. The first was Christian and Ingrid's daughter, Ingre, born in September 1887; then a son, followed by a second son and another daughter.

❖❖❖ 9 ❖❖❖
At the Homestead

JOSEPH HENRY THE UTAH FARMER

While Ingrid was rebuilding her life with Christian Lilya at Silver Creek, Joseph Henry and Hannah at West Jordan were living through a similar experience, but perhaps a more painful one since they were having to face deep hurts, and the moral and spiritual issues that lay behind them. To what extent they were able to face these issues may never be known. One can only hope that they found the courage to do so, and then go forward in faith together to build a happy and stable future for their children. The trauma of Joseph Henry's trial, and his ex-communication from the church, had affected them deeply, but their marriage survived and the unity of the home was preserved.

There were good reasons for this. It was a custom in the Mormon Church that, when a member was in deep waters, those he had come to know in the church would stand by him and help him back onto his feet. Joseph had many friends in the church in West Jordan, and had close ties with some of the leaders. Amongst them were the Goff family, into which his sister Ann had married. She and her husband, Isaac Goff Jnr., lived in West Jordan. Her husband's brother, Hyrum Goff was a bishop in the church. Joseph Locke, Catherine Sisam's brother-in-law, who had brought the Sisams into the Mormon Church years before in England, was a high priest and lived in Salt Lake City; and there were several senior officials of long standing in the West Jordan church, who knew the family well. Certainly there were faithful friends who could stand by Joseph Henry and help him not only to face what had gone wrong but find repentance and forgiveness before God. In point of fact, excommunication did not mean total exclusion from church gatherings. Joseph Henry was able to be present at the blessing of his children born during the years when he was waiting to be re-instated in his church. At the same time rehabilitation and rebirth, by its very nature, was a matter of time; but it came about. There is no surviving, written account of those years that shows to what extent Joseph Henry welcomed the hand of friendship, or how deep was his commitment to serve God in his own personal life and in the world around him. If outward appearances are anything to go by, then the probabilities are that he did come to a new and deeper commitment of his life to God. Records show that in 1892, after a period of nine years, he was re-baptised and accepted once more as a full member of the church. Hyrum Goff, who had known the family for many years, officiated at the ceremony. It must have been a moving yet very happy occasion for the family who were present. In due course, in 1906, Joseph Henry was again elected an elder, an office he held for the rest of his life.

Joseph Henry was fortunate during the troublous years of domestic, legal and social uncertainty, that he had the solace of the family farm to occupy his mind and energies. These years, and the many years that followed, were a time of steady progress at the homestead on State Road. By 1888 the household consisted of Joseph Henry and Hannah, his parents, Joseph and Catherine, together with the three children, Annie age 10, Berta Andrew 4, and Alma Neils 1. The house had been expanded to accomodate everyone and the acreage of the farm had been increased. Between them the family now owned a total of about 38 acres in various blocks in the neighbourhood, of which the farmhouse and its outbuildings stood on a plot of about 23 acres. The surrounding rural area was comparatively thinly populated, with a few houses and stores scattered here and there. With the increased acreage, the farm now produced all the food the family needed; as well as the saleable crops such as wheat, hay and sugar-beet.

But it was not all work. There were simple pleasures as well. Life in the community followed very much the pattern set by the early pioneers. Hard though their life was, and strict though the rules of behaviour, the importance of relaxation and entertainment was not overlooked. The tradition and customs of the prairie emigrants were continued. On the overland journey, when the day was done, they used to gather in the circle of wagons and dance to the fiddle, squeeze-box and banjo. So, in West Jordan, the settlers would have a weekly night of relaxation and enjoyment. It was not on Saturday night for that was bath night, when the tin bath was filled with hot water from the kitchen stove and, starting with the youngest child and ending with father, the whole family bathed one after another. Entertainment night was during the week in the Rock Meeting House, built of stone in 1859 to replace the original log hut of 1848. As soon as it was sundown families would gather there, the children being put to bed in the vestry while the grown-ups spent the evening dancing the Virginia reel, the waltz and the polka. At midnight there was supper, to which each family contributed homemade dishes. Afterwards dancing went on until the small hours. These weekly get-togethers became an institution, which Hannah Sisam in her old age recalled with much pleasure.[6]

During those years Joseph Henry gained a reputation for his wheat-growing. Adequate irrigation of the land was the key to good cropping, and the local farmers all depended on it. The main source of water was the streams flowing from the surrounding mountains. Joseph Henry was well acquainted with the irrigation system, and quite early on had served as Water Master for the district with responsibility, especially during the crop-growing season, for directing the waterflow to the different farms. This was done every eight days in daylight hours, then every eight nights. The work also involved inspection of canyon streams in the mountains, and the irrigation channels they fed, making sure both were free from vegetation and from debris washed down from the upper slopes.

He also had an interest in several business enterprises, which increased in number as the years went by. Being a wheat-producer, it was a natural step to become a stockholder and director of the West Jordan Milling Company. As a participant in the local irrigation system he invested in the East Jordan Irrigation Company. He also ventured further afield and, in the course of time, held investments in the Utah-Mexican Rubber Corporation, the Beaver Mining Corporation, the Neva Mining Company, and the Tabasco State Rubber Company of Mexico. He was a man who was enterprising in his use of money, though his main financial base was always the Sisam farm, itself a viable and prosperous family concern.

In the early 1900s life at the State Road homestead was pleasant enough, and proceeded in a stable and well-ordered fashion. The family had increased, and Joseph Henry and Hannah had seven children living and working at the homestead, four boys and three girls,

The new homestead on State Road, West Jordan, near the outskirts of Salt Lake City.

The Old Rock Meeting House in West Jordan where the evening barn dances were held.

ranging from Berta Andrew in his early twenties, to the youngest child Laverne. The single-storey, wooden farmhouse was of a reasonable size. A porch ran the length of the front, in the centre of which was the front door, opening on to a corridor leading through to the back. On either side of the entrance corridor, facing to the front, were bedrooms formimg two separate suites, left and right. At the back were larger rooms: one on the left serving as a kitchen and one even larger room on the right. This was the family dining room and living room, complete with a large table in the centre. Beneath the kitchen was the cellar, where milk, butter, and other provisions were kept. It was a comfortable home, but like most pioneer houses had no indoor running water. A well outside provided water, and of course there was no indoor sanitation.

There were horses on the farm for ploughing and hauling, two or three cows to provide milk, as well as chickens and pigs. They always kept pigs, and produced their own bacon and hams. In addition to the farm crops of wheat, potatoes and hay, they grew vegetables, gooseberries, strawberries, apples, and there was a fine walnut tree. Gooseberry pie was a universal favourite. All the boys worked on the farm, and the girls as well. Laverne remembered getting up early in the morning before it was light to help her mother milk the cows in the barn; and going out in the fields, where her father was working, to weed potatoes. The family employed hired men on the farm, who were paid a dollar a day. A good deal of the potato crop was taken into Salt Lake City and marketed. The going rate was 'a dollar a hundred', i.e. a dollar for a hundredweight. Wheat was the other main crop. In the busy threshing season, Hannah would cook an enormous midday meal for everyone. To the children especially this was 'a regular banquet', and was eaten indoors in the family dining room, sitting round the great table.

Hannah was a good cook. She worked by instinct and experience. She never measured anything. It was always just 'a pinch of this', and 'a pinch of that'; and that is how she replied when asked for her recipes. For the younger children there was a special drink known by the intriguing name of 'angel tea'. It was really quite simple, hot water with milk and sugar, and was much in demand. What is not so clear is the significance of the name 'angel tea'. Either it meant a drink suitable for little angels, or it was reminiscent of the early days when the concept of angels was a real one, and when grown-ups drank 'Mormon tea' made from a desert plant, since normal tea and coffee was always considered harmful. Saturday was a big cook-day, as very little cooking was done on Sunday. That was a day of rest for both men and women, and the family would usually go to church in the morning. In the evening after dark Joseph Henry would read to them from the Bible, while Hannah crocheted and tatted, or perhaps worked on a bedspread. In the summertime, in the cool of the evening they would sit on the front porch.

At Christmas time there was a Christmas tree in the farmhouse, decorated with popcorn, home-made from home-grown grain, as might be expected. On the top of the tree was a star. Later, the star was replaced by an angel and there was great excitement among the girls as to who should have it. Thanksgiving Day saw an even greater celebration and gathering of the family. But at other times of the year, whenever an unusual pause in the farmwork allowed, the whole family would down tools and set off for a day out in the equivalent of today's family car – the 'surrey with a fringe on top'; so named from the original four-wheeler originating in Surrey, England. This was a rare occasion as usually there was too much to do on the farm. Joseph Henry would drive, with the family squeezed into the two seats as best they could. Perhaps as he drove he marvelled as he recalled the covered wagon he drove across the desert 45 years back, when he was but a lad of sixteen. Here, they were making for Wandamere Lake where there was a park and plenty to amuse youngsters, both boys and girls. Laverne won a doll here on one occasion, which more than made up for any Christmas angel that may have evaded her. Such days were memorable for children and, like the great family meals at threshing-time, a day at Wandermere was also a 'banquet' to Laverne, and that is how she always referred to it. Wandermere Park was a happy place where as evening descended men would play the harmonica and there was dancing of the Virginia reel.

The children went to school locally, but attendance depended on the seasons and the work needing to be done in the fields. For the girls there was in the home that essential training in cooking and housecare, which Hannah gave them. At times it may have seemed burdensome but she knew it would stand them in good stead in years to come, when they had families of their own. Hannah did not often go away from home but, when in later years she did go away for a few days, Laverne stepped into her shoes and had no difficulty in coping. She knew exactly what to do and, equally important, what to do next. 'We were taught' she said, 'how to keep things very clean'. When Hannah returned home the house was as fresh and clean as a new pin.

As the years rolled by, and Joseph Henry's sons each in their turn grew up, the future of the homestead seemed less and less certain. Although they had worked the family land since childhood none of them, even the eldest Berta Andrew, showed any strong inclination to continue in farming. In any case, although the farm had prospered, it is doubtful if it would support more than one son, together with whatever family he might raise. It was a very different situation from the day when Joseph Henry began helping his father till the first plot of land in West Jordan in 1868. Joseph Henry had known the horse and buggy days; but now, at the beginning of a new century, his sons were growing up in the age of the automobile and electricity. In both these areas America would soon become a world leader. The machine age had come to stay and the younger generation were becoming attuned to it. Many saw that their future lay in a new direction.

Joseph Henry was not a man to shut his eyes to progress. He knew that his sons must make their own way in the world, and being a generous father he was prepared to help each one financially to follow his calling. His aim was thereby to prime the pump, in expentation that it would continue to run efficiently and with ever increasing productivity thereafter. But, like all hopeful fathers, he knew it was an act of faith and that each son would have to make his own decisions and accept responsibility for them.

Another factor that may have influenced these family decisions was that West Jordan itself was changing. When the Sisams first came there it was in more or less open country but now, with the rapid expansion of Salt Lake City, it was becoming more and more urbanised. State Road, where they lived, was soon to be known as State Street, and it was not long before street cars were running from West Jordan to the City, now the capital of a fully recognised State of the American Union. With these developments came industrial development. There were now several smelters in the district, and their smoke fumes were already affecting crops.

A new century was about to begin and a new world was emerging. As the old century was slipping away, Joseph Sisam, the patriarch of the family, reached the end of his life.

He died on January 13, 1899, at the age of 79. He had started as a young farmworker in England, amongst the meadows and lanes of Warwickshire, where he met and married his wife, Catherine. His life had been an eventful one, and at times dramatic. He saw his brother transported for life to Australia when but a young man, for the theft of a gun and a few clothes. The lives of his own family were transformed by the faith they found through Mormon missionaries at work in Warwickshire. He and Catherine made the courageous decision to emigrate with their family to America. There, in Utah on the distant frontier of civilisation, they settled on virgin land and built a new home. Joseph the father was the pioneer, and his son Joseph Henry was the builder; for on his father's foundations he founded a dynasty. Catherine, who became blind in her old age, lived on until 1908; long enough for her to know that the dynasty was well and truly established.

10

Automobiles & Electricity

THE UTAH SONS AND THEIR DESCENDANTS

In 1893 two brothers, Charles and Frank Durya, produced America's first practical automobile. It had a one-cylinder gasoline engine, eletric ignition, and sold steadily for the next twenty years. They were soon followed by other pioneers whose names were to become famous. Random Elis Olds produced the Oldsmobile, known as the 'modern buggy' that gave 'one chug per telegraph pole'. By 1905 there were 15,000 on the roads and the Oldsmobile had become the best known automobile in the country. The Cadillac appeared with patent leather seats and brass lamps, and in Detroit a Scottish plumber, David Buick, made the first Buick. Soon afterwards the Hudson came on the scene capable of almost 50 miles an hour. All of this was made possible by man's inventiveness and enterprise, and also by the Dangley tariff of 1897 which imposed a 45% duty on the importation of European automoblies thus enabling the American industry to become established. But the greatest leap forward in road transport came, as the world knows, through the Detroit engineer, Henry Ford, with his Model T of 1903 and the establishment of the mass-production assembly line ten years later. In 1915 the production rate of the Ford Model T reached 300,000 vehicles a year. They were rugged, reliable, easy-to-drive and provided a family automobile that was within reach of the ordinary man's pocket.

Side by side with the development of the internal combustion petrol engine went the development of electricity. In the 1870s and 1880s there had been major improvements in the dynamo and electric motor, and soon afterwards Thomas Edison of Newark, New Jersey, perfected the electric light bulb. By 1900 most of the main American and European cities had a public electricity supply for street and domestic lighting. The Niagara Falls were harnessed to generate electric power, and at Salt Lake City the Ogden River and various cataracts in the Cottonwood and other canyons were put to similar use. This was the new world into which Joseph Henry's three oldest sons would soon be stepping. All were farm-boys by upbringing, but he gave each the freedom and backing to choose the path they wished to follow, and allowed them to take with them the inheritance he had set aside for them.

Of these sons Alma Neils, the second of the three, was the first to leave the farm. At the age of 19 he travelled east across the continent to Albany, New York, where he worked intensively for two years on a Mormon Mission. It was good, all-round character-training, as is the experience of young Burmese who serve as Buddhist priests for a period, or of young Americans and Europeans who volunteer for overseas service in the Third World.

When Alma Neils returned home in November 1908 he knew what he wanted to do; it was to become an electrical engineer. He underwent training, obtained his qualifications, and set up as an electrical contractor. He married in 1909 at the age of 22. Like his brothers he was tall and dark. His bride was 23, tall and blonde. She was Edith Lillian Bess, from Holladay on the far side of the Jordan valley. They had a marriage ceremony in the Mormon Temple that stood with its six slender spires in the centre of Salt Lake City. The heart of the marriage ceremony was a sacred and solemn giving of vows and a dedication by the couple of their own lives to God's service. It was followed in the evening by a dance given by the bride's family. The couple made their home in Browning Avenue, Hawthorne in south Salt Lake City, not far from the city centre.

While he was still on the family farm, Alma Neils became close friends with his younger brother Wilford Martin, and remained so throughout the years. The year after Alma's wedding Wilford also married. He was 21 and working on the farm with the oldest brother, Berta Andrew. Wilford's bride was Mary Elizabeth Butterfield, whose family name suggested English forebears living long ago in rich meadow country. She was from Taylorsville a few miles north of West Jordan. The Sisams knew the Butterfields well for Wilford's elder sister, Annie Catherine, had married David Butterfield, Mary's brother, some years previously. Mary was now a farmer's wife and went with her husband Wilford to live on the Sisam farm. This was in 1911.

The future of his sons was not the only question occupying Joseph Henry's mind at this time. He was conscious of a another cloud hanging over the future of the farm itself. It was an actual cloud, partly visible and partly invisible, of smoke and fumes from the gold, silver and copper smelters in the district, in particular from the United States Smelting Company's plant on West Center Street. For the last eight years the family at the homestead had suffered increasingly from sickness and respiratory trouble, and their crops had been seriously affected. Four acres of potatoes had been lost one year and, over the years, lucerne, grass, beets, oats, fruits and berries had been spoiled by sulphurous fumes. Joseph Henry took the company to court and claimed damages of $1,000. The company appealed against this on the grounds that there were other smelters in the district. But experts refuted the appeal by presenting scientific evidence on the the direction of the prevailing winds. Finally, on October 21, 1911, the U.S. Court of Appeals awarded Joseph Henry $750 compensation for the crops, and $50 for personal discomfort. The pollution continued for some time, but gradually public pressure brought about restrictions which gave some improvement. What was not known was the long-term effect of pollution on the health of the people of West Jordan.

In the same year, 1911, there was another wedding in the family when Joseph Henry's eldest son, Berta, married Margaret Louise Green of Murray, Utah. Berta, like Alma Neils, was one of the new generation of technically minded young men eager to be part of the new age. Alma Neils had chosen electricity. With Berta it was automobiles. He too had taken a course of training, both theoretical and practical, and was now an automobile engineer, qualified to undertake the maintenance and overhaul of the growing number of gasoline-driven vehicles on the roads. This meant that of the younger generation left on the farm there were now only Wilford Martin and the youngest son, Amil Arthur aged 16. It looked as if Wilford might inherit the farm eventually, since Amil Arthur showed little interest in it; and no doubt Joseph Henry hoped that this would be the pattern of events. Unfortunately, as the years passed, Wilford became increasingly disenchanted with the

1910 Model T Ford saloon.

The Mormon Temple in the centre of Salt Lake City. Some Sisams had a temple marriage ceremony here.

The United States Smelting company on Center Street, West Jordan.

homestead. Whether it was the surroundings, or the proximity to the smelter that caused him to doubt, or something deeper, is difficult to assess. He continued for three years carrying the major part of the farm-work, during which time two daughters were born, Myrtle Leone in 1911 and Violet Elizabeth in 1913. It was in 1913 that the question of the future came to the point of decision. Joseph Henry genuinely wanted the best for his sons and took great pains to try and understand their aspirations. Wilford, however, was undecided. His father now made him a generous offer. He had heard that there was good land available in Idaho and was prepared to buy a farm there for Wilford. So the two of them set off together in search of a suitable property.

Idaho had much to recommend it and had attracted a good many settlers from Salt Lake and elsewhere. In the south it had large expanses of level, fertile land and in the north wide and well-watered valleys running from the foothills of the Sawtooth Mountain Range. This is where Ingrid, Joseph Henry's second wife by a plural marriage, went with her children when the Federal Legislation against plural marriages compelled Joseph Henry to part from her. The trip that he and Wilford were now making, twenty-eight years after those unhappy times, may well have included a visit to Ingrid and her family; and particularly to Joseph Willard Sisiam, Ingrid's son by Joseph Henry, whom she brought up in Idaho. This son, Joseph Willard, was now married and living with his family on a plot of land in Cassio County beside the Big Wood River. Unfortunately no record or family memory exists of such a visit, only that there was contact from time to time.

Joseph Henry and Wilford travelled about a good deal in Idaho and looked at a number of locations, but none of them appealed to Wilford. Perhaps it was dawning upon him that farming was not for him. Be that as it may, the trip was an interesting experience for both of them and helped to clarify Wilford's mind. When they reached home Joseph Henry, who had been very patient until now, finally said to Wilford, 'What do you really want?' Wilford replied, 'I want to go to school. I want to become an automobile mechanic.' So his father sent him to college in Kansas City, Missouri. This was a thousand miles or so from Salt Lake City, for there were few if any technical colleges west of the Missouri River. As the Oklahoma cowboy sang in the musical show, 'Everything's up-to-date in Kansas City. It's gone about as far as it can go.' But what the cowboy had in mind was the fun to be had in that fast-moving city. Wilford wasn't drawn to the bright lights. He had come to work and to study. He had ability, which his father recognised and on which he was prepared to gamble. In the event Joseph Henry was not disappointed. The engineering course normally took one year and a half. Wilford completed it in eight months. He had a deep interest in his subject and studied day and night, returning to his lodgings after classes and working on into the small hours. This fascination with book-learning was something that stayed with him throughout his life. In later years his daughter remarked of him, 'He wasn't a swot'; it was just that he had an insatiable appetite for knowledge. During the time in Kansas City he was more than a little homesick and longed to be home again. His dedication to study though admirable must have tended to cut him off from the world around him, depriving him of some of the stimulus and widening of horizons that a modern metropolis like Kansas City might have offered. When he returned to Salt Lake City his immediate need was to earn. He looked around for a while and then went to work for the Cullins automobile engineering company.

Joseph Henry was now in his early sixties. The troubles of the past had receded into the mists of time. He had been reinstated into the church for over twenty years, and was enjoying a well-earned prosperity. One by one his sons had married and set up homes of their own, as had two of their daughters, Annie Catherine and Laura May. There remained the younger daughters, Irene Leone aged 14, Laverne the youngest of them all, aged 11, and the youngest son, Amil Arthur, aged 18. Joseph Henry and Hannah could look with equanimity on their large family, knowing that they had done their best thus far to give them a good start in life. Like most grandparents he and Hannah were much loved by their grandchildren, of which seven were born during the period 1911–1916. The older ones visited regularly. They remembered that their grandfather had a small moustache, as was fashionable in those days. But especially they remembered the handfulls of wheat he gave them to chew. 'This is your gum', he would say, and very often they would be sent to the barn to help themselves. Before they went home Hannah would feed them with her home-made bread spread with butter and jam or pickles from her store.

The farm was a pleasant place with an orchard at the front planted with apple trees. Behind the house was a walnut which in the fall was a magnet for the children eager to gather its nuts. This was a trial to Hannah because their clothes inevitably became covered in black stains from the outer husks. Sometimes they would find their grandfather in the orchard making cider with a small apple-grinder. The apples were ground by hand, with a pitcher under the spigot to catch the juice. Once Ruth, Alma Neils' small daughter, asked her grandfather, 'What happens to the worms if there are some in the apples you grind?' He laughed and replied in his humorous down-to-earth fashion, 'Cider is much better with a little fresh meat in it.'

It was in these later years that Joseph Henry began to build a smaller house on part of the farm property adjacent to Center Street, where they might spend their remaining days. It was about three-quarters of a mile from the homestead, next to an already exisiting house which he owned. This existing house he sold to his son Wilford Martin, who moved in with his wife, Mary, and their two children, Myrtle and Violet. Wilford set up a workshop there. For him the going had been rough. After leaving his first job at the Cullins workshops he had not found it easy to set up on his own as an automobile engineer. For a while he was a driver on the electric trolley cars running along State Street near the homestead, but he suffered a severe burn while at work and had to give up. Undaunted he began studying electricity and gained his journeyman's licence. This gave him two strings to his bow, enabling him to undertake electrical installations as well as the maintenance of automobiles.

In 1917 Amil Arthur, the youngest of Joseph Henry's sons, reached the age of 21. Up until now he had been living at home helping with the farm. From an early age he had been a high spirited boy, full of mischief. He and his sister Laverne were close to each other in age. She never forgot the day she was walking home when Amil, who had been hiding behind the hedge in front of the house, suddenly sprang out at her with a loud 'Boo!'. 'I thought I was going to die,' Laverne said afterwards. When Amil boasted to his mother about his exploit, Hannah admonished him sharply. 'Don't you ever do that again', she told him in no uncertain terms. As a young man he was a bright spark always ready for a lark, but the time inevitably came for him to face the future. His father put the same question to him that had been put to his brothers, 'What do you most want?' The answer came back, 'I want the fastest horse and buggy in town.' A buggy was a smart light-weight carriage, intended to make a dash. The horse and buggy duly appeared and from then on Amil seemed to spend most of his time riding about the town in it. But this was

Laverne in 1990 clearly remembered her young brother Amil Arthur's skylarking.

Amil Arthur: 'I want the fastest horse and buggy in town'.

1917, the year in which the German threat to ocean-going shipping brought America into World War I. Very soon there would be 1½ million American soldiers in Europe. Amil went into the United States Army, but was not drafted to Europe, and performed his military service within America.

In the same year of 1917 the family were shaken by two sad events within a short time. On July 23, Joseph Henry's oldest son, Berta, who was an established automobile engineer, was struck down and killed by an automobile while walking home only a short distance from the family farm. He left a wife, Louise, and three young children, Delilah, Vera and William. He had been a steadfast man, a good father and much loved at the homestead where he and his family had been part of the household. Two months later in the month of September Joseph Henry himself died. He had been feeling unwell for some time. He was 65 years old.

To his friends Joseph Henry was always known affectionately as 'Harry'. At his funeral in Midvale there was a large gathering to bid him farewell. The service was led by Bishop John Aylett. Many paid tribute, and a solo was sung by one of the Goff family, with whom the Sisams had had close links ever since the early settlement days. He was buried nearby in a peaceful setting of green grass and open sky, where his tombstone looks out towards the Oquirrh mountain range, from which flowed the precious mountain streams that had turned the arid land into fertile and productive acres.

❖ ❖ ❖

The following year, 1918, saw the ending of World War I and the beginning of the lengthy peace negotiations in Europe, in which America played a prominent part. The next years, although free of major military conflict, were an unsettled period of social and economic instability, characterised by extremes of wealth and poverty, industrial strife, unemployment and the loosening of family ties. It would be a testing time for young couples seeking to raise and care for their families for it was an age of change, when old values were challenged and new paths were offered.

Hannah remained at the homestead for a year or two after Joseph Henry's death, while the house he had begun to build for her was completed. It is not known whether he left a will or how he disposed of his money and investments, but he transferred to Hannah by a legal deed the farm and all the land he owned shortly before he died. He had already given generously to his sons on their coming of age. Before she moved to the new house, Hannah sold the homestead to the Malmstroms, a Swedish family, and 25 acres of the farmland to her son-in-law David Butterfield, husband of her eldest daughter, Annie Catherine. She retained about 20 acres herself which she farmed, raising wheat and beans. Her youngest son Amil Arthur, who had not yet left home, stayed and helped her for a while. In additon she had the support of Alma Neils, now the senior man of the family since the death of Berta. He came to see her regularly and helped her with her business affairs.

Laverne her youngest daughter, who had attended a local high school for two years, went with her to the new house. Laverne had been well trained by Hannah and knew how to look after a home. She was the only unmarried daughter left as the others all had families of their own, the last one being Irene Leone who married Leo Tripp, a neighbouring farmer's son, in 1919. About the same time Amil Arthur, the 'bright spark', married and moved to a home of his own. His bride was Elesta Mae Robertson. Laverne was conscientious by nature and caring. She said later, of the period immediately after her father's death, 'Mother was a widow so I figured she needed some help, so I got a job at a laundry. Then I worked for Sweet's candy company for a while. I didn't want chocolates for a while after that!' Finally in 1923, by which time Wilford and his family were well settled into the house next-door, Laverne married a man from South Jordan. But unhappily the marriage did not work. Her husband had a roving eye, and did crazy things although he was a Deputy-Sheriff. She felt she had to divorce him, and not long afterwards married again. Her nieces summed up the situation very aptly. 'He was just a chaser', they said. 'Aunt Laverne had a bad husband the first time but she got a good one the second time'. This was Uncle Robert, Marvin Robert Greathouse. Uncle Robert, they said, was a good man and 'such fun'. He and Laverne were devoted to one another and they made a wonderfully happy life together.

Hannah was the natural hub of the family. In the difficult years that followed she fulfilled her role as matriarch with modesty, generosity and a loving care for all who came her way. In many ways her life continued in the much the same pattern as before. The seasons came and went and she always kept open house for her children and grandchildren. The grandchildren, who lived some distance away, adored visiting grandma's farm. The house, which was meticulously kept, was comfortable but had a certain frugality about it. There were two windows facing the street. One was the dining room and the other the parlour, which had an organ. Hannah did not use the parlour much and the children had to ask permission to go into it. There was also a bedroom in the front part of the house. At the back was the spacious kitchen and a large bathroom which was very cold in the winter. The dining room was heated by a small 'monkey' stove which was only lit on Saturdays and Sundays. During the rest of the week the kitchen stove provided the warmth. The visiting children usually made for the barn and went sliding down the haystack, and when they said goodbye they never left without some goodies from her store. Hannah's generosity remained constant through good times and bad. On a farm there was usually some produce available even at the worst of times. Whatever Hannah had she shared.

In the first few years after World War I there were economic difficulties both in Europe and America. For many families there were shortages of basic necessities. Trade reached a low ebb and, like many others, the automobile business slumped. Wilford's family found it hard to make ends meet. They often lacked the means to heat their home in winter. Their house was not far from the railroad tracks. The children would often go and stand by them and wait for a slow freight train to come by. When the crew of the locomotive saw the children the men tossed out hunks of coal for them to take home. It was like gold to the family for then they could have a fire in the evening. Violet, Wilford's second daughter, when recalling these days in later years, spoke of them without bitterness or regret. 'I am glad', she said, 'that I was born in the time that I was, when we had poverty, because I knew the value of the dollars. I wouldn't have missed those days for anything.' For she felt the youngsters growing up around her today had no understanding of the value of things. Everything came easily to them and they knew nothing of sacrifice or doing without, or of the compassion for others that the experience of hardship brings.

Hannah meanwhile would come in every day from her house next door to help Violet's mother with the household, and if there was a sick baby she came every morning. This she did thoughout the next ten years during which the rest of Wilford and Mary's children were born; they were Donald, Darrell, Robert and Patsy. Wilford's children were not the only ones Hannah took on. When in 1924 Louise Sisam, Berta's widow, died of tuberculosis Hannah had their three children, Delilah, Vera and William, to live in her home in Center Street and brought them up. They stayed with her there until they married.

Alma Neils seems to have had better luck with his business than Wilford. He succeeded in establishing it at an early stage and in 1918 it was incorporated as a company under the name of 'Sisam Electrical'. Alma had begun the business single-handed and had worked hard to establish it. It involved installation work and long hours of evening study after work, in order to keep up with ever increasing technical developments. He and Wilford were very much alike in that they worked hard and studied hard throughout their lives. As their families said of them both, 'They never quit learning'. As soon as Wilford came home from work he would bury himself in a book. Usually he would sit down with it in the middle of the kitchen floor, deep in its pages and lost to the world. Sometimes when the children were at home Mary, wanting them to be noticed, would call out to him when he was reading and say, 'Speak to the kids'. There was a pause and more often than not the reply would come from the floor, 'What kids?' Both men were good fathers and beloved of their children nevertheless, despite their long hours of work. Alma Neils was successful financially and his business prospered. Wilford, although a trained automobile engineer, never made much money; yet he did not begrudge his brother's success.

Alma and Edith had four children in all, three boys and a girl, their daughter Ruth being their firstborn. As the children grew older the family would sometimes accompany Alma on his regular visits to Hannah. The high point of these for Ruth was to be with her father, and she was not above playing tricks to achieve her heart's desire. The whole family rode on the trolley car: Ruth, her parents and the three boys. On the journey home she would pretend to feel unwell, whereupon she and her father got off the trolley and walked the rest of the way, while her mother and the boys continued on their journey, by trolley. She now had her father to herself, much to her delight. In later years she told Alma about this ruse. He laughed and said, 'O, I knew you weren't that sick.'

Alma and Edith lived a full life. She had the children to care for. He had his work, his after hours study, his share in bringing up the children and the responsibility for Hannah and her farm; and always there were his close links with Wilford and concern for his well-being. Yet amidst all these responsibilities Alma and Edith played an active part in their church at Hawthorne. They contributed greatly to it but it was also a source of inner strength to them. Their faith was in fact the key to their lives.

Ruth their daughter grew up to be a warm-hearted and high spirited young woman, but with a mind of her own. At the age of 18 she lost her heart to a gentle, lovable young man, slightly older than herself, by the name of Carl Ernest Moulton. Her father and mother were not sure about Ernest. He did not appear to belong to any church. This was important to Alma and Edith. He had already been married once, but unhappily, and his wife had died in childbirth. It was a difficult situation which was further complicated by Ruth's sudden disappearance. She had eloped with Ernest. However Alma and Edith very soon realised that the couple genuinely loved one another and that Ruth knew her own mind. There was a reconciliation after which a wedding was celebrated. It proved to be a truly happy marriage.

The year was 1929, the year of the Wall Steet crash and the beginning of the world economic depression. The impact on America of the collapse of the stock market was immediate and sooner or later affected almost every home in the land, whether rich or poor. It also lasted a long time. Many of Alma Neils' clients had difficulty in paying him for work done. Some simply could not pay. He did not press them. 'O.K.', he would say, 'then we'll mark it off the bill', and that was that. Wilford Martin had to seek work at an iron smelting plant where, true to character, he soon succeeded in transferring to the carpenter's shop, taught himself the skills and became a qualified craftsman. Ruth and her husband, Ernest Moulton, struggled to maintain their home and feed and clothe their two young children. Ernest was an automobile engineer and, like Wilford, found work hard to come by. Ruth was getting assistance from a welfare organisation and he was helping at a greengrocer's to earn some income. At the end of each day the grocer would give him unsold vegetables such as lettuce and carrots to take home. The daytime heat had wilted them but Ruth stood them in cold water and they revived. Hannah at the time was her usual kind self, and gave her daughters and granddaughters flour and butter from the farm for their families. Alma Neils' electrical business managed to weather the difficult years of slump. With his daughter Ruth happily married there were now just the three sons living at home, Alma Leslie, Henry Whitney and Lorne Richard. Sadly, Henry Whitney died a month before his fifteenth birthday. In the same year Alma Leslie, who was a musician, married Marge Hansen in August 1933; but within three years he also died leaving one daughter, Claudia Gay.

When slowly the economic situation began to improve, Ruth's husband went back to his work with automobiles. Unfortunately he developed severe asthma, which was aggravated by having to work in confined spaces filled with gasoline fumes. At that point Alma Neils asked him if he would like to become an electrician and work for 'Sisam Electrical', where he would spend more time in the open air. Perhaps Ernest's entry into the business as a younger man, filled the void in Alma's heart caused by the loss of his own two older sons, just at the age when one or both of them might have come into the family business. After a few years Ernest took a course in electricity at the University of Utah and qualified in electrical engineering. He continued with 'Sisam Electrical' and eventually took charge of their contract work.

Wilford stayed with the carpentry department of the smelting company. As ever he remained an avid reader, always eager for knowledge. When his daughter Violet reached the age of 15 the ukulele era was in full swing. One day she said how much she would like to have one. 'Okay', he said, 'I'll make you one.' Knowing how absorbed and absent-minded he used to get over his books, the family said, 'That'll be the day. He'll have a beard before that happens!'. But he made the ukulele and the family still has it.

Amil Arthur remained an enigma. When he married in 1920 he moved away and settled in Murray. He went his own way and his appearances on the family scene became less and less frequent. In the earlier years when he was hard up he would sometimes visit Hannah and make his needs known. She very rarely, if ever, refused him. No one quite knew if he had a regular occupation, or if so what it was. Like several members of the family before him he worked for a while at a smelter. He was a tapper. The work was tough and had its dangers, for tapping was the drawing off of molten metal from the high-temperature furnaces. He had eleven children in all, so it looks as if he made a success of whatever he may have set his hand to, perhaps inheriting something of his father's business acumen.

Hannah lived to a good age. Throughout her life she had shown courage in the face of upheavals and difficulties, and was constant in her care for the family. In her later years she broke an arm and afterwards was unable to straighten it fully. She never complained about it and went on with her household duties as if nothing had happened. No one in the family

Automobiles & Electricity 103

Wilford Martin Sisam.

Alma Neils Sisam.

The ukulele made by Wilford for his daughter Violet.

ever mentioned her arm, until one day one of her granddaughters out of natural curiosity asked about it. One subject that Hannah would never discuss was Joseph Henry's plural marriage to her sister Ingrid in the early days. It had hurt her deeply but she remained loyal to Joseph Henry, serving the family and bringing up their children. She lived long enough to rejoice at having 39 grandchildren and 25 great-grandchildren. Her life spanned a childhood in Sweden, emigration to America, the founding of a dynasty, and drew to a close on the eve of America's entry into World War II. She died in October 1941, at the age of 83.

❖ ❖ ❖

For the next four years America was deeply involved in World War II, both in Europe and the Pacific, with the nation's economy and resources geared to preventing the domination of the world by evil and totalitarian philosophies. It was a commitment that in one way or another touched a great number of families, some very deeply, and others hardly at all. For some it meant service in the armed forces, or longer hours of work, and for many a strengthening of family ties.

Wilford Martin's two older sons were amongst those who were drafted overseas. His eldest son, Donald Wilford married in January 1941. Within a year or so he joined the U.S Marines and served on Midway in the Pacific. His younger brother Darrell was killed in Italy in October 1944, when the building in which he was taking cover received a direct hit. Wilford Martin himself retired early from the Midvale smelter in 1955 for health reasons, but went on busily working at home. When his daughter Violet and her husband, Morrell Seal, moved house to Riverton he did most of the carpentry work in the couple's new home. He also returned to his first love, automobiles, and worked on them until the day before he died, at the age of 80. In addition to Donald Wilford he left another son, Robert Arlon, and three daughters.

Of Berta's children, whom Hannah brought up after their mother died, all three married; the two daughters and their younger brother, William Albert. William, like his father, followed the trail of the automobile and spent most of his life in the freight business, driving Mack trucks along America's highways. He was a warm and open hearted man. He had a son and two daughters.

Alma Neils' only surviving son, Lorne Richard, went into the family business, 'Sisam Electrical', after graduating in electrical engineering at the University of Utah. He worked closely with his father and later took over the contract work when Ernest Moulton retired from the company. Richard worked alongside his father both inside and outside the business. The family acquired a plot of land in the upper reaches of Cottonwood Canyon, where Richard and his father built a cabin among the tall conifers and quaking aspens. Well accustomed to keeping up with modern developments, they saved time and labour by buying a do-it-yourself kit of pre-cut logs and finished timber. It took them three years to complete, working as and when they could at weekends. It served the family well as a holiday home within easy reach of the city, reminding them of their pioneer history, though of course the cabin was fitted with modern comforts.

In 1954 Richard married Colleen Moore whose family came to Salt Lake City from a Kentucky mining community south of the Ohio River. Her home was in the village of Russell, near Greenup, in the vast coalfield of that name. Her parents named her after the

Lorne Richard Sisam.

popular movie star of the 1930s, Colleen Moore. She and Richard had two sons and two daughters. Richard inherited the 'Sisam Electrical' business when his father died in 1971. The work of the company was wide-ranging and took him far afield into Nevada and other locations outside Salt Lake City. He was no stranger to hard work, nor did he limit his working hours to his business. Ever since as a young man he had gone on a two-year mission for his church, he gave generously of his time and energy to Mormon church activities. He was an elder for many years, and became a bishop in charge of a ward (parish). Most evenings he would be out on some assignment or another, and often at weekends would help to run youth camps and orienteering programs.

Richard's home in his later years was in the southern foothills of the Wasatch Range. It faced westward, looking out across the level Salt Lake Valley towards West Jordan. There in the distance lay the old homestead where the Sisams from England first settled. There too were the old meeting house where the barn-dances were held, the farmland which supported the family, the churches where they worshipped, and the green meadow where their forebears' tombstones still stood; and beyond them the line of the gold, silver and copper-rich Oquirrh Mountains. Living in the valley below were the new generation of Sisam sons and daughters, whose visions, heart's desires and decisions would determine their future and that of the whole family.

Joseph Henry and Hannah's four married sons and their families had to make their way through difficult days. Theirs is a story of struggle, of disappointment and also of triumph over difficulty. There is another parallel story that needs to be told. It is the story of Joseph Henry's other family, the story of Ingrid, Hannah's sister, and of her son and daughter who grew up in Idaho. So it is to Idaho that we now turn.

11
The Westerners

THE IDAHO SISIAM FAMILY

Idaho's Big Wood River rises amidst spectacular scenery in the Sawtooth Mountain range. The place-names of this region of mountains and valleys suggest grand vistas, rich vegetation, abundant wildlife and the romance of the great outdoors. There is Redfish Lake and Salmon River, Elk Peak and Bear Valley. There is Sheep Mountain and Shepherds Peak, Sleeping Deer and Cougar Point, Pistol Mountain and Dagger Falls, and the famous, gold-rich Thunder Mountain immortalised in Zane Grey's romance of the same name.

The great Salmon River flows north and east from the Sawtooth Range, whereas the smaller Big Wood River runs south, creating a fertile valley of sheep and cattle-grazing, corn fields, ranches, hot springs and silver mines. In Joseph Willard Sisiam's day it was dotted here and there with settlements like Gannett, Picabo, Hailey, Ketchum and

Typical scenery in the Sawtooth Mountains, Idaho.

Bellevue. Here in future years would be built the Sun Valley ski resort, site of the Winter Olympic Games, and here at Ketchum the writer and sportsman Ernest Hemingway spent his last days. It was an area in which men of the open-air lived – shepherds, farmers, miners, fishermen, lumbermen, cattlemen, railroad maintenance men, and men of the saddle.

As soon as he was old enough Joseph Willard Sisiam went to work on the family farm by the Little Wood River, helping his mother and his Lilya step-father. When they were old enough the other children followed suit. At about the age of eighteen, when there were now eight mouths to feed in the Lilya household, he left home to make his way in the world. He did not have to travel far, for the world for him was the world bounded by the great mountain ranges and the rivers and valleys of that part of Idaho. He settled in the Big Wood River Valley, and bought a plot of land near Silver Creek, to the south east of Gannett. The plot was on the banks of a small branch of the creek, known as Stocker Creek. He probably had some money put by from wages earned at casual farmwork or from money Joseph Henry had sent to Ingrid for his use. Perhaps Christian Lilya, who seems to have been a kindly man, also helped him. The plot of land was in a pleasant situation at the foot of a ridge of hills, facing across the water towards the floor of the valley. It was also good farmland.

Since Silver Creek was not all that far from the Lilya home, Joseph Willard kept in close touch, and the rest of the family knew of his progress and the kind of place in which he was living. Shortly afterwards, round about 1897, the Lilyas also moved to Silver Creek, taking their family with them. There was Alice aged 13 (Ingrid's daughter from her first marriage and sister of Joseph Willard), together with Ingrid's Lilya children, Inge aged 9, Christian 7, Martin 5, and Anna aged 2. Another son, Golden, was born two years later. They settled by Silver Creek a short distance upstream from Joseph Willard, and there Christian built a house on a hill above the water. It was an idyllic spot for the children. No doubt the older ones would spend much of their time helping on the farm, but once the chores were done the waters of the creek would provide plenty of fun with fishing, swimming, boating or just playing.

Joseph Willard was able to support himself from his own plot of land, raising crops and keeping a few animals, supplemented by occasional work for other settlers. As yet he had no wife to keep house and make a home for him. But now that the Lilya family, including his mother and his own sister Alice, had moved to a new home and were living close by, a sensible arrangement was made whereby he lived with the family while at the same time he continued to work his own plot.

Joseph Willard Sisiam married an Oregon girl, Ruth Hurst, in 1908. They made their home on Joseph Willard's land, by Silver Creek in the Big Wood River valley. It was a simple home. It consisted of a small house, a lean-to for horses and cattle, a pen for chickens, and a small plot on which to grow produce for the household. Seven children were raised here, four boys and three girls. In order to provide for this growing family, Joseph worked for farmers and ranchers in the vicinity. He made friends readily, and gladly lent a hand to neighbours when it was needed. Whatever spare time he had was spent in fishing and hunting, for which he had a great love. His children in later years remembered him as 'honest, jolly, a hard-worker and a good provider'. He had had very little schooling. Educational facilities were few and far between in these newly settled Western areas. He had been taught mostly at home by his mother, Ingrid. He could read but had difficulty in writing.

His wife, Ruth, proved an excellent mother. She put the children first. She made their clothes, yet still found time for fancy needlework, embroidery and crocheting, and making of costumes for the children's school play. There was a small school nearby with a typically rural name, called the Pumpkin Center School. On Saturday Ruth and the girls would bake. On Sunday morning they would set off at 6 a.m. for church at Gannett. They went in the surrey, with goodies packed for the trip. After church they would have a picnic and then return home. The rest of the week Ruth would spend on household duties and helping the children with their schooling.

Having had practically no schooling himself, Joseph Willard was anxious for his children to have an education. In 1917 he sold the Big Wood River Valley homestead and moved to the nearby town of Bellevue, to a house that stood opposite the schoolhouse. There were three other houses in the street in those early days. At the time of the move the eldest boy, Richard, was seven. The other boys were Nelse, Roy and Wilford; and there were three girls, Stella, Helen and the youngest Virginia. Soon after the family arrived in Bellevue, Joseph Willard went to work for the Union Pacific Railway in a track maintenance crew, for by now the railway network had penetrated the more remote areas of the West. The particular branch line that served Hailey and Bellevue, though owned by Union Pacific, was known as the Oregon Short Line. Joseph Willard worked for Union Pacific until he retired. All four of his sons grew up in their home locality and all, in one way or another, lived an outdoor life. They were men who lived close to nature, surrounded every day of their lives by magnificent scenery. At the same time, like the

A Borax mule-train in Bellevue, Idaho.

Sisams in Salt Lake City, they too had to cope with rigours of finding work in the depression years.

Richard, the oldest of the four, was a man of many parts. During the next 60 years or more, he worked as a shepherd, farmer, silver miner and lumberjack. Some of this was during the depression years when jobs were provided by federal government projects under President Roosevelt's Works Progress Administration. It undertook work such as renewing roads and trails in the forest areas, which in turn helped the lumber and mining industries to get back on their feet. Lumberjacking took Richard high up into the Sawtooth Range. Many is the time he and his mates, after a hard day's logging near the Galena Summit, would strip off and plunge into one of the natural hot springs of that area before going home to supper. He also worked in two of the main mines in the Big Wood River Valley – the Triumph and the Queen's. He bagan by working underground, drilling the hard rock for the insertion of dynamite sticks that would blast the rock and release the lead, zinc or silver ores. There were no wet drills then. The dry drills produced clouds of dust that could 'cut the lungs like glass'. He then transfered to the ore trains, which carried the ore from the rockface to the hoist. Later he operated the hoist itself on the surface. From there the ore was sent by railroad to the smelting plants. Richard moved to surface work in time to avoid contracting silicosis. In 1935 he married Ruby Turner. They had one son Wayne Joseph born in 1936, and seven years later a daughter Geraldine May. Richard's regular work at the Triumph Silver Mine continued until he retired. He was a man who loved the wild country in which he had spent the whole of his life. Shortly before he died in 1988, he asked that his favourite song be sung at his funeral. It was *When it's Springtime in the Rockies*, a traditional song of the West, expressing simple, yet universal sentiments of the heart.

After leaving school Nelse became a shepherd and looked after flocks of sheep grazing the mountain and valley pastures. In 1940 he married Helen Richardson. They had one son Virgil Nelse, born in 1945, and one daughter Jo Anne born three years later. In 1963 Nelse married again. His second wife was Carolyn Black. He worked for the Highways Department for a good many years, and latterly was employed on a number of ranches, and drove horse-sleighs in winter at the Sun Valley resort. He liked the open air and had a good knowledge of horses.

Roy, like his father before him, worked on the Union Pacific Railway until he retired. Wilford, the youngest of the brothers, on leaving school followed in the footsteps of Richard and Nelse and became a shepherd. He worked for a sheep company at Shoshone, a settlement named after the Indian tribe that had ranged these mountains and plains for centuries. In between seasons he went haymaking. But he was not a farming man by nature and soon transferred to the Triumph Silver Mine where Richard had also worked. He was there several years, but during that time was away two years serving in the army during the Korean War. He had married Juanita James in 1947. They had one daughter Vicki Lynn, born in 1956. After marrying, he went to work in his brother-in-law's coal business, then ran a Texaco Service Station and Motel with his wife, Juanita, and finally bought his own gas station. Later he sold out and worked for the City of Hailey in the Water Department.

All four of the Sisiam brothers were true Westerners. That is not to say they wore guns, though on one occasion in a family row, when tempers flared, a gun was produced. But nothing amiss happened. They were practical men who could turn their hands to almost

Richard and Ruby Sisiam.

Nelse Sisiam.

Wilford Sisiam.

Roy Elmer Sisiam.

anything – handling horses, automobile repairs, carpentry, crop-raising, care of animals – whatever the situation required. They were in the direct tradition of the old frontiersmen, independent and self-reliant. They had the mannerisms as well. Like that other Westerner, the Wyoming-born film actor Gary Cooper, their talk was often characterised by long silences, interspersed with an occasional 'Yep', 'Nope', or 'Mebbe'; but underneath the silence there were hearts of gold. For although very little might be said there was plenty of caring thought, from which sprang many kindly acts.

Time and circumstances had separated the two branches of Joseph Henry's original family, and placed them wide distances apart from one another, the one in Salt Lake City and the other in Idaho. To what extent the Sisams and Sisiams kept touch with one another is difficult to know. There were a number of occasions when there was probably close contact. That Joseph Henry sent money regularly to Ingrid in Idaho for the upbringing of their two children, was clearly remembered by the older members of the family in Salt Lake City.[7] Ingrid herself made a number of journeys there to visit her own parents soon after the Lilya homestead was established in Idaho. Two of her Lilya children were born in Salt Lake, a son in 1890 and a daughter in 1895. It is likely that she would have seen her sister, Hannah, at that time and probably Joseph Henry as well. Joseph Henry and his younger son Wilford, as we have seen, visited Idaho about 1911 to look at farms; and probabably visited her at the Lilya homestead. About two years later Albert Walter Tripp a near neighbour of the Sisams, whose son Leo later married one of Joseph Henry's daughters, planned to take a wagon load of produce to his Tripp relations in Idaho. Hearing of this, Joseph Henry sent with him a load of potatoes for Ingrid from the Sisam homestead.

After Joseph Henry died Hannah received a letter from Joseph Willard in Idaho inquiring whether he and his sister were to receive any inheritance from Joseph Henry's estate. This letter has survived.[8] It is quite short and not very clearly expressed. It seemed to come from a man who had difficulty with the written word. There is no record as to how Hannah replied to this letter, but shortly afterwards Joseph Willard took his son Richard by train to Salt Lake to see Hannah. Richard remembered this event very clearly by the fact that they had to change trains three times. What happened between Hannah and Joseph Willard no one knows, but Hannah's was a warm and generous heart, and she is likely to have made sure there was a fair settlement. It was shortly after this visit that Joseph Willard moved his family to Bellevue so that the children could have a better education. Perhaps whatever arrangement Hannah made helped them with the move to Bellevue. It is interesting that, at the end of her life, Ingrid moved to Bellevue so that she could be near both lots of her grandchildren. She is buried there.

Both families, the Sisams in Salt Lake City and the Sisiams in Idaho, put down solid roots. They also spread further afield and branches have sprung up in Oregon, Nevada, South Carolina, and Hawaii, all descending from the 16 year-old wagoner's son of Alcester, England, who drove a covered wagon to Salt Lake City in September 1868.

12
To the Antipodes

EMIGRATION TO NEW ZEALAND 1862 AND THE MAORI WAR

A few years before Joseph Sisam and his family emigrated from Alcester to North America, three Sisam brothers had left Arrow Mill and travelled even further, to New Zealand. The three who had decided to try their fortune in the Antipodes, Tom aged twenty-one, Walter aged twenty, and Alfred John aged eighteen, had all grown up in a farming community. They were primarily millers rather than farmers. Tom and Alfred had worked with their father at Arrow and Walter with his eldest brother, William Henry at Harvington. Both those mills had a certain amount of farmland attached. Whether the ultimate aim of the brothers was farming, milling or some other profession we do not know.

As they sailed from London's East India Docks for Auckland, in the *Matilda Wattenbach* in May 1862, their minds were full of the idealistic concepts of the Albertland Settlement scheme. The passengers on board were in high spirits and full of expectation. Amongst them were a large group from Nottingham. The women of Nottingham had made for them a lace-edged silken banner to be flown from the ship as it left England. It had the city's coat of arms on it in gold braid on a shield of crimson plush. It survived the voyage

The 'Maltilda Wattenbach' which carried the three Sisams of Arrow Mill from England to New Zealand in 1862.

and has recently come to light again, and after careful restoration will be housed in a New Zealand museum. As was natural, the promoters of emigration presented glowing prospects to those seeking opportunities on distant shores. Whether they, or anyone else at that time, had a clear picture of the situation in New Zealand is a moot point. Today we are still seeking to understand the complexities of the intermingling of European civilization and the older civilizations of the world. In New Zealand the Maori people, after the first shock of contact with the Western world, had welcomed white settlers for the benefits they brought. But increasing numbers of settlers arriving, hungry for land, brought conflict. In that conflict good and evil on both sides were revealed. The Treaty of Waitangi of 1840 sought to establish a peace. Not all Maori leaders signed and few, if any, understood what its wording, drawn up in Whitehall, really meant. To the British it meant the establishment of British rule throughout the land, annexation in fact. To the Maoris it was seen as a kind of protective association, allowing them the freedom to rule themselves as their leaders thought fit. The situation was further complicated by unscrupulous land agents who acquired land contrary to the Treaty. This led to various armed clashes and finally to the war which began in 1860, two and a half years before the three Sisam brothers sailed southwards on the *Matilda Wattenbach*.

The voyage to New Zealand took about three months. About 300 miles off the Cape of Good Hope there was a near disaster when a sudden squall struck the ship, carrying away the mizzen topmasts, as a result of which it was impossible to steer the ship. The situation was saved by the crew, who cut away half the remaining section of the mast and rigged jury masts. By means of this they managed to reach Auckland on September 8, without having to put into Cape Town for repairs.

Drama of a very different kind awaited them in Auckland. These travellers to the Promised Land suddenly found themselves faced with a war situation, a war between the Maori people and the European settlers supported by the Government. Before travellers could disembark, officials would arrive and search baggage for arms and ammunition, in case passengers might be planning to sell arms to the enemy – for Auckland itself was reckoned to be in the front line and in imminent danger of attack.

When dawn broke the morning after the *Matilda Wattenbach* had anchored, the immigrants transferred to a paddle steamer, the *Tasman Maid*, which took them up the harbour to the Auckland landing. There a reassuring vista opened up before them of high hills covered with 'beautiful green trees and ferns, mixed with a kind of lilac blossom, and all looking fresh after the early morning spring shower'. It was indeed spring, and within a few months they would be celebrating Christmas in the heat and sunshine of summer. The town itself was quite small, not much larger than a village. As the settlers walked up from the landing stage, where Fort Street is today, and went up Queen Street, there were very few shops; roads and foot-paths were laid with scoria, or small pieces of volcanic lava, for Auckland was built on extinct volcanoes. In front of the main shops there was flagstone paving. The houses had wooden verandahs but no waterspouts; the rainwater pouring down clay channels into the street.

At first the new arrivals were given accommodation in Princes Street, Howe Street and Freeman's Bay. There were caretakers in charge of these living quarters, but the settlers had to do their own cooking and provide their own bedding. Two days after their arrival they were welcomed by the town's leaders on the green near the Council Chambers. They learned that the blocks of land forming the Albertland Settlement were in uncleared bush

Auckland as it was in the 1860s.

some seventy miles inland, but with no roads leading to them. The only access was by boat up the coast to Mangawai and a twelve-day slog across country by rough tracks, the total journey taking about sixteen days.

Very few of the Albertland settlers were experienced farmers. Most of them were tradesmen, craftsmen or professional people, and were not emigrating primarily in order to farm but to make a living as best they could. Whether they could practice their particular skills in a remote and undeveloped area, with almost no communication with civilisation, must have been a matter of concern to them, the more so for those who had come with wives and children. Many were disheartened by the prospects and especially by the dangers and uncertainties of the Maori War. Some abandoned their land claims and went to the southern part of New Zealand to the sheep-grazing areas; others to Australia, particularly to Melbourne – the gateway to the goldfields. Gold had been discovered there two years previously, and in September 1862 the *Great Britain* had sailed from Melbourne carrying 106,659½oz of Australian gold,[9] worth £400,000, (that is about US $36,000,000 by present-day standards). This indicates the size of the mining industry which was creating jobs and opportunities not only in mining but in all walks of life.

Unfortunately very few family papers have survived to reveal what went through the minds of the three Sisams at this point. Walter, being of a bookish nature, kept a diary from the day he arrived in New Zealand until the day he died, but it was thrown away during a final house clearance.

Most of Alfred's papers were burnt in a disastrous farm fire. Nothing of Tom's has survived. All that can be done, therefore, is to try to reconstruct the course of events from contemporary records and from recollections handed down within the family.

There are two interesting clues as to what the three brothers decided to do. Amongst Walter's survivimg possessions is a much-used, leather-bound copy of *Webster's English Dictionary*. Inscribed on the fly-leaf in his handwriting are the words, 'Walter Sisam, Melbourne, 1862.' This is supported by a story handed down in the family that Walter worked temporarily for a farmer near Melbourne planting potatoes. It is also known that there was a Joseph Coombs in Australia whom Walter may have wanted to see. Coombs was a friend of Walter's old colleague in England, Fred Bomford. He had emigrated to Australia and was working as a solicitor's clerk at Castlemaine, north-west of Melbourne. The other clue is in a book, *The Albertlanders* published in 1920, and written by two Albertland settlers who sailed on one of the first coastal boats carrying passengers up-country to Mangawai to inspect their plots. In it they state that there were two Sisams on the boat with them. The question is which two?

It is possible that they were Alfred and Tom, and that, in view of discouraging reports about the Albertland site and the war situation, Walter may have gone immediately to Melbourne to see if it would be wiser for all three of them to go there. The journey up-country to Albertland would have been within a few weeks of the disembarkation from the *Matilda Wattenbach*, probably at the end of September. After an arduous journey the two brothers reached Albertland. The allocation of sections of land was by ballot. Their section was either in the upper reaches of the Oruawharo estuary, somewhere near present day Port Albert, or in the region of Paparoa and Matakohi. What they found was not what they had expected. The ground was so stoney and on such a steep slope that they reckoned it to be uncultivable. As Alfred said afterwards, 'It was so steep that if a hen laid an egg on it, the egg would roll away before you could pick it up.' A grazing ground for goats seemed all that the place was good for. By the terms of their land tenure, the Albertlanders were prevented from selling off their plots until after five years, during which period annual rates had to be paid.

Alfred wrote a poem some years later, which has survived, describing their misadventures. It is semi-humorous, but has a ring of truth about it. He recalls how when they arrived they missed the share-out of farm implements, to which they had contributed, and on reaching the settlement found that their land had not been surveyed. But they made the best of it, built a hut to live in, and decided to stay for the time being. They had with them a twelve-months' stock of provisions. Alfred bought a pig-dog to hunt the wild boar in the bush, of which there was a plentiful supply, and there was a ready demand amongst the settlers for the fresh meat which they provided. If the land had been cultivable, the work would have been daunting even for experienced farmers. The bush would have had to be cleared, then ploughed, and the ground either seeded for grazing, assuming livestock was available, or planted with crops. It is uncertain whether there would have been any willing and available manpower amongst the settlers, or the friendly Maoris of the area. The two brothers, being unmarried, had no family to help them or provide domestic support.

An even more serious factor affecting the situation was that Tom was taken ill, and had to return to Auckland. Exactly when he became ill is unknown, but it is said to have been very soon after the brothers arrived in New Zealand. By the time Tom got back to Auckland, and Alfred probably with him, Walter may have returned from Australia. If word had reached Walter about the land and particularly about Tom's health, his affection for Tom would more than likely have sent him hurrying back.

Albertland 1862
(By one of the Others)

Back in the Sixties, the old "London News",
Gave to its readers some very fine views.
Nearly nine hundred Nonconformists and Others,
Bound for New Zealand, leaving Fathers and Mothers,
Booming of cannon, flags, cheers and the band
Marked our departure for famed Albertland.

Amongst the good Settlers, for we all paid our way,
Was a Parson and Doctor, but they did not long stay,
And a Journalist the proprietor of the Albertland Gazette,
But waiting for the railway he has not got there yet.
We brought out farm implements, paid one pound a share,
When the manager divided them we were not there.

Welcomed in Auckland when we landed; that day
Clergy and City Fathers had plenty to say.
One with a long coat advised us that now
The first thing to do was to each buy a cow.
The cow in New Zealand would soon have a calf,
Which a mother would be in a year and a half.

Compounding the increase at the same rate,
Five years from purchase our yards would be full.
The speaker retired, and the laughter was great
When asked for advice "should the calf be a bull".
From the look of the block there was someone to blame
But goats would have suited - a good milking strain.

We were asked our impressions of the City every hour.
We likened it to London, with the Windmill for the Tower.
It was no greater libel, though it worked like a charm,
Than to say we were farmers, or my section was a farm.
For many years I paid the rates, and thought it rather smart
When I met a man land hungry, and changed for his cart.

I took I think about twelve days from the City to the block,
With luggage and provisions, we had a twelve month stock.
There was just a slight omission - the sections not surveyed.
It did not seem important, for we built a hut and stayed.
I never knew my section, although it was very dear,
For after idling there awhile I thought it best to clear.

Poem written in later years by Alfred John Sisam recalling the brothers' experiences in Albertland.

But larger events were looming and were soon to affect the lives and affairs of the three brothers. The Maori War had suddenly taken a more serious turn. Hitherto the main fighting had been in the Taranaki area to the far south-east of Auckland. It had been inconclusive. Maori strategy and tactics had prevented the government forces achieving victory. In the meantime the tribes of the Waikato area immediately south and south-west of Auckland had united for the first time to resist any further land encroachment. Faced with this large-scale armed opposition the Government brought in reinforcements from England and Australia; and ordered an advance into the Waikato territory, in an attempt to destroy the bulk of the Maori forces. General Cameron was placed in overall charge of the war operations.

Letters written by Walter during 1863–4, now kept in the Alexander Turnbull Library in Wellington, describe the situation in Auckland. They were sent to his old friend Fred Bomford of Atch Lench, in England. Writing on August 2 he says:

'The times are serious with us now. Every man capable or judged capable of bearing arms is a soldier or liable to be should his name come to the ears of the authorities. All the rifle volunteers that were available at the time, ten days since, have left town for one of the outstations – Papakura, and I believe there are some at Wairoa. There are daily accounts of skirmishes, attacks, murders, intended attacks.'

Some time before placards had appeared throughout Auckland and its suburbs calling for volunteers for the newly formed Colonial Defence Force, a cavalry corps under the command of Colonel Nixon, and based at Otahuhu nine miles south of the city. Good horsemen were invited to join. Horses, a carbine and sword, and appointments would be provided. The daily pay was 7/6 for sergeants, 6/6 for corporals, and 5/- for troopers, each providing his own rations. In a few days over a hundred men, mostly settlers, had applied. The two troops stationed in the Auckland district became known locally as 'Nixon's Cavalry'.

In his letter of August 2, Walter wrote that Alfred had already enlisted. 'Alfred is a soldier. He is in the Cavalry Defence Force under Col. Nixon. He had, last Saturday, already been in three skirmishes in close contact with the enemy. This must not be known. Don't let it go further than yourself and confidants.' Walter was thinking of the family at Arrow, and wanting to spare them anxiety.

What had happened was that Alfred was working as a share-farmer with a certain James Rutherford on his farm, which was beside the South Road out of Auckland, not far from Pukekohe. This was the communications and supply road for General Cameron's army during its advance into the Maori-held territory south of the Waikato River. As such it was an obvious target for Maori guerilla bands. Rutherford's farm was being threatend, so Alfred and many other young settlers moved to live in the Mangere area and began drilling at Mangere School House. Alfred was attached as a military cadet to a Mr. Tuck for training.

Colonel Nixon, who had his headquarters at Otahuhu, was living at Mangere at the time and invited those of the settlers who could ride to join his Colonial Defence Force. Alfred joined in June 1863, his regimental number being No. 46. The first 50 men enlisted were all young settlers from the Otahuhu, Howick, Pukekohe and Onehunga districts.

The skirmishes Walter mentioned in his letter to England had all taken place near Keri Keri in the Manukau tribal area to the south of Auckland. On July 9, 1863, as the government troops were preparing to advance into Waikato country, all Maoris who had not taken the oath to Queen Victoria were required to move out of the Manukau and

Waikato frontier area to south of the Waikato River. Alfred's troop were ordered to ride south and begin driving the Maoris towards the Waikato River. They went by a night march to Papakura where the settlers and their families had taken refuge in a church. By the time they arrived the Maoris had left. Next morning Nixon's Cavalry joined a large body of regular infantry and swept the ranges driving the Maoris before them. At one point the Cavalry led by Nixon and Major Walmsley charged up a hill, but on reaching the top they almost rode into an ambush; for in front of them was a large body of armed Maoris in a strong position in fern-covered terrain, while the rest of the Maoris had retreated into a pa (a Maori fort) at Keri Keri. Being newly enlisted the Cavalry were as yet untrained in light-infantry movements, so they quickly dismounted, sent their horses to

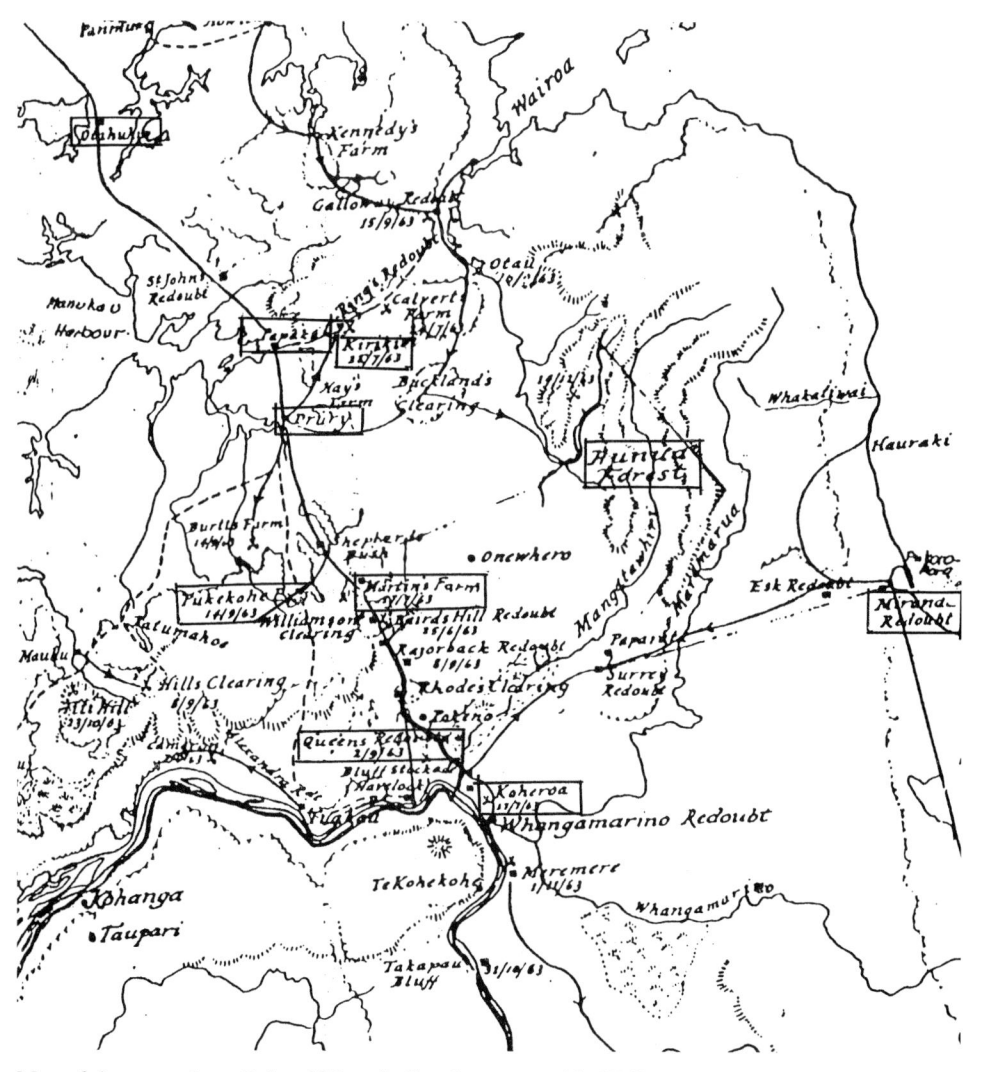

Map of the area where Colonel Nixon's Cavalry operated in Waikato country south of Auckland.

the rear and took what cover they could. Since they were at very close range, they were ordered to each cover one of the enemy. Two clergymen, one of whom was Bishop Selwyn of Auckland, were then sent to parley with the Maoris to persuade them to leave peacefully. The Maori chief, said to be laid up with rheumatism and unable to move, remained in his whare (Maori hut) during the negotiations, though according to Alfred the wily old man was lying on top of his gun and ammunition. This was on Saturday, July 13. It was finally agreed to extend the date for leaving until the following Monday, so that Sunday could be observed. In the early hours of Tuesday morning most of the Maoris dispersed into the bush. A heavy rainfall ensued, making troop movements difficult. Meanwhile, a group of Maoris had re-occupied the pa. The Cavalry together with other troops moved to the attack. The Maoris were taken by surprise and there was no opposition. The chief and eighteen men and women were made prisoner, and a flag, a keg of powder (on which a Maori was sitting) and twelve stands of arms were captured.

The Colonial Defence Force was involved in further action on July 17 in rescuing a convoy that had been ambushed. It took place further south at Martin's Farm near Drury. The convoy had been surprised by Ngati Poa warriors who overpowered the escort and hotly pursued them down the road. The convoy was rescued by Nixon's Cavalry and other reinforcements, but lost 'some horses, several carts and sixteen men killed and wounded – one-third of the escort's strength'. The Maoris lost one or two men. It was a busy day, July 17, for the government forces. While these engagements near Keri Keri were taking place General Cameron, heading the main advance, had led 553 men in a successful attack at Koheroa a few miles north of the Waikato River; but he was dependent on his convoys and the supply line from Auckland. Further manpower had to be deployed to protect it and the mounted units of the Colonial Defence Force were in much demand.

In the next three months Alfred's troop, led by Colonel Nixon, Major Walmsley and Captain Pye, were attached to a Flying Column of 300 men charged with clearing the country on the east side of the South Road as far as the Waikato River. The Column included the famous Forest Rangers commanded by Captain William Jackson. The group also included Gustavus von Tempsky, a colourful and courageous ex-Prussian officer, expert in guerilla-warfare from his fighting experience with the Misskito (Mosquito) Indians of Central America. This Flying Column was sent to relieve a church at Pukekohe which was under attack and then to move from Drury to reinforce the engagement at Bald Hill near Mauku. They arrived just as the Maoris were withdrawing, but were ordered to await the arrival of infantry which had left Drury at the same time but had not been able to move as rapidly. They then moved to Selby's Farm where they camped for a month, a mile or so from the Queen's Redoubt on Pokeno Hill. This was in November 1863. While there Alfred's troop acted as a mounted escort to General Cameron. In December, 50 of Nixon's men returned to Auckland, Alfred with them, and were shipped to Pokoroko near Thames as part of a force of 1,000 men, including the Auckland Naval Volunteers. They landed on Pokoroko Beach three days later and made a long march to the spot where the Miranda Redoubt was later built. Alfred was transferred, probabaly temporarily, from Nixon's Colonial Defence Force and attached as orderly to the 18th and 43rd Regiments; possibly because of his education and familiarity with paperwork. He was sworn in for twelve months or until discharged, with pay of 5/- a day.

❖ ❖ ❖

In Auckland meanwhile Walter was on military defence duties several nights a week, and would have been posted to the out-stations had he not been running a school for boys. As for Tom, he was better in health and Walter was looking after him as best he could. But Tom was by no means cured. The illness had been diagnosed as heart trouble and doctors told him he must return to England as soon as he was fit enough and a passage available.

In October that same year, Walter wrote that he had been soldiering at the Papakura outpost, replacing another man whose wife had been taken ill. He left Tom in charge of the school, expecting to be back in a few days. He was kept on duty at the outpost for a whole month. This caused the school to break up and Walter was forced to abandon it. That was a great disappointment to Walter as the school had been doing well and could have accommodated a hundred pupils. He would probably have made teaching his profession if it had not been for the war. With Tom in poor health and Alfred in the cavalry, it was essential for Walter to earn. After the school closed, he had what sounded a good offer of work from a Scots farmer some three miles out of town. The farmer promised good wages if Walter would get his part-time military service transferred to a local unit. No sooner had the transfer been made than the farmer went back on his word and would only pay a low wage. The transfer suggestion had been a ruse to get cheap labour. As soon as the initial week's work was over, Walter left.

By now Tom's condition had deteriorated. Writing to Fred Bomford on October 13, Walter said:

'Poor Tom has been very much worse. This last fortnight, in fact, he has been all but gone. He went into hospital on Monday. . . . As it is you may expect to see me when the *Ida Ziegler* (a ship to England) arrives, sh'ld Tom be strong enough to start. I shall be sure to come with him. . . . I shall, be very sorry to leave New Zealand, but I shall come back again. But I wont come back without a wife or mother or sister. To be here without sufficient means to keep an establishment, to be continually shifting from place to place without a home or female friend, is a hardship which exceeds all others. It may be that I feel it on account of poor Tom, as I have had considerable difficulty at times in getting him comfortable lodgings, and then being obliged to be separated from him. . . . I shall feel sorry to leave Alf alone here, particularly in his hazardous engagement, but I trust God will preserve us all to meet again. . . . Tom, poor Tom. I am afraid he will never recover his strength again. It is sad so young, formerly so merry, and now so weak and helpless. I trust he may live to see his friends, to gaze upon those scenes he left in such good health and good spirits. There is a chance he may recover. He may get well, but that chance is a poor one as yet.'

He continued the letter a few days later, on October 30, 1863:.

'I am ordered off to the front tomorrow. I go in the midst of dangers. For myself I care not, but for poor Tom I do. . . . Last night I was on guard and consequently had little sleep. If Tom is well enough and the Dr.'s opinion be favourable, sh'ld I ever return from this campaign safe, we will start for England via Sydney as soon as we can. But sh'd he not live, I won't say what I will do. But certain it is my life, or fear of that event, has received a fresh bias, and once more I feel roused to action to preach, to warn, to pray and work.'

Happily, both Walter and Tom survived their respective crises. The medical archives in Auckland show that Thomas Marshall Sisam was discharged from hospital in Auckland on November 23, 1863.[10] He probably left Auckland for England soon after that, not by the *Ida Ziegler* but some other vessel that went via Melbourne. For family tradition has it that in Melbourne he was successfully treated by a Chinaman. He reached home safely, and Walter remained in New Zealand.

The war meanwhile continued. On February 20, in the summer of 1864, a large force of infantry and cavalry penetrated Maori territory in the Waikato region with the object of luring the main Maori force into the open and destroying it. About 90 miles southwest of Auckland the government troops approached an unfortified Maori settlement at Rangiaowhia, which was a main Maori supply centre and part of their main defensive system on the Hairini Ridge. It was a peaceful and beautiful place. Nixon and his troopers galloped forward to open the attack, firing warning shots as they went. At that time the settlement itself was occupied mainly by women and children, the Maori warriors having taken cover in a strategic position nearby. Nixon's men surrounded the huts and demanded surrender. This was met by a volley of rifle fire from the twelve courageous defenders. Nixon was hit and fell from his horse mortally wounded. His troop suffered heavy casualties. But inevitably the superior numbers of the main invading force quickly overwhelmed the defenders. There were also casualties amongst the Maori women and children. The government force withdrew to await reactions. The Maoris re-occupied Rangiaowhia and began fortifying the ridge. It was attacked and driven back, after which the main Maori force were compelled to withdraw to a second line of defence to the south.

At the subsequent battle of Orakau, the Maoris had encamped in 'an orchard of peaches, apples and nuts' where they had built a pa. It was an ill-chosen defensive position, with no escape route if withdrawal should become necessary. The attacks on the position were skilfully directed but were met with vigorous resistance. Gradually the government troops surrounded the fortification and when Maori reinforcements arrived they could not get through the circle to reach their comrades. The tide of battle swung inexorably in favour of the attackers. Both sides knew the end was in sight. At the last moment, taking their enemies completely by surprise, the besieged Maoris broke out in a brilliant charge, cut through a line of government troops and escaped; and despite hot pursuit were able to withdraw even further south. The net result was that serious fighting in the Waikato area virtually ceased. The war moved south to the Tauranga area, and the danger clouds that had hung over Auckland were now almost entirely dissipated. Following Nixon's death the Colonial Defence Force was disbanded. In September 1864 Alfred John was discharged at Papakura.

In the *Albertland Gazette* of February 3 of that year, the same month as Nixon's fatal charge, there was a report of a meeting of settlers at Oruawharo in Albertland. It was called to discuss the building of a chapel. A collection was taken and the list of the contributors contained the entry, 'A.Sisam'. This suggests that Alfred was on leave at that time. In a volunteer regiment men could take leave of absence if circumstances permitted. Alternatively, it may have been Walter, with his interest in church matters as well as in the Sisam property, who went to Oruawharo and for some reason made the contribution in Alfred's name.

The town of Auckland had made rapid progress, and had changed a good deal in the two years since the brothers first came there. In September 1864 Walter wrote:

'Formerly you could take a quiet walk of an evening without meeting many people and with little interruption. But now the principal streets are crowded. Two theatres and a circus are kept going, while "'ot, pies! Pies all 'ot!" "Oranges! Oranges! Only 2d. cash, fine oranges.!" "Apples! Apples 4d. a pound, apples." "Buns, cakes be 1d. each, only 1d."

These are ringing in your ears and the vended articles are thrust under your nose. Shoe blacks are set up. It's a change, indeed. Two fresh banks are started and the whole town is vastly improved and bids fair to rival in time some of its comperes and superiors in Australia.'

By now, Walter was in steady work, eight hours a day, at a newly established market-garden at Epsom on the outskirts of Auckland. In one of his regular letters to Fred Bomford he described the crops being grown in Auckland in September – equivalent to March in England or North America.

'You can sow now at all times in the year, excepting the dry weather. You will find in the garden the following list at nearly all stages; cabbage, cauliflower, peas, potatoes, kidney and French Beans, parsnips, carrots, celery, onions, lettuce, radish, spinach, thyme, parsley, sage, rhubarb.'

His pay was reasonably good. He was earning 86 shillings a week with board and lodging included, and was able to put by a pound a week in savings. The work was pleasant, providing him with the necessities of life and enabling him in his spare time to follow what he felt was his basic calling which was to help people find a faith. He was especially active amongst the Baptist churches in Auckland and sometimes preached in them. But here he ran into a kind of snobbishness which, being a sensitive man, he found hard to bear. He was conscious that certain people engaged in professional or business occupations regarded him as a labourer and looked down on him. He felt this was the reason that, although he was active in the churches, so far no family had asked him to sit down with them to a meal. This was sad for a lonely bachelor, all the more so since he was a cultivated man and had come from a good home. That home remained vividly in his memory, and his loneliness in a strange country made his longing for a home of his own all the greater.

13
Alarms & Excursions

ARMED CONSTABULARY AND TWO MARRIAGES

By 1864 Walter and Alfred had now been in New Zealand for two years. The expectations they had when they left England had hardly been fulfilled, at least not in the way they had envisaged. Their land settlement had failed and their individual paths had, through unexpected circumstances, led in different directions. They kept in close touch and by the spring of 1864 had jointly invested some of their savings in an enterprise, initiated by Alfred, which was showing a 100% return. Assuming this venture continued to prosper, they calculated that they would be able to build up 'a good financial basis for the future'. In his letters to England Walter mentioned this enterprise but without revealing what it was. It may have been connected with Alfred's purchase of some land at Glenafton, near Huntly, which he afterwards sold and where, ironically, coal was later discovered. In 1866 Walter and Alfred's finances were such that they were together able to purchase some land. They drove in a horse and cart from Auckland through the bush into the Waitakere Ranges and looked at a plot there. Alfred did not think much of it. However, they bought it jointly. It was 130 acres and cost £100.[11] In June of that year Walter married.

The bride was Mary Ann Mason from Derbyshire, England, aged 24. She had travelled with her father William Mason, her step-mother and her two brothers to New Zealand on the *Matilda Wattenbach* at the same time as the three Sisam brothers, and they may have met during the voyage. She was known in the family as Polly. They lived in Edwards Street, Auckland where her father was known locally as 'the preacher'. Her two brothers set up as 'hairdressers and perfumers' at 264 Queen Street, now a modern shopping centre. The wedding took place in her parents' home in Edwards Street. On the marriage certificate, the bride's father gave his occupation as 'missionary'. How Walter and Mary Ann resumed their acquaintance is not known. Quite likely it was through Walter's involvement with non-conformist churches in Auckland. In 1862 Walter had written to Fred Bomford in England from Vine Cottage, Edwards Street, which was the same street in which the Masons lived for a period. Edwards Street (now known as Airedale Street) ran from the Town Hall in Queen Street to Symonds Street. After their marriage, rather than remaining in Auckland, Walter and Mary Ann set up home in Thames, about 140 miles south-east of Auckland. There had been severe unemployment in Auckland, and many able-bodied young men had been leaving the town daily for Thames, where prospects were greater. Walter, no doubt, felt that his chances of work would be better there.

It might have been expected the couple would settle on the Sisam property in the Waitakere area, of which Walter was a part owner. It was a beautiful place. It lay in and along the slopes of the valley of the Waitakere River, with magnificent kauri trees dotted over the landscape. Not far away were the impressive waterfalls, known as the Cascades.

The original owner of the Sisam plot, George Bacon, had built a shack near the river, but made little or no attempt to clear the virgin bush. It was a remote spot, reached only by rough tracks over the hills. Although it was an attractive place, it was not very good farming land. The ground was undulating, so that growing crops would have been difficult. Most of the property was uncleared bush that could be made suitable for grazing if cleared and seeded, but this would have needed a good deal of labour. Walter no doubt realised that in its existing state it was not an ideal place to which to take his bride, nor was it a suitable place in which to bring children into the world. Much work would need to be done before the land became productive. Besides, Walter was not all that robust. These considerations, together with the fact that some of Mary Ann's family were against such a move, may have made Walter decide to settle at Thames.

By October 1864 Alfred, having received his discharge from the Colonial Defence Force, was now back in Auckland and was able to give his mind to the care of such land as he and Walter possessed. At some point, probably when he was discharged, it seems likely that Alfred made use of the Waitakere property. He certainly kept two troop horses there, possibly the ones he rode in Nixon's Cavalry. He may well have lived on the spot in the old shack. This would have been no hardship for a single man trained in the armed forces and used to bivouacing and outdoor living. While there he is likely to have begun clearing the bush. In 1867 the five-year restriction on the disposal of the original Albertland sections expired. Walter and Alfred were now free to sell their two plots. If Walter disposed of his at this time, the proceeds would have helped with maintaining the home in Thames. Alfred's Albertland poem, written in later years, states that he exchanged his plot with a 'land-hungry' settler for a cart, and subsequently sold the cart for £30.

So far the main sphere of operations in the Maori War had been to the south and south-west of Auckland in the Waikato area. On the East Coast there had been only a number of small-scale guerrilla actions by individual Maori chiefs. There were two main causes of these actions. One was the increasing confiscation by the Government during 1864–5 of Maori lands. The other was the emergence of Pai Marire ('The Good and the Peaceful'), also known as 'Hauhauism', a basically idealistic, religious movement amongst the tribes who had grievances against the British. This united them in a common body of hostility to the Government. Initially it was peaceful and spread quite rapidly, but as it spread it had violent offshoots. In 1865 one of these offshoots led by a fanatical chief, Kereopa Te Rau, attacked the town of Opotiki in the Bay of Plenty, some hundred miles north of Taupo. The minister of Opotiki's St. Stephen's church, Carl Volkener, regarded rightly or wrongly by the Maoris as a government spy, was murdered. Another group of Maoris, on July 2, 1865, killed Lieutenant James Falloon on board the naval cutter *Kate* in Whakatane harbour. In response to these attacks, a punitive force of 500 men occupied Opotiki in September 1865, and turned the church and its surroundings into a fort and military barracks. The troops included the Taranaki Military Settlers, the Wanganui and Patea Rangers, the Yeomanry Cavalry, the Wanganui Maori Contingent and the right wing of the 1st Waikato Regiment.

The Maoris who supported 'Hauhau' were punished by the confiscation of their coastal lands in the Bay of Plenty, north of a line running from Mount Edgecumbe to the Waimana River near Opotiki.[12] At the same time there were military expeditions against the Whakatohea, who had taken part in the Waikato War of 1863–4. They had a pa at Ohiwa near Opotiki and, with other Maoris, were cultivating the coastal flats. This was highly fertile land producing good crops, while the coastal waters provided bountiful supples of

Garrison at St Stephen's Church, Opotiki, including the 1st Waikato Regiment called in to defend the town, following the murder of the Rev. Carl Volkener by 'Hauhau' Maoris.

fish, enabling the Maoris to trade their surplus produce. The partial transition from inter-tribal warfare to land cultivation was to a great extent due to the work of missionaries. In 1866 these lands were also confiscated as a warning against engaging in any future hostilities. They were divided into plots and given to militia soldiers as military settlers, particularly to men of the 1st Waikato Regiment, in order to stabilise the area. The displaced Maoris were forced to become labourers or, being deprived of the means of growing crops, to eke out a living either solely by fishing or from the traditional wild produce of the forests. Resentment continued to burn, therefore, and there were attacks on government mail-carriers. A Maori mailman, Wi Popata, was ambushed and killed by 'Hauhau' at Ohiwa in 1866. In June the same year another mailman, Bennett White, was killed near Opotiki at the Ohiwa ford, and his head displayed on a wooden stake. This was partly an act of revenge, since White had been a witness at the trial of the two Maori chiefs who earlier killed Lieutenant Falloon at Whakatane. They were subsequently hanged.

The Government in Wellington were anxious that hostilities should not escalate into a total war, as they had done in the First Maori War of 1845. With this in mind, an Armed Constabulary was formed in 1867 primarily for the defence of Auckland. It was a partly civilian body, but recruited mainly from men with previous military experience, particularly from the best men in the volunteer militias. It was fully subject to British military discipline. It's role was to maintain law and order in outlying districts and it could assist the regular military forces when needed. The pay was good and as an armed force it played an important role in the latter part of the war. The following year, in January 1868, a contingent was sent to Opotiki to take over from the 1st Waikato Regiment which was in the process of being disbanded.

Six months later an event occurred that sent a shock-wave of excitement and alarm throughout the East Coast region. On July 10 the much feared Maori leader, Te Kooti, having led a brilliantly-planned escape of prisoners from the Chatham Islands off the East Coast, landed in Poverty Bay, south-east of Opotiki. He was a skilful military strategist and a spiritual leader of his people. He had previously fought alongside government troops against 'Hauhau' revolutionaries, but was imprisoned by the British for treason; accused, probably by jealous rivals, of firing blank cartridges in battle. In the two years he was in custody he evolved a religious faith, 'Ringatu' (the Upraised Hand), which was adopted by a good number of leading tribal chiefs. He inspired loyalty. He was also a man of wide experience, having been a trader, sailor and skilled horseman, and he understood the European mind. On July 15 he marched inland. He and his band were chased throughout July and early August by a large force of government troops, as he headed west for the safety of the Urewera Forest which lay to the south of Whakatane.

By this time Colonel Whitmore, who was moving up from Turanganui (Gisborne) in pursuit, was joined by a unit of 52 of the Armed Constabulary sent from Opotiki under Major Fraser. Te Kooti took up a strategic position in the Ruakituri River gorge, which Whitmore's force had to negotiate in single file. Te Kooti's snipers picked off many of Whitmore's men as they made their way up the gorge, and when Te Kooti charged Whitmore's force was only saved from annihilation by a surprise attack on Te Kooti's rear. Even so, Whitmore was forced to withdraw. For the next five months Te Kooti kept on the move, sometimes defending himself in fortified pas, repulsing attacks and making clever escapes, and sometimes taking the offensive.

In October Alfred John, who had been keeping his two horses in the Waitakere and had had four years respite from military affairs, now took his two mounts and rode due south from Auckland to Hamilton. There he enlisted on October 30, 1868, under Colonel Moule in the Armed Constabulary and was posted to No 4. Mounted Constabulary Unit. His enrolment number was 339, and he was recorded as being five feet ten inches in height, with blue eyes and brown hair. In the Mounted Constabulary each man had to provide his own mounts, forage and uniform. The latter consisted of a close-fitting buttoned tunic, breeches, riding-boots, pill-box cap, and a protective breastplate. All were armed with a breech-loading Snider carbine, a revolver and a sword. There followed a period of training and much drill. When Colonel Brannigan assumed command at Hamilton, Alfred and four other troopers were assigned to the East Coast. They immediately began night patrols in the Tauranga district and then maintained communications with Colonel McDonnell, and with Major Fraser of the Armed Constabulary and the units taking part in the pursuit of Te Kooti. This regular contact with the forces in the field involved Alfred in a ride of some 150 miles each way from Tauranga and back.

On January 1, 1869, in the height of summer, Whitmore attacked Te Kooti at Ngatapa, to the north of Poverty Bay. Fraser's Armed Constabulary from Opotiki, occupying an exposed ridge, held their position gamely under heavy fire with great steadiness and bravery. The pa was surrounded, but still Te Kooti and his band escaped; this time by lowering themselves over a precipice on the north side of Ngatapa. They not only escaped but made their way to the Urewera Forest where, amongst the Tuhoe tribe, they built a settlement and bided their time, while seeking new allies and fresh supplies. Then Te Kooti turned his attention to the tribes near Whakatane and Opotiki. He visited the Whakatohea pa at Ohiwa and compelled their support notwithstanding the fact that their

Alfred John Sisam as a trooper in the Mounted Armed Constabulary, in which he enlisted in 1868.

land had been confiscated for previuos participation in hostilities. Soon afterwards he emerged from the Urewera with a force of 150 and sacked and burned Whakatane, killing the miller at the Te Poronu cornmill. A force of militia came out from the Opotiki garrison to deal with the situation, but Te Kooti slipped away into the forest.

By this time, Whitmore was under considerable pressure from the Government to get the war finished, and was determined to deal with Te Kooti once and for all. Whitmore brought a large body of troops by sea to Opotiki in April and launched a three-pronged advance into Urewera Forest against Te Kooti. One unit of the Armed Constabulary set up a redoubt on the shores of Lake Waikaremoana in the heart of the forest, while another built a string of forts along the Rangitaiki River valley on the western side. The most important of these was Fort Galatea, where there seems to have been a mounting anticipation of great happenings to come; not least on the part of the correspondent of the *Southern Cross* who, reporting from the fort, stated with glowing excitement, 'The whole of the Armed Constabulary are now here.'

In October 1869, a year after he joined the Constabulary, Alfred was transferred to Opotoki. The Government had now begun to wind down the military role of the Armed Constabulary. Many of the personnel whose age, character and experience made them suitable candidates were offered the opportunity remain in the Armed Constabulary and act as mounted constables in a civilian situation. The Government were also concerned for the protection of mail and despatch deliveries, following the ambush and murder of the two mail-carriers in the Opotiki district. Certain Armed Constabulary men were selected for this role who had a good 'mana' or reputation with the friendly Maoris. Alfred was appointed both constable and mail and despatch rider. He carried dispatches and mail between Opotiki and Whakatane once weekly for the next ten years. In those days it was a

Armed Constabulary Force, New Zealand.

CERTIFICATE OF APPOINTMENTS.

Issued to Mounted Constable _Alfred Swain_   No. 334

No.	Article.	Date of Issue.	In what Condition when Issued.	Remarks.
One	*Snider* Breech-loading ~~Rifle or~~ Carbine	27 June 1871	Serviceable	A. McL...
	Sling			
One	Cleaning Rod			
	Wire Cleaning Brush			
One	Snap Cap and Chain			
	Cap Pocket			
One	Pouch and Belt			
One	Revolver			
One	Revolver Sheath			
One	Revolver Ball Bag			
One	Sword			
One	Scabbard, steel			
One	Sword Belt, b.l.			
One	Saddle			
One	Numna			
One	Girths, leather			
Two	Stirrup Irons			
Two	Stirrup Leathers			
One	Breastplate			
One	Crupper			
Two	Wallets *Single*			
One	Headstall			
Two	Reins *plain*			
One	Bits			
One	Curb Chain and Hooks			
One	Picketing Rein ✓			
One	Straps { Cloak			
Two	Straps { Wallet			
Two	Straps { ~~Holster~~ Bit			
One	Carbine Holster			
	Headstall, stable			
	Handcuffs and Key			
One	Rules and Regulation Books			
	Memorandum Books			
	Extracts from Colonial Acts			
One	*Surcingle*			
One	*Sword Knot*			

_____ Signature of Officer issuing.

_____ Signature of Constable receiving.

This List is to be produced prior to a Constable receiving his Monthly Pay, and a Certificate inserted by the Officer paying in the Occurrence Book of the state in which he finds the articles enumerated, and noting any deficiencies.

In the event of any Constable absconding and taking with him any of the articles mentioned in this List, he will be prosecuted for felony.

Any Constable losing or defacing this Certificate will be charged 5s. for a new one, and it will be presumed that he had been provided with every article mentioned above.

In case any of the above-named articles are lost or damaged, the amount of the cost of the article will be charged against the Constable to whom they were issued.

Form No. 18.

Official List of Alfred John's kit in the Mounted Armed Constabulary.

The Whakatane River gorge in the Urewera Forest.

Te Kooti the Maori War leader who campaigned to the south east of the Urewera Forest and used it as a hide-out and base.

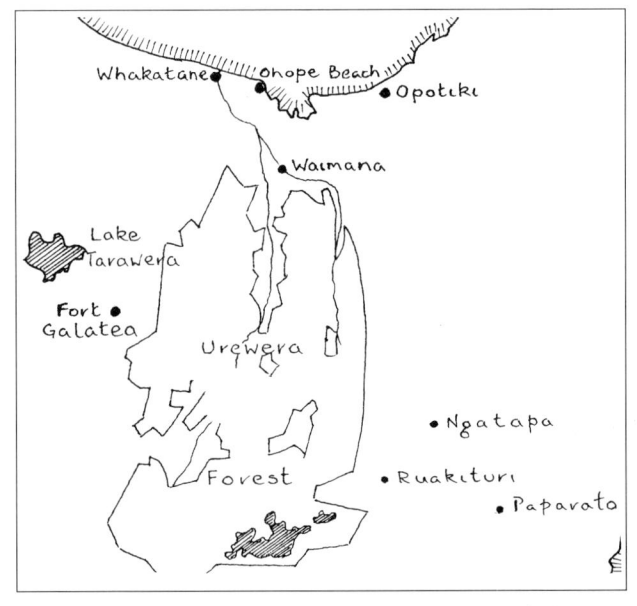

Map of the area of Te Kooti's operations in the Bay of Plenty.

hard ride and involved the crossing of three tidal rivers and Huntress Creek, there being no ferries or bridges. At Waiotahi, where the mailman Bennett White had been murdered earlier, once the water had risen to half-tide level it was a question of swimming across with the water well over the saddle. Delay was not possible because a link-up had to be made with despatch riders coming from Tauranga.

At one point during the campaign against Te Kooti in the Urewera, Alfred was detailed to take despatches to Fort Galatea. The route followed the wild and rugged gorge of the Waimana River valley up into the forest, and then across the mountains to the fort. It meant finding a way through a maze of tracks, across rivers, streams and valleys, and up precipitous slopes. He took with him a Maori guide. After travelling some distance the guide suddenly stopped and refused to go any further. He was terrified of penetrating deeper into the forest for fear of attacks by Te Kooti's followers, who would show him no mercy. An argument ensued. Alfred, knowing the urgency of his despatches, pulled out his revolver and levelled it at the man. The man chose the most sensible option. There was no further trouble and the journey was safely completed. This was one of the more innocuous stories of his wartime adventures that in later years Alfred John used to tell to his children and grandchildren.

In spite of the establishment of Fort Galatea, and the infiltration of government troops into the forest, Te Kooti still evaded capture. He expected to be attacked sooner or later and took up a strong position in a gorge deep into the interior, but the attack never came. The lines of communication of the government troops had become too extended and supplies were running out. Sickness was also taking its toll; Whitmore being one of the casualties. Gradually troops were withdrawn and later Fort Galatea was abandoned. Te Kooti had in fact won this round. He knew that the forest was on his side, for to Maoris it had long been known as a death-trap to invaders. He left the forest unopposed and slipped away to the safety of the Waikato area in the far west. He was pursued there but the pursuit was never pressed home. The Government had had enough and did not want to engage in a further war against the powerful tribes of the west, who had welcomed Te Kooti and given him refuge. The numbers of his followers had diminished to a small band, but he remained there unmolested. The war came to an end in 1872. Te Kooti was eventually pardoned and was given a plot of land on which to live in the Bay of Plenty, only a few miles from Whakatane – the town which he had sacked and burned in March 1869.

Once he had begun his new duties at Opotiki, Alfred's life took on a more ordered and stable form. His duties were regular. He lived in one place and he usually returned there each evening. In addition to despatch-riding he was also drill instructor to the Bay of Plenty Volunteer Cavalry. In Opotiki he came to know a military settler and his family, Henry Knights, who had served in the 1st Waikato Regiment and on its disbandment had received land at Opotiki. Alfred became friends with the Knights' daughter, Maria, an attractive young woman of twenty-three. The friendship ripened into love.

❖ ❖ ❖

Henry Knights had been born in Lambeth, London in the year 1818. He was the son of a shoemaker. He married Mary Ann Wickham and their first child, Ellen, was born in England in 1841. Most of his life was spent in the army. He was over six feet tall and well built. Because of his physique he was enlisted in the 10th Hussars, a distinguished cavalry regiment, in which he reached the rank of sergeant. He saw service for a while in Ireland,

and later in India where for most of the time he was based at Kirkee, a British garrison near Poona. He had his wife there with him and three more children were born at Kirkee, a son who died in early childhood and two more daughters, Maria and Emma. Although they lived in a remote part of the world, their's was a happy childhood. There was plenty to interest and delight them. They had toys, among them a peepshow in the form of a folding concertina-like box with a series of receding cut-out scenes giving a three-dimensional effect. The subject was the Thames Tunnel. What the girls remembered most clearly were the human figures in it, which included an Indian with a magnificent turban and a lady in a red dress. The peepshow has survived.

Just before the outbreak of the Indian Mutiny in 1857 the family left Kirkee, as Henry Knight's regiment was moved to Melbourne, Australia. Very soon the regiment was disbanded and men were given a grant of land at Melbourne, where Henry and his family now settled. He also had a pension from the 10th Hussars. While there he served for a time in the Australian Mounted Police, after which he went to the Ballarat goldfields. There were close ties then between Australia and New Zealand, for in its early years New Zealand had been governed from Sydney. After the Second Maori War broke out in New Zealand in 1862 recruits were sought in Australia, especially amongst men who had seen military service. Henry Knights decided to enlist. He enrolled for the Waikato Militia in September 1863. In the following year he set sail for Auckland, with his wife and three daughters, to report for duty. In June 1864 he was promoted from Private to Lance Corporal.

Mary Ann, his wife, was very pretty as a child and in the village where she grew up had been chosen Queen of the May. As a woman she was vivacious, and attractive, with her high cheekbones and finely modelled features. She loved the life in India and in Melbourne. Henry, though well-built and of impressive appearance, was stolid and of a quiet nature, rarely taking any initiative, preferring to stick to familiar routines and avoid trouble. Nor did he care much for going out. Mary Ann, on the other hand, had a great capacity for enjoying life. She liked to go the theatre and the races, and never lacked for male companions to escort her. She acquired in India a good collection of jewellry, inlcuding a garnet brooch surrounded by ivory leaves. She also had a flair for nice clothes. She sometimes wore pink silk stockings, which was considered very daring at that time and other women would look askance at them.

The three daughters, Ellen, Maria, and Emma, were high spirited like their mother. Henry's sobriety and serious-mindedness does not seem to have inhibited their natural vivacity. During the voyage to Auckland, Emma, the youngest, met a young Englishman, Edward Woodford. He was extremely good-looking and of a kind nature. He had been educated at Harrow School in England and now, after staying with the Governor of New South Wales, was on his way to Auckland; from where he later planned to embark for the South Island of New Zealand.

The Knights went to live in the Onehunga district of Auckland, quite near the sea. This delighted Emma who used to go down and collect oysters from the rocks. Young Edward Woodford was a frequent visitor to the house. As he walked out to their home he would gather posies of wild manuka flowers along the way to give to Emma. Theirs was a mutual attraction and by now Emma was deeply in love with him. She made her love known and was eager for an engagement. Her mother, however, said she was too young and should wait until she was 18 before marrying. This was not good enough for Emma. She did not want to let Edward slip through her fingers. When the day came for him to sail for the south she got a boatman to row her out to the departing vessel. In an impassioned reunion she threatened to throw herself overboard if Edward did not take her with him to the South Island. From the ship she could see her parents approaching in a rescue boat, but they were too late. The anchor was already weighed and the vessel was moving off. So Emma escaped capture and eloped with her sweetheart. They travelled as brother and sister and, in December the following year in Christchurch, they were duly joined in holy matrimony. Emma gave her age as 23, when actually she was 15.

This must have been a heady experience for Emma's sister, the seventeen-year old Maria, who had been a witness of that daring and romantic escapade. In the family events continued to move at a rapid pace. Within four months her oldest sister, Ellen, was married at her parent's home at Onehunga to Henry Charman, a Trooper in the Colonial Defence Force. Not long afterwards the family moved from Auckland, and Maria once more found herself living in a military enclave. For her father Henry Knights, still in the Militia, had been posted to Tauranga in the Bay of Plenty north-west of Opotiki. He was now part of the 1st Waikato Regiment stationed at a fort known as Camp Te Papa, in the front line of a war.

Tauranga was at that time a key military centre in what became known as the Tauranga Campaign. As recently as May and June of 1864, there had been decisive battles around Tauranga itself. One was at Gate Pa, when the Maori Chief Rawiri Puhirake, in the face of very large and heavily armed force, outwitted and defeated General Cameron. It was a humiliation for the British, but it also gave rise to great bravery and great humanity. One of the Maori commanders was a chief named Henare Taratoa. A unit of British troops had fought its way into the pa but twenty of their officers were killed or wounded, and their men retreated leaving them lying there. Chief Henare himself tended the wounded throughout the night. One English colonel asked for a drink of water, but there was none in the pa. Henare crept out and found his way in the darkness through the British lines and, dodging the sentries, came back with a calabash of water. On his way back he was shot and wounded. When the British counter-attacked, Henare was killed. On his body were found the orders for the day, which ended with the text in Maori, 'If thine enemy hunger, feed him; if he thirst, give him drink.' This selfless act, though not widely known, was not forgotten. Many years later the first bishop in New Zealand, George Selwyn, when he left New Zealand to become Bishop of Lichfield, in England, had a stained glass window erected in the episcopal palace in Lichfield to Henare's memory.

Soon after the Knights moved from Onehunga to the stockade at Te Papa there was recorded on August 3, 1866, in the list of births to soldiers and their wives in the Tauranga District Register, the birth of a daughter to Maria Knights. The father was listed as Thomas Squire, a sergeant in the 1st Waikato Regiment. The child was called Marie Olivia. No record has been found as to when, or whether, there was a marriage, nor of what happened to the sergeant. Military records show several men named Thomas Squire or Squires, but none in the 1st Waikato Regiment. It is impossible to tell whether any one of them was the father of Maria's child.

The 1st Waikato Regiment, Henry Knights' regiment, was formed with the aim of providing the country with military settlers; that is, men who would farm land but be available for military training and military service when required. While still stationed at Tauranga this regiment had been allocated the Opotiki area for settlement; and each man was there and then assigned his plot of land. Henry Knights was given a town plot in Opotiki and 80 acres of land at Waimana East, named from the Waimana River. Men were not allowed to leave the Tauranga fort to take possession of their land until 1867, when Henry

Marie Olivia Sisam known by the name of 'Tottie'.

Knights moved to Opotiki with his family. Once they had staked their claim the military settlers were struck off the pay list, given twelve month's rations, and for the next three years were on stand-by for military duties; but otherwise were free to cultivate their land.

It was some time after the Knights had settled in Opotiki that Alfred and Maria met and fell in love. Their wedding took place in Opotiki on September 22, 1870. This was the beginning of a very happy union, for Alfred loved Maria dearly throughout their life together. Maria's child, Marie Olivia, was brought up as his own child and was always treated as such. It is likely that none of her brothers and sisters ever knew that this was not so. She was known by the affectionate name of 'Tottie'. In years to come her marriage certificate gave the name of Alfred John Sisam as her father. A treasured possession of Tottie's descendants is a Bible given to the little girl by her mother. The inscription in the Bible reads: 'Marie Olivia Sisam. A Birthday Present from her Mamma with her best love, 27th June 1877, this being the eleventh anniversary.'

Alfred and Maria embarked on their life together in Opotiki. Alice, known as 'Allie', was born in 1871 and over the next five years more children were born. In the 1870s Alfred and his family were living in Church Street, in the centre of Opotiki. Church Street was so named from St. Stephen's Church at its northern end, where the Volkener murder took place, and around which was built the redoubt where the Armed Constabulary based. Alfred's duties as Mounted Constable, mail-carrier and despatch rider continued and his horse was still stabled in the old redoubt buildings. Little Allie used to listen anxiously at night for the clip-clop of his horse's hooves, as her father passed their home on his way back to the stables.

14
The Waitakere

WALTER'S FARM IN THE BUSH

When in October 1868 Walter's brother Alfred had joined the Armed Constabulary, he embarked on a course of events that determined the future pattern of his life. It distanced him from Walter, for it took him away from Auckland to the Bay of Plenty area and involved him in the latter stages of the Maori War.

Walter and Mary Ann having settled at Thames, remained there for ten years, during which time two children were born to them, Walter Henry and Caroline Mary. We can only guess at what Walter did at Thames. Almost certainly he would have been involved in preaching and other religious activities, and probably in teaching. He may also have continued with market-gardening.

In the spring of 1876, Walter and his family made the momentous decision to move from Thames to the Waitakere property and make a living from it. It was a courageous venture: some might say a foolhardy one, others that it was a venture of faith. Walter suffered from asthma and an open-air life suited him but, as a farmer, he would need to hire labour for the heavier work. Mary Ann's brother was strongly opposed to his sister's going to 'such a place'. But the couple held to their conviction and moved the family, taking up residence in the original shack. Here they stayed until Walter could build a new house. When the time came for this, timber was split from trees felled on the property, enough for a single-story wooden house with fireplace and chimney. The site was on a piece of high ground near a small creek. The creek fed into the Waitakere River flowing behind the house and along the valley below. The land stretched to left and right, the river marking the eastern boundary. In its upper reaches the river formed a series of precipitous waterfalls, known as the Cascades. But all around was thick bush, which Walter had to clear. This contained enormous kauri trees, up to a hundred feet high, each with a life of several thousand years if left undisturbed. Such trees were extremely straight, fine-grained, durable and free from imperfections. With these outstanding characteristics it is not surprising that, in the early years of the century, the British Navy used New Zealand's kauri trees for ship's masts. It is said that at the Battle of Trafalgar the British kauri masts proved far superior to those of the French ships and thereby contributed greatly to Nelson's victory.

Although the Waitakere River valley was a romantic and beautiful spot. Its wild, natural state together with its remoteness, meant that life would be hard for Walter and Mary Ann, especially for Mary Ann. Yet they seem to have been happy there. Every morning before breakfast Walter read from the Bible and conducted prayers, with all the family on their knees. To start the day in this way was a Sisam family tradition and had been the custom at Arrow Mill in England. There was no school within reach, but Walter taught the children

The Waitakere Ranges looking towards the Waiktakere River valley.

The Waitakere River flowing behind the house and along the valley below. All around was thick bush.

their lessons, and encouraged them to write letters and read such books as he had been able to bring with him from England. One of these was a precious copy of John Bunyan's *Pilgrim's Progress*, published in 1836 in Derby by Henry Mozley and Sons. It had been bought at a shop in the High Street, Alcester, from 'E.M. Wright, printer and book-seller'. Walter made a present of the book to young Walter Henry a few months after they came to Waitakere. He had also brought with him from England a set of drawing instruments, a folding writing desk, and the old muzzle-loading shot-gun, used at Arrow Mill in England to frighten the sparrows off the corn.

The nearest point for provisions was two miles over the hills, by a rough forest track. Walter would walk or ride there. It was not a store so much as a small supply depot, used by a storekeeper named Fred Baxter who brought out goods by packhorse for the logging camps in the area. Walter's account book for November and December 1876 shows that on his farm he already kept cows and chickens and was supplying modest quantities of butter and eggs to Baxter, buying groceries with the proceeds. On November 24th, for instance, he supplied eggs and butter to the value of 19s. 4d. and bought tea, sugar, soap, rice, baking powder and salt to the value of 5s. 9d, and took home the difference, 13s. 7d. in cash. It was subsistence farming rather than farming for profits, but it enabled Walter and his family to live there happily, albeit very simply.

Their main household provisions, such as flour and other perishables, were kept in two large chests, six feet long, lined with zinc. One of these was the chest Walter's father had

The forest trail leading over the hills to the nearest store.

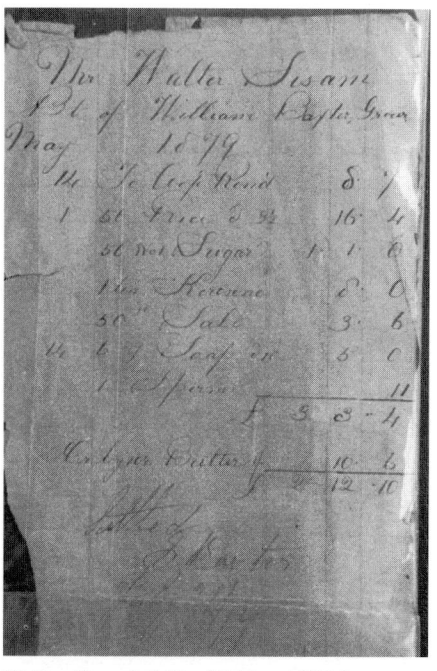

Walter Sisam's bill of 9 May 1879 for groceries, showing the credit given for butter supplied in part payment.

given him when he left England. The other was probably Tom's. These proved ideal for keeping out mice and damp. The family wash was done outdoors down by the creek, as it was easier to boil the water there than carry it up to the house. They baked their own bread and, to help the dough rise, they wrapped it in Walter's old great-coat which he had bought in Australia in 1862. The nearest flour mill was about 3½ miles over the hills in the direction of Riverhead, a town situated on an estuary leading to Auckland's natural harbour. On occasions Walter walked the seven miles there and back, carrying the sack of flour home on his shoulders. It was a heavy load but, having worked in England at Arrow and Harvington mills, he knew how to lift a heavy sack of flour and carry it without injury.

Walter proudly named their new home Arrow Farm, after the river which flowed along the boundary of his old home in England; for the English Arrow was a small river, like the Waitakere, and marked the boundary of the Arrow property in England, just as the Waitakere did that of their new home. For the two children, Walter Henry and Caroline (Carrie), it was an isolated existence. They had no schoolmates or playmates of their own age. However, they had one good and faithful friend, and this was their grandmother, Caroline Sisam, in England, whom they had never seen. She wrote to them regularly, always thinking of things to tell that might interest them, despite the mails taking three months to reach them. On May 29, 1877, she wrote to her grandson nine-year old Walter Henry:

'Thank you so much for writing me such a nice letter too. I can't remember if I wrote to you last March or not, but I sent you some mignionette seed which I hope you got and I shall be glad to hear if it grows. I hope there was enough for Carrie, too, to plant in your little gardens. How much I would like to have a peep at them, but more especially at the

Caroline Sisam of Alcester, Warwickshire, grandmother to young Walter Henry and Carrie.

little gardeners. There are some beautiful Lilies-of-the-Valley just in blossom at Arrow Mill. I dare say your dear Papa remembers them, they are very sweet. Your Papa tells me you have some nice flowers in New Zealand. I am glad to hear you got your little books all right. Aunt Alice and I send it between us so that it is only half Grandma's present. With much love, dear Waltie, to Carrie and yourself. Believe me, ever your loving Grandma.'

When she wrote this letter, Grandmother Caroline was living at a house called The Priory in Alcester, the town near Arrow Mill. Her husband, Henry Sisam, Walter's father, had died in 1870; whereupon Walter's younger brother, James Leonard, had succeeded to the lease of Arrow Mill. Caroline refers to correspondence from Walter who, it seems, was a faithful letter-writer. Aunt Alice was Walter's sister, married to a local Arrow farmer. Little Carrie was, of course, named after her Grandmother Caroline.

Walter became a well-known figure in the Waitakere area. From his earliest days there he regularly travelled the hills and valleys. For in addition to the exacting work of the farm, he also remained faithful to the spiritual calling he had felt in England. In emigrating to New Zealand under the Albertland scheme he had no doubt visualised the settlers founding a community that had a religious base to it, in which he could play a part, but this was not to be. The poor quality of the plots of land and the uncertainty caused by the Maori War had put an end to that hope. During his stay in Auckland he did some preaching and a good deal of work amongst the non-conformist churches. But, as we have seen, he had found his humble occupation at that time as a market-gardener barred him from being accepted socially by some of the church members who, in the nation's first capital city, tended to have their eyes more on the social ladder than on the ladder to heaven. There were no such barriers in the Waitakere, and here he could follow his calling.

He was soon in demand as a preacher. There were few chapels yet built, so he preached wherever there were small communities. He found himself at gatherings in barns, houses, public halls, wherever people could meet together, including in days to come the railway station waiting room at Swanson. The public hall at Pomona was run by a local committee and used for all kinds of purposes. The village school was based there, and various religious denominations made use of it for services. Over the years he was regularly welcomed at Pomona, Taupaki, Swanson village, and Kumeu. To reach Kumeu he walked four miles over a hill, and did this frequently. It became known as Parson's Hill. His preaching was a stimulus and encouragement to the building of further permament churches that appeared during the next years, and this quiet, faithful, yet unpaid service to the community, played its part in the development of the area and the creation of communities out of scattered farmsteads.

During these first three years at Arrow Farm the many miles he had walked and ridden over the bush trails, whether to obtain supplies or to preach, gave him a sound knowledge of the topography of the district. In addition he was respected and trusted as a man, just as his brother Alfred was to be in the Bay of Plenty area. Very soon he was asked to undertake official public work on a part-time basis. In the 1877 records of the local authority, the Waitemata District Council, he is listed as a 'fence viewer' for Waitakere East, a person whose duty it was to see to the errection and maintenance of boundary and highway fences. Two years later, in 1879, he was appointed 'valuator', an assessor of property value for rating purposes. This included both occupied land and forest areas. Sometimes he took young Walter Henry with him to help. This was all part-time work and as such was not all that remunerative, but nevertheless provided a welcome addition to the family income. It was congenial to be in the open-air and brought Walter in touch with people in an area that was sparsely populated compared with Thames or Auckland. He seems to have had a natural understanding of people, and had always felt that it was in this sphere that his real bent lay, whether in normal human contacts, or in teaching or preaching. At the same time, he worked hard on his own farm, on which he and his family depended for a living. He knew that a man's horizons needed to be able to expand, and not remain constricted and static. Opportunities to broaden one's horizons in the Waitakeres were few, but he seized what there were, knowing that whatever stimulus he found through his wider contacts, he could share with his family at Arrow Farm.

The children, meanwhile, were flourishing like wild flowers in a wilderness. Their faithful Grandmother Sisam in England, ever mindful of their welfare, continued her letters to them in spite of her advancing years. On January 1879, the year of Walter's appointment as valuator, she wrote to Walter Henry, then nine years old:

'I was so glad to hear your Papa has given you a cow for your very own. I think Daisy a very pretty name for her. I hope you will have better luck with your poultry this season. It gives me great pleasure, my dear Boy, to hear from your Papa how good and useful you are. You quite shame the boys and girls in this country. They go to school until they are much older than you, and are not allowed to do any work until they are 13 or 14. But, I think it is a pity it should be so. We have had such very sharp frost now for some weeks, and lots of people go skating on the ice. I suppose skates would be of no use in New Zealand. I wish your Papa would bring you all to England, and I hope you will be able to go to Opotiki after a bit, and see your Uncle and Aunt and Cousins there. And now my dear Boy I must say good-bye. May God bless you. . . . Believe me with much love, ever your fond Grandmamma. C. Sisam.'

With their limited resources and isolated dwelling-place, Walter and Mary Ann did what they could to equip their children for whatever life might have in store for them. The children learned to work and to be useful in the household. They acquired the skills needed on a farm. They learned to read, to write letters, and to do arithmetic. Walter Henry learned to handle money and to keep simple accounts, and also to keep a diary like his father. His father, although busy with preaching and with his work as a local official, was neither neglectful of his children nor failing in his appreciation of the part they played in the homestead.

Walter knew that development involved the whole person, body, mind and spirit, and like every good parent sought to maintain the right balance. He tried to pass on what he had been taught by his parents. Hence his birthday present to the young Walter Henry when he was 12 years old. It was another book, this time a copy of *Uncle Tom's Cabin*, and on the frontispiece was written:

'Walter Henry Sisam. A present from his affectionate Father, given on his twelfth birthday, 28 August 1879 – a reward for his industry and care when the giver had been absent from home. With the prayer that the Grace of God be with him.'

By 1880 the new and roomier farmhouse was completed. Made from kauri trees felled on the farm, it was roofed with shingles of split kauri timber. The children helped the hired man fix the roof by keeping him supplied with shingles, fetching and carrying them as he needed them. They remembered the occasion because he told them stories, and drank frequently from a bottle of 'painkiller' as he worked. The steady supply of shingles no doubt speeded the work and made up for time spent in pain-killing and story-telling.

Previously, the children had watched the kauri trees being felled by two men working with axes. One, as the axe struck, would let out his breath, making a 'ho' sound. The other, as his axe struck, in turn made a 'ha' sound. Perhaps this was to help clear the air from the lungs, just as athletes let out a shout at the peak of their effort. To the children it was exciting to watch, and the regular chopping and ho-ha sounds made a pleasant and almost musical rhythm. A few years later, the young Walter Henry was himself beginning to use an axe, and, all his life, remembered the day he felled his first tree. He was about thirteen. He remembered it, not only as an achievement, but because on that occasion his mother brought out a blackberry pie for him to eat, freshly made from the wild fruit growing on the farm.

As the local postal services were now functioning smoothly, it is likely that Alfred and Walter continued their regular correspondence with one another. Alfred would have been kept posted with news of Walter's family, and especially of young Walter Henry's progress as the years went by. When the boy was fifteen he was taking a full share in the work at Arrow Farm. He kept a diary at this time. The entries were brief and to the point, and were about cultivation, the collection of gum resin from the kauri trees, care of live stock, particularly cows, and the simple pursuits and pleasures of farm-life. Among the entries for the summer and autumn of 1883 were these:

'Jan. 23rd. Went scraping gum, getting wood. Papa found Topsey's kittens. Finished digging potatoes out of 2 beds.

'Jan. 25th. Very showery. Papa and I cut bush. Mended fence. Sissie (Carrie), Fred (Fred Cottle, the farmworker) and J. (Jo, otherwise Equilio Pizzini, another farmworker) scraped gum. Had a bathe. Found cat up a tree. Papa went fishing.

'May 1st. I went after Peggie, Primrose and Cowslip (various cows sent into the bush to graze). Found them. Sowed seed. Cherry could not be found.'

In the winter of 1888, Walter Henry and Carrie, who had been away from the farm all day on a visit, were making their way home in the late afternoon sunshine. As they came along the hill track leading to Arrow Farm, Walter Henry saw a movement of light and shade on the trees. At the same moment he had a strong presentiment that his mother was no longer alive, but he said nothing to Carrie. As they reached the summit of Pukematakeo Hill a few minutes later, they were surprised to see Walter, their father, coming towards them. When they met he told them that, while entertaining visitors at the farm, Mary Ann had suddenly and without warning collapsed and died. Knowing the children would return at any moment, he had immediately set off to tell them. As soon as Walter Henry heard his father tell what had happened, he told of the premonition he had had near the top of the hill when he had seen a strange light on the trees, and he knew that his mother was dead. It is easy to read things into a moment like this, but the incident reveals the youth's sensitivity, and the close affinity he felt with his father, enabling him to speak openly of the secrets of his heart. Perhaps, too, he had inherited something of his father's visionary nature, and spiritual perception.

Mary Ann was buried at Waikumete in Glen Eden, a small settlement not far from Auckland; there being no burial ground as yet at Swanson, the nearest township to Arrow Farm. The suddenness of her going, breaking as it did the even tenor of life at the farm, was a great blow and loss to Walter, and to his children. They were now aged about twenty-one and seventeen. When the news reached her in England, Caroline Sisam was deeply grieved. She felt for them all and, despite failing eyesight, wrote to Walter Henry

Pages from Walter Henry's Diary for January and May 1883.

Family washing day beside the creek on the Waitakere farm.

and Carrie hoping, more fervently than ever, that they would still be able to visit their cousins in Opotiki. The ocean mails of that time were slow by modern standards, so it was after Christmas in the following January, before Caroline was able to reply to the news of Mary Ann's death:

'How much I wish I was near you, Carrie dear, that I could come in and assist you a bit sometimes in your household duties. You must indeed miss your dear Mother very much. I feel so sorry for you all. You must try and comfort your dear Father as much as you can. I am thinking how lonely he will be when you are at Uncle Alfred's, but I hope you will have a good time and enjoy yourselves. I wish I could be one of the party. I was invited to a children's party on Monday evening but I have a bad cold so did not go. The cousins from Alcester and the Mill, and Katie from Harvington were there. I think they had a pleasant time. We all wish you, Father, Walter and Carrie, a very happy New Year. You must please give my dear love to your father. I wrote to him not long since. I hope he keeps pretty well. Carrie dear, do you do your washing yourself or how do you manage that? I often wonder how you get along. Your brother Walter seems to think you are a capital housekeeper and I've no doubt you are.

I spent my Christmas at Harvington with Uncle William. We had such a beautiful mistletoe-bough hung in the hall, and plenty of berried holly about the house. Have you any mistletoe or holly where you are? Write to us soon again please, and with dear love to you both. . . .'

There is a contemporary photograph of Walter standing with Carrie and Walter Henry in front of their house, taken in the Waitakere farm by a photographer, F. Will, in 1889, a year or so after Mary Ann died. Walter, Walter Henry and Caroline are dressed in their best

The photograph of Walter, Walter Henry and Carrie outside their Waitakere farmhouse, taken by F. Will of Auckland.

clothes. Walter wears a dark suit and a bow tie and a pointed, velour hat. Walter Henry is in his shirt sleeves but is wearing a waistcoat, collar and tie and straw hat. Carrie is also in a straw hat, with a ribbon and bow, and a neat fitting, ankle-length dress with a high neck. Topsey the cat is nestling by the front door, and there are flowers in the bed beneath the window, with some wire-hooped edging to keep the animals out. Rough paving stones are laid in front of the house, and the neat rows of kauri shingles can be clearly seen on the roof. The bush is growing thickly in the background. It is possible to date this photograph exactly because of the entry in Walter Henry's account book, which reads: 'October 24th, 1889. For Assisting F.Will taking views, 4/0.' The fact that Walter Henry was helping the photographer is probably why he appears in the picture in shirt-sleeves. F.Will was an itinerant photographer from Auckland, who does not seem to have had any studio or office, but preferred roaming about the country photographing whatever pictures pleased him and living on the the sale of prints.

It took some time before the visit to Uncle Alfred's family, materialised. There was much to be done at Arrow Farm, and it was difficult for Walter to do without Walter Henry's help. In the end Walter Henry stayed with his father, and only Carrie went on the visit. But there were also other events that made postponement necessary; and these concerned the fortunes of the Sisams in Opotiki.

15
Founding Families

OPOTIKI AND WHAKATANE – WAITAKERE WEDDINGS

In the early 1860s Opotiki had consisted of little more than a wharf on the waterfront and a church, and it was not until 1863 that the first European child was born there. In the next 25 years it became a thriving, commercial centre. It was in this setting that Alfred's family grew and flourished during the next years.

By the 1880s they were living in what had become the main street of a busy town, where there was always something interesting going on. Where they lived, on a corner of Church Street, they had an interesting and varied number of neighbours. A directory for 1880 lists the occupants of the houses and shops. Next door to the Sisams, on the west side of the street, was the medical practitioner Dr.Leslie. Beyond were Richards the county clerk, Tabb the bootmaker, Eliot the postmaster, Constable Gordon of the Armed Constabulary and the town lockup, Bush the resident magistrate, the Masonic Hotel, Richards' general store, Geary the bootmaker, and the Maori chief Wiremu Kingi. Opposite them were, amongst others, the Constabulary Headquarters, the Opotiki School, Geoghan the baker, Turner the tailor, Clay the saddler, Filmer the blacksmith, the Bank of New Zealand, the vicar (the Rev. A.C. Soutar), Bates' general store, Croon the builder, and Te Tatane the Maori chief.

The Sisams had very quickly become part of this fast-growing community of merchants, shopkeepers and professional people. Maria herself opened and, for a while, ran a small haberdashery business. She had inherited something of her mother's flair for nice clothes. She once ordered a new hat for herself. Her instructions to the local hatmaker were quite clear: 'Let it be handsome'.

Maria's young sister, now Emma Woodford, reappeared on the family scene at this time. Having lived for a while in the South Island, following her marriage, she and her husband now took up residence in Opotiki in King Street, near to the Sisams. Despite her whirlwind romance, Emma had settled down to a quiet married life, and now had two children. Whatever she may have been like as a teen-age girl, she was the one daughter most like her father. What she most wanted was a quiet, settled life. It was this longing that probably induced her to take bold and drastic action to secure Edward Woodford as a husband. But sadly Edward was quite unfitted to make his way in the world. It seems that in England he tried to become a doctor but soon gave that up. Unfortunately he had no particular training or qualifications. On an Opotiki list of residents for 1880 he appears, surprisingly, as a butcher. It seems that Alfred John, not knowing quite what to advise him to do, noted that there was then no butcher in Opotiki and there was a good opening for one. But the enterprise did not last long. Alfred John used to get exasperated with the young man because he did not grip anything. Apparently a young boy was drowned in a

Residents listed in the district in 1880

OPOTIKI STREET DIRECTORY, 1880:

River Street, North Street, and Albert Street, no occupants; Victoria Street, PATON, Robert, farm contractor, private residence; Princess Street, Hira te OKIWA, private residence; High Street (north side), MURPHY, John, market gardener, BALL, George, private residence; High Street (south side), VILCOQ, Mrs, private residence; Gray Street (north side), SUNDREY, Mrs, private residence; Kelly Street (north side), PARKINSON, John, senior (vacant), Roman Catholic Mission House, quarters of Officer Commanding A.C. Force, Sergeant-major Powell; Kelly Street (south side), PEEK, Richard, saddler, ELMSLIE, J. G. storekeeper, private residence; Main Street (north side), ARTHUR, J. C., painter, etc, MCDONALD, R., Masonic Hotel, Bates and Walmsley, bakery, DETTE, Charles, Opotiki Butchery, CONNELLY, John F., storekeeper, McCABE, John, constable, private residence, NICHOLSON, John, bricklayer; Main Street (south side), FILMER, John, blacksmith, private residence. MOODY, Samuel, farmer, private residence, police station; King Street (north side), PARKINSON, John, junior, Royal Hotel, DAVIS, Mrs, private residence, CLARKE, Mrs, private residence; King Street (south side), HUBBARD, Mrs, private residence, KING, Robert, J.P., private residence, FORBES, Robert, farmer, private residence, REECE, George, blacksmith, shop and private residence, WOODFORD, Edward, butcher, private residence; Richards Street (north side), Resident Magistrate's quarters —R. S. BUSH Esq., R. M. FLANAGAN, Charles, constable, private residence, CONNELLY, John, senior, farmer, private residence; Richards Street (south side), PARKINSON, John senior, lemonade etc. manufacturer, FILMER, John, cook, private residence, PARKINSON, James, storeman, private residence, DETTE, Charles, butcher, private residence; Ford Street (north side), LITCHFIELD, C. D., storekeeper, private residence, McCARTHY, Mrs, private residence, DAWSON, Thomas, farmer, private residence; Ford Street (south side), PARKINSON, Benjamin, brickmaker, SMITH, James, contractor, private residence, SAVAGE, James, constable, private residence, BAKER, Charles, master S.S. Staffa, private residence, CRAPPS, S., Public Works Department, private residence, DUFFUS, J. W., private residence; Bridge Street (north side), GEOGHAN, William, baker, private residence, LAVIN, Michael, private residence; Bridge Street (south side), KELLY, John, contractor, private residence, KELLY, Mrs, private residence, LAW, William, constable, private residence, LAW, Mrs, private residence, PARKINSON, Alfred, constable, private residence, CUTHBERTSON, George, painter, etc. private residence, MAHONEY, Mrs, private residence, ABBOT, Charles, carpenter, private residence; Wellington Street (north side), McLEAN, Thomas, bushman, private residence, McGOUKIN, Thomas, farm contractor, private residence; Wellington Street (south side), THOMPSON, Robert, farmer, private residence, DENNING, James, gardener, private residence, MONAGHAN, Patrick, farm contractor, private residence, LEE, Williams, carpenter, private residence, ABBOT, Robert, builder and contractor, private residence, ABBOT, Thomas, carpenter, ABBOT, Miss, dressmaker, McCAULEY, William, farm contractor, private residence, HAMILTON, James, farmer, private residence; Duke Street and Forsyth Street, no occupants; Union Street (west side), FITZGERALD, Patrick, farm contractor, private residence; Brabant Street, no occupants; Nelson Street (west side), SOUTAR, Reverend A.C., parsonage, WEBSTER, Mrs private residence, MAHONEY, Stephen, farm contractor, private residence; Wharf Street (east side), BOCKET, C. F., grain and flour store, ABBOT and WHITE, builders and contractors, TURNER, J., tailor, private residence; Church street (west side), KINGI, Wiremu, native chief, private residence, GEARY, Jeffry, bootmaker, WRIGHT, Richard, general store. McDONALD, R., Masonic Hotel, Resident Magistrate's Courthouse — R. S. BUSH Esq., R. M., John Thomson, clerk, Opotiki lockup — constable in charge, W. R. GORDON, Post and Telegraph Office —Samuel Eliot, postmaster and telegraphist, COOK, Mrs private residence, — Mechanics' Institute, TABB, John, bootmaker, KIDD, H. L. private residence, RICHARDS, Loftus, county clerk, secretary to Highway Board, commission agent, surveyor, etc., LESLIE, Dr A. private residence, SISAM, A. C. constable, private residence; Church Street (east side), Constabulary Quarters, officer in-charge — Sergeant Major Powel, Opotiki School, head teacher — Thomas E. Wyatt, assistants — Miss Parkinson and Miss Tinling, GEOGHAN, William, bakery, PARKINSON, John junior, Royal Hotel, TURNER, J., tailor, CLAY, John, saddler, FOSTER, Edward, engineer, S.S. Staffa, FILMER, John, blacksmith's and wheelwright's shop, Bank of New Zealand — agent Isaac Carley, BATES and WALMSLEY, general store, Church of England, clergyman — Reverend A. C. Soutar, LITCHFIELD, C. D. general store, licensed interpreter, commission and general agent, SMITH, Angus, branch of junction store and bakery, CROON, Frank, builder and contractor, McDONALD, Mrs, private residence, Te TATENE, native chief; St John Street (west side), DELANEY, John, junior, private residence; St John Street (east side), CONNELLY, Charles, constable, private residence, IRWIN, Daniel, contractor, private residence, CAPPER, Samuel, bushman, private residence, SAVAGE, Benjamin, bootmaker, private residence, BELL, A., private residence, BELL, the Misses, milliners and drapers, FORBES, George, private residence, DUGLEAUX, L. P. baker, private residence, BOCKETT, C. F., solicitor, Opotiki Town Hall; Goring Street (west side), CRIMMINS, Thomas, carter, private residence, TINGLING, Andrew, farm contractor, private residence; Buchanan Street (east side), HENNESSY, Christopher, carter, private residence, RYAN, Samuel, drayman; Stewart Street, Malcolm Street, and Newry street, no occupants.

Opotiki Street Directory of the 1880s, listing Alfred Sisam living on the west side of Church Street and Edward Woodford on the south side of King Street.

creek that flowed past the back of the Woodford's house but Edward never fenced it in, even after this accident. It is not clear how he made a living. He earned a little writing letters for people and perhaps from other odd jobs. The Sisam and Woodford families kept closely in touch with one another. They went on many picnics together, visited each other's homes and usually spent Christmas together. It is remembered that the Woodfords were always late. The education of children in Opotiki was a problem. The Sisam children were particularly fortunate as the Opotiki School was in the street where they lived. In this they were luckier than their cousins in the Waitakere who, at their remote farm, had no school to go to. Allie Sisam did especially well at the Opotiki School, and as she grew older remanied there as a student-teacher until 1882.

In the outlying country districts near Opotiki there was a sizeable population, though somewhat scattered. The people were mainly engaged in farming, most of them being veterans of the Maori War. Henry Knights was one of these, his farm being some way out of Opotiki at Waimana. As a property owner he had voted in the 1871 parliamentary election. The election was conducted informally at a meeting which Henry Knights attended, when the voting was carried out, not by a secret ballot, but a show of hands. The man elected was W. Kelly, an enterprising Irish immigrant who came to Opotiki in 1863 and later built the town's first hotel down by the old wharf.

There were also Maori settlers in these districts, some who had never been involved in the fighting and some who played a leading part in it. The once-dreaded Maori war leader, Te Kooti, when he received his government pardon in 1883, had come out of hiding and settled just outside the town by the banks of the Maraetara Stream. Maori and Pakeha settlers lived amicably side by side in this area, cultivating their lands and raising maize, and sometimes they inter-married. Among them was a romantic and legendary figure, J. R. Rushton, whose land was at Paewiwi, on the coast of Ohiwa harbour. He had served during the war in the Patea Rangers and the Opotiki Volunteer Rangers, both based at Opotiki, and for a while had been in the same unit as Alfred John. His comrade-in-arms and close friend was David White. Their comradeship was complicated by the fact that they both fell in love with the beautiful Maro, daughter of a Whakatohea chief of the Kareka clan. Maro was fond of both men but was afraid to commit herself to either for fear of breaking their friendship. Finally they made an agreement that whomever she chose the other would bear no jealousy, and that if anything happened to the one she chose the other would take care of her. David White and Maro married. The next year David was leading a party of scouts up the Whakatane Gorge in pursuit of Te Kooti, when he was shot and killed while fording the river. Rushton, when he heard the news, went to comfort Maro. Not long afterwards they were married at Tauranga, and for nearly forty years lived a simple life cultivating their crops and fishing from their canoe.

Alfred's position in the Armed Constabulary at Opotiki – responsibile for law and order – and the fact that the family lived in the heart of the town, brought them into the mainstream of what was now a minor boom-town. His appointment seems to have been as much due to his character as to his experience during the Maori War. He was, like his brother Walter, a typical Sisam in that he was straight-forward, upright and Godfearing. Yet, at the same time, he was an able man and worldly-wise.

Over these years much of the original wartime Armed Constabulary was gradually disbanded to be replaced by what was New Zealand's first civilian police force. At the end of 1884 the Armed Constabulary post in Opotiki, which had consisted of two men, was

Alfred John and Maria Sisam's children in Opotiki. Back row: Alice (Allie), Alfred (Alfy), May, Caroline Marshall (Lena). Front row: Leonard Wilfred and Walter Holtom. Their youngest child Kenneth, being only a baby, was not included in the picture.

closed down and Alfred was transferred to the regional headquarters at Taupo, under Major Scannel. There he learned that the field force of which he had been a part was soon to be disbanded, and that men could apply for a discharge at once if they wished. Having a wife and eight children, and knowing that there was no Armed Constabulary pension coming to him, Alfred resigned on January 2, 1885. He received a gratuity of £25 and twelve months pay. As far as the future was concerned his position was precarious. He had received no land grant either for his Armed Constabulary service or his service in the Colonial Defence Force under Nixon. For nearly ten months he was without an occupation. Then, on October 22, 1885, he was appointed Mounted Constable in the Police at Opotiki where he was made Clerk of the Court for the town under the resident magistrate, Mr. Bush.

In 1887, with these upheavals behind him, there came the happy occasion of the first wedding in the family on High Street. It was on New Year's day when, in the Presbyterian Church in Opotiki, John Alexander Campbell Lamont married Olivia Marie Sisam. This was Tottie the eldest of the family, now aged 20. John (Jack) was 21 years old and a school teacher from Tryphena, a small town on Great Barrier Island off the east coast near Auckland. He had been born in Ireland, his father being a house contractor. Tottie gave her occupation as housekeeper, since for some time she had been helping her mother care for the large household of children. Maria would miss her very much now that she was leaving to set up home with her husband in Auckland.

In 1889 Alfred John and Te Kooti came face to face with one another over a matter of the law. Te Kooti had settled down happily by the Maraetara Stream and adapted quite well to living in peace. But sometimes he may have found it a little dull. During this year he was hauled up before the magistrate in Opotiki for 'riotous assembly' and was ordered to find sureties for £1500. Alfred was the Constable who put him in the Opotiki lockup and had charge of him while he was there. A friendly relationship subsequently developed between the two men. There was a another 'eruption' during this time, of a somewhat different kind, which put police forces on the alert. The volcano of Mt. Tarawera, some fifty miles distant, erupted. The sky went dark, Maori villages were engulfed and a thick dust descended over the Opotiki area. Many of the overland trails leading out of the Opotiki district, which were the only means of communication, were blocked.

With the pressures of war now removed, all kinds of business enterprises were springing up in the town. Inevitably there was crooked dealing, intimidation and law-breaking. Something of this nature occurred over the operation of the long-established brewery. There was serious drunkenness in the town and there were also customs duty irregularities involving the brewery. Alfred made an investigation and sent a preliminary report to the Inspector of Customs in Wellington. But there were influential local men involved, including a land-broker, S.Bates, who also owned the town's newspaper. They knew that Alfred could not be intimidated and would follow through the case until the truth was uncovered. The Inspector of Customs came down in person. There were powerful forces at work behind the scenes to get Alfred transferred to Whakatane, so that he could no longer follow up the case. Alfred sought legal advice from a friendly solicitor in Church Street, who appealed to the Minister of Justice on his behalf. But Bates had friends in high places. On July 5, 1890, Alfred's solicitor, Mr. Bockett, called at the Sisam home and showed Maria a telegram from the Minister of Justice to say that the appeal had been dismissed and they must leave Opotiki.

Alfred was away from home at the time on police duties. Maria singlehandedly had to pack up the family home, children and all, and take the hazardous boat journey across the river mouth. Then they had to travel along the beach which was the only route to Whakatane. To reach it meant negotiating the notorious sand-bar of Opotiki Harbour, where at high tide the depth of the water was only six to eight feet. When Maria finally set out on July 15, with the children and all her household goods, the boat could not get over the sand-bar and had to turn back. Kind Opotiki friends came to Maria's aid, especially her neighbours: the Parkinsons who kept the Royal Hotel in Church Street, Mr. Connors, and the clergyman Mr. Wills from the vicarage. Next morning the boat made a second attempt. Maria wrote in her diary:

'Left Opotiki and got out all right. How I held my breath crossing that old Bar, for I just dreaded going back over and over again.'

But her spirit was resilient. A week or two later she was writing:

'Whakatane is just a lovely place with its grand high hills. Just fancy a few short years ago old Te Kooti was careering about them and frightening the people, both here and at Opotiki, out of their wits. Now the farmers sheep are feeding peacefully there. And the river is a glorious picture, I had a view of it from McGarvey's store room this evening. The sun was just setting and the beautiful shades of light he threw out over the smooth water, where two or three boats were sailing about so prettily, just charmed me.'

It looked as if this was going to be a happy home for the children, and a place where they would thrive. There was plenty to amuse them, not least the exciting exploration of their new surroundings. Soon after they arrived Leonard, who was 11, fell off a rock at the top of a hill, about 60 or 70 feet, and came an awful cropper. He was badly cut and bruised

Whakatane Waterfront with the Maori 'pa' on the hills above.

Alfred John Sisam.

Maria Sisam (née Knights).

about the face and head, and sprained his knee. For some time he went about on crutches, but he recovered and was soon travelling about the country with his father helping to take the census. The post of Constable also carried with it the position of Postmaster in charge of mails, a custom which no doubt went back to the days when the Armed Constabulary were the mail-carriers. The usual procedure in Whakatane was that the Constable's family ran the post office, so Allie became postmistress. Her sister Lena meanwhile taught music.

Maria found the people of Whakatane welcoming and kindly, but certain social distinctions were nevertheless observed, as she found out when different groups of ladies began to call on her. In her diary she records with some irony the social distinctions she met in the way people were described to her:

'The leading ladies are Mesdames Swindly, Enas and Buckworth. Then comes Mrs. McGarvey – Mr. is only a storekeeper, Mrs. Wilkins and Mrs. Chalmers are only farmers. All the rest seem honest working folk. Then there are a number of half-castes, ladies who count. Mrs. McGarvey, Mrs. Buckworth and Mrs. McAllister have called on me. All three can boast of Maori blood.'

Maria came to know Mrs. McGarvey very well and the two women became great friends. They were near neighbours and were in and out of one another's houses frequently, helping each other in times of illness and other domestic crises.

In mid August 1890, soon after they arrived, Alfred and Maria made a home with them for old Henry Knights, Maria's father, after his wife, Mary, died. Henry and Mary had lived quietly together in Opotiki for about twenty years. Their life was a simple one. They cultivated their plot of land which supplied many of their needs, though seeds for sowing vegetables were difficult to come by in those days, especially garden peas. Like many folk they would keep the pods and cook them when the peas were finished. Mary was of a generous nature and, in later years, gave away a good deal of her beautiful jewellery to anyone who was kind to her and her husband.

Early in 1891 there was an interesting sequel to the brewery affair in Opotiki. The men responsible for Alfred's sudden removal to Whakatane, subsequently overreached themselves. The headmaster of the Opotiki School, Thomas Wyatt, who was a heavy drinker and part of the brewery clique, was reported by the clergyman, Mr. Wills, for being drunk and disorderly while in charge of the children at school. A gang of youths including Fred Bates, the son of the man who engineered Alfred's removal, beat up the clergyman in the street. One youth named Wyatt, son of the delinquent headmaster, hit the Rev. Mr. Wills several times across the face with a loaded whip. In her diary Maria commented on these events in no uncertain terms:

'Every honest person in Opotiki knows that Mr. Wills has only done what was right in exposing Mr. Wyatt. The old man is a drunkard and an Atheist and is not fit to teach young people. Yet they all pity him, but when my husband, who neither drinks nor never owed any man in Opotiki one shilling, but went without many a comfort that he might pay his way honestly, yet those people were against him, those who are for Mr. Wyatt.'

When charged in court the youths were let off, one of them getting a small fine. But Mr. Wills sued S.Bates the newspaper proprietor for libel in his reporting of the case. Bates' son was one of the ringleaders in the mugging of the clergyman. Mr. Wills won the case and Bates was bound over for £100 to appear in court if he offended again. So justice was at least partly done and the wrongdoers were shown up for what they were.

In the midst of these excitements Allie, who had been running the post office in

Whakatane, became engaged. Her fiancé was William Parry Browne, a skilled carpenter and cabinet-maker. He made the most beautiful furniture and his work was meticulous. He was also what is known as 'a character' in the community, and was always referred to as 'W.P.' Browne, never by his first name. Allie retired from being postmistress, and her place was taken by her sister Lena. The wedding took place on May 6, 1891, not at Whakatane but in Opotiki; since it was a registry office wedding rather than one held in church. This was a disappointment to Alfred and Maria, but it was otherwise a happy occasion. The weather was perfect. The wedding dance was a great success, and over fifty people sat down to supper, including many distinguished guests from the neighbourhood. Maria described it:

'From Opotiki there was Harry (nickname for Edward) Woodford and his two daughters, Eva and Rosie. They looked really pretty in pale blue dresses. Then came Mr. and Mrs. Arthur Parkinson and Clare, Mr. and Mrs. Jim and Alf from Whakatane, Major and Mrs. Swindly, Mr. and Mrs. C. Buckworth, Mr. and Mrs. R.Wright, Mr. and Mrs. McGarvey, Miss Elliott, Mr. Grant, Mr. Broderick, and Mr. Pratt, and all the other nice people here. I believe everyone enjoyed themselves, as so they should for neither trouble nor expense was spared to make it a success.'

By now the winter was approaching and, after five weeks of fine weather, it was becoming unsettled. Maria wrote in her diary:

'There was a tremendous downpour of rain last night and one of the water spouts in the hill (at the back of Swindly's butcher's shop) has burst, doing a great deal of damage to

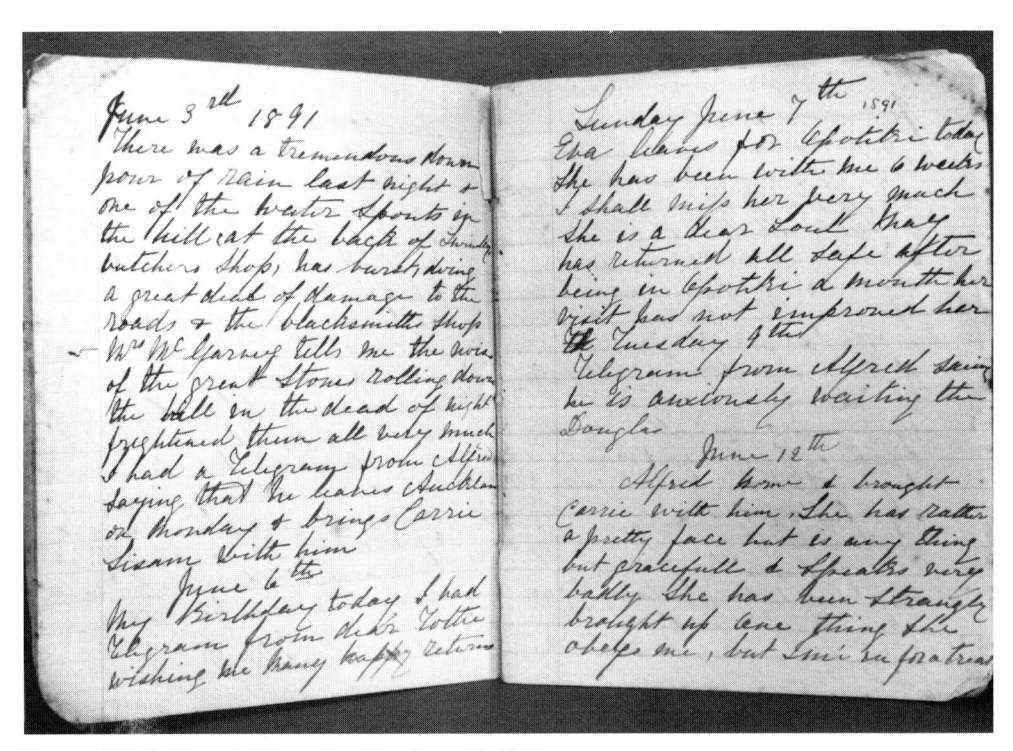

Pages of Maria Sisam's Diary, June 3 to June 12, 1891.

the roads and the blacksmith's shop. Mrs. McGarvey tells me the noise of the great stones rolling down the hill in the dead of night frightened them all very much.' Then she adds: 'I have a telegram from Alfred saying that he leaves Auckland Monday and brings Carrie Sisam with him.'

❖ ❖ ❖

Now at last the long awaited visit of Carrie Sisam from the Waitakere was actually to take place. It was unfortunate that Walter Sisam could not spare young Walter Henry and his sister had to come alone. For this was a visit which Grandmother Sisam, in England, hoped would give the children contact with others of their own age and widen their horizons. She was by now a young woman of twenty and already quite set in her ways, and was no longer the malleable child she was when the visit was first suggested.

Maria's comments on her twenty-year-old niece were as follows:

'She has rather a pretty face but is anything but graceful and speaks very badly. She has been strangely brought up. One thing, she obeys me, but I'm in for a treat.'

This was a down-to-earth and candid observation, but perhaps does not make allowance for a childhood spent in the bush from the age of six, without any formal schooling. Carrie's father had done his best for her. His children and grandchildren in later years remembered his admonitions, even if they paid little attention to them at the time. He had very clear ideas as to how well brought up children should conduct themslves, especially young girls, and time and time again, when things got out of hand, he would say to them: 'A young lady would not behave in this way, or speak in this way.'

Caroline Sisam (Carrie) daughter of Walter.

The house in Whakatane built by William Parry (W.P.) Browne for Allie after their marriage. It is still in use.

Carrie had already met one of the Whakatane family a few months earlier. The newly engaged Allie had paid a visit to Arrow Farm at a time when Carrie had begun walking out with William Hieatt, a neighbouring farmer's son and a friend of her brother. Carrie and Allie no doubt had much to talk about together. None of the Waitakere family have left any recollections of Allie's visit, but her family remembers that she didn't care much for the pork that was offered to her. Allie was apparently an outspoken person with a mind of her own, and was an excellent cook, who became known for her cakes. Now that Carrie had come to Whakatane she renewed her acquaintance with Allie, as Allie and her husband W.P. Browne were living in the Sisam household until they made their own home.

Very soon after Carrie joined the Whakatane family, a visitor called at the house in connection with Alfred's work as Constable and Clerk of the Court. The visitor was Te Kooti, the former Maori war commander, who had to attend a meeting in the district with the Minister of Native Lands from Wellington. Te Kooti, as well as having been a remarkable general and war leader, was said to have a penchant for attractive females. He immediately took a fancy to Carrie. Maria described what happened:

'He came into the sitting-room and wanted us to have some beer with him, and the old rogue kissed Carrie's hand. I think him a wonderful man to have the power he has, both with white and black men. Twenty-two years ago we used to live in dread of him and there was one thousand pounds reward for his head and now he is free to roam about with his followers just as he pleases.'

Carrie was thrilled. Maria seems also to have fallen under the old warrior's spell, though it is said she terminated the coquetry rather abruptly much to Carrie's disappointment. Unfortunately Carrie does not seem to have had an entirely happy time at Whatakane. Somehow the family did not manage to reach her heart. The children were some years younger than Carrie, Lena being 16, May aged 14 and the boys younger still. Probably the children couldn't resist making fun of her ways, or teasing someone whom they discovered had a fiery temper. Maria's diary for October notes:

'Carrie has been four months with me and I have done everything in my power to teach her all I can. The children don't get on very well with her. I hear them nightly quarrelling in the bedroom and in the morning before they leave their bedroom. I have even heard Carrie stamp her foot with rage. May is just as bad only she is fooling while Carrie is in earnest.'

Not long after Carrie returned to Arrow Farm, she and William Hieatt became engaged. The Hieatts were an English family originating from the farming village of Souldern in Oxfordshire. It is a picturesque place quite near to the great estate of Aynho, and lies at the end of a quiet lane, which dwindles to a woodland footpath and vanishes into the trees.

It has changed very little since the 1850s when their ancestor, William Hooper Hieatt, lived there. The old church is still standing where Hieatts had been buried from at least the late 1600s. William moved to Lincolnshire in search of work, married there, and like so many country folk was forced by the agricultural depression to move to one of the fast-growing towns spawned by the industrial revolution. He settled at Mexborough, Yorkshire, not far from Sheffield, and went to work at iron smelting for 2s. 6d. a day. Life was hard for the family. His childen never had meat to eat and he could not afford to clothe them properly in winter as well as pay for their schooling. When, on a bitterly cold day, the school clerk told him to sell the children's petticoats to pay the school-fees he owed, William was so incensed that he there and then decided to emigrate to New Zealand. They left in 1883, father, mother and eight children. They travelled fourteen hours by train to the Devonshire port of Plymouth, having nothing to eat or drink on the journey. At Plymouth they boarded the steamship *Doric* for New Zealand, with only ten shillings in their pockets. As they came on shore at Auckland, the ten shillings was lost in the water when they came down the gang-plank.

William Hieatt was a man of character who did not allow misfortune or hardship to embitter him. He was also an upright man. Long before they left England he and his wife gave up taking the customary beer, which was cheaper than tea, simply because one day they found one of the children sipping it and feared she might become addicted, as many did. William lived to become one of the true family patriarchs of the country where his family had settled. When he died at the age of 88, a friend said of him, 'Mr. Hieatt never had nor did he ever desire any of this earth's material gifts, but he was, I think, the richest man I ever met.'

William Hieatt's first job in New Zealand had been at the Onehunga ironworks. After about four years there, he took a forty-acre farm plot near Swanson, not far from the Sisams of Arrow Farm. Walter Henry became good friends with young William Hieatt. The two would go out on jobs together wherever there was work to be had in the district. Walter Henry also worked for his father at Arrow Farm during this time, for wages, but there was not enough of that work to support him, so the two young men took on anything that was going – digging for kauri gum (used for making varnish), road-building, bush-felling, corn-cutting and mill-work.

Carrie came to know William Hieatt quite well so it was natural that they should become sweethearts. On the death of her mother Carrie had taken on the running of the household at Arrow Farm, and had continued this faithfully for four years. Carrie and William married in 1892 and set up house at Avondale, between Henderson and Auckland, a few miles from Arrow Farm.

In Swanson, the nearest settlement to Arrow Farm, there was now a permanent store, from which Walter fetched supplies, and a church in which he preached. On one of his preaching trips across the hills, Walter had met a woman named Nellie Hewitson at a church gathering at the Pomona Hall, Taupaki, where her family had connections. She was well educated and had been to a ladies' boarding school at Bamburgh, Northumberland, in England. She was 43 and he was 51. They were married in February 1893, the year after Carrie's wedding. The intrepid Nellie journeyed into the bush and took on the running of the home, where she soon made her mark.

Nellie and Walter had a good deal in common as she came from a Christian family. She made a good home for him, 'attractive, with comfortable and cleanly surroundings', as he put it. There was a religious calendar on the wall, which was renewed every year. There had always been a spiritual influence in the home. This did not dampen the ardour of youth. There was another wedding the following year. Walter Henry married William Hieatt's sister, Fanny Jane, in Auckland in May, 1894. Walter Henry had managed to buy a hundred acres not far from Arrow Farm, when some government land came up for sale, and there the couple settled. Later they moved near Thames, where Fanny Jane had relations. Walter and Nellie during this time made a home at Arrow Farm for Nellie's elderly mother, who was bedridden. Walter put a ceiling into the house at that time to make it nicer for her, and he and Nellie looked after her until she died. She was the first person to be buried in the Sisam plot in the new burial ground at Swanson

Walter and Nellie Sisam.

16
Two Valley Farms

ALFRED ACQUIRES FARMLAND – DEATH OF WALTER

The year 1894 had been a happy one at Arrow Farm, with three family weddings in just over two years. But for the Whakatane Sisams, on the other hand, 1894 was a year in which troubles came thick and fast. Two of Maria's married daughters, Allie and Tottie, were going through difficult times with illnesses, frequent childbirths and miscarriages. Tottie's husband, Jack Lamont, was quite ill, and at Whakatane Maria's eldest son, the semi-invalid Alfy, was far from well. Alfy had been born a perfectly healthy baby but suddenly became ill. Some think he may have been dropped as an infant, but it is probable he caught some infection. Maria's diary records these days:

'Jan. 7th. 1894. Allie's baby arrived today. Poor little love. He has taken to us all, and is quite happy.

'Jan. 25th. Alfy still very ill.

'July 21st. A telegram from Lena saying Jack is worse. I suppose it means the end. Poor boy, he has had a sad time. It seems dreadful for one so young to be taken away from his wife and family. Again I pray God help them. It will be a sad holiday for my poor Lena, too, but I think God put it into her heart to go just at this time so as she would comfort poor Tottie. I am thankful Alfy is better and quite himself again. Poor Mrs. Buckworth left here for Tauranga with her baby ill.

'July 22nd. Mrs. Buckworth's baby died on the way up. I am sorry for the poor soul.

'August 2nd. A telegram telling us poor Jack died today.

'Nov. 1st. I was called to Mrs. Creek tonight.

'Nov 7th. Mrs. Creek died this morning at half-past four. If there's a heaven she is there. Last month Tottie ran down from Auckland just to see us. I really forget the date. She came and went by the same steamer.

We have had a letter from her telling us Allie is with her. Has seen the Dr. She is going to have an other baby. It seems just dreadful. She was getting on nicely and then for this to happen. It is just a case of murder on one side and suicide on the other.'

This is the last entry that Maria wrote in her diary. On July 22 the following year, 1895, she died at the age of 48, possibly a victim of the hardships and stresses of a pioneering existence. She is buried in the Whakatane cemetery, which has both Pakeha (European) and Maori graves.

The responsibility for the home at Whakatane, bereft of the capable hand that had ruled and ministered to it, now devolved upon Lena, age 20, the eldest of the unmarried daughters, closely supported by her younger sister, 17 year old May. As Lena also ran the Whakatane Post Office and operated the telephone, May carried a great deal of the running of home. The rest of the household consisted of their father, Alfred John, and the boys –

John A.C. Lamont (Jack).

Maori headstones in the Whakatane Cemetery and beyond them in the distance the white headstone of Maria Sisam.

the sickly Alfy, now aged 23, Lennie 16, Walter 15, and the youngest one, Kenneth ('Ken'), who was 7.

May was an attractive person. She had inherited the family good looks and had dark hair and sparkling eyes. She was somewhat scatter-brained and unconventional, but the family survived. She was highly entertaining. Nothing seemed to bother her and she appeared not to have a care in the world. In order to help the family, Maria's younger sister, Emma, and her husband, Edward Woodford, took young Kenneth to live with them for a spell at Opotiki. Emma described the boy as, 'funny little Kenneth Sisam', having discovered him one day sitting forlornly amongst the lupins in the Opotiki sandhills, eating something from the family larder.

Not long after Maria's death, an event occurred the following year which was to have a profound effect on the family's future. In 1896 the Government offered a large area of land to the public by ballot, in blocks ranging from 50 to 315 acres. It lay in the Opouriao Valley about ten or so miles south of Whakatane and had been confiscated from the Tuhoe tribe during the Maori War. The Sisams had no land as, unlike the military settlers, Alfred did not receive any grant on the termination of his war service. A verbal promise had been made to the men of the Colonial Defence Force that they would have the same land privileges as the military settlers, but there was no written record of this and it was conveniently forgotten. A considerable number of families in Whakatane put in for the 1896 land ballot. One member of the Sisam family was lucky and drew a plot of 100 acres. The lucky person was Tottie, now the widowed Mrs.O.M. Lamont, who had recently lost her husband, Jack. She at once gave the property to Alfred for the family's use. He sent his two sons, Leonard Wilfrid and Walter Holtom, to clear the land and cultivate it. The property was in a fertile valley and seemed only to need enterprise and hard work to make it a profitable undertaking.

Another event of that year which stirred the community was the violent death of a gifted artist and writer named James Forsyth, a Scotsman in his early thirties. He was a familiar figure in the district, who frequented the waterfront bar of the Whakatane Hotel with a few companions and lived alone in a shack amongst the sand dunes by Ohiwa Bay. He had contributed articles to various newspapers and did attractive watercolour sketches. No one knew his origins, but it was believed that he was a remittance man, whose family in Britain had paid him to disappear abroad. He had become attracted to Lena, who by now had grown to be a tall and elegant young woman. He called at least once at the house and wrote her a number of letters with delightful illustrations. He also sent her a small book of his writings and sketches, but the friendship developed no further. Shortly afterwards James Forsyth was found lying dead in his shack with an axe in his skull. An inquest was held and a verdict of suicide was returned. Friends erected a tombstone to him on the sea shore. This has survived and has been rescued from the shifting sands. Not many relics of him remain: amongst them are some framed watercolours he gave to one of his friends, and the charming book of paintings and his illustrated letters that Lena kept. Recently Forsyth's art has attracted the notice of local historians. Some years later Lena married a young Auckland optician, Edward von Sturmer, whose father was the Anglican Rector of Heapham, in Lincolnshire, England. Edward and his brother had both emigrated from England to New Zealand, and his brother became editor of the *New Zealand Herald*.

Meanwhile, in the Opouriao Valley, Leonard Wilfrid and Walter Holtom were making progress on their one hundred acres. It was alluvial land, flat and in grass, with no

The Opouriao Valley.

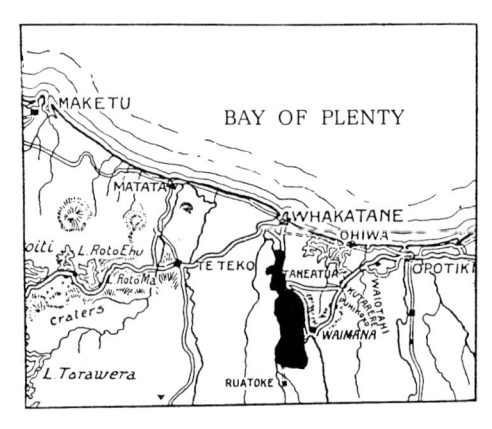

The whole of the Opouriao Estate (shaded in black).

Plot Number 2 of the Opouriao Estate won by Tottie in the Ballot. Next to it is Plot Number 3 (Hautapere) which the family later bought.

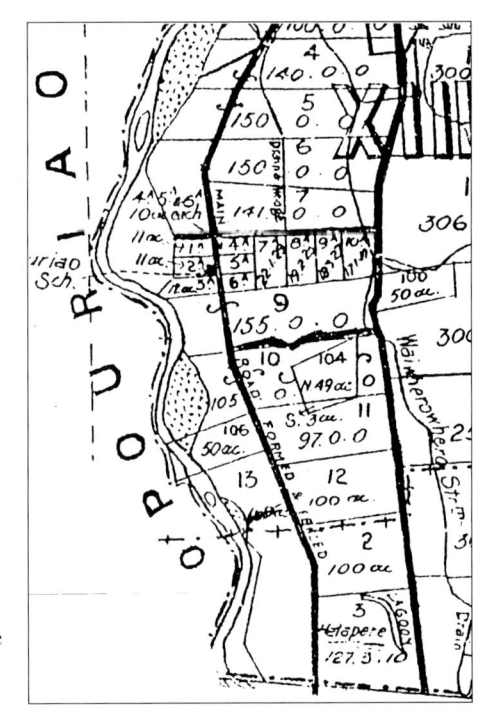

intersecting streams, but there were springs near the surface and a lagoon on the southerly boundary. It adjoined the main road and was already fenced on that frontage. Within the next two years the family were able to buy a further block of 300 acres in the valley from an absentee owner. This included further flat, grass land, that was well watered and some bush and fern-covered hills.

Their mode of life was simple and spartan. They lived in a 'bach' (bachelor camp or shack) doing for themselves. Their first undertaking was to plant maize. There were no tractors in New Zealand at that time and very little farm machinery in the Opouriao area. Ploughing was with horses and many farmers had to sow seed by hand. Maize was usually sown in October-November, during the spring, when the frosts were over. Their first crops were encouraging, but in the next two years there were freak frosts, some lasting right up to Christmas Day in the height of what was normally the summer season. Crops were almost totally destroyed. This experience made the Sisams switch to cattle-raising. They bought stock in Gisborne and drove them across open country and through the Waioeka Gorge to be fattened on the farm. Later they were driven to the railhead at Rotorua, where they were sold for transport to Auckland. There were no roads or bridges on the trails. Swamps had to be negotiated and rivers to be crossed by swimming. It meant long hours in the saddle, making camp in the evening, and moving on at first light the next day. The experience gave them a unique understanding of horsemanship which was to last them the rest of their lives.

Their youngest brother, Ken, after his stay with the Woodfords at Opotiki, had returned home and was now going to school at Whakatane. The school in those days, was very small and not much to look at. The family described it as 'a storage shed'. Whatever it may have lacked as a school was compensated for by the atmosphere in the home. It was culturally stimulating. There was always music, for Lena was an accomplished musician. She was a gifted person and it was she who formed Ken's early life. It was she who brought him up and was his favourite sister.

During this period, Alfred was driving one day along the sandy shore at nearby Ohope with Ken when they met Te Kooti. Te Kooti was on horseback. Ken was scared of Te Kooti and afraid that he might say something which would offend the old warrior. Alfred and Te Kooti fell into conversation. Te Kooti suddenly stopped and, looking down at young Ken, said 'Your boy looks hungry. Do you think he would like a nice piece of plum cake?' Whereupon he put his hand into his saddlebag and produced the cake, which Ken happily demolished.

The Sisams were all avid readers. The big event for them was always the arrival at the local library of new books from England. Ken developed a liking for books and became a keen reader. Then there was the sea, which was to become another of his absorbing interests. He began to enjoy himself with boats and sea fishing. This caused some alarm as Whakatane, like Opotiki, had a dangerous bar near its harbour mouth. His father became anxious for his safety. In addition to this, Ken had cut his head badly in some accident. To keep him out of mischief, Alfred John sent him up to the farm to be with his two older brothers. This was in 1897. He was ten at the time and, although it was a solitary existence, roughing it in the open air probably did him a great deal of good. In their Whakatane home the Sisams had always had a good selection of books. The 'library' at the farm was not so extensive. It consisted of: Prescott's *History of Peru*, Josephus' *History of the Jews*, a translation of Victor Hugo's *Les Miserables*, a volume of

Restoration Plays, and the *Encylopedia of the Horse and its Diseases*. Of these *Les Miserables* was Walter's favourite. Ken's was the *Encyclopedia of the Horse*. He read it again and again. He knew everything there was to be known about the horse. On the farm, the only other book-learning he acquired was at the tiny local village school at Opouriao, which he was now attending. There was only one teacher. He was a highly intelligent young man who was saving up to train as a doctor. Under his care, for which Ken was always deeply grateful, the boy had the chance to develop unusual intellectual qualities.

From time to time Ken had a holiday with the Woodfords at Opotiki. Emma Woodford was astonished at his voracious appetite. At the mealtable he would cram his mouth full of food, then, resting his chin on the table, would slowly chew what was in his mouth. She commented, 'I've never seen a boy eat like he did'. Once they took him to the Auckland Agricultural Show. He wasn't particularly interested in it, but scooped up all the food he could and disappeared into the bush with it, plus a book. But, in the course of time, his appetite seemed to decrease. In fact, he became unusually abstemious. At the farm, when walking to school, he would usually give his lunch packet to a dog he had made friends with which used to wait for him at spot where the path crossed a stream. As he grew older, this practice of abstemiousness remained with him and going without lunch became a habit.

Ken spent four years at the farm, where he helped his brothers with the work. It gave him a knowledge of farming and a genuine fondness for animals. He described the shack in which they lived as 'a kind of square box without any furniture'. The day started at 4 a.m. and Kenneth did much of the cooking, including plenty of custard. At the end of the four years he astonished the family by winning a scholarship to Auckland Grammar School. This happened for several reasons. One was that a system existed by which scholarships were reserved for children from country schools with only one master, like Opouriao. The other was that the young schoolmaster was a good teacher, and Ken was undoubtedly clever.

Winning a scholarship was one thing, getting a young boy to Auckland and back was another. There were three possibilities. There was the paddle steamer which travelled up the coast but might at any time be forced to seek shelter from sudden bad weather. There was no food on board, other than a coil of sticky pudding off which pieces could be torn, or perhaps if the steamer were badly delayed a sheep could be had from a farmer en route by putting into some harbour. The voyage could take as long as a week. Another possibility was to ride alone about a hundred miles across barren and uninhabited country to Rotorua and take a train; but it was a difficult ride as the 1886 eruption of Mount Tarawera had laid waste the country, leaving only one mountain pass open which was just wide enough for one horse to pass through. The third way, which Ken preferred, was to ride with his brothers when they were droving sheep or cattle to Auckland.

When he started at Auckland Grammar School he soon found there was a great deal he did not know. He was backward in certain subjects, for instance in mathematics, compared with the other boys, who were mainly city dwellers. In one maths class the question came up as to which was the Derby winner at some date in the 1870s. Ken instantly knew it, but gained no credit for only knowing that kind of information.

English became his special subject at school. It happened because he and his classmates wanted to outdo a particularly bright boy who was always coming top in every subject. They couldn't stand it, so they agreed that each would specialise in one subject in which to beat him. English fell to Ken and he set about mastering it. The boys' plot worked and the poor fellow who had been top never recovered his nerve. This was the beginning of Ken's deep interest in English. About the same time he discovered Anglo-Saxon. Browsing in the Auckland Public Library he came across the first fascicle (instalment) of the Oxford *New English Dictionary*, which was coming out in monthly parts. Pouring over it he became fascinated by the subject of language.

While at school in Auckland Ken lived with the Farquhar family, whose niece Naomi he was later to marry. He only went home for the long summer holidays. With the rough overland tracks and the slow, uncertain transport, it was not worth making the journey at other times. The summer holidays, which included Christmas, he spent at his home in Whakatane with his father, Alfred John, and his sisters Lena and May, and the invalid Alfie. He no doubt visited the Opouriao farm and would have seen a good deal of his two older brothers, Len and Walter. In Whakatane he was reunited with his beloved dog, Hutter, a clever but failed sheepdog. In the evenings, he would take his elder sister Lena rowing when she had finished her day's work in the Post Office. After he had gone back to school, Hutter would go down to the Whakatane wharf to meet every steamer from Auckland in the hope of seeing his master return.

By now Alfred John's very active life in the saddle and his exposure to the elements and the hazards of cross-country despatch riding had begun to tell on him. The frequent crossing of rivers with the water over his saddle had seriously affected his legs with rheumatism, so that eventually he could scarcely mount his horse and needed help to dress himself. Even the thermal waters of Rotorua failed to help. In November 1897 he resigned from the Mounted Police, with a year's pay. It meant moving out of the official Constabulary residence which had been the family home since they first came to Whakatane. He probably went to live in one of the three cottages he owned opposite the Constabulary. May continued to keep house for them all and he was able to continue his close interest in the progress of the farm. Several of the family lived within easy reach: Len married and moved from the farm to King Street, whilst Walter remained at Opouriao. Allie and her husband W.P. Browne were also in Whakatane. In 1905 Lena married and went to live with her husband, Edward von Sturmer, in Auckland where they had two chidren, May and Maude. During his retirement Alfred served as a Justice of the Peace, from 1908 for eight years. Alfie died in 1913. In 1916 Alfred finally retired from participation in the affairs of the farm and went with May to live next door to Lena in Woodside Road in the Mount Eden district of Auckland.

Young Ken meanwhile had for some time being spending the shorter school holidays not far from Auckland with his Uncle Walter and Aunt Nellie at Arrow Farm in the Waitakeres. There is an old photograph of Arrow Farm and its setting as Ken would have known it. It shows some of the terrain, the rising ground and surrounding forest, and some of the farm sheds, with figures in the foreground. On the left is one of the farmhands (there were two) and, on the right, Nellie is holding a pet lamb, the farm having started to raise sheep. Walter is in the middle distance, leaning on his stick, and looking quite elderly.

It was a contrast to cosmopolitan Auckland, but Ken was accustomed to bush life and enjoyed being at the farm. He fished in the river and one day appeared at the farmhouse carrying a huge eel, with its head dangling down his shoulder and its tail trailing along the ground behind him. At the same time, he could not help remarking on the unusual mode of

In the evenings Kenneth would take his elder sister Lena rowing, when she had finished her day's work in the Post Office.

Caroline Marshall Sisam (Lena).

Arrow Farm in the early 1890s showing the surrounding forest terrain. In the distance Walter stands with his stick. Nellie is with the sheep on the right.

life at the farm. He noted that his uncle, who had strict notions about the sabbath, would not pull up thistles on a Sunday however much they proliferated, and instead built a cairn of stones over them so that he could go back and eradicate them on Monday. Ken also thought the method of dealing with the live stock rather quaint. In the autumn the cows were turned loose in the bush until the spring, when the dog would be sent in to bring them home. It appeared to Ken that the dog would set off but spend the day sleeping behind the first bush he found. Nevertheless, he and his uncle got on well together, and Walter always spoke of the boy with genuine affection. Ken was about 15 at this time and had some first hand knowledge of farming, and would certainly be aware that his uncle was getting on in years. In fact a few years later, Walter sent for his son Walter Henry to return to the farm with his family and help manage it. In his observations Ken was reflecting the view that the Alfred Sisams took of Walter and his farming efforts, but neither Ken nor his family may have appreciated the problems of that particular farm.

❖ ❖ ❖

Although Walter Henry, Walter's married son, had been settled near Thames for some years, he responded loyally to his father's request for help, knowing that someday he would have to take on the property. He and his family made the journey from Thames to Arrow Farm in January 1907. They took the paddle steamer from Thames to Auckland and from there the newly opened railway to Swanson, thence the five miles over the hills to the farm. By now Walter Henry and Fanny had three children, Martha Mary, aged 11, Ivy Rose, 6, and Walter Leonard, 1½ years old.

This final part of the journey through the bush took some time, and it was getting late. It was especially tiring for Fanny, as little Walter Leonard would not leave his mother, and she had to carry him the whole distance. In the darkness the party lost their way and managed to get on the wrong side of the creek. As they neared the farm, Walter Henry called out in the darkness. Almost immediately they saw the welcoming glow of a lantern as Walter senior opened the door of the farmhouse. He came down to the creek and guided them to the bridge, which took them safely across the water and home.

With a larger family at the farm, additional living space was now needed. There is an entry in Walter Henry's diary for September 27th of that year which chronicles the steps they took: 'Began again to work for father at 25/- per week. Started to saw timber for his house.' This refers to the building of a new house for Walter and Nellie a little further down the valley. Walter Henry hired a carpenter named Upton, known locally as 'Tuppie', and the two of them set about felling some of the remaining kauri trees on the farm, and cuttiing up the timber with a two-handled long-saw in a saw pit. The hollow shape of the pit and the two kauri-log end-supports were still to be seen there in the 1980s. The house was completed before the end of the year 1907. Then Walter Henry began work on a separate house, this time higher up the valley, for himself and his family. It was known as the Cottage.

Building a new house was a major expense for Walter, but it was made possible by a loan from his younger brother, James Leonard Sisam at Arrow Mill in England. James Leonard had inherited the lease of the Mill from his father and was now running the

Walter's original house and the new one built in 1908.

business. It was a reasonably prosperous undertaking, so that he was in a position to help. He and Walter had been very close in their early years and Walter had a special regard for this younger brother, who named one of his own sons after him. In due course the family repaid the loan.

Living close to their grandfather was a new experience for Walter Henry's children. At first they were somewhat overawed by his solemnity and strict behaviour, and were usually very careful what they said in his presence. He was rather a puzzle to them and they could not understand his studious preoccupations. 'Grandfather is ever sitting writing', they used to say. But they found he had a kind heart and a sense of humour, and could laugh at himself. He was working outdoors one day with the children playing nearby, and said to them, 'Go up to the shed and get the whatsit for me.' They were mystified but went to the shed to look for it. They couldn't find it so went back to him. He said, ' It's on the thingamy'. Then, seeing their blank looks, he realised why they could not understand what was wanted. He laughed and went to get it himself. The children helped on the farm, which, in addition to cattle and chickens, now carried sheep, for which a shearing platform had been set up near the original farmhouse. But the farm was plagued with thistles. The burrs caught in the sheep's fleeces so, before shearing, the children were sent to pick off the burrs one by one. It was a task they remembered for a very long time to come.

Unfortunately and perhaps understandably, Walter Henry and his father sometimes had strong differences of opinion and heated arguments ensued. The older man was a firm believer in keeping chickens, but Walter Henry could not abide them. Once, in exasperation, Walter Henry was on the point of hitting his father when Fanny stepped between them. Walter Henry quickly realised he was getting into dangerous waters. He said to Fanny afterwards, 'Thank you, Fanny. I could have regretted what I might have done.' Both father and son were carrying the burden of a farm that was not really viable, and felt the strain of it. The soil was poor and the terrain difficult and neither man was physically fit. Walter had arthritis and was feeling his years, and Walter Henry had an unsuspected heart condition.

As far as spiritual matters were concerned, Walter Henry did not follow the same pattern as his father. There were no evening prayers in Walter Henry's household, nor was there grace at meals. Walter Henry took the view that a man should thank God at all times, and not just at mealtimes. He was a man with a definite faith. But, as with every new generation, he needed to find his own way and follow his own inner conviction.

Sadly, in 1909 Nellie became ill. Doctors were not within easy reach, and at first the family thought the illness was a passing one and not serious. But when Walter sent a detailed account of the symptoms to a doctor, the resulting diagnosis was that there was no hope of recovery. Nellie died in December 1909. Walter continued to live in the farmhouse by himself, and Walter Henry and Fanny arranged for the two girls, Martha Mary and Ivy Rose, to go down each morning and do the outside chores for him. When they had finished they would call to their grandfather, 'All's well', and he would answer them. Sometimes he would come to the door with a sweet for each. Then they ran off, eager to follow their own pursuits. They were not to know that he would only be with them for a little longer. In later years they wished they had spent more time with him in his last solitary days.

One April day the following year, household supplies were getting low and a trip to Swanson was necessary. Walter Henry was unable to go as he had injured his leg. Fanny was going to be away on a visit all day with young Walter Leonard, so it was decided that Ivy Rose would accompany Grandfather, who also wanted to get some chicken feed. Martha was to stay and keep house. The memory of that day remained vividly with Ivy Rose:

'Grandfather was going to the store at Swanson and I was going with him. Martha gave me a little list of goods to get and we set off. As we passed Meikle's place, we saw that Mrs. Meikle was saddling up their horses and she said I could ride on their packhorses, which I did. On the return journey, Grandfather left first and Mrs. Meikle and I caught up with him going up Redhill. Grandfather had to walk his horse, Rangi, the whole distance of 5 miles, because the horse was so loaded up with packages, one big one right on the top of the saddle. As we passed him, he told me to be sure to feed the fowls when I got home. I said that I would and promptly forgot all about the request. Those fowls never did get fed on that day, April 28, 1910.'

Martha remembered that evening: 'Towards evening as darkness approached, we became a little concerned because Grandfather did not appear. It was dark when Ned Meikle, the son of our neighbour, half a mile away, came to us and told Father that his mother had found Grandfather lying dead by the unopened gate past the cutting. Rangi his horse, was cropping the grass nearby.' Walter was lying there beneath a large and beautiful Puriri tree and Mrs. Meikle was much struck by the peace and beauty of the scene. She said afterwards to the family, 'Don't worry about where he has gone. He had the most beautiful look on his face when I found him.'

A stretcher was made out of sacking and all the family went up to bring the body home to the farmhouse. The next morning, everyone was astir early as Walter Henry had to make his way to Auckland to report the death, and the two girls were to go to the farmhouse to see to the chores. This included milking the cows and meant taking the milk into the dairy inside the house. Ivy didn't want to go in the house, but her father reassured her: 'Your Grandfather would never have harmed you when he was alive and most certainly would not do so now.' With that, they went off contented to their duties. In some ways Walter's death marked the end of an era. The period of pioneering was over, and it was time to reassess.

A few months after Walter's death, his nephew Kenneth, who had spent school holidays at Arrow Farm, was, at the age of 23, preparing to go to England. During his six years at Auckland Grammar School he had gone from strength to strength. It was a first rate school academically. From it he had won a scholarship to the University College of Auckland, where in due course he became President of the Students' Association and graduated as Bachelor of Arts in English, Latin, French, Maths, Jurisprudence and Constitutional History. He then sat for his M.A. and graduated in English and Latin with first class Honours. In English, he had been fortunate to be tutored in Anglo-Saxon by Phillip Arden, who had recently studied at Oxford and had read English there at a time when Anglo-Saxon was a comparatively new subject. The press reported: 'Professor Egerton, English Professor at Auckland University College, writes that he believes Mr Sisam to be in many respects the most promising student that he has ever had.' After gaining his M.A. Kenneth was awarded the coveted Rhodes Scholarship to Oxford University. This was on account not only of his academic excellence but also his proficiency at sport. He had done remarkably well at both rugger and cricket, and had proved himself at tennis and hockey. He was the opening batsman not only at Auckland Grammar School, but also at Auckland

University. In addition, he was a fine leg-break bowler. He had practiced as such so regularly and methodically that he could drop a cricket ball on a halfcrown coin at will. It was as a leg-break bowler that he was offered the chance of being trained to play professionally for Australia, but academic studies were more important to him.

He set off for England in 1910, and went first to the Priory, Alcester, where he stayed with his uncle and aunt, James Leonard and Letitia Sisam, James Leonard having recently retired from Arrow Mill. Here, with the help of his aunt Letitia, he kitted himself out with such things as silverware, cutlery and the various requisites of a university undergraduate about to take up residence in an ancient and distinguished Oxford college. Kenneth took up his quarters there in the early autumn, when the leaves were turning yellow and red in the waning warmth of the sun, and the soft evening mists were heralding the chills and damps of the approaching English winter.

❖❖❖ 17 ❖❖❖
Across the River

Farm Expansion – 'Sisam & Sons'

The two brothers, Walter and Alfred Sisam had both acquired land in New Zealand at different times and under different circumstances. Walter's farm began with an outright purchase; Alfred's was an unexpected windfall, a quirk of fate, as it were. Walter's farm in the Waitakere seemed to be idyllic but unfortunately it was not profitable. Alfred's land at Opouriao was also in a pleasant location, but it was fertile and had potential. Both farms were near rivers, but in the Opouriao Valley the Whakatane River flowed through broad, flat pasture, whereas the Waitakere River cut through rough hilly country, in which there were few level areas.

In the Opouriao Valley, Alfred's two sons were fortunate in their switch to cattle-raising. It proved a commercial success. However, from the outset when the family had first acquired the property, Alfred had stipulated that any profit should be ploughed back into the farm and not spent on the luxuries of life; and so it was. Within ten years the two brothers and their father had prospered sufficiently to increase their holding to a total of 527 acres. This was through the purchase in 1904 of the plot next to their original one, which an elderly farmer and his wife were vacating. It was known as Hatapere and was described in the sale notice as 'excellent alluvial flat, in grass' and included a ten acre lagoon 'which could easily be dried by deepening the present drain.' There was a lived-in house already on the site.

The following year, 1905, Len married. His bride was Mabel Jane McGarvey. The McGarveys, on their Irish father's side, had long been traders in the Bay of Plenty area, and in Whakatane they kept the general store. They were near neighbours of the Sisams, and Mabel's mother and Len's mother had been good friends since the Sisams first came to Whakatane in 1891. As a boy of twelve, at the Whakatane School, Len had sat next to Mabel. On her mother's side, Mabel had historic Maori connections. Her great grandmother was Princess Puihi Ruawahine who was directly descended from the Maori Chief Toroa, commander of the war canoe *Matatua*, one of the seven Polynesian war canoes that colonised New Zealand in the 14th century.[13] The *Matatua* reached Whakatane, and the landing is commemorated by a full-scale replica canoe, placed beneath the great Pohaturoa rock in the centre of the town, and by a plaque on the sea-shore. Princess Puihi was of the Ngati-te-Rangi tribe which lived in the Tauranga area, and, in the Maori War, fought vigorously for the Maori cause not only in that area but on other fronts far from their home base. They are the tribe who were involved in the battle of the Gate Pa, Tauranga, in 1864, where they won the respect of their opponents for their courage and humane treatment of prisoners.

As a young woman, Mabel was a brilliant horsewoman, sharing Len's love of horses,

Historical plaque on the seashore at Whakatane, commemorating the landing of the 'Matatua' canoe in 1340 bearing one of Mabel McGarvey's Polynesian ancestors.

and was a fine Maori scholar, speaking the language fluently. The blending of their two backgrounds made it an intriguing marriage, not least on account of the participation of Len's father, Alfred John, in the Maori War, Alfred's involvement with Maori affairs after the war, and his acquisition by ballot of former Maori land. There was some opposition to the marriage, not so much on racial grounds but from the fact that the McGarveys were Catholics. It seems that neither parents attended the wedding ceremony. Daniel McGarvey, Mabel's father, had gone away together with his family, and left the house locked with Mabel's wedding dress inside. The atmosphere was such that later when Len's sisters called on the new bride they were not made welcome. The memory of this lingered on for many years. It must have been a difficult beginning for the young couple as they set up house together.

Their first home was the Hatapere farmhouse at Opouriao, on farm land next to the original Sisam plot. It was a simple, one-story wooden building with living room, kitchen, a brick chimney, two bedrooms, and a verandah at the front. Next door was the bachelor shack Len and Walter had shared, and where Walter and the farmworkers continued to live. The two brothers worked closely together, and a picket gate gave easy access between the dwellings.

Len and Mabel made a happy life together in the Opouriao Valley. The nearest settlement was Taneatua village, reached by the road running the length of the valley. Approaching the village the road crossed the Waimana River by a ford not far from its junction with the Whakatane River. Mabel used to drive to Taneatua regularly with the horse and buggy, and at the ford the water was often so high that it would flow through the buggy. Four childen were born there in the next years, Leonard Alfred (Pete), Doris Mabel, Mona, and Harold Walter(Mannie). The farm prospered. Cattle raising and dealing increased. Len and Walter continued buying stock in Gisborne for fattening at Opouriao. Horses were an important feature of the farm. Clydesdales, which were to play such a vital part in the future, had been introduced for the first time as work-horses, as also were hacks for riding. Len set up a breeding stud for both under the name Hatapere. Local farmers would hire the stallions. It was probabaly about this time that they started a herd of Aberdeen Angus beef cattle. The valley now had a flourishing annual Agricultural Show to which the Sisams contributed cash prizes as well as participating, and Sisam-bred horses took part in the races. There were also regular Sheep Dog Trials, which Walter helped to organise.

For the two brothers the years ahead were to be years of expansion, made possible by dedication and sheer hard work over twenty years or more, and by their father's foresight and ever-watchful eye. As a result 'Sisam and Sons', the name of the partnership under which the family operated, was ready when a potentially golden opportunity presented itself. In 1914 a block of over 10,500 acres of land on the other side of the Whakatane River became available for purchase. It lay in and around the adjoining valley of the Owhakatoro, another tributary of the Whakatane river. Alfred, with Len and Walter, put in a bid under the name 'Sisam and Sons' for certain sections of the new land. Their assets at the time were reckoned at £50,000. The property consisted of fertile river flats, and hilly slopes covered in bush. It was traditional Maori land and contained a number of ancient

Leonard Wilfred and Walter Holtom played an active part in local agricultural shows and competitions.

pas in which artifacts were often found. It had been held originally by the Tuhoe tribe, a number of whom lived in the nearby Urewera Forest, and had been confiscated from the Tuhoe by the Government during the second Maori War. The Sisams acquired some acres of this land and also made an offer to purchase 5,000 acres then owned by the Ngati Awa tribe. But since, according to Maori custom, the ownership was communal, it took some time to negotiate these purchases with all the parties involved. It was not until 1918 that the purchases were finally concluded.

In the meantime, in 1914, Walter had married. He met his bride-to-be, Rose Stansfield Allen, in Whakatane while she was there on a visit. Her father owned and operated a banana-plantation in Fiji. The wedding was held, in Suva Cathedral, Fuji, where Rose used to play the organ. Gifted and musical, she had lived a protected life in a home that had plenty of servants, as was the custom in planter households. For her the move to the Opouriao farm was a dramatic change. But she was very game and ready for adventure. She was once asked whether she found coming to the farm a daunting experience. Her answer was: 'No, it was Romance with a capital 'R'!' She and Walter moved into the simple Hatapere farmhouse, which Len and his family had now vacated. Len had bought a house on the edge of Whakatane, which had come on the market. It had been built originally by Len's father-in-law, Daniel McGarvey, for his wife Jane. With it came 15 acres of land. It was a good central place for Len as the senior son in the family. It enabled him to keep in touch with local business and farming affairs, and with his father Alfred. At the same time he could continue to work closely with his brother Walter in the running of the farm, and would go over to Opouriao most days.

In his retirement, Alfred contemplated the family prospects with equanimity. The farm was in the safe hands of his two sons Len and Walter, both of whom were married. Plans for the expansion of the farming enterprise into the Owhakatoro Valley were already beginning to be implemented. The future looked promising, and there were already grandchildren to continue the family line. But his mind ranged further than the well-being of his own family and their future. He thought of his brother Walter Sisam who had died a few years before at the Waitakere farm, and of his children and grandchildren, and the fact that Walter had had very little to leave to them apart from a subsistence farm. He thought especially of Walter's grandson, Walter Leonard, now a boy of nine. He knew that this was a crucial age when a boy's mind would soon begin to open out and reach for knowledge and experience as he progressed to manhood. He also knew that the future, bound as it was by the limitations of circumstances and situation, did not have very much to offer the boy. So, in 1915, the same year that plans were forming in Whakatane for the farm expansion, Alfred offered to have young Walter Leonard to live with him in Auckland, put him through Auckland Grammar School, and afterwards set him up in farming at Whakatane. It was a generous and exciting offer, and one that might set a boy's heart and mind astir.

How the offer was made is not known. Probably Alfred wrote a letter. The response must have been a surprise to him, perhaps a shock. The boy's parents were uncertain and declined the offer. Fanny Jane, his mother, was non-committal and said that the boy must decide. Walter Henry told his son he must do whatever he thought would make him happy. At this age it would have been difficult for a young boy to make such a decision on his own. Circumstances had been such that education was not something that had loomed large in the life of the family, and they may not have seen the point of it. The only education Walter Leonard received was what his mother and father gave him, for there was no school within reach of Arrow Farm. Perhaps it was felt that the farm would need him, or perhaps there was an understandable reluctance to accept charity from the more prosperous side of the family.

At the Opouriao Valley farm during these years Walter and Rose had begun to raise their children. A daughter, Dulcie Rose, was born first, and then another daughter, Joan Cecily. As was the custom, a local womam came in to attend the births. She was a Mrs. Kerr, whose first name was Cecily. She was the mother of a local farmer, and Joan Cecily was named after her. Within a year or so, in 1918 and 1919, the valley, like much of the rest of the world, was stricken by the epidemic of Asian 'flu. Fortunately all the Sisams survived it, but there were many deaths in Opouriao and the next and much larger village of Ruatoki. Many of the Maori people lived there, and the crowded conditions caused the disease to spread very rapidly. The Opouriao people, though they were suffering badly themselves, gave what help they could to the people in Ruatoki. Walter went into many of the whares, or cottages, and cut windows in them to let in fresh air, and Rose killed most of her hens to make broth for the sick.

In 1921 'Sisam and Sons' sold their last plot of the old Opouriao land, and Walter and his family finally crossed the river to make a new home on the land they had acquired in the Owhakatoro Valley. They had waited the better part of seven years for legal formalities to be completed. It was a daring move because once across the river the family would be cut off, since as yet there was no bridge across and often the rapidly rising water could be dangerous to navigate. The river had to be crossed either by boat or on horseback. Some of the village women thought the Sisams were out of their mind to go there, and said that they would not live there for all the tea in China. Dulcie, who was six years old at the time of the move, remembered the event very clearly. What struck her was how tiny the house was. It was, she said, 'a pokey, little house'. A double bed occupied the whole width of the main bedroom, and you could only get into bed by climbing over the foot. They were all in fact waiting for a new house to be built. It must have been a squeeze in the meantime. There were already four children: Dulcie, Joan and Walter John, and a new-born baby, Allen Leonard. As in most farmhouses of the time, the bath was an iron tub placed in front of the kitchen fire. At Christmas time there was great concern because the chimney was clearly so small that Santa Claus had no hope of getting down it, so the front door was left open all night for him. Fortunately in New Zealand Christmas is at the height of summer.

In the early years at Owhakatoro the Whakatane River ruled the lives of the whole family. Getting to school across the river was a problem as it was too dangerous for Dulcie to negotiate. So she was sent to stay with her aunt Lena in Auckland and went to school there. This was a wrench for a child so young. In later years, when the other children were ready for school, the reliable and competent Dulcie, aged 10, returned home and rowed them across by boat. The children walked the rest of the way barefooted through muddy paddocks to Taneatua village. In wintertime, the schoolmaster had a bucket of hot water ready for them so they could wash their feet and put on the shoes they had carried with them. Sometimes when the river was high they would miss school for weeks on end. As the family grew and money was short, they had to make do and mend. By this time they were in their new house. The only other children on their side of the river were Maori children, with whom they often played, and whose fathers probably worked on the farm. To feed the horses oats were grown. The children especially remembered the chaff-cutter used in the preparation of the feed. On Sundays, Rose would drive them all in a gig to the little church at Taneatua, crossing the river at a ford known as 'Sisam's Crossing', which was a good wide one opposite Old's Road. Rose also played the organ in the newly-built church. This was a change for her after playing in Suva Cathedral in Fiji.

It was a long time before there was a bridge across the river, so when the family bought their first car, an American Oakland, they had to leave it at Charlie Old's place and row across. When built in 1925, the bridge across the river at Pekatahi was intended only for the railway trains, but cars began to use it, straddling the tracks and running on the narrow planks on either side. Pressure from settlers resulted in its being converted to a combined road and rail bridge with full decking and sides, which was completed in 1928. Drivers of vehicles had to keep a sharp lookout for any sight or sound of a train approaching, for it was apt to come round a bend and loom up suddenly. It was with some trepidation therefore that Walter decided to bring the car all the way home and drive it across the bridge.

In 1926, on Easter Monday, disaster struck the homestead. The house caught fire and was burnt to the ground with practically everything in it. Fortunately everyone escaped without hurt, but all family papers and possessions were lost. Rose was away in Auckland at the time with two of the girls, Joan and the youngest, Isabel. Three of the children – Allen, Walter John and Dulcie – had been out for the day with their father, Walter Holtom, at an event in Taneatua, dressed in their best clothes. In the evening they returned home for supper. After supper they noticed an acrid smell of burning in the house. A thorough search was made but nothing was found, so they all went to bed thinking it was someone burning old tyres nearby. At eleven that night, Walter Holtom was woken by the sound of window glass breaking, and found the house ablaze. He promptly got the children out of bed and out of the house with their bedding to keep warm in the cool night air. Allen didn't wake up and was carried out wrapped in his bedclothes. Dulcie and the boys had put their clothes away before going to bed and so lost them. Their father had hung his over the foot of the bed and was the only one with clothing. He just had time to ring a neighbour, Charlie Old, who got out his horses and turned up to take the children back to his home, where Mrs. Old provided them with some clothes. The only things saved from the fire were a drawerful of bedding, Dulcie's doll and doll's pram, and some office records. Young Walter John remembered for the rest of his life standing near the clothes line, wrapped in a blanket, watching the fearsome flames leaping out of the upstairs windows. The heat was so intense that socks hanging out on the line, fifteen or twenty metres from the house, were burnt. Walter telephoned Rose in the early hours of the morning. Her immediate concern was for the children and then for the household belongings. Isabel remembered hearing her mother's stricken cry of 'Oh Wally, not everything, not everything', on hearing that all had been lost.

The young girl who worked for the family got out safely from her first floor bedroom, though the floorboards were very hot, the source of the fire being just below. Apparently, earlier in the day she had done the washing and, after clearing the ashes out of the firebox under the boiler, had put a partially burnt log back into the woodbox. When the family came back from Taneatua in the evening, Walter had put his saddle on that very woodbox. It was this that produced the strange smell of burning they had noticed.

A new single-story house was built after that, and this is still standing. It is situated on the site of the previous house, using the undamaged chimneys. It stands on rising ground just above the main farmyard buildings, beyond which a tree-lined avenue leads down

'In the task of clearing the bush from the steep hillsides the powerful Clydesdale draft horses were matchless.'

through meadows to the public road. Immediately behind the house is a steep hillside on which there are the remains of a fortified Maori Pa. This would have contained dwelling houses or whares, and as the Sisams began their cultivation of the surrounding land they often discovered Maori artifacts.

This land in the Owhakatoro Valley was different terrain from the Opouriao farm. Although it had similar alluvial flats of silt loam suitable for grazing or cultivation, much of it was hilly country of scrub and fern that had great potential for raising sheep. The hill country carried a soil derived from the volcanic ash fall-out of the Mount Tarawera eruption. Both soils responded well to fertilizer. There was also some virgin forest. In the task of clearing the bush from the steep hillsides the powerful Clydesdale draft horses were matchless; and later after discing and harrowing, when the slopes had been seeded and become pasture, the Clydesdales were again used to haul the sledges loaded with top-dressing. This was spread by hand as the men walked over the hillsides, replenishing their supplies from the sledges as they went.

The whole property now covered a considerable area, and totalled well over 10,000 acres. The possession of such an extensive farm demanded very hard work, and the expansion of the work-force, and it required careful management over many years to come. It was a challenge which was met by a spirited response. But there were difficult times, nevertheless, during the twenties and again in the thirties. As early as 1915 Len and Walter, together with other farmers in the district, had acted as guarantors in the setting up of a meat-freezing works at Whakatane. But in 1921, through mismanagement and technical failure, it ran into severe financial difficulties, and by 1924 went into liquidation. The guarantors were called upon to meet the liabilities. Many farmers were brought to the

Alfred John Sisam in his later years.

verge of bankruptcy, and many lost their properties. The Sisams lost their £500 investment, and money they had loaned to help another farmer to invest, as well as what was lost as guarantors. They managed to survive and over the next years were able to recoup their losses.

    The storm waves of these events were bound to have disturbed the placid surface of the Auckland household, where Alfred John was living. Although no longer able to be on the spot, Alfred John at least had the satisfaction of seeing the farm pull through these acute difficulties. He was a tireless letter-writer. He corresponded frequently with his youngest brother in England, James Leonard, who had continued at the old family home of Arrow Mill in Warwickshire. Above all he wrote every week to Kenneth, his own youngest son in

England, of whom he was justly proud. This he did for well over twenty years from the time Kenneth first went to Oxford in 1910 until the end of his life.

In Woodside Road, Auckland, Alfred John was well looked after by May who by now had learned how to handle her patriarchal father. She served him cheerfully and was not unduly put out if he hammered on the floor with his stick, when she had been out visiting and his morning coffee had not arrived on time. Like many elderly men he could be irascible. Once, when he had been unwell for a while and began to feel better, he went out for a walk. In the street he met an old friend from Whakatane days who had come to see how he was. When asked about his health, Alfred John replied, 'I'm very well, thank you, and I have no time to talk to you today now that I am well. You never came to see me when I was sick.'

He could be brusque like this, and even blunt, but he would tell the story to the family afterwards and laugh at himself. Having been a constable for many years he never lost the habit of admonishing and correcting others. It is said that some years earlier he met a man at a river-crossing who was standing for election and was anxious to have Alfred John's support. But Alfred dashed his hopes. 'I shall not vote for you' he said, 'because I don't think you are a suitable person to hold public office.' He was certainly a shrewd judge of character, yet he had a warm heart and a generous nature.

May, or 'Auntie Bunny' as she was affectionately known by her nephews and nieces, was a character in her own right, and had always been a great source of affectionate amusement to the rest of the family. She had strange ways about money. She disapproved of banks and would hide pound notes under cushions and in between the pages of books on the bookshelves. She once received a statement from her bank which read, 'No pounds, no shillings, no pence'. Yet she was especially sensitive to the material needs of others, and was extremely generous. Nothing seemed to dismay her. Once she received from a well-known shop an account stating, 'We venture to draw your attention to the fact that this is overdue'. She scrawled across the account, 'Nothing venture, nothing win' and returned it to the shop. Sometimes she was over-economical. She would say 'Never throw away an empty tea packet', for she always kept empty packets in a cupboard, so that if she ran out of tea she had the particles left in them for a reserve. May had something in her of the character of her vivacious grandmother, Mary Knights, in that she liked nice clothes and going out. There was not much scope for either when she lived in Whakatane. Much later in life she once bought a secondhand orange velvet dress, which she could not resist. It was covered with a mass of minute, scintillating ornaments. Her family and friends remembered it because as she moved she looked like 'a flash of lightning'.

Next door in Woodside Road, Lena's two daughters, Maude and May, had grown into attractive and able young women. May, the elder girl, passed music exams with honours and composed crossword puzzles for the *Auckland Star* when only a schoolgirl. Maude was also gifted musically. She worked for an insurance company. Sadly, both girls were stricken with a mental illness in the 1930s and had to spend the rest of their lives in an institution. Lena sought every line of medical advice, but in those days nothing could be done. She visited the girls faithfully every week for as long as she lived.

Alfred died in May 1928. His tombstone of black marble looks out over Auckland and the waters of the bay. It was a Maori tradition to bury chiefs on the hilltops. Like the Maori chiefs he too, as the chief of his clan, lies on a New Zealand hilltop.

Alfred John's last resting place in Hillsborough Cemetery overlooking Manukau Harbour, Auckland, is marked by a black marble headstone (centre foreground).

18
Forest Ranger

WALTER'S GRANDSON AND HEART'S CONTENT

With the passing of Alfred in 1928, both branches of the family had lost their pioneer forefathers, the two brothers, Alfred and Walter Sisam. When Walter died in 1910, many changes took place at the Waitakere farm. When his son, Walter Henry, inherited the property the sheep were disposed of, and Walter's beloved chickens. The farm was turned over to dairying. The small milking parlour was improved and an Alfa Laval cream separator installed, and very soon up to 25 cans of cream were being supplied daily to local customers. In winter some of this was delivered over the muddy tracks by horse-drawn sledge. The switch to dairying was a wise move and one which many farmers were making at that time. Arrow Farm, although it had several neighbours within reach, was still remote from the rest of the world. The main currents of contemporary life scarcely touched it, nor did the farm have many visitors. An exception was the arrival of Alfred's son, Walter Holtom Sisam, in 1914. Having recently married in Fiji he arrived at Arrow Farm carrying a huge basket of bananas from his father-in-law's plantation. The basket of bananas made a lasting impression on young nine-year-old Walter Leonard.

Under Walter Henry's care the farm improved, but he barely lived long enough to see the dairying fully established. It was his final legacy, for he died in 1920, only ten years after his father, at the age of 53, from heart trouble. Fanny Jane's brother, Fred Hieatt, the close boyhood friend of her husband Walter Henry, now urged her strongly to sell the farm on the grounds that whatever type of farming was adopted it was never likely to prosper sufficiently. But she stayed on, and her family with her. They were Martha Mary who was 25, Ivy Rose 21, and Walter Leonard 15, all able-bodied and capable between them of running the dairy. Some time earlier Fanny, who was a warm-hearted person, had taken charge of an abandoned baby girl, and cared for her. Later she adopted the child and called her Nancy. By now Nancy had grown into a promising young girl, and was a helpful member of the household.

There was still contact between the two branches of the family. Fanny and Ivy Rose used to visit Alfred John in Auckland during his latter years, and Lena next door to him. Unfortunately, as the older generation died out, there was less and less contact between the Waitakere family and the Whakatane folk. That a distancing should have occured between them is sad, though understandable.

For years now the area surrounding Arrow Farm had seen extensive foresting operations as timber companies felled more and more of the trees. This was now becoming a matter of public concern, as people became aware of the wholesale destruction of the environment for commercial purposes. In 1923 the Auckland City Council had been besieged with appeals to step in and prevent the destruction of the few remaining blocks of virgin bush near Auckland city. One of these blocks was just across the river from the Sisam farm. Some of it had already been felled, and the rest was due to be cut at any moment. The Kauri Timber Company. who then owned the bush, intended to blow up the Cascades waterfalls, a well-known local beauty spot, build a dam and float logs down the Waitakere River, but the City Council designated the whole area a protected Kauri Park, including Arrow Farm. The scheme allowed Fanny to remain at Arrow Farm for as long as she wished.

The standing kauri trees on the edge of the Sisam property were still being climbed for the valuable gum. The gum was exported and used extensively in the manufacture of varnish. It could be collected by tapping the tree or digging it from rotted tree trunks embedded in the ground. The tapping or 'bleeding ' of the trees was done using a very sharp folding knife with a 6 to 7 inch blade. The lowest branches were usually at about 80 feet above the ground. A young man came one day to climb the trees for gum. He did so with the aid of boots with toe spikes and climbing hooks for each hand. He had a fishing line tied to his belt which, when he was in position on the branch, he pulled up. Attached to the end of this was a strong rope and a wooden seat. This he later used to lower himself to the ground with his load of gum. He and Martha became acquainted. There was something romantic about him. He was born in New Zealand of Italian descent, his family having come originally from the fishing village of San Vito Chietimo in Italy. His name was Benjamin Copedo. They were married in 1926 and went to live near Waitakere station. About the same time a man named John Devenport came to work on the farm and took over the dairy herd. He married Nancy. About three years later a neighbour's son, Victor Christian, who had returned from the 1914–1918 war and had found his father's farm insufficiently productive, leased some additional grazing at Arrow Farm. He married Ivy Rose.

Until 1925 Fanny Sisam's son, Walter Leonard, had helped his sisters on the farm. In that year, when he was 20 years old, he was approached by the Auckland authorities and asked to become a Forest Ranger in the newly designated Kauri Park. This he accepted and, although continuing to live at Arrow Farm, he was no longer closely involved in the daily running of the dairy-farm. His work as a Ranger was to look after the forest, keep the tracks and trails open, care for the wildlife, note their numbers, and watch out for gum poachers. He also had to escort visitors, and maintain the fencing and fire-breaks. There would be up to six local workers assisting with the manual labour. He was left very much to his own devices and only once in a while reported to the City Council. The job seemed tailor-made for him.

A life spent in the open air, roaming the kauri forest, appealed greatly to him, not only because of the beauty of the natural surroundings but because of the freedom he enjoyed and the chance to meet interesting people. In the late 1920s and early 1930s there was a growing interest in natural scenery and wild life. It drew many discerning visitors to the Waitakere area and to the Kauri Park in particular. One day. Leonard fell in with a young camper who was interested in the local flora and fauna. In talking with him, Leonard discovered his name was Bernard Ferguson, son of the Governor-General of the same name. Leonard joked and said to him, 'I suppose someday you will also be Governor-General'. The young man laughed at the idea. A keen naturalist who used to walk the ranges and talk with Leonard was the young Edmund Hillary, the future conqueror of Mount Everest. Two well-known botanists also frequented the area. One was Arnold Weil,

Walter Leonard Sisam, Forest Ranger in the Waitakeres.

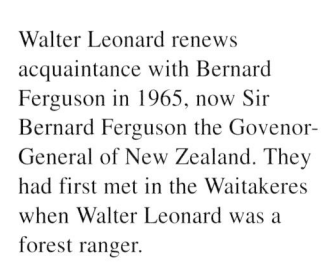

Walter Leonard renews acquaintance with Bernard Ferguson in 1965, now Sir Bernard Ferguson the Govenor-General of New Zealand. They had first met in the Waitakeres when Walter Leonard was a forest ranger.

the Professor of Botany at Canterbury University, Christchurch. The other was Lucy Cranwell. They had many discussions with Leonard and later she and the professor jointly published the authoritative volume, *The Botany of Auckland.* The new Governor-General at that time, Lord Bledisloe, was greatly attracted by the Waitakere. He visited Arrow Farm, and had lunch there. He was much interested to meet the Sisams, and said there were Sisams living on his estate in Wiltshire, in England.

By the late 1930s it was clear that the days of Arrow Farm were numbered. Although the Auckland City authorities had allowed Fanny to remain at the farm, and did not exercise their powers to purchase it compulsorily, they naturally wished to take possession of it as early as they could. In 1940 she and Leonard finally decided to sell it and move away. The price they received was around £5,200, or £40 an acre – quite good for those days. Leaving the farm was not a great wrench. The family had been there a long time and it had been a hard struggle. When the house was being cleared, Fanny came across her father-in-law Walter's original diary, which he had kept from the day he set foot in New Zealand in 1862 to the day he died in 1910. Fanny asked if anyone wanted it. No one did. It was burnt along with the rubbish, and with it the detailed history of the family.

Fanny went to live with her daughter Martha. Benjamin and Martha Copedo lived in the newly established township of Waitakere. Leonard had already married in 1935. His wife was Winnifred Hansen the daughter of a Danish settler family. Leonard bought a farm at Pokeno, south of Auckland. But he had been a ranger too long and never took to farming. He disposed of the land in 1942, retaining only the homestead, and did some shepherding for a while. By now he had three children, Richard Kenneth, Margaret (who later married Kenneth Allan) and Peter Leonard. Peter went shepherding in the southern part of the North Island, much of the time near Gisborne. After some years the eldest son Richard set up a building business on the family premises, specialising in prefabricated work. In the 1950s, Leonard and Richard made two visits to the Sisams who were farming near Whakatane. It was in the summer time and, true to his ranger's instincts, Leonard preferred to camp out under the trees. The folk at the farm thought this most strange.

All his life Leonard had loved the freedom of the open-air. He was at one with the natural surroundings for they were conducive to contemplation and spoke to that strange inner, mystical sense of a 'presence' that so many people experience in the solitudes of nature. There is no doubt that in some of the Sisams this was an inherited trait, and with it often went an instinctive understanding of the spiritual meaning of life, a familiarity with the power of intuition and even, from time to time, a glimpse of the visionary. These characteristics are often accompanied by the gift of a vivid imagination. The first Walter Sisam, before he came to New Zealand as a young man, clearly had a sense of the spiritual that shaped the rest of his life, and moulded his character. He too responded to the solitudes of nature. Intuition was something that his children experienced on occasions. Walter Henry had a premonition about the unexpected death of his mother as he journeyed home the day she died. There was a similar occurrence the day that Walter Henry's father was found lying dead on that same forest trail when returning home from Swanson. His grand-daughter, Ivy Rose, who had forgotten to feed the chickens for him, was waiting in the house for his return. She recalled the incident:

'Towards evening that day I looked through the gateway in the stone wall behind our cottage and looked down the broad track to Grandfather's place. For a moment I thought I saw Grandfather walking and holding onto his stick. Later, when I knew he had already

Walter Leonard Sisam at Pokeno in 1985, with the old flint-lock gun that his forebears brought to New Zealand from Arrow Mill in England.

died, I was a little upset by this incident and wanted to go and tell father about it, but I was afraid he would laugh at me. Many years later, I told Mother and she said she wished I had spoken out as she was sure he would have understood.'

Her brother, Leonard, for most of his adult life did not show much outward sign of an inner spirituality, but his grandfather Walter's life had a great influence upon him. 'He was a great believer' was how Leonard described him. In his later years Leonard did have a very specific experience that occurred in very everyday circumstances. For some time his health had been poor and he was under the doctor's care. The latter had been urging him to give up smoking, for he was quite heavily addicted, and prescribed some medicines. These had little effect. About that time he went somewhat unwillingly to a pentescostal gathering. Not long after, he was sitting one day in his room when he suddenly became aware of a bright light shining for a few seconds. At the same time very clear and definite thoughts came into his mind in the form of specific instructions. These were to throw away his medicines, and his pipe and tobacco. This he did. His health immediately began to pick up and he never smoked again. These characteristics of intuition, premonition, vision, imagination, and consciousness of a divine presence are spiritual gifts. They are part of the makeup of human beings, and the spiritual is as important an ingredient of human life as the physical. The Sisams, like any other family are an example of the mixture of the spiritual and the material.

A very happy memory for Leonard during those years at Pokeno was in 1965, when the then Governor-General was visiting the area. Leonard renewed acquaintance with him, much to the Governor-General's delight, for he was none other than the same person whom Leonard had met as a young man camping in the Waitakeres nearly forty years before. He was now the second Sir Bernard Ferguson to be Governor-General of New Zealand. Leonard's light-hearted prophecy in the 1920s as to the young man's destiny had come true. Afterwards Sir Bernard wrote to Leonard from Government House. He said, 'I write this short line to say what immense pleasure it gave me to see you again after 39 years. I well remember my camping in the Waitakeres. . . . I still remember the water was the coldest I have ever bathed in.'

In the 1980s, when he was in his eighties, Leonard made a nostalgic visit to the Kauri Park nature reserve and the site of Arrow Farm. The old buildings had disappeared, but the river was still flowing sweetly beneath trees of the virgin forest, the hollow where the old sawpit had been was still there, and the kauri trees where the young Copedo had tapped gum were still standing on the farm boundary. Other visitors were also there. The Mayor of Auckland had come to inaugurate a new footpath trail into the bush, starting from that same group of kauri trees. As the first Forest Ranger appointed to area, Leonard was interviewed by a TV crew and appeared on television the same evening, recalling the happy days of roaming the forest and protecting it for posterity.

19
Oxford

KENNETH THE SCHOLAR – THE OXFORD UNIVERSITY PRESS

When Kenneth Sisam went from Auckland in 1910 to take up residence at Merton College, Oxford, it was as if he had stepped from the twentieth century into the Middle Ages. Merton, the oldest college in Oxford, was founded in 1274. It was built on a monastic pattern. Narrow arches led from one quadrangle to another, around the sides of which the students' and tutors' rooms were situated, each group of rooms with its own staircase. There was a communal dining hall and chapel, and in one of the quadrangles a small staircase led to the beautiful library.

Although a distinguished college, Merton was comparatively small numerically, but had a reasonably good mix of students. When Kenneth arrived on the scene there was a large number of rugger-playing toughs, with no pretensions to learning. They respected Kenneth. He was strongly built and robust-looking, as well as being slightly older than most of the undergraduates. There was in the college an undergraduate, Hubert Phillips, who was small of stature and of spare physique. He was of an intellectual bent. The toughs rather despised him. They were always tormenting him, so he would take refuge in Kenneth's room. The rugger-players were all frightened to come in, because Kenneth was regarded as a formidable sage. Being a big man physically he seemed to have had this protector strain in his nature. Hubert Phillips gained a First in his final History examinations, and kept in touch with Kenneth all his life. He earned a living partly by playing bridge professionally, and also became well-known in the world of journalism. He had a regular column in the *News Chronicle* under the pseudonym 'Dogberry' and in the *New Statesman* as 'Caliban'. He was a clever composer and compiler of puzzles and published several books of them.

Kenneth had come to Oxford as a graduate, having already obtained B.A. and M.A. degrees at Auckland University. His original purpose at Oxford was to read for the Oxford B.A. in English. He started working to this end under Professor A.S. Napier of Merton College, at that time Professor of English Language and Literature. Kenneth had originally applied to go to Balliol College, but the Rhodes Scholarship Trustees placed him at Merton, probably because of Professor Napier.

Now that he was in Europe, Kenneth naturally wanted to see something of it, not least because he was interested in all things medieval. He took the opportunity in vacation time to go on a European tour. But the place that captured his heart was Lake Lugano in southern Switzerland, so much so that later, when he wanted to escape from the damp, English winters he returned there as often as he could. He liked boating on the lake, and much regretted at Easter time having to return to Oxford before the wistaria blossomed. He usually spent these holidays alone but during at least one of them he was joined by an old and special friend.

Kenneth Sisam, graduate of University College, Auckland, and Rhodes Scholar of Oxford University. A photograph taken shortly before he left New Zealand to go to Oxford.

Merton College, Oxford, was Kenneth Sisam's college. A view from Christchurch Meadows.

In Auckland, when lodging with the Farquhar family, he had met his hostess's niece, Naomi Gibbons, who was his contemporary at Auckland Grammar School and like him went to Auckland University where she took a B.A. Kenneth had been president of the students' union and excelled in sport as well as in scholarship. Naomi, who was an elegant and attractive young woman, was a daughter of a well-known timber merchant. Her father Robert Pearce Gibbons, who had ten children, was either very rich or very poor, depending on the state of the timber trade. When he died he was rich enough to leave £3000 to each of his seven daughters. In the meantime, Naomi had fallen in love with Kenneth and knew that he was the man for her. After Kenneth had left New Zealand for Oxford, Naomi and three of her sisters, on the strength of their father's legacies, set off on a world tour which brought them to Europe. They all met Kenneth in Switzerland. Having completed the world tour, Naomi then remained in Europe and took a teaching job for a living. Her reason for staying was that she wanted to be near Kenneth. She taught the English language in a school in Switzerland, at the same time improving her own knowledge of French and German. She was a good linguist, not so much academically as in her ability to speak a language. She had a quick ear which enabled her to learn rapidly.

In Oxford Kenneth was working hard on his B.A. studies. As might be expected he was in considerable demand as a cricketer at this time. He knew that his studies must come first, and that he could never give the time to cricket that would have been required if he were going to realise his full potential as a cricketer. So he limited himself to playing for his college. The first time he tried his leg-break bowling technique he found the air in Oxford was quite different from that in New Zealand. The ball swerved all over the place, because of the humidity. This had to be mastered. In the winter and spring months he played hockey. But these activities were soon to be curtailed. Despite his normal robust health, early in 1913 Kenneth began to feel ill. The cause of this was a mystery.

At this time the Bodleian Library was by arrangement open on Sunday mornings to a select group of academics for study purposes. A small coterie would gather there, each of whom was pursuing some particular subject, and they would fall into conversation. Among them was Professor Napier. Another was Sir William Osler, the learned medical man. Kenneth was privileged to be admitted to this group of senior academics. It was Osler who helped Kenneth to have the best medical treatment then available. He was operated on for appendicitis, which was then a new and major operation. But it failed to cure him, and all his life he remained subject to abdominal pain. In addition he seems to have contracted some kind of wasting disease, perhaps undulant fever from infected milk. The symptoms persisted, and a later medical opinion diagnosed overwork, which rest and some kind of electrical treatment and time would cure.

Professor Napier soon discovered that Kenneth was a promising medievalist, and as he himself was in declining health he asked Kenneth to take on some of his lecturing and tutoring. As the professor's assistant it became inappropriate for Kenneth to sit the Final Examination for B.A. with his pupils. He transfered to research for the B.Litt (Bachelor of Literature), which was at the time the only research degree at Oxford. The special subject which Napier suggested for Kenneth's thesis was an unpublished tenth-century Latin psalter, the *Salisbury Psalter*, which had an Anglo-Saxon gloss added between the lines of the original text. In the course of his study of the *Salisbury Psalter*, Kenneth consulted the distinguished liturgical scholar Edmund Bishop of Downside. Tne two of them became lifelong friends.

Naomi Gibbons
of Auckland

Kenneth had now embarked on what was to be an arduous stint of tutorial teaching, together with five or six lectures or classes a week during each term, and this was to continue for nearly five years. One of his pupils was J.R.R. Tolkein, four years Kenneth's junior. When World War I broke out in 1914, Kenneth was found unfit for military service, on account of his ill-health.

Naomi, who had been teaching in Switzerland most of this time, was trapped there by the war. After the Battle of the Marne, in September 1914, she managed to make her way to England. She and Kenneth were married in Oxford on January 12, 1915; Kenneth looking gaunt and frail, as if he had not long to live. He desperately needed someone's loving care, and she wished for nothing more than to be with him and look after him. She was to be his salvation.

He had almost no money. His Rhodes Scholarship funds had come to an end: he had a small scholarship from his college, and earned modest fees for lecturing and tutoring. His financial situation compelled him to drive himself, for scholars, even in Oxford, did not make fortunes. Naomi still had a sizeable amount left from the legacy that had financed her world tour. The original sum had been £3,000, which was considerable in 1915. Kenneth saw to it that it was wisely invested. Out of their joint funds they rented a house on Boar's Hill, Oxford, in a healthy, rural situation on high ground well above the city. They hoped that this would help Kenneth to regain his health.

Kenneth's work-load was still daunting. He completed his thesis satisfactorily in June, and was now not only tutoring and lecturing but, as Professor Napier's health failed, more and more of the work of teaching English Language in the university fell on his shoulders. Although his own health was slowly beginning to improve, he was compelled to conduct tutorials lying on a couch. Yet his academic reputation continued to grow. He was asked to do occasional work for Henry Bradley on the preparation of the 'S' volume of the New English Dictionary. He was also approached by the Clarendon Press, the academic and central publishing department of the Oxford University Press. He took on one assignment for them, the revision of Professor Skeat's edition of *The Lay of Havelok the Dane*. It might have been expected to take two years. Kenneth was given three weeks, and in that time carried out a complete revision of the edition. He became known for his speedy, accurate work, and for his ability to get to the nub of the subject and deal with it effectively. Later, the Clarendon Press, eager to make use of his knowledge and ability, offered him a small retainer fee for his services.

Napier had died in May 1915. He was a man for whom Kenneth had great admiration, whom he acknowledged as having taught him everything he knew. Kenneth was now officially in charge of the teaching of English Language in the University, a task which, owing to Napier's indisposition, he had already been carrying for the last two years. He was appointed as examiner in the Final Honours Examination of English Language and Literature. To do this an Oxford M.A. degree was statutorily required, and so, very abnormally, an M.A. by decree was conferred upon him.

Gradually, supported by the devoted Naomi, his health began to pick up and by 1917 he was fit enough to join the Ministry of Food, where he had a special lean-back chair in which he could sit comfortably. He and Naomi moved from Oxford, and she joined the Ministry of Pensions since, in the Civil Service, husbands and wives were not permitted to work in the same department. They took with them to London a minor problem. After they were married they acquired a dog from, Robert Bridges, the Poet Laureate, whom they knew well. Bridges, being a classical scholar, had given it a Greek name, Teknon, meaning 'child'. Kenneth did not consider this a good name for a dog so he called him Tecko, which sounded something like the original. Tecko was highly bred. Naomi gave him a bath one day and his colour changed from brown to white. He had long curly hair and looked smart; but Tecko was almost blind. For some reason, the Government had imposed restrictions on the movements of dogs, and Kenneth wanted to move Tecko from Boar's Hill to London. The Ministry of Agriculture, situated opposite the Ministry of Food, was dealing with the case and had a large file on it. During the lunch hour Kenneth would stroll across the street to the Agriculture Ministry and talk to the man there. Kenneth knew that to get round civil service regulations you would need to show that your dog was different from other dogs and therefore a special case. He remembered that Tecko was nearly blind, so he said to the man, 'My dog is blind, you know, and do you realise that a blind dog can't come down a spiral staircase?' Whereupon the man said, without inquiring whether Kenneth had a spiral staircase, 'Oh, is that so? That's very interesting', and was so impressed that he exempted Tecko from the restrictions.

When World War I ended food supplies were still short, and would remain so for some years. Kenneth dealt with bacon and its pricing, and had to handle the Ministry's supply of bacon to merchants all over the country. He became a director of bacon contracts in August 1919. After the war there was a dispute between Britain and Canada about bacon contracts, which finally came to court in 1923. Kenneth had left the Civil Service in October 1922 and gone for his first holiday to New Zealand. His holiday was cut short when he was recalled to England to be the chief witness for the Government. The Government won the case, thus saving impoverished Britain several million pounds. Kenneth was offered the choice of a knighthood or £3,000. As a penniless young man with life ahead of him, Kenneth chose the latter. It enabled him to buy land on Boar's Hill on which in due course a new home was built, named Yatsden.

In 1922, the Clarendon Press had offered him the post of deputy to the Assistant Secretary, which he accepted, and took up this new assignment in June 1923. Within two years he himself became Assistant Secretary, and from then on he carried a large part of the administrative work of the Press. In 1925, when the post of Professor of Anglo-Saxon became vacant, the short list of applicants contained two names, Sisam and Tolkien, his former pupil. When the votes were cast the result was a tie. The Vice-Chancellor of the University held the casting vote and voted for Tolkien. When Kenneth came home in the evening on the day the announcement was made, he said little about it. He never held it against Tolkien. Kenneth would have liked to become Professor of Anglo-Saxon and to have devoted himself to academic study, but he knew that the job at the Clarendon Press was much more important.

Kenneth and Naomi continued to live on Boar's Hill, where their two children, Hugh, born in 1923, and Celia, born in 1926, grew up amidst pleasant surroundings. Kenneth laid out the garden which he landscaped from scratch; for he was a garden-lover. The orchard was his pride and joy and contained a selection of traditional varieties of apple. There were congenial neighbours, among them the writers and poets, Robert Bridges, John Masefield, and Professor Gilbert Murray. Kenneth shepherded Robert Bridges' *Testament of Beauty* through the Clarendon Press, and later Bridges appointed him his literary executor.

Yatsden was a great joy to Naomi. She worked hard to make it comfortable. The question arose in the late 1930s of having a wireless. Kenneth would not hear of it. He did not want the nice drawing-room, with its period furniture, spoiled by some new-fangled gadget. Naomi very much wanted a wireless, and she was shrewd at going about it. She had a friend whose son was interested in wireless. He made a set for her and mounted it behind an 18th century front. She smuggled this into the drawing-room. When World War II became imminent and broke out no one was a more avid listener to the BBC news than Kenneth.

A similar thing happened over the question of a cat. Kenneth liked dogs but felt cats should live outside. The rest of the family wanted an indoor cat. They smuggled in a white kitten. Kenneth wouldn't have anything to do with it. They did not tell him it was a female. The cat used to sit at his feet as he rested in his lean-back armchair, and gaze adoringly up at him. One day it jumped up into the chair, and in the end he accepted it, but made it sit at the back of the chair and not on his lap. Then this white cat had kittens, and of these one solitary black one was kept. The white mother-cat trained this kitten very thoroughly and he developed into a very intelligent cat. He was known as Toby. This was the cat to whom Kenneth became devoted.

Kenneth kept in close touch with the family in New Zealand. He and his brother Len exchanged letters regularly, and when at one point during the inter-war years the farm was in financial straits, he provided a loan. Because this loan was linked with the farm property it could not legally be paid back to Kenneth until 1952, by which time the New Zealand Government restrictions on land transactions had been eased. He also corresponded regularly with his sister Lena, who had meant so much to him in his boyhood days. In 1936 she came over from New Zealand and stayed with Kenneth and his family at Yatsden for a year. When World War II broke out she and her sister May generously sent parcels of food from New Zealand to Kenneth and Naomi. The food was sewn up in cotton bags, which could be used as pillow-cases. This was appreciated since materials as well as food were rationed in England.

In the years immediately before World War II the Jews in Nazi Germany were suffering increasing persecution; they included many scholars and academics. At Oxford the Clarendon Press and Balliol College did all they could to help those fleeing from Germany, and in this Kenneth Sisam took a leading part. Several were found work at the Press. One of these, an eminent professor of Greek, Paul Maas, came to tea at Yatsden every week. Kenneth also introduced him to the Gilbert Murrays nearby.

Kenneth was promoted to become The Secretary at the Clarendon Press in 1942. He remained in charge of the Press until 1948. This period included the crucial years of the Second World War and the immediate postwar period, when a steady hand was required on the tiller, and a mind ready to cope with the vital changes and innovations and to look beyond day-to-day affairs. The war years were hard. At the Clarendon Press Kenneth had only one fellow administrator, A.L.P. Norrington, since the juniors, including Kenneth's assistant, John Mulgan, had gone to the war. The Press printed a great deal of Government work, and continued its academic publishing. During those war years Kenneth never took a day off. In his twenty-six years at the Press he was involved in numerous publishing projects, both popular and academic, many of which he personally saw through to completion. Among these were *The Oxford Book of Modern Verse*, (edited by W.B.Yeats at Kenneth's suggestion), the first of a scientific series headed by Dirac's *Principles of Quantum Mechanics*, the various *Oxford Companions to Literature*, *The Oxford Histories of England* and *The Oxford Histories of English Literature*; also *Classical Roman Law*, and *The Oxford Dictionary of Place-Names*. The last named, a standard work by Eilert Ekwall, was one of many books written at Kenneth's suggestion. Kenneth took personal charge of the publication of scientific and mathematical books and delegated the arts subjects to others. Through his efforts the Press gained a reputation for books on scientific subjects.

The Oxford University Press or Clarendon Press, in Oxford. As head of the Press, Kenneth Sisam's office was in the centre building.

The administrative structure of the University Press was somewhat complex. The Secretary, whose full title was Secretary to the Delegates of the Oxford University Press, represented the University and was in overall charge of all publishing. He had under his control the five aspects of the Press: academic publishing, general publishing, the printing works, the paper mill and the bindery. He was in fact the chief executive. At the same time the Secretary was manager in charge of the academic publishing. He was also titular head of all overseas branches of the Oxford University Press. At the London offices of the Press there was a representative known as the Publisher; technically he was answerable to the Secretary in Oxford, who was his senior. The London Publisher was responsible for all Oxford University Press' non-academic books and general publishing, such as the World's Classics series; while the Secretary in Oxford dealt with the learned books which bore the imprint of the Clarendon Press. The Publisher in London was the person whose name appeared on all Oxford University Press books, and was therefore more familiar to the public than the Secretary in Oxford. This strange situation goes some way to explain why Kenneth was not better known.

In 1945 a young Balliol graduate from New Zealand, Daniel Davin, presented himself to Kenneth at the Press for the vacant post of Assistant Secretary, recommended by the head of his college. Kenneth interviewed him. According to Davin the interview went like this: 'I see you have been in the Army. Did you ever play rugby football? I notice you have got a First in Latin and a First in English in New Zealand, and a first in Greats over here, so you could be very helpful to us. Of course, it will be five years before you can be of any use. It will take that time to train you. So we would like you to undertake not to leave before that period.' Despite this somewhat daunting introduction, Davin took the post and in the years that followed, as Kenneth Sisam's assistant, he was able to observe how he ran the Press. At the same time Davin became aware of Kenneth's human qualities.

Not long after he joined the Press Dan Davin came to work one glorious, sunny morning when Kenneth called the staff together and said, 'It's a fine day such as we rarely get. The war is over. We'll all have a holiday. Anyone who wants to come up to my house on Boar's Hill can do so.' Everyone did and had a delightful day. This human quality permeated all that Kenneth did, despite the fact that he was an austere man who did not suffer fools gladly.

He lived by a well-ordered routine. He rose early, made the tea, read Latin or some other improving literature to his children at breakfast, and then went by bus to his office. There he would sit at his desk placed in the middle of the room facing the open door, so that no one could go by without his seeing them. So, if any of the girls arrived late, he would say to them smilingly, 'Transport's awfully difficult nowadays, isn't it?' But they took note. He had about five secretaries at any given time. He liked to recruit them straight from school. He chose intelligent girls who, if grants had been available in those days, would have gone to a university. He trained them carefully. He would deliberately put mistakes into his draft letters to see if they picked them up. He taught them to go to the files and read the background to the correspondance they were handling. Thus they would take more and more responsibility; and he made sure they all knew everything that was going on.

He took a great interest in people. He knew all his staff, all 130 of them. He never ate lunch. He had a pint pot of tea and four biscuits brought to him at his desk. During the lunch period his door was open, and anyone in the office who had a problem, a private grievance or some other difficulty, could come in and seek his advice. Kenneth knew that most people worried about things that were not worth worrying about, but to talk them out with someone who was understanding and considerate was usually the way to resolve them. He was a good tutor to his students, and took great pains over the training he gave to each member of his staff.

A very large number of manuscripts for possible publication passed through his hands during his management of the Press, so that he very soon acquired a sound judgement as to what made a book worthy of publication. It is interesting that in later years, Professor Eugene Vinaver, an authority on Malory, said that Kenneth's real greatness was to be discerned in the number of prefaces of books published in which he is thanked by the author as the man who really made the book. There seemed to be no book that he looked at in which he did not find a way of making some improvement. On the other hand, he used to say, 'It's no good trying to improve a second-rate book. You'll only waste your sweat and months and months of work over a poor author, and even if he adopts your suggestions it will still be a second-rate book.'

Kenneth was not only a fine scholar but also an astute businessman. There is no question that the business acumen that served him well at the Ministry of Food was in later years to serve him well at the Press. He was particularly knowledgeable about the pricing of books. He once spoke about the popularity of the *Concise Oxford Dictionary*. 'Remember', he said, 'if you put a penny on the price of the *Concise Oxford Dictionary*, and you are selling a quarter of a million a year, then that is quite a lot of money. But you've got to watch out. If you put sixpence on, someone out there is going to say, 'Well, we can produce a dictionary nearly as good as the *Concise Oxford Dictionary*, but we will make it cheaper.' So the sales of theirs would go up and cut into ours.' He was a man who thought ahead. During the Second World War he persuaded the Delegates of the Press to buy up most of the dwelling houses near the Press, as they fell vacant. As a result, when the war ended and the Press needed to recruit more staff rapidly, he had living accomodation to offer them which they could acquire at a reasonable rent. He therefore had no difficulty in obtaining the staff he wanted.

Being a publisher he was inevitably involved in lawsuits. The art, he explained, was to go to counsel as the counsel's name would then terrify the opposition. But it was essential to tell him what to say and, since counsel was no fool, the odds were that you would win your case. In point of fact Kenneth never lost a case throughout his time at the Press.

It must be admitted, though, that such an independent-minded, capable and dedicated man as Kenneth Sisam was not all that popular in the University. Partly it was because of his no-nonsense practical approach to matters. This was especially true of his letters. Davin said they were like boiled eggs. 'As soon as you took the shell off you were at grips with the egg, and as soon as you opened a letter of Sisam's the first sentence had you right into the businees straight away. The English were accustomed to talk about the weather or something for the first paragraph. Then they come to the nitty-gritty. Sisam's letters had the nitty-gritty at the start. Some recipients, accustomed to skipping the first paragraph, often missed the point of his letters.'

One of his weaknesses, which though very human could be frustrating to others, was that he loved winning arguments. Davin commented on this point, 'Many a time I was right, but I never won an argument. But then he was a big man. He was a big man as I see Churchill, or General Freyberg. There are very few of them. They make mistakes. They fool themselves. They have always got a great deal of generosity, as well as a slight tendency to tyranny. You had to stand up to Sisam. I had to take a stand. But he never held it against me.'

'Middle Carn' the house which Kenneth built at Hugh Town, St Mary's in the Isles of Scilly.

Kenneth in his retirement in the Isles of Scilly.

Kenneth and Naomi retired to the Isles of Scilly in 1948, where for many years the family had spent their holidays. It was Naomi who had discovered the delights of these islands. In 1931, while holidaying with the children at Marazion in Cornwall, she and Hugh went over on a day trip. The next year Kenneth and the whole family began to holiday there. For some years they took lodgings. Then in 1937 Kenneth built a holiday house at the sea's edge facing the Atlantic Ocean. When he retired from the Press they could no longer afford to continue at Yatsden. The house in Scilly was the alternative they chose. They adapted it for permanent occupation as best they could within the post-war building restrictions and made it their family home. It was named Middle Carn from the great rock or carn below which it stood.

When the time came for the move there had to be a great clearing out of books, for the house was full of books, most of them Kenneth's. Only a fraction of them could the house in Scilly possibly contain. Kenneth had the ability to be quite ruthless with his own possessions. He parted with many things he loved and cared for, both books and furniture. About a third of the books were sold, including some of the most treasured. He gave his extensive collection of books on Middle English to his daughter Celia. Naomi chose the books she wanted to take with her, mainly novels and a choice of poets. Kenneth chose the books he needed for further study in Anglo-Saxon, and a selection of fiction classics. Toby, the clever black cat, also went with him.

Scilly was a place that reminded Kenneth of New Zealand. He immediately immersed himself in the life of the islands, a life of boats, fishing and gardening. He would sit on a bench by Old Town harbour and make friends with the islanders and join in the talk. He listened with delight to their tales of times past and wrote them down. His nearest neighbour was a flower farmer, Roland Gibson, whom he visited every day. He interested himself in local people, helping them to sort out their problems, so that some thought he must be a retired lawyer. Toby the cat adapted well to Scilly. He had every reason to. His master would go out regularly to catch fish for him, as well as for the household. Kenneth also collected shrimps, winkles and limpets and other such delicacies – a welcome change for Toby from the stale cods' heads of wartime Oxford. The cat became quite famous in Old Town, where the family lived, and used to sit in the window and watch the passers-by on the coast path. It was a pleasant life and Kenneth made very few expeditions to the mainland, but many old friends and ex-colleagues came to visit him.

For Hugh and Celia it must have been somewhat difficult to follow such a gifted scholar as their father. However, they in their turn were also endowed with considerable scholastic abilities. Hugh, being a firstborn son, was a boy for whom his father naturally had great hopes. Before Hugh went away to school, Kenneth read to him every morning at breakfast time from the Latin Classics: Virgil, Horace, Catullus and the like. The boy was precocious and was reading these Classics himself at the age of 9 or 10 quite happily. He was brilliant in that field. Kenneth was immensely proud of him. He won a scholarship to Winchester College, one of England's premier schools, and at the end of his time there he passed out top in the examination for scholarships to New College, Oxford. There, in his first examinations in Classics he obtained a First Class. World War II interrupted Hugh's Oxford studies. He went into the Navy, serving in minesweepers in the Mediterranean as a Sub-Lieutenant, and twice his ship was sunk. He thoroughly enjoyed his naval service, and then returned to Oxford in 1946 and began working for his final examinations in Ancient History and Philosophy. His earlier success at Oxford in classical subjects reflected his natural

Hugh Sisam, scholar of Winchester College and of New College, Oxford.

Celia Sisam, Fellow and Tutor in English at St Hilda's College, Oxford.

ability in the classical languages and the excellent education he received at Winchester. Philosophy and History were new subjects which required different skills and hard work. It soon became apparent that all was not well. He did not apply himself much to his studies but hoped to get a First nevertheless. In the end he got a Third. However, he had a beautiful literary style, which he retained throughout his life. After leaving Oxford he made a career for himself in the City of London, until poor health made him unfit for work.

After leaving school Celia, who was three years younger than Hugh, went to Lady Margaret Hall, a women's college at Oxford and, following in her father's footsteps, graduated in English, specialising in medieval studies. She was awarded a senior scholarship at Lady Margaret Hall to do research, and started work on a collection of twelfth-century English homilies under Professor Tolkien. After a year, unexpectedly, she was offered a post at Queen Mary College, London University, to teach medieval English. So she abandoned her research degree. After four years she returned to Oxford as Research Fellow of Lady Margaret Hall. In 1957 she became a Fellow and Tutor of St Hilda's College, Oxford, another of the few women's colleges of that time, where she lectured in the University and taught students of English language and literature for many years, until she retired in 1986.

In December 1957 her mother, Naomi, was taken seriously ill, and in February went into hospital in Cornwall for a major operation. Hugh came down from London and Kenneth and Celia joined him as often as they could. Hugh remained with Naomi and cared for and comforted her until she died in hospital a month later. Kenneth lived on alone in Scilly for another thirteen years. He had good friends there. Amongst them was Alfred Jenkins who tended his boat, servicing the engine each year. He was a good engineer, a kind and helpful friend, always responding to any calls for assistance. In his later years Kenneth was looked after by Mrs. Arthur Sherris who shopped for him and came each day to cook and run the house, while Celia was working in Oxford. During the university vacations Celia came down to Scilly for as long as possible. Kenneth was a contributor to the *Scillonian*, the islands' old established magazine, and he continued his academic studies and writing. In these years he completed *The Oxford Book of Mediaeval Verse* (1970), which he edited with Celia. He died in 1971 in his 84th year.

He was a remarkable man. Dan Davin, who later became the Academic Publisher at the Clarendon Press, was quite clear on that. He went even further. He referred to Kenneth as 'a great man, a very great man', and this may well be right. Kenneth came, as it were, out of the bush in a then remote part of the world and, by sheer ability and hard work, reached the highest levels of scholarship. Although a modest man who never sought preferment or honours, men and women everywhere recognised his ability and his clear and original mind. The British Academy elected him a Fellow of their distinguished society. He was a Professorial Fellow of Merton College and an Honorary Fellow after he retired. He had an Honorary Doctorate of Literature from Reading University, and Iceland made him a Grand Knight of the Icelandic Falcon. He was also elected to the Finnish Societas Scientiarum Fennica. Eugene Vinaver described Kenneth as 'a king among medievalists'. At the Clarenden Press he is remembered today with respect and gratitude. He is one of the long line of Secretaries who have built up the Oxford University Press to be one of the most wide-ranging international establishments of its type in the world. There were many personal tributes to his qualities. The quality of his work is perhaps best expressed in the words of the distinguished Anglo-Saxon scholar, Professor Dorothy Whitelock. She referred to him as 'My mentor and model, Kenneth Sisam'.

20

King Street & Owhakatoro

THE NEXT GENERATION IN THE BAY OF PLENTY

When Kenneth Sisam left New Zealand in July 1910, his two older brothers, Leonard Wilfrid and Walter Holtom, were hard at work on the land the family had acquired in the Opouriao Valley. With the subsequent move across the Whakatane River in 1921 to the larger Owhakatoro property, the future of 'Sisam and Sons' looked especially promising. The story of the farm, situated in the part of New Zealand so aptly named 'The Bay of Plenty' by Captain Cook, was in the coming years to be the story of these two brothers, Leonard and Walter, and their descendants. Walter and his family, as we have seen, had made a home on the farm itelf, while his brother, Len and his family, were living on the outskirts of Whakatane in what became King Street.

The partnership of 'Sisam and Sons' had been formed in Alfred John's lifetime, the partners being Alfred and his three sons, Leonard, Walter and Kenneth, all holding equal shares in the farm. Later Kenneth withdrew, having settled in England to follow an academic career. From the beginning the partnership was conducted in a spirit and manner to ensure the participating families a fair share at all times of the income from the farm. It was also in Alfred's mind that the property would remain in the family and not be divided up or have portions sold off by any who wished to strike out on their own. At the same time, there was no legal bar to anyone withdrawing if they so wished. The secret of success in such an arrangement would undoubtedly depend upon the spirit in which business affairs were conducted. The years ahead, as new generations gradually assumed control, would clearly present a stimulating challenge.

Len, being Alfred John's eldest son, was now the head of the family, and although he and his brother Walter worked closely together in running the farm, the home in Whakatane was the natural hub of the Sisam's farming enterprise. When Len and Mabel first moved there from Opouriao they already had four children, and as the family grew the home became a busy, highly organised but hospitable family centre. Pete (Leonard Alfred), the first born, was his father's shadow, eager to learn about the men's world of farming. Doris, as eldest daughter, was her mother's right-hand woman, and was kept busy with the ever-growing family and consequent chores. So much so that when Lorna, the fifth child, was born she declared that if there were any more babies she would 'put them through the wringer'. But despite her sharp words, arising from the pressures she felt as the eldest daughter, she was at heart a dedicated member of the family and played her part loyally. It was just as well, for Mona, the third child, was a tom-boy and a rebel, not at all interested in things domestic. All the daughters had minds of their own and knew the direction in which they wanted to go. As one by one they reached maturity the family scene was greatly enlivened by their independence of spirit and readiness to take adventurous steps in their own lives. The next child to be born was Mannie (Harold Walter). When they were quite young, both Mannie and his sister Mona had rheumatic fever, an illness that often affects the heart. Mona, although she was quite ill during her teens, excelled in all kinds of sports. Mannie also lived a fully active life and learned to pace himself and live within his strength.

Sisams seemed to have had a penchant for nick-names. In this family some were born dark and some were born blonde. Pete and Doris, the eldest son and daughter, both had their mother's colouring, black hair and olive-skin, whereas Mona was extremely fair. Pete and Doris used to tease Mona and say she must have been adopted, until Mannie arrived and he too was fair. At that point the parents began to call their two daughters 'Mrs. Black' and 'Mrs. White'. Doris being the older daughter objected, but Mona, all her life, was known in the family as 'Whitey', or 'Mrs. White'. Two more daughters were born to Len and Mabel: Lorna, tall with black, curly hair and olive complexion, and Eileen, quick, petite and with soft brown hair. Finally there was the baby of the family, Ken (Kenneth Charles), who also had soft brown hair.

As did most of the children Pete, the eldest, went to school in Whakatane. He worked hard and, like his uncle Kenneth before him, won a scholarship to Auckland Grammar School. There he boarded with his grandfather, Alfred, and his Auntie May in Woodside Road. It looked as if he might go on to university as his uncle had done. He had become deeply interested in law and this could have been his course of study. But time and events were against him. This was in the early twenties when farming fortunes were at a low ebb in the Bay of Plenty. The collapse of the Whakatane freezing-plant in 1921 had hit most farmers badly, including the Sisams. Pete's father had to sell part of the valuable land he owned at Ohope Beach in order to redeem their guarantees to the freezing works and to save the farm from retrenchment. For Len the payment of university fees was out of the question. The farm had to be saved. Pete was called home. He was now fifteen. His father said to him: 'Now it's time for you to start work', and start work he did.

He did so with a will because he loved the farm, having lived so close to it during his early boyhood. By this time the family enterprise was very much dependent on its cattle-dealing and needed drovers. Pete set about learning to become a drover. His father provided him with a horse, a saddle and dogs. He would set out in the early morning on the three-day ride to Gisborne on the coast, complete with packhorses and food, and camp out overnight wherever there was suitable grazing for the animals, all of which had to be carefully organised in advance. At Gisborne cattle were sold and fresh cattle bought from local farms to be driven home for fattening. The drovers came from different farms and worked together, many of them farmer's sons like himself. Pete not only drove cattle for his father but took assignments from other farms as well. Sometimes he journeyed north to Thames and often to Rotorua, the railhead.

He learned how dependent a drover was on his dogs. By day there were hazards on the roads and on the rough tracks. Cattle could not be driven in the heat of the day, and a drover had to know where there was water for them. If sheep were being driven, they would become drowsy towards the end of the day and would sleep in the early part of the evening, only to wake up first thing in the morning and become restless. Someone had to keep watch all night. A drover had to be observant at all times.

For Pete it was a time rich in experience, gained in the rough and ready fellowship of the road. The older men never missed an opportunity to teach the greenhorns a lesson, often in the form of practical jokes. Pete did not escape this form of education even from friendly neighbours. One of them was visiting the King Street home when Pete called in on his way to the Coromandel Coast with cattle. The man said to him: 'I know where there's a fine paddock you could use for grazing on your trip', and told him exactly where to go. So Pete took the advice, found the spot and made full use of it. The next morning an irate farmer appeared threatening to have the police on to Pete. When he heard about it the family friend laughed, and said: 'O, did that man get mad? Good, I've been trying to get one over on him for years!'

It was an effective training school and Pete developed a keen business sense, so much so that after six years of this work he was approached by a stock firm in Hamilton and went to work for them. Then he was approached with an offer of work in the Argentine; but, at the same time came an opportunity from the New Zealand Loan and Mercantile Company to manage their Whakatane office and act as their agent in the district, which job he accepted. Management seemed second-nature to him, and he had a good touch with the farming community, who were his potential clients. He developed a passion for this work, and the ability to strike a hard bargain.

Pete's younger brother Mannie, took his turn at the Whakatane school but disliked it, for he was not a book man. His one ambition was to be a drover like Pete. While still at school he began to help his father on the farm and felt a real hero the first time he rode

Entrance to the Owhakatoro Farm.

through Whakatane with a herd of cattle. He felt it gave him status which he did not have at school as an academic. When he left school in April 1928 he began full-time work on the farm. He lived with his Uncle Walter and Aunt Rose at the Owhakatoro homestead, together with one of the farmworkers, Tommy Gee. He was at once in his element working with dogs and horses. During this time he had his first long cattle drive. He rode for six days to Tokomaru to pick up cattle, and then 29 days driving them round the coast road and home. His speciality became the breeding and training of sheep-dogs, and participating in local sheep-dog trials. He had entered his first dog in a trial when he was still at school. He was to continue this for over 50 years without a break.

Mannie's younger cousins, Walter and Allen the sons of Walter Holtom, spent their boyhood at the Owhakatoro homestead. Having been brought up to the saddle from an early age they soon became good horsemen, and as the farmhouse was close to the Whakatane River they learnt watermanship at the same time. The river was actually a mountain watercourse, capricious and sometimes dangerous, in which the water level could vary suddenly and currents become swift. For much of the time it could safely be crossed on horseback. Walter and his brother had many adventures and escapades in its waters, when their skills were fully tested. They had ridden to school in Taneatua one day when the river rose rapidly within hours. Rose, their mother, telephoned the school to tell the boys to come back by the railway bridge, rather than risk swimming the horses across. But it was twice the distance and the boys reckoned if the water level was below the horses' backs it would be safe. The water had risen higher but not quite over the horses' backs. The two boys knelt on their horses to keep themselves dry and started across. In the process a parcel they had collected from the Taneatua Post Office fell out of Allen's school bag and floated off in the current. He turned his horse downstream but could not catch the

The farmhouse at Owhakatoro where Walter and Rose and their family lived.

Walter Holtom Sisam.

Rose Stansfield Sisam.

parcel. Walter, being in front, rode across to the far side, galloped down-river along the bank, re-entered the river, rescued the parcel and rode back. On the way home, with horses and feet dripping wet, they were met by a distraught mother who, looking from her window, had seen them through the willows enter the water and disappear. Time elapsed and fearing the worst she had gone to look for them. They were duly contrite. The parcel contained two surcingles their father Walter Holtom had ordered, worth thirty shillings.

Walter Holtom was a great teller of tales, to the delight of the younger children. He made up stories with local settings and characters such as Robbie Rat and Freddie Fish, and most of these contained a subtle moral. He was a man of quiet disposition who unobtrusively helped those in sad or difficult circumstances. Few people knew of this. His advice was sought on many local matters. He helped to organize the first Taneatua Cricket Club, for which he frequently played. He was also, with his brother Len, a staunch supporter of the Whakatane Agricultural Shows and regularly took part in them. Being a quiet man he avoided politics, but backed good causes that would benefit the farming community. For years there was no road access to the farms on the western side of the Whakatane River. During all but three months of the year cattle, sheep, produce, feedstuffs and manure had to be carried across the river by boat in small quantities. Yet this was the farmers' only link with Whakatane. They paid rates towards the Whakatane Harbour but could not make proper use of its facilities. The County Council had promised to make a road, but nothing happened. Walter Holtom was chosen by the farmers to lead a delegation to the Council demanding action. This he did and presented the case in strong and forthright terms. After the road was built, the only adequate crossing of the river was still by the railway bridge that had neither decking nor railings. Walter rode round the neighbouring farms on his large white horse, organising a petition to have the bridge made safe. He then presented the petition to the local member of parliament. The improved bridge is still in place and well used. In all his work he was far-sighted in his thinking and planning. One of his favourite sayings was, 'We must look forward to the next hundred years'.

As regards the farm itself, the year 1931 was a crucial one. The world economic slump was now seriously affecting New Zealand agriculture. All kinds of pressures were bearing down on farmers and many anxieties beset them. Soon after his handling of the bridge petition Walter Holtom had become unwell, and for the next two years he had to rest. Dulcie returned from school in Auckland at this point to help her mother. At the height of the haymaking season of 1931 Walter was greatly concerned that the vital hay crop should be safely gathered. He rose from his sick bed, saddled his horse, and went to join in the haymaking. Tragically, he collapsed and died shortly afterwards, leaving two sons, Walter John aged 12, and Allen Leonard aged 10, both at school, and three daughters, Dulcie, Joan, and Isabel, and their mother, Rose. He was only 50 years old when he died.

Rose remained in the main Owhakatoro farmhouse. Her two sons were now approaching manhood. Walter, the oldest, showed an aptitude for figures. On leaving school in 1936 he went to work daily at a Taneatua branch of the Union Bank of Australia, which later became part of the Australia and New Zealand Bank. In October the same year Allen left school. He had farming in his blood and went to work at the age of 15 with his cousin Mannie, 9 years his senior. Their mutual love of horses was a bond between them. During those days they developed a good working relationship, which was to bear fruit in the years to come.

Len, on whose shoulders the main responsibility for the farm now rested, undertook, in a new and deeper way, responsibility for looking after the interests of his brother's family. Rose took Walter's place in the partnership of 'Sisam and Sons', and Len made it his concern to see that the upbringing and education of Walter's children continued unhindered. Three of Len's own children had already reached adulthood, but this still left a total of eight youngsters in the combined families who needed shepherding, with ages ranging from six to sixteen. These changed circumstances focussed even more sharply the importance of maintaining and strengthening the viability of the farm.

The situation had become especially difficult by 1931. For some time the farm had each year kept a number of yearling Jersey heifers until they were almost ready to milk and then sold them. This year 300 yearlings were taken to the Whakatane Saleyards to a special sale that had been well advertised. Only twenty were sold, and at a very low price. There was clearly no market so the sale was stopped and the heifers driven home. Len was worried as to what to do with the animals. Pete, who was living in the family home at King Street, but working for the New Zealand Loan and Mercantile Company in Whakatane, suggested milking them on the farm. This seemed to make sense because there was a slump in the beef market due to a severe drought, and it was therefore prudent to cease cattle-droving at this juncture. Len had always been against getting into dairying, but agreed that this was the wisest course to take.

By now, Mannie and Tommy Gee had moved out of the main farmhouse into a small house, where they kept one Jersey cow for their own supplies. They milked it by hand each day sitting beside the fence. As the yearling heifers withdrawn from the sale came into milk, the responsibility for the ever increasing hand-milking of these fell on Mannie and Tommy. A third man came to help them, Barney McCoogan, and they built a wooden race along the fence to channel water for the waiting animals. The new heifers were pretty wild, so at an appropriate moment the young men, feeling tough and wild, would spring on the new animals and bring them to the ground, so that they could then be tethered.

As time went by the hand-milking took longer and longer. If permanent dairying was to be undertaken on any profitable scale, milking sheds and proper facilities would have to be provided; and this the farm could ill afford. Apart from the recession, the loss of Alfred John in 1929 and now of Walter Holtom, imposed heavy death duties. The farm was exceedingly short of money. Many local farmers were in a similar position and finance companies were not providing credit. It was at this stage that Pete's four years experience in the financial field proved useful. After much perseverance he managed to negotiate a substantial loan from the Australian Mutual Provident Society. This saved the day. Eventually four milking sheds were built. Relations and friends took them on as share-milkers, on a profit-sharing basis. By the time the first one was completed there were 35 milking heifers. One of the first in the family to take on a shed was Len's eldest daughter, Doris, and her husband, George Symmans. They moved into the house on the farm where Mannie and Tommy Gee had been living, while Mannie and Tommy moved into a bach. Others of the family and their friends followed until all the milking-sheds were manned. The farm benefitted and jobs were created in the community at a time of need.

Pete was a busy man at this time. He was so committed to business that no one in the family thought he would ever marry. Nevertheless, he did have some social life. He was invited one evening to a small party at a house in King Street, where he met Edna List whose Norwegian forebears had emigrated to New Zealand some years before. At the end of the evening Pete, to whom she had scarcely spoken, offered to drive her home; despite the fact that he did not have his car with him and had to go home and fetch it. While he was gone, five other girls said they would also like to go home with Edna. So Pete took six girls home. But, as in his business dealings, he knew what he wanted. He kept in touch with Edna and invited her to go to the pictures with him at the Whakatane movie house. It was rather like a barn and was said to harbour rats, but her friends insisted that she go. Afterwards he took her to family supper at the Sisam home in King Street. There she met Mannie, Lorna and young Kenneth. From time to time after that they went on picnics together, often combined with business visits. On one occasion it was to buy pigs. Pete's evenings were usually taken up with phone calls, as he knew that was the only time he could reach his farmer clients. Sometimes he went down to his office in the evening and would take Edna with him. While she sat and worked at her embroidery on one side of the table, he would be making phone calls on the other. It was at about this time they decided to get married. The wedding took place in December 1933, at the height of the New Zealand summer.

From his six years at droving Pete had saved a thousand pounds. This enabled him to build a new house for Edna on land which he already owned. All in all, their future prospects looked more than satisfactory. The post he held in Whakatane was a good one. Originally the area operations of New Zealand Loan and Mercantile had been centered in Tauranga. They were now transferred to Whakatane, with Pete in charge. The days became even busier. Often they began at five in the morning. Sometimes Pete would get calls from farmers before they started work at four in the morning, if they wanted anything urgently.

On the Owhakatoro farm the milking enterprise was proving a success. The first milking shed run by Doris and George Symmans had rapidly reached a total of 280 cows daily. When the second shed was built half of the cows moved to it and another relative took charge of it. The herd increased meanwhile and the project progressed until all four sheds were operating. Each shed was a self-supporting unit, fenced in and complete with equipment. Each also had its own piggery. In this lay the beginnings of what later became a kind of pioneering family 'settlement', whereby different households were established on the farm, each with its own farming responsibility, yet linked together as a single enterprise.

Len's responsibility for the farm, following his brother Walter's death, was a demanding one requiring a constant and vigilant dedication. In the household at King Street a strict routine was followed. Just before daybreak Mabel would be up before anyone else, when her footsteps could be heard padding down the hall to a softly whistled tune. The stove would be filled, the kettle put on, and family breakfast followed – porridge, cream, eggs boiled or scrambled, bacon and sausage hot off the range, and toast made with a long-handled fork held over the glowing embers. The large kitchen table was formally set, ready for when Len appeared dressed in snake-proof trousers and white collarless shirt, face freshly shaven and an immaculate moustache. After the meal he would move to a chair by the kitchen window, pull on his boots left ready polished by Mabel, gather any gear needed and leave punctually for his inspection of the farm. Any intending passengers had to meet the deadline as there was no waiting about. Departure time was usually 7 or 7.30 a.m., depending on what calls had to be made on the way.

Arrival time at the farm was the same each morning, the destination being the house where Doris and George Symmons lived. Here Len would saddle up his horse and ride off

The Sisam home on King Street, Whatakane.

A street sign in Whatakane near the Sisam home on King Street preserves the family name.

on his rounds. If he was working close enough he would return to Doris for a hot, midday dinner at 12.30 p.m., rest for three-quarters of an hour and then ride out again. About 5 p.m his farm day ended and he would ride in, unsaddle, attend to his horse, and drive back to Whakatane for 'tea'. At King Street, if it was a Monday, there would have been the family wash. The washing was carried from the house across the yard to the wash-house. The copper was stoked for boiling, tubs would be filled with water, the scrubbing board would be readied, together with the wooden hand-wringer, and every scrap would be washed by hand. Even when washing machines came in, Mabel continued to do her laundering by hand, leaving her daughters to use the machine. Tuesday was ironing day, another long day, when an electric iron was used. All linen was starched, damped down with a sprinkler, then ironed. Following these two busy days, there was the house-cleaning, food perparation, gardening and, of course, everyday there was the care of the children.

In the haymaking season there were extra demands on the household. Mabel would be up at 2.30 a.m. to bake and prepare food, ready for transportation to the hayfields. All the workers involved in haymaking were fed and watered throughout the period as they raced against the weather to get the hay in. For the children it was a fine holiday. For the grown-ups it was very hard work indeed. Whatever she may have been doing during the day, Mabel was always ready to greet Len on his return. He would go to the same kitchen-window chair, remove his boots, leaving them neatly placed for cleaning, before retiring to the dining-room with the mail and newspapers of the day, until called for the evening meal. Normally after supper everyone congregated in the dining room. Other members of the family and friends would call in to discuss business or catch up on events. The youngest child present would sit on Len's knee for a cuddle before bed, while Mabel would be busy darning or stitching on the other side of the large fireplace. Just as it was in his father Alfred John's time, so in Len's household there was music and literature.

All Len's family were musical and loved a sing-song around the piano, one member playing the accompaniment, or joining in singing to a phonograph. Len was a voracious reader and kept a large collection of books. These were arranged in bookshelves reaching from floor to ceiling and extending almost the full length of the exterior wall of the dining-room. Family and friends were able to avail themselves of a wide-ranging selection and some used it as a lending library. The family reckoned there were as many books out on loan as there were on the shelves. The collection was always growing as everyone gave Len a book on gift-giving occasions.

On the 15 acres of land attached to the house grew plums, peaches, walnuts, nectarines, pears, grapes, gooseberries, grapefruit, passion fruit, Chinese gooseberries (Kiwi fruit), lemons, oranges and apples to be taken in season or preserved. Hens gave a plentiful supply of eggs, and two cows enough milk for the household and all the 'town' family members, as well as the local convent. The household made its own butter. In charge of the outdoor work was Jack Hewa, a Maori of the Tuhoe tribe and a follower of Te Kooti's

Leonard and Mabel and their family at King Street in 1940. Standing (L–R): Doris, Lorna, Harold Walter (Mannie), Mona, Eileen. Seated (L–R): Kenneth Charles, Leonard, Mabel, Leonard Alfred (Pete).

beliefs. He lived alone on the premises in a room next to the wash-house and ate his meals there which were prepared in the kitchen. The children knew that if no adults were about, Jack would always be generous and share his sugar sandwiches with them, a delicacy of which he was very fond.

Mabel found time to be involved in the local community as a member of the Lyceum Club, the Gardening Club, the Tennis Club and the Croquet Club. She was a founder President of the Country Women's Institute. Many Maori people would call at the house when she would talk to them in their own language. The children were fascinated by one elderly Maori lady who visited from time to time. She travelled in a horse-drawn dray which she halted in the drive-way, then she would sit under her conveyance in the shade, smoke her pipe and talk with Mabel. There were also the more formal occasions – garden parties, tennis and croquet parties – held on the lawns and in the garden, all kept immaculate by the handyman Jack.

As Len and Mabel's children grew up, each found their own way in life, not at all inhibited by the strict yet loving discipline which had characterised the household. The loyal, though sometimes protesting, Doris knew what she wanted to do. At the age of 15 she had packed up her schoolbooks, refused to study any more, and worked at home until she married George Symmans. He was a farmer's son who, in the depression years, pioneered a flourishing car-hire service when buses scarcely existed and few people had cars. Later he and Doris took one of the family milking sheds and spent the rest of their working lives on the farm.

Mona won a junior scholarship to Whakatane High School, then one to Auckland Grammar School, staying, as her brother Pete had done, with Grandfather Alfred and Auntie May at Woodside Road. Like her mother, she was a keen sportswoman. She played hockey, tennis and golf for the province. Having done well at school she took up teaching. In 1931 on February 3, a few days after the beginning of the school year, she was caught in the earthquake at Napier. It was at playtime and she was sitting at the school piano. A wall of the classroom collapsed, trapping her legs. Fortunately she was rescued unhurt. She immediately gave away all her spare clothes and money to those who had lost everything in the quake. A week later, as soon as the roads were cleared of the earthquake damage, she hired a taxi and travelled the 193 miles home to Whakatane. She arrived unannounced, walked in with only the clothes she stood up in and asked her father Len to pay the driver. This he did. A year later she went to Nelson to visit a young soldier, Guy Fowler, who had been one of the Army contingent sent to clear up the earthquake devastation in Napier. While she was in Nelson, Len and Mabel received a telegram from her on a Friday saying she and Guy were getting married the next day. At the time this caused some consternation in the family. However, Mona and Guy made their first home happily at Blenheim in the South Island. As he was a professional soldier, they subsequently moved house several times.

Lorna grew up to be a tall, slim young woman, rather like her Sisam aunts, Len's sisters. A popular person, she played golf and took part in local mannequin parades with Pete's wife Edna. One day she met an attractive Irishman at a dance, Geoff Fogerty. He was a gentle, handsome man, and they became devoted to one another. After they were married in 1939 they went share-milking at Kati Kati, near Tauranga, and later ran one of the milking sheds on the Sisam farm. In the last years of her life, after her husband's death, Lorna was a Justice of the Peace in Whakatane and a Marriage Celebrant conducting civil marriages for many young couples.

Eileen and Frederick James Harold (Buster) McCracken.

Like the others, Eileen went to school in Whakatane. The school was burnt to the ground during one summer holidays. When the winter term began, the children were taught in large tents, while the new school was being built. Eileen went on to Marlborough College, Blenheim, for a year, staying with Mona and her husband, Guy Fowler. Eileen blossomed and became a first-rate tennis player. She did a further year at Whakatane High School, playing cricket, tennis and basket ball; emerged as a smart young career woman, and went to work in a Whakatane solicitor's office. While there she took a business course in Auckland. Soon after this she brought home a tall young man by the name of Frederick James Harold (Buster) McCracken. He was the son of a local farmer and worked in a bank. They were married in 1944, and soon began farming on McCracken property close to the Sisam farm.

Ken, being the youngest of the family, was the apple of the family's eye. It was he who got a new bicycle, the others had hand-me-downs. He was a bright pupil at school and like Eileen he went on to Marlborough College, Blenheim, where he stayed for two years. Here he became proficient at languages. He was a good horseman and tennis player. He began work in an accountant's office in Whakatane and then moved to the New Zealand Loan and Mercantile Company, where, no doubt, Pete kept a watchful eye on him.

As the war clouds gathered, first over Europe and then the Pacific, New Zealand began to look to her defences. Recruitment for the part-time Territorial Army was increased. Walter working in a Taneatua bank and Allen at the farm, both being keen horsemen, joined a local mounted unit of the Territorials. Mannie, their cousin and an equally keen horseman, tried hard to enlist but each time was turned down for medical reasons. The final rejection was a great blow to him. He went back to the farm and for a long time could not bear to visit Whakatane. Guy Fowler, who was a professional soldier, was soon posted overseas with the first New Zealand contingent, to Egypt. This was a short time before his third child was born. Ken, twenty-one and as yet unmarried, was called up in due course. When World War II broke out, Walter and Allen had been mobilised and posted to a mounted defence regiment, the Auckland East Coast Mounted Rifles. But horses, though providing good local mobility, were soon outmoded. After Japan came into the war, Walter and Allen no longer rode horses but American 'Honey' tanks. While Walter was with his unit at Pukehohe, he called one day at the Union Bank of Australia. There a young woman working in the bank, Noeline Ogden from Devonport, Auckland, noticed him. They met again later at a dance and soon became engaged, undeterred by the wartime uncertainties. When the situation in the Pacific eased in 1943, and an invasion of New Zealand seemed less likely, the two brothers were posted overseas to Europe, Walter to the 20th New Zealand Armoured Regiment and Allen to the 18th. Ken, their cousin, was also posted to the 18th with Allen, and became an army interpreter on account of his gift of languages. The destination of all three was Italy.

❖ ❖ ❖

For the farm the war meant a shortage of man-power, equipment and spare parts, and a heavier workload. Fortunately Len had Mannie as his right-hand man throughout this difficult period. The work was hard but Mannie was determined not to let his physical weakness, dating back to his childhood rheumatic fever, prevent his making a maximum contribution to the farm. He often breakfasted at 3.30 in the morning, and was out riding all day until the evening mealtime, for he loved the farm. He knew he was following his calling, and he was therefore at peace within himself. His eleven years there had given him a wide experience, not least as a stockman concerned with sheep, cattle and horses; and many is the time, when the rivers and streams were in flood, he would be out getting the stock on to the high ground out danger of the flood-water. All three areas of the farm livestock operation were now in a healthy condition. The milking sheds were all in capable hands and continuing to function efficiently and profitably. The farm had made a complete recovery since the severe depression years. It seemed as if everything was now in place, ready, as it were, for an era of further progress and development.

Len, in these years, had the support and advice of Pete, who, as the area agent of the New Zealand Loan and Mercantile Company, held a key position in the local agricultural affairs. Now in his middle thirties, he too, like all those involved in farming then, had a full work-load. He and Edna were still living in the four-roomed house he had built when they married. Sadly, they lost their first child, Marlene, in an accident when she was quite young. In 1940 a second daughter, Rosalie, was born, and in 1942 a son, Peter, then finally in 1945 another daughter, Margaret.

The family at the Owhakatoro homestead was now much smaller. Dulcie, the eldest daughter, had married Percy Ingley in 1938. They went to live in Port Jackson at the end of the Coromandel Peninsular, where Percy had been working for some years. It was a remote place, only accessible by sea or a precarious road. There was no electricity.

Dulcie Ingley.

Walter John and Noeline Sisam.

Isabel and Graham (Andy) Quick.

Joan Stewart.

Supplies came once a week and Dulcie made her own bread. There were no medical facilities. Later they moved to the Hauraki Plains and finally to Thames. Dulcie became very well known in both these places for her church and community work, and also for her embroidery. Dulcie's two brothers, Walter and Allen, were serving overseas in the New Zealand armed forces. There remained at home their mother, and their sisters Joan and Isabel. Like their brothers and cousins, they went to Whakatane High School.

In 1929 Joan won a three-year scholarship to Auckland Grammar School and stayed with her aunt Lena in Woodside Road. When the scholarship ran out she continued school at Whakatane, after which she returned to Auckland and took a two-year course at the Teachers' Training College and gained a B.A. degree at the University. She returned to Taneatua and taught at the school, where she was joined by Isabel. During World War II she and Isabel together with a friend, Adele Nankivell, were the main stay of the teaching staff at Taneatua.

Isabel, the youngest of the three sisters, had had an adventurous start in life in which the old familiar Whakatane River featured. Rose, her mother, had realised that birth was imminent at a time when her husband was away on the far side of the farm. She had no means of getting across the river to the hospital; she waited anxiously for him all day and had already sent a basket of her clothes across the river in advance. He finally arrived at nightfall. They walked half a mile to the river, rowed across and Walter raced to a neighbour's where the car was kept. He drove back along the shingle bed of the river to where Rose was sitting, and furiously drove her the fourteen miles to Whakatane hospital. The baby, Isabel, arrived fifteen minutes later. Isabel seems to have had an affinity for the river. Some years later the children were swimming there when Isabel was seen floating face downwards with her fringe of hair spread out. Dulcie fished her out and all was well.

As a school teacher in later years Isabel taught in the Waikato, and through playing representative basket-ball she met and later married a young newspaper reporter, Graham (Andy) Quick, who became Sports Editor of the *Waikato Times* in Hamilton. Isabel did much work for her church and the community, particularly in the Citizens' Advice Bureau. Their second daughter followed her father's leaning towards sport, became a middle and long distance runner representing New Zealand, and made her name in the marathon when on an athletic scholarship in the United States.

Joan first met her husband-to-be during her year at Whakatane High School, where she came to know a promising student, Alan Stewart. Seventeen years later in 1950 they were married. In the meantime he had served in the Royal Navy during World War II, after which he took up a delayed Rhodes Scholarship to Oxford. Later he lectured at Massey College in New Zealand and then worked for the British Milk Marketing Board at Thames Ditton in England, where he and Joan made their home for several years. Whilst there they came to know Joan's cousins, Celia and Hugh, and their parents, Kenneth and Naomi, which was one of the highlights of their time in England. Alan became Principal of Massey College and when this was made a multi-faculty university he was appointed Vice-Chancellor. In 1981 he was knighted for his services to education. As well as fulfilling her official duties on the campus at Massey, Joan continued her own commitment to education as a member of the Federation of University Women and spent many years in voluntary work in the cause of Adult Literacy in New Zealand.

21
The Broad Acres

STEADY PROGRESS AT THE FARM – 'PETE' O.B.E.

Once they left New Zealand for Italy in 1943, the three Sisams -Walter, Allen and Ken – had very little contact with one another. They were in different units and had gone overseas at different times. For a while Walter and Allen, and possibly Ken, were fighting on the same front, but in different sectors. After that their units went in different directions in pursuit of different objectives. The common front had been the holding of the line at Cassino, where the allies were seeking to break through the massive German defences that barred the advance northwards. Allen was operating with an advanced reconnaissance unit of armoured cars, and Walter with a troop of Sherman tanks. When the breakthrough came, both reconnaissance and tank units headed north towards the river Po. Walter's squadron was the only tank unit to get across the river at that stage. The tanks then had to keep on going to provide support for the infantry, as they moved towards Bologna and Padua. The infantry were well rested because they had been relieved regularly during the advance, but not so the tank crews. They were very tired by the time they reached Padua.

North of Padua, on April 29, 1945, Walter's tank troop was ordered to seize an enemy-held bridge across the River Brenta. In the early hours of the morning when it was still dark Walter led the tanks and infantry for several miles until, coming under fire, he pressed home the attack so vigorously that they overran two enemy armoured cars, the enemy infantry, and at point blank range put two 105mm guns out of action. Three hundred enemy infantry were captured with their vehicles and equipment. He was subsequently awarded the Military Cross, the citation for which read:

'Through his bold action Second Lieutenant Sisam prevented the enemy demolishing a very valuable bridge which was afterwards used as the 'access' for the whole division. His complete disregard of personal safety and his exemplary leadership and courage were an inspiration to the whole squadron at all times.'

After his troops crossed the Brenta they were diverted from the main advance and sent to take control of recently liberated Venice. Since the city's thoroughfares were canals, tanks could not be taken into the heart of the city. They were left in a huge car park on the outskirts, while their crews were billetted in Venetian houses. After setting up a recreation centre for New Zealand troops, they themselves had the chance of a well-earned rest. On the day they left Venice to rejoin the main column, heading towards Trieste, they heard on their tank radio that the war in Europe had ended. Walter's tank crew celebrated with the only refreshment they had – one bottle of warm beer between the five of them.

Four months later, when the war with Japan ended, the New Zealanders began to leave Europe for home. Allen was among them, but not Walter. By a quirk of fate he had been part of the eleventh reinforcement to arrive from New Zealand, and being an officer and unmarried was posted for duty in Japan. The married men were exempt. The single men had no choice and consoled themselves with a little song, the chorus of which went: 'We wish we were married before we left home.' In the end Walter did not have long to wait. After a six month tour of duty in Japan he came home at last. That same year, 1946, he was married to the faithful Noeline Ogden, who had waited for him for three years.

Allen had returned to the family farm at Owhakatoro in January of that year, where he went to work again with Mannie. For Allen and Mannie this was the start of a new and close association which continued for over 26 years. They were to serve the farm well. No one thought Mannie would ever marry, but he surprised them all in 1947 when he and Adele (Del) Nankivell married. She was the same Adele Nankivell who, during the war years, had taught in the Taneatua School with Joan and Isabel Sisam. They went to live in Whakatane, moving later to the farm. Six weeks after Mannie's wedding his cousin Allen married Hazel Cave. They settled on the farm and made a permanent home there.

Walter went back to work for the Australia and New Zealand Bank and was posted to Palmerston North, a city of about 40,000 people, some 70 miles north of the capital, Wellington. Later he was moved to Te Kuiti, then to Christchurch, and finally to Wellington itself. His work in the bank involved some unusual assignments. One was the setting up in 1958 of a central stationery supply organisation for the bank, by which branches throughout the country received their requirements monthly instead of yearly, from one central and purpose-built depot in Christchurch. This cut costs dramatically, saving losses from over-stocking, and enabled the bank to make bulk purchases of stationery supplies at very economic rates. In 1968–9 another assignment was to take charge of the bank's conversion to computer operation. For this he was able to hand-pick his team for the job. As he said afterwards, 'They knew they were my choice and gave their very best.' It was not surprising that he was later made Chief Manager, Personnel and Services for the bank. He also became chairman of the computer processing company for the five trading banks in New Zealand.

While fully aware of the value of computers, he also knew how vital the human element was. He emphasised this aspect in all he undertook, as this quotation from him in the Chamber of Commerce Journal indicates:

'Perhaps the most important area of concern for leaders is the field of human relations, particularly industrial relations. In a country of small businesses industrial harmony is more easily maintained while the businesses remain small than when they grow. As top management becomes further and further removed from the work floor, managers need to give greater thought to the impact of their decisions upon the people who must implement them. It is only by the co-operation of all the people in the business that real progress is made.'

Ken came through the war safely, as did Mona's husband, Guy Fowler, and there were happy reunions at King Street, Owhakatoro and other homes. There were rejoicings in both the Owhakatoro and King Street families in these next years over weddings and then the arrival of grandchildren. The bumper year was 1950 with three family weddings, those of Joan, Isabel and Ken; when Joan married Alan Stewart, Isabel married Andy Quick and Ken married Joan Burnard of Gisborne.

In 1945, before Walter and Allen came home from the War, their cousin Pete Sisam, was promoted from the Whakatane branch of the New Zealand Loan and Mercantile Company to the Wellington headquarters. The purpose was to groom him for a senior post, in two

216   *The Broad Acres*

Allen Leonard Sisam.

Hazel Sisam, wife of Allen.

Adele Sisam, wife of Mannie.

Harold Walter Sisam (Mannie).

years time, when the occupant would retire. Although his heart was in the family farm, this was a chance too good to miss. It was not a complete severance from old ties, for Pete kept in close and constant touch with his father by telephone through the following years.

He set about the move to Wellington in a characteristically business-like way. He and Edna had two children at this time, Rosalie and Peter, and another was on the way. The need was urgent, so he rented an apartment and had a friend drive the children to Wellington from Whakatane. Auntie May, who had faithfully looked after her father, Alfred John, in his later years, joined them for a while. Pete was immersed in business affairs, so, after the birth of their next child Margaret, it fell to Edna to go out and look for a permanent home. However, Pete then saw a house at Lower Hutt which he felt was the perfect place. Edna was not so keen. It was not as near to the centre of Wellington, but unlike much of Wellington it was on level rather than hilly terrain. In the absence of a car Edna could get about on her bicycle. He said to her, 'You've got to be near some shopping and it's close to some schools. Those are the two important things.' Pete's judgement, though disconcerting, was sound. They moved in and stayed for 30 years, but retained a holiday home at Ohope Beach, Whakatane, to which they went every summer.

These 30 years were also a time of steady progress at the farm, when it entered into a period of continuing prosperity. In 1952 Len, with his long experience with horses and horse-breeding, bought the farm's first Arab horses, a fine Arab stallion 'Shereef' and two mares to put to him. This was the beginning of an Arab stud which became the largest in New Zealand, and produced many leading show jumpers. Arabs were mated with hack mares and the progeny sold as two-year-olds, much in demand as riding horses and for the show ring.

As Len advanced in years, Mannie and Allen assumed more and more of the responsibility for the daily running of the farm. Len still kept a close eye on everything, which Mannie naturally sometimes found irksome. Often Len would complain that when he went out to the farm to talk to Mannie he could never find him. As he became older his lonely rides over the hilly territory caused some anxiety as it was not always possible to keep him in sight. But he loved the farm and was totally committed to it, and insisted on this daily inspection.

Maori farmworkers had always played a part on the Sisam farm. It could not have operated without them. They were superb horsemen and cattlemen, expert at looking after the animals. When it came to the hard work of ditching and road-making, there were few who could equal them. Many of the Maoris lived in the nearby village of Ruatoki, higher up the valley towards the Urewera Forest. In the forest during the Maori War, the war leader Te Kooti had eluded his pursuers, of which Alfred John had been one. The men who worked on the Sisam farm knew they were working on land confiscated from their people, and that the Sisam homestead was built on the slopes of a Maori pa, or fortress, but this did not prevent their giving their best skills or regarding the Sisams as their friends. Len was regarded both with respect and affection by them. They knew that Mabel, his wife, was of Maori descent. They also knew Len was a straight and honest man, concerned with their well-being. They called him by his first name, which he appreciated. When any of them got into trouble, as sometimes happened, the police would call Len who would go down to the Whakatane gaol, collect the offender and take him home. Once, after one of these episodes, as Len was having a fatherly talk with him, the man said, 'Well, Len you have your fun at the Auckland Show every year. You must let me have mine here in Whakatane.' That was a difficult one to answer.

Len and Mabel were true grandparents and whenever their grandchildren came to stay they treated them in exactly the same way as they had their own children. They set them standards. Life was strictly ordered, but love surrounded and bound the whole family. Len expected good manners. At the kitchen table the two youngest would be sat on either side of him and the rest in ascending order of age towards the other end of the table, where the two oldest would be on either side of Mabel. In the morning the children would have their nails, teeth and face inspected to be sure they were clean. Then, and only then – provided the hair was combed and tidy and clothes neat – could they take their places at table. There was a great scramble not to be last, or Len would name the late-comer, 'the last rose of summer'. Table manners were strictly policed and good behaviour rewarded, either with cuddles or lollies, or even 2/6 to spend like a millionaire. Every child was brought up to be a caring and responsible family member, supportive of each person in the extended circle, and strongly rooted in the home. Towards the end of their lives Len and Mabel found themselves alone, with all their children married, and they now needed help in the home. Lorna and her family moved into the King Street house to be with them and run the household. Lorna, in due course, inherited the house and its contents.

❖ ❖ ❖

In the early 1950s, despite his commitments in Wellington, Pete still dreamed that he might one day return to the farm permanently and play a more direct role in it. It was a deep longing in his heart. About that time he completed, with Mannie, a short film of the history of the farm, made mainly during the family holidays. Pete wrote and recorded a commentary to it. There was a grand showing to the family. It was on this visit that he probably realised his dream could never come true. He could see that his brother Mannie was firmly based there, and needed to be there. The farm had made a life for Mannie where he had the freedom to go at the pace that suited him, and to rest when he needed to. Pete could see there was no room for him as well, and that he must stand aside and let his brother enjoy the life that had been given to him. The closing words of the film commentary, as the various members of the family appeared on the screen, were, 'And now we must say goodbye to them all and go back home to Wellington.' These were simple words, and Edna felt that for Pete they had a deeper meaning and a sad finality, marking the end of a dream. But for the rest of his life he served the farm in every way he could. That same year, 1956, Pete's mother, Mabel Sisam died – descendant of a Maori princess, outstanding horsewoman, scholar, and loving mother to her family.

Len lived on another five years after Mabel's death. The farm was his life and remained so until he died in 1961 at the age of 82. In the press it was written of him: 'He was the soul of honour to all men . . . he was beloved and held in high respect by all for his repeated generosity and help to those less fortunate than himself.' In October 1966 the *New Zealand Herald* ran an article chronicling the development of the 10,640-acre farm, in which it said: 'Owhakatoro must rank amongst the largest mixed farms in New Zealand' and which ended: 'Owhakatoro and the Sisams who have built it represent a chapter in New Zealand history.'

Credit for a great deal of the farm's development should be given to Len. He served the farm for over 60 years. For many of those years, after his brother's death, he alone carried the ultimate responsibility. He laid the foundation which later made possible the

'After Len, the reins fell naturally into Mannie's and Allen's hands.'

The part of the farm known as Sisam Valley.

consolidation of the farm during the economically buoyant and expanding market following World War II. This ensured an inheritance for the next generation.

After Len, the reins fell naturally into Mannie's and Allen's hands. They became joint managers of the farm, on behalf of the family partnership, and they sought to continue the spirit of that partnership as originally envisaged by their grandfather, Alfred John Sisam. The principles of fairness and equal participation were maintained, no matter the difficulties or misunderstandings that might arise from time to time. Their own children were now growing up fast. Mannie and Del had one son, Harold Robert, and two daughters. Harold studied forestry and accountancy. Allen and Hazel had six sons, but no daughters. Later three of their sons studied for degrees in agricultural science. In May 1968 Allen's mother, Rose, who had always taken a keen interest in the life of the community, died at the age of 81.

There were further developments and transformations on the farm after Len's death, under the joint management of Mannie and Allen. More amd more land was brought into pasture which by 1966 totalled 8,000 acres. The spreading of fertilizer was now carried out by aircraft, using six different landing strips. The number of sheep increased to 13,500 including 7,564 Romney ewes. The original small herd of Aberdeen Angus beef cattle was steadily expanded. There were now 750 Jersey milking cows and 725 Jersey yearling heifers, and 'Sisam & Sons' also went into deer farming. All this was possible as the pastures improved. There were 4 shepherds on the farm and 12 general hands, as well as the 4 share-milkers. The breeding of Arab cross-breds, introduced by Len, was further developed. The cross-breds were much in demand at home and overseas, so that the breeding of them became one of the farm's most important facets. High-class Arab stallions were purchased in New Zealand, and were also imported from Australia and Holland. Two of their best known were 'Crescendo' bought in Australia, and 'Dynamit' bought from Holland. Allen made this his speciality, and Sisam-bred horses very soon made a name for themselves as shepherds' hacks, show jumpers, and 'endurance riding' horses. A Sisam-bred horse, 'Syndicate', was part of the New Zealand team at the 1980 Tokyo Olympics.

On the death of Len, Pete had succeeded him as Chairman of the Board of Trustees, and as such continued to make regular visits to the farm. He was also fast becoming a leading figure in New Zealand business and government circles. He devoted a great deal of his energies to facilitating the merger between New Zealand Loan and Mercantile and the international export-import group, Dalgety. This was successfully completed in 1961, and he was appointed General manager of Dalgety (New Zealand). In Pete's family household 1961 was a memorable year for other reasons as well. For years he had strenuously refused to have a television in the house. 'No way', he would say, 'We are not going to have a television.' So, to celebrate the Dalgety merger, the family secretly clubbed together and bought him a set. He took to it like a duck to water. He would come home after a busy day, turn on the set and forget all his worries. The children were more than delighted.

In the late 1960s the Government encouraged the planting of radiata pine, and special tax benefits were available for planting trees. The farm already had small plantations of pines. On a visit there Pete noted that there were large areas of scrubland which could also be used for forestry, and suggested that this should be undertaken. In 1970 'Sisam and Sons' began a major planting extending over 2,000 acres, which Allen supervised.

The years in which Mannie and Allen shared the responsibility of the farm were fruitful

Farm uplands with shearing sheds in the distance.

Cross-bred Arab horses carrying the Sisam brand mark.

'Sisam & Sons' farm truck.

Leonard Alfred Sisam OBE.

ones. Both lived on the spot. Allen was at the Owhakatoro homestead where his father had lived, and Mannie and Del had built a house near the farm entrance. Like their fathers they knew every inch of the property, and on it spent years of great fulfilment and joy. They had seen significant developments take place, and began to see the next generation coming onto the farm, some with families, each taking responsibility for different aspects of the work. In 1977 Mannie retired, leaving Allen and the younger generation to carry the new developments to full fruition.

In Wellington Pete had an even heavier workload than before, which involved frequent visits to London, and elsewhere. At that time Dalgety was a household name in New Zealand, with branches in every town. Pete was also on the London Board of Directors. There was a welcome break every summer when he spent the holidays at Ohope Beach with the children. He could scarcely wait to get there when the time came, for he was a real family man and loved his home. When there he would potter in his garden, with its fountain which he had made and enjoyed, doing nothing in particular. There was no golf or organised leisure activity, just lazing and enjoying his family. In 1972 in Wellington he was suddenly stricken with a serious heart attack. His first instruction to Edna was to telephone Dalgety and arrange for three months leave. There were several other practical things he wanted done. One was immediately to buy a new car (which was overdue), and another was to send to the Wellington Club the ninety cents that he owed. He made a good recovery but had to relinquish most of his responsibilities on the board of Dalgety, of which he was then chairman. In a way it was a relief for him, and he was more than happy to be able to go and live quietly at Ohope in their beautiful home which was right on the beach, facing the Pacific Ocean. In 1979 he received the OBE for services to New Zealand agriculture.

In 1982 the farm was faced with an unexpected financial crisis just at a time when everything seemed to be secure. Ken, Pete's youngest brother, who had also worked for New Zealand Loan and Mercantile, had died in 1968 after a long spell in hospital. On coming of age his two sons and their sister would inherit a share in the farm, left to them by their grandfather, Leonard Wilfrid. They wished to take their capital out of the trust. The hidden danger that looms over all large family enterprises had now materialised. All the trustees, including Pete and their accountants were greatly concerned, as this posed a threat to the farm's viability. Finally, in 1982, an arrangement was made with the Tasman Forestry Limited whereby 'Sisam and Sons' would borrow the needed money from them and the company would have all rights to harvest the forest in due course. The loan would thus be repaid from the proceeds of this harvesting. This plan was only possible because in earlier years Pete had the foresight to urge the planting of a large acreage of trees. If the farm had not had to dispose of the timber in this way it would have brought in greater profit than all the rest of the farming operations put together. That same year Pete, who had been frail for some years, died in the month of July.

Five years later, in the summer of 1987, there was a great family reunion at the farm of the descendants of Alfred John Sisam. It was to honour him and his wife Maria, 125 years after he and his brothers landed in New Zealand. Allen and Hazel acted as the hosts and organisers. A marquee was set up in the paddock. There was tea and coffee for folk arriving in the morning from a distance, and a full-blown lunch at midday. It came by road just before 1 o'clock in a Whakatane caterer's trucks all freshly prepared, and in ten minutes it was all set out on the long trestle tables. The cutlery was put out in neat piles

Part of the crowd at the Reunion. Allen Sisam stands on the left.

Peter Sisam, Chairman of the Board of Trustees of the family farm and son of 'Pete', made the welcome speech at the Reunion.

Some grandchildren of Alfred John cutting the celebration cake. Sitting (L–R): Celia Sisam (Guest of Honour from England). Ian McCarroll (descendant of Tottie), Dulcie Ingley, and Mannie Sisam.

and everyone helped themselves, as suited young or old appetites. All ages, in fact, were present. An ice cream van came in the afternoon for the children. They were also taken for rides round the outback in a tractor-trailer, driven by Allen's son, Bruce, and grownups were transported in trucks. Every family was group-photographed, and there was an exhibition of old family pictures. Celia Sisam from England, daughter of the Oxford academic, Kenneth Sisam, was the guest of honour, and made a speech about the origin of the Sisam name. There was also a speech by Peter Sisam, Pete's son, now Chairman of the Board of Trustees who managed the farm.

It was a truly happy event, and in a way marked the end of an era, the era which the older generation had nurtured. It was a fitting climax of the years in which Allen and Mannie had run the farm, for within two years they both died. It was these two cousins who had seen the farm through one of the most important periods of its history.

22
Arrow & After

JAMES LEONARD, PATRIACH OF ARROW MILL, AND HIS HEIR

It is often said that Britain unwittingly exports a good deal of her best ideas and manpower, as if this tight little island could not contain all its burgeoning vigour and creativity. The Sisams at Arrow certainly responded to the call of distant horizons and made their contribution to far away places. The family had already sent some of its men to New Zealand. These maintained close links with their old home by regular correspondence, and many of the values, traits and even customs of Arrow re-emerged in a new land. Sometimes their descendants, like Kenneth Sisam, returned from distant shores and made their contribution to the homeland itself and from there to the world at large. The emigration from Arrow and elsewhere in the 1860s naturally caused some shrinkage in the English family line, as did the natural hazards of illness and accident, together with the occasional reluctance of some male Sisams to embark upon matrimony.

In 1870, when his father died, James Leonard Sisam inherited the lease of Arrow Mill. He was 25 at the time and single. In the previous year his eldest brother, William Henry, had married Helen New of Winchcombe. Within a few years James Leonard married Helen's younger sister, Letitia. Both weddings took place in Winchcombe's medieval, limestone church that dominates the centre of the town.

Letitia proved to be an exemplary and house-proud wife to James Leonard. Not long after moving into Arrow Mill, and probably as a result of her propensity for tidyness, she found in one of the attics the family's copper tea urn, covered in dust and cobwebs. She cleaned it and put it into use and many were the times her kitchen maid was told to polish it; for the regime in Letitia's household was well ordered, correct and probably strict. She kept two maids and was very particular about the washing-up of dishes. Everything had to be washed twice, in separate tubs, then rinsed in a third tub of cold water and dried. The tubs had to be wooden, and china and metal were never allowed to touch.

James Leonard was a quiet man, gentle in manner but with strong convictions about right and wrong. He had beautiful hands, so much so that at first sight it appeared that he had never done a day's manual work in his life. But that was far from the truth. He was a working miller and a practical one at that. His character combined two remarkable qualities. He was a natural gentleman and an able businessman. In his hands Arrow Mill progressed.

For centuries milling at Arrow had been by the use of millstones, as was the general practice. All flour was stone-ground, and retained the health-giving bran fibre. But in the late 1880s, in the days long before health foods, there was a growing demand for the new white flour which had originated in Hungary. It was considered to be more elegant and more palatable and though less nutritious it was, for those with weak stomachs, easier to

Arrow Mill and Mill-pond as it looked in James Leonard Sisam's day.

A typical mill grindstone which produced coarse-grained brown flour.

Oversley Mill in the late 1930s when more and more country corn mills were falling into disuse.

digest. Millstones could not produce the highly refined, bran-free flour, so the switch to steel rollers in place of millstones began. James Leonard, like his father during his occupancy of the mill, knew that Arrow Mill must move with the times. He installed steel rollers in Arrow Mill in the late 1880s.[14] Steel rollers, on the other hand, could not handle the production of provender, or coarse grain, for cattle-feed. This led to the renting of Oversley Mill a mile or so upstream from Arrow for that purpose. It was owned by the Throckmorton family who had been landowners in the district for many hundreds of years, and in 1605 were involved in the Gunpowder Plot to blow up Parliament. From the same estate two farms were also leased, Primrose Hill Farm and Castle Farm, both of which stood on the hill above Arrow Mill. Various members of the family occupied them from time to time. Primose Hill Farm took its name from the carpet of primroses that covered the hill in early spring; now, alas, destroyed by modern pesticides. Castle Hill Farm was so named because it had a white tower. It was known in the family as 'The Castle'.

As the years went by, other properties were added to the Arrow Mill enterprise. One of the earliest of these was South Arrow Farm. This lay a short distance up Arrow Lane, a narrow road leading out of Arrow village towards Inkberrow. Apart from the crops it grew, the farm was a useful place to keep spare cart-horses. A foreman-in-charge lived there. In 1909, not long after the acquisition of South Arrow Farm, James Leonard made purchases in the Cotswold village of Ebrington near Chipping Campden. One was Pudlicote Mill Farm for £3,800 and another the land adjoining it for £121, both south of the village. The third consisted of three stone cottages in the middle of the village, two with thatched roofs and one with slate, for £125. Two years later for £3,400 he bought Marfurlong Farm, near Pudlicote. All these properties had tenants whose leases continued. These transactions reflect the prosperity of rural flour mills at that period. James Leonard's last purchase was in 1919, in his later days, when the Throckmorton family disposed of some of their land: he bought Castle Hill Farm.

Throughout his time, as in the days of his father and grandfather before him, flour was delivered to customers by wagons drawn by teams of carthorses, all immaculately turned out. On average the mill kept fourteen horses and five wagons. The meadows, which surrounded the mill and formed part of the property, provided good grazing for the animals and a crop of hay each year. The flour was supplied mainly to local bakers and to a few large-scale bakers in Birmingham. The wheat for milling came from a wide area, some of it from farms on the Cotswold Hills. There was a good rapport between James Leonard and the farmers who supplied the grain, in which mutual trust was a major factor. It is said that many farmers never bothered to keep an exact record of the quantites they supplied, as they knew they would get an honest tally from Sisam the miller; which they did.

The children who grew up at Arrow Mill were fortunate to live within walking distance of schools. From the late 1860s Arrow village had its own primary school just across the meadow from the Mill; and in Alcester, three-quarters of a mile away, there was the Grammar School, an old foundation going back to around the year 1490. Amongst Alfred John's papers in New Zealand there was a picture postcard of this school looking very much as it was when he attended it. He was followed by generations of Sisams until the 1930s when young Harry Sisam, James Leonard's grandson, was the opening bat for the school cricket team. The school itself still flourishes but has moved to new buildings. The originals have long since disappeared.

Although there were scholarships offered for children to attend the Grammar School, and some Sisams won these, most parents had to pay tuition fees. Naturally parents expected good value for their money. As James Leonard had his three sons at the school – Henry, Frank, and Walter – he was in a good position to judge the quality of the education they were receiving. The school records show that in 1891 James Leonard Sisam was involved in a hot controversy. On behalf of 34 other parents in the district he sent a petition to the governors complaining of 'the inefficiency of the school: drawing not being taught, shorthand only occasionally, drill exercises now discontinued, the management is not good, the master often being called out, manners not taught, boys after being there become degraded.' The complaint was not so much about the school's scholastic standards as its standards of discipline and organisation. But the governors strenuously denied the charges, and objected to the use of the word 'degraded'. The complainants courteously agreed to moderate the expression used, but held strongly to their main contentions. There was a marked improvement in the school after that, and the headmaster engaged a second master to assist him.

James Leonard Sisam.

Newport's Free School, later known as Alcester Grammar School.

The three Arrow Mill boys at the school, like their uncles of the previous generation, were known as Sisam I, II and III, and like their uncles performed creditably. The same was true of their older cousin Alfred, youngest son of William Henry and Helen, who was at the school at the same time and was know as Sisam A. In December each year there was a school examination conducted by a visiting academic and in 1891 the examiner was the Rev. Mr. Stoneman, the Vicar of Longborough, near Stow-on-the-Wold. The subjects covered included Latin, French, English Grammar, Arithmetic, Geography, History, and Divinity. Sisam A (cousin Alfred) came second in Geography, Sisam II (Frank) was first in Divinity and second in Arithmetic, and Sisam III (Walter) was overall second in all subjects in the Junior Class.

The household at Arrow Mill was very much a family centre, and there were frequent comings and goings. Letitia Sisam had always been close to her sister Helen who, as she lived in Alcester, visited Arrow Mill every week bringing her small daughter Peggy with her. James Leonard, who had blue eyes and wore sideburns, was very fond of children, especially of this little niece. He called her 'the lamb'. She looked up at him one day, gazing at the sideburns, and said, 'Then I shall call you 'ruff'un''. Peggy in fact was a step-niece, for Helen's first husband, William Henry Sisam, James Leonard's brother, had died and Helen had married again. When Caroline, Helen's elder daughter by William Henry, came to be married, she had no real father to give her away. It was James Leonard who took his brother's place at the wedding and did the honours. He was kind to everyone, especially to those in need.

He kept up a regular correspondence with his brothers in New Zealand, offering financial help at a difficult period, and for years watched over his brother Tom, who returned from there in ill-health. At the same time he carried wide responsibilities. There were the many properties to oversee and, in addition to Arrow and Oversley Mills, there was also Harvington Mill, which the family had rented for many years and for which he became responsibile. His output was all the more remarkable considering that he was of a delicate constitution. That he lived as long as he did was because Letitia looked after him. In his later years, after he retired from Arrow Mill, he spent much of his time sitting in his armchair. But when grandchildren came to visit he would as likely as not get his cane and walk them down the street to the sweet shop; or perhaps take them for a spin in the pony and trap through the dappled sunlight and shade of the leafy lane leading to South Arrow Farm.

When James Leonard's oldest son Henry reached manhood he was uncertain whether he wanted to take on Arrow Mill when his father retired. The representative of the flour industry magazine *Milling*, who visited the mill in 1909, wrote of him that 'the young gentleman is credited with having more ambitious ideas'. Be that as it may, when James Leonard finally retired the following year, Henry Leonard did take on the mill. His father and mother then went to live at a pleasant corner house in Priory Street, Alcester, known in the family as 'the Priory'. The family had owned it for some years, and it was from here that James Leonard's widowed mother, Caroline Sisam, had written her early letters to the Sisam grandchildren at Arrow Farm in New Zealand.

❖ ❖ ❖

Henry, the new master of Arrow Mill, had always been somewhat of an enigma. Unlike his two brothers, Frank and Walter, who were open-hearted and outgoing by nature, he was shy and retiring, and at times morose. He was a good son to his parents, but none of the

The Arrow Parish Council. Amongst those standing: Tom Rouse (4th from left), the head gardner to the Marquis of Hertford and Henry Leonard Sisam. Seated are: The Marquis of Hertford, the Rev. J. Stannus (vicar of Arrow), George Clarke the Arrow wagon and coach builder.

family thought he would ever marry. He became firm friends with Tom Rouse, a local farmer's son. They served together on Arrow Parish Council, and there is a contemporary photograph showing them in a group with their fellow councillors. It includes the top-hatted Marquis of Hertford (lord of the manor), his estate agent, his head gardener, the Rector of Arrow, the church sexton, the church clerk and the village wagon-builder George Clarke. They were all interesting characters. George Clarke was a superb craftsman and built wagons and coaches for customers throughout the district, some of which are now preserved as museum pieces. He also used to shoe the Arrow Mill horses, and in winter would 'ruff' the shoes to prevent slipping on the ice. This was done by fixing wedge-shaped 'frost' nails to the shoes.

Tom Rouse's family had come to the district recently from a remote farm at Par in Cornwall, in the extreme south west corner of England; an area which was isolated from the rest of the country by its geographical location. The farm the Rouses moved to near Alcester was in a way also remote, not only in distance but in atmosphere. There had been a homestead there for a very long time. It had the daunting name of Cold Comfort Farm, sometimes written Colcomfort Farm. The origin of this was unknown, but local legend has it that Shakespeare called there one day and asked for some refreshment, only to be given a drink of water.

Much to everyone's surprise Henry did marry, in 1910. His bride was Mary Westlake Rouse, Tom Rouse's sister. The wedding took place at Par, in Cornwall, rather than at Arrow; probably so that the many Cornish Rouse relations could attend. This was in the same year that Henry's father retired from Arrow Mill. Henry having now taken charge of the mill, which included a good sized dwelling house, was fortunate to have found a partner and companion with whom to share the future. He soon showed himself to be a capable, intelligent, and hard-working man, with a good business-sense and a reputation for honesty. In milling he moved with the times. By 1910 the population of Britain had increased to the extent that home-grown corn could not meet demand, and there were increasing supplies of grain coming into the ports from Canada and Australia. Henry obtained his imported grain direct from the Avonmouth Docks at Bristol, where a supply of sacks bearing his name and imprint were stored. The filled sacks were delivered by rail to Alcester station, where they were collected by the wagons from Arrow Mill.

Both Henry and Mary were approaching middle-age when they married, and Mary was 40 when their son, James Leonard Jr., was born. She was a warm hearted and kindly person, but reserved and not much given to conversation. She found it difficult to deal with her un-communicative husband. Sometimes there were days when scarcely a word was spoken. Mary unfortunately did not take to Arrow Mill, and felt the river with its slippery banks was an unsafe place for a child. She feared for her young son Jim (James Leonard Jnr.). She knew that just across the meadows in Arrow churchyard there was the tombstone of an 11 year old David Sisam, drowned in the Arrow River in May 1833. So great was her concern that, while busy in the kitchen, she would tether Jim to the kitchen table leg with a strap, to prevent his wandering too far. The boy, on the other hand, as he

Henry Leonard Sisam.

Mary Westlake Rouse.

grew older, thoroughly enjoyed living in a mill and was forever playing at being a miller. To his delight his father gave him a toy wagon bought in a shop in Birmingham. Jim's name and address had been painted on it, just as his father's was on the big mill wagons. Henry had taken the toy wagon to George Clarke, the Arrow wagon-builder, and asked him to put the boy's name on it.

Arrow Mill stood in 50 acres of grass, which were grazed by the 12 or 15 draught horses that hauled the mill wagons. Some hay was produced and there were a few cows. The latter were looked after by a farmworker who lived in at the mill. In addition to cows there were pigs. There was a vegetable garden growing, amongst many other things, Russian comfrey. Flowing water dominated the setting. The River Arrow ran the full length of the eastern boundary and, with the tributary mill-stream running under the mill to the millpond, it formed a green island on which stood some of the buildings. Fish and water birds abounded, especially moorhens, kingfishers, coots, and occasionally swans. Sometimes this presented problems. Once one of the mill workers arrived at the kitchen door with a dead swan he had somehow managed to kill, and wanted Mary Sisam to cook it for him. She refused to have anything to do with it. Perhaps she knew that in England swans were royal property.

The mill building itself was not a good spot in which to work. It was damp and in places awkward. The labour involved was hard. There were heavy sacks to lift, machinery to tend, and a constant vigilance to be maintained. Henry was a slimly built man and not all that robust. Yet he never complained. He would buckle into the job, saying that he did not mind the hard work so long as he could do a good day's work. The mill ran 24 hours a day in two 12-hour shifts, except for Sundays when it was still. It started up again at 10 p.m. each Sunday evening and ran without stopping until 10 p.m the following Saturday. Two men worked the night shifts during the weekdays and five or six the day shifts. The rumbling of the machinery could be felt throughout the building, including the family living quarters. Mary thought it was like heaven when the rumbling ceased on Sundays. The flow of the river had to be watched constantly as it affected the level of the water reaching the turbine propellers. Control of the water was effected by adjusting sluice-gates where the millstream left the main course of the river. If there was too little the mill would stop. If there was too much the turbines could suffer damage and the mill machinery would turn too fast.

By day, from time to time, there would be deliveries of grain from the port of Bristol, and regularly wagon-loads of flour would leave the mill for delivery to customers. Once a fortnight the miller would visit customers to receive orders. During the 1914–18 war white flour was in scarce supply. Most people had to make do with the coarse, wartime mixture containing a high precentage of bran. When people were ill they craved for white flour since it was easier to digest, and members of the family would come to Arrow Mill to beg some of their strictly rationed white flour. When the war ended Henry Leonard bought Oversley Mill which the family had previously rented. By his outright purchase of Oversley Mill for £1,500, he gained complete control of the flow of river water to Arrow Mill lower downstream.

With the War over Henry acquired his first automobile in 1919, an American 14 h.p. Trumbull. He bought it secondhand from a man at Coughton near Alcester. It was a two-seater and Jim sat on his mother's lap. The gearbox was on the rear axle. However it was easier to start than many cars as there were taps on the cylinder block so that petrol could be poured directly into it. Nevertheless, Henry frequently had difficulty starting it and became increasingly frustrated with the car. He pulled up at a garage one day and discovered that one of the rear wheels was nearly off. On inspection both rear wheels were found to be held in place with a piece of wire. The last straw was when the car broke down at Binton station as the family were on their way to Frank Sisam's farm. Henry abandoned the car there and then and reverted to a pony and trap. He was a man with a hot temper, and both people and machines endured his wrath.

As the years went by Henry began to have severe trouble with his legs, due to much standing in the mill and the lifting of heavy sacks. His doctor warned him that the work was too hard for him. The upper storey of Arrow Mill, where a good deal of the work took place, had a low ceiling so that it was impossible to stand upright. Henry asked the landlord, the Marquis of Hertford, to raise the roof. The Marquis declined to do so on the grounds that it would make the mill visible from his home at Ragley. Finally, when the lease of the Mill was about to run out, the Marquis gave Henry notice to quit. This was in 1921. Thus nearly a hundred years of Sisam occupation of Arrow Mill came to an end. Almost immediately the mill was sold outright to a firm of local millers, Adkins and Thomas of Broom. The first thing the new owners did was to raise the roof.

The year 1921 was also the year in which James Leonard Sisam died. He had been a patriarch in the best sense of the word, and had exemplified the virtues that had long been associated with the family, and continued to be so after his death. Writing of him, the *Evesham Journal* commented, 'By his conscientious and straightforward dealings he was well-known and highly respected, not only in the immediate district, but throughout a very wide area.'

When his lease of Arrow Mill came to an end, Henry was uncertain what to do next. He thought of continuing in milling and investigated a possible purchase of the large flour mills on the River Avon at Evesham. But he found that they had been used as a canning factory during the 1914–18 war and all the mill machinery and been taken out and disposed of. Instead he decided to take up farming, and bought a property named Radbrook, near Preston-on-Stour, a few miles from Stratford-upon-Avon.

He and Mary and five year-old Jim moved into an imposing, Georgian house which had decorated ceilings, oak panelling, and a fine, Adam-type tiled fireplace and flag-stone floors. It was a cold house, and one severe winter the chamber pots froze. The only water supply was from an outside pump in the courtyard. The property had been run as a dairy farm but had been neglected and no hedges had been laid for forty years. Henry spent a considerable amount of money on the place and put it into good shape, with everything in order and every gate opening properly.

The extent of the farm was about 239 acres, to which Henry added another 13 acres rented from the neigbouring Alscot Park Estate. He used most of the land for grazing cattle and pigs, as the wet subsoil made all but a few fields unsuitable for corn-growing. The pasture was good but it was not an easy farm, for being in a river valley the wet land made both cattle and pigs susceptible to disease; and there were no antibiotics available then. Four or five men were employed permanently with seasonal labour when necessary. When the price of beef fell, Henry reduced his herd of Hereford-Shorthorn cattle and increased the pig-breeding. At one time he had over thirty sows, which was a considerable number for those days.

Radbrook was an isolated place away from the village and there was little social life. Henry did not go out of his way to make friends there. An exception was Harvey Smith of Lower Farm, Preston, a neighbour who seemed to understand him. Henry was by

Radbrook Manor, Preston-on-Stour.

profession a miller rather than a farmer. Harvey Smith did his best to help him become established at Radbrook, but he found that Henry did not welcome advice. Like most of the farmers in the neighbourhood, Harvey was a member of the local hunt. Henry was not a member and refused to follow the custom of removing barbed wire from his hedges during the hunting season. Harvey went to see him about it and managed to persuade him. They became good friends and Harvey would drop in at Radbrook of an evening. Henry would say to him, 'You know where to find me. I'll be in the barn', for he would spend most evenings, not at the family fireside, but in the barn mending sacks.

When Henry was in the house young Jim had to be very quiet and was not allowed to get his toys out of the cupboard and spread them on the floor. Sometimes Jim would ask his mother wistfully, 'When is father going out?' Radbrook was a lonely place for the boy. Longing for companionhip, he would often jump up beside the drivers of lorries calling at the farm, and ride with them on their rounds. In due course he went to the village school in Preston. There he made friends with a farmer's son, Andrew Bishop. It was a friendship that lasted, and though their paths went different ways it was resumed in later years. Jim's father had many things on his mind during these years. There were the problems of the farm and of his own health. Because he was short-tempered Mary became afraid to approach him on any subject. She avoided answering the telephone for fear of being upbraided for saying the wrong thing. Henry's apparent inability to take Mary into his confidence caused her to turn more and more to her son for companionship, and to centre her life on him. She bought his clothes out of her own pocket, and also her own. She and Jim were inevitably drawn together and she spoiled him. This did not help the boy to overcome the hot temper he had inherited.

Since Radbrook was a remote spot it was necessary to go to Stratford-upon-Avon to shop. Jim and his mother often caught the bus into Stratford. They drove from the farm by pony and trap as far as the bus stop and left both with a neighbour. But the pony died suddenly one day and was not replaced; so from then on they had to walk to the bus and back, carrying the shopping home. Most of the time it was muddy, especially where the cattle congregated round the farm gates. When setting out they would take a clean pair of shoes each, which they put on when they neared the main road. The dirty shoes they would hide in the hedge until they returned.

Henry's brother, Frank, who farmed about twenty miles from Radbrook and kept in touch with Henry, was much concerned at Jim's isolated upbringing. Frank felt deeply about it and poured out his heart to his other brother, Walter. It seemed to them both that Jim needed a break from the closed-in atmosphere of Radbrook, and that a good boarding school might be the answer. As a boy Frank had gone to Dean Close School, in Cheltenham, and had benefitted greatly from it. When approached Henry responded to the idea, but Mary would have none of it.

So Jim remained at the village school, but was also tutored by the headmaster for a scholarship to Stratford Grammar School. He won the scholarship and went as a day-boy. It was a step forward but it did not free him from the confines of Radbrook. His cousin Peter, Walter's son was already at the Grammar School but as a boarder. In 1928 Jim began going daily; cycling to the end of the lane where he left the bicycle at a neighbour's farm and caught the bus. Later he cycled all the way there and back, a full ten miles every day. Like many boys when he first arrived at the school he was subjected to bullying. Another boy Vernon Carr, known as 'Boy' Carr, somewhat bigger than Jim, saw what was happening and stepped in to side with him. The two became firm friends. Vernon had difficulty with his homework. Jim, who had a quick brain, was a great help to Vernon and would often assist him or let him copy his work. That was the beginning of another lasting friendship.

Jim enjoyed the wider horizons that the Grammar School offered. He found that there were boys from all round his neighbourhood cycling into Stratford every day to the Grammar School. He responded to the comradeship of his peers. He had a sense of humour and enjoyed a joke, especially the ones the boys played on their long-suffering schoolmasters, for as he once said, 'I can't help being mischievous.' At the same time he had a good brain and did well at his work, and in the evenings at home he kept at his homework conscientiously. From time to time he bumped into his cousin Peter in the playground during the morning break periods. But they were in different classes and their paths did not often cross. Sometimes, when Jim's mother came to Stratford to shop, the two boys would meet after school and she would take them to have tea and cream-cakes in the town.

Jim would have liked to continue beyond the final school-leaving examinations and perhaps have gone to college or university. He had shown a growing interest and enthusiasm for mechanical things and machines of all kinds. But in the middle of the autumn term of 1933, in October before he had a chance to take the school-leaving examination, his father's health had so deteriorated that Jim had to leave and help with the farm. The hard years at Arrow Mill had taken their toll of Henry. For some time now his leg trouble had been getting steadily worse. He was compelled to rest whenever he could and kept two old egg skips near his chair as foot-rests. He was scarcely in a fit state to give his mind to Jim's future. Within eighteen months he died suddenly and quite unexpectedly of a kidney infection and Jim, ill-equipped as he was, took on the farm.

23

Sons & Daughters

WARWICKSHIRE FARMING HAZARDS AND WORLD WAR II

Jim was now master of Radbrook at the age of 18, not long out of school and with no experience of running a farm. He had had little opportunity to acquire the qualities a farmer needs – practical knowledge, foresight, the ability to handle labour, and an understanding of the value of money and how to manage it. All who knew him, his uncle Frank Sisam, his cousin Leonard, his Rouse relations and many others, could see the dangers that lay ahead and were more than ready to give help and advice. Among them was Harvey Smith, his father's friend. Unfortunately the advice, even when sought, was not implemented for Jim thought he knew what to do.

Troubles came thick and fast. A heifer bought in a sale calved and then went almost to a skeleton. A vet was called in. Shortly after his visit the herd developed Johne's disease, which was common at the time. It was always thought that the vet had brought the disease with him as he had come straight from another farm where there was an outbreak. The disease spread through the drinking ponds used by the cattle, and several beasts had to be slaughtered. For a year the farm was closed to the outside world, and it took nearly three years to clear the land of infection. In 1936, the year after his father died, the rainfall was such that hay needed for animal feed could not be cut until August. Then further rains ruined the crop before it could be carried. At the same time labour was hard to find in the area. If Jim had had but one or two brothers the situation might have been different.

Within three years World War II began, and severe restrictions were imposed on agriculture throughout the country. Local War Agricultural Committees, who controlled what crops farmers should grow and in which fields, were not always staffed with experienced men; and these certainly did not possess detailed local knowledge. Jim found himself instructed to plant crops in fields at Radbrook that were entirely unsuitable, and the crops were lost, but as far as local officials were concerned they provided satisfactory statistics of areas ploughed and sown. To make matters worse the only labour available was from the pool organised by the Womens' Land Army. Three or four semi-trained girls would arrive at the farm on the day required, expecting to work for an experienced farmer. Seeing young Jim and taking him for a farmworker they would exclaim, 'Where's the boss?' It was an unnerving situation.

There were other problems such as the shortage of tractors and farm machinery, and the difficulty of trying to borrow them from other farmers when there were breakdowns. Both Frank Sisam and George Clarke, nephew of the wagon-builder, tried to lend help; but with the petrol shortage it was difficult. Jim had a certain amount of machinery on the farm. He had bought a threshing machine at a time when most farmers employed contract harvesters. It was not in very good condition, and eventually the main driving belt snapped. Jim seized the belt and swung it round and round his head in exasperation, only to hit and damage the weighing machine standing in the yard. Like his father, he found machines tiresome if they failed to work. He arrived one day at the garage in Alderminster with his 10 h.p. Morris car. One of the front wings was badly damaged. When the garage men asked what had happened, he replied, 'I lost my temper with it and gave it a good hiding.' He had taken the starting handle and beaten the wing.

The farm never recovered from the early disasters caused by cattle disease and bad weather, and the difficulties of wartime. In those war years every farmer and farmworker worked long hours. All were in the Home Guard (the home defence organisation) and had frequent periods on duty. Jim served along with Harvey Smith's son, Harry, and the two became friends. Harry, aware of Jim's isolation, tried to get him to mix with people. Jim did not belong to the popular Young Farmers' Club, whereas most of his contemporaries did. During this period of World War II both Jim and Harry had been directed to remain on the land in order to raise vital food supplies. In the evenings Harry either worked on his father's farm or had to do Home Guard duty. On the few nights he had free he would go over and visit Jim at Radbrook. Eventually, towards the end of the War, he persuaded Jim to come with him to a Young Farmers' dance at Moreton-in-Marsh. There Jim met Elsie Ireland from Aston Magna. He was immediately taken by her happy outgoing personality. Some time later he went to visit the Smiths. Harvey Smith, Harry's father, who had been a good friend to Jim's father, liked Jim and thought well enough of him to appoint him one of his executors. On this particular evening Jim told him about meeting Elsie. Harvey held old fashioned views and, being a practical down-to-earth farmer, thought that farmers' sons should pick their brides out of the potato field and not off the dance floor. Jim was

James Leonard Sisam Jnr. (Jim) and Elsie Ireland, 1946.

not to be put off. He knew that Elsie was a farmer's daughter, used to haymaking and keeping livestock, as well as being an attractive personality. Their relationship blossomed and within six months they were married at Aston Magna in 1946, after the harvest. Elsie proved to be a constant support for Jim in the years to come.

That summer, at a crucial point during the ripening of the corn, it rained heavily for two to three hours a day for weeks on end. Much of the crop was never harvested and wheat began to grow out of the ears. The wet summer was followed by a very severe winter of frost and snow. In addition the farm was overdrawn at the bank and further credit was refused. The strain of the last years was beginning to tell. Jim felt he could not continue to carry the load. The upshot was that he and Elsie decided to sell up and leave. Radbrook fetched only a moderate price despite its fine house, as the upturn in land values after the war had yet to materialise. Jim's mother had already moved into a cottage in Preston, kindly made available by Mrs West of nearby Alscot Park. Mrs. West and her husband were large landowners in the district, and she knew Mary Sisam from working with her in the village church. Jim and Elsie went to live nearby at Brailes in a large, brick-built period house standing back from the road and here they stayed for seven years.

Having been born in a flour mill and spent his early childhood in one, Jim had milling in his blood. When he moved to Brailes it was to milling that he turned. He took a post at Clark's, an old-established, family milling business in Banbury, producing a high-quality flour for biscuit-making. They supplied the leading biscuit manufacturers: Huntley & Palmer, Crawford, Cadbury and Peak Frean. Here Jim was in the midst of the bustle and hum of milling, working as a miller. It was a setting in which he felt at home. He hoped he could remain there and work his way up to a senior position in the business, but in milling men usually stay there for life, and the man above Jim would not be retiring for a long time. There seemed no way of advancement.

During this time, in the year 1950, a daughter was born to Jim and Elsie and was christened Gloria Mary. In 1955 the family moved to Willicote, near Radbrook, and Jim joined Lucy's flour mill at Stratford-upon-Avon, cycling the four and a half miles morning and evening. He began by working in the mill itself, and later moved into the office for he was meticulous with his paperwork. But again at Lucy's there was little chance of advancement, especially for a man approaching middle-age. Then a shortage of drivers arose and Jim was asked if he would go out on the road. He made frequent long trips to Avonmouth Docks at Bristol, the same docks which had supplied his father with wheat for Arrow Mill. The trucks he drove were old and frequently heavily overloaded. Sometimes he had eight tons on board a five-ton truck. Elsie, meanwhile, was caring for Jim's elderly mother who had come to live with them. Elsie showed great kindness to Mary and looked after her until she died in 1956.

Lacking any promotion possibilities at Lucy's, Jim set up a corn-dealing business at Aston Magna where Elsie's family still lived. Corn-dealing, though not the same as milling, was a trade associated with it. But in the early 1960s the chance came to acquire a small corn mill at Long Buckby, near Northampton. It was a temptation Jim could not resist. The mill produced mainly animal feed. He used to refer to it as 'the smallest corn-mill in Britain'. But, viewed realistically, there was no future in it. Jim was clinging to a dream of the days of the rural flour mill that his forbears had known. Such rural mills were fast disappearing especially the smaller ones. Modern milling had moved to large, centralised establishments, mainly at the ports, since imported grain was now the nation's main standby. It was a losing battle for Jim and in the end, though bravely fought, was bound to be lost. 'Milling was my life' he once said and kept a handfull of wheat ears, carefully preserved, to be buried with him when the time came.

Life at Long Buckby was hard. The mill itself did not provide an adequate livelihood. Elsie took on a local shop and Jim went to work at the Hovis mills in Northampton to supplement the family income. He cycled the twenty miles each day by way of Althorp Park. Sometimes, having worked all day in the mill at Northampton, he would come home to his own mill and roll barley all night, then go to work again the next morning as usual. After Hovis closed down he was for several years with the construction engineers, Gilbert Ash, handling wages at the building of the Watford Gap section of Britain's first motorway, the M1, some six miles from Long Buckby. At the same time Jim and Elsie were doing their best to give Gloria a start in life. They sent her to a private day school in Northampton, and later to a technical college.

Of these years, no one could say that Jim lacked resolution and courage. He had no false pride and was prepared to tackle wholeheartedly and good-humouredly whatever came his way. He hated to be idle. By the end of the 1960s he finally came to terms with the fact that small-scale milling in a rural location was no longer a viable occupation. They moved to Leamington Spa where Jim, now in his mid fifties, went to work for Benford and Company, a firm making concrete-handling machinery. It had recently won a contract suppling machines for the construction of the Thames Barrage. His work was in the stores department. It was detailed work requiring accuracy in the handling of a great number of different items, some 2,500 in all. He was concientious and reliable and he remained there until retirement. Sadly, within a few years Elsie died, in 1971, after a long and serious illness. Jim felt this loss deeply.

They had known much happiness together, and for their daughter Gloria the years the three of them had together were her dearest memory. Jim and Elsie had their differences, and at times Jim was difficult and uncaring, yet at heart he was a loving husband, and their love for one another was such that it was able to encompass and absorb the many traumas that befell them. Elsie, like her mother before her, was a loyal Methodist and in the spirit of John Wesley fought nobly for her husband's soul. More than once in times of difficulty between them she would ask him to kneel with her and pray. Jim himself attended church and frequently drove the elderly and infirm to Sunday morning service, when otherwise they might not have been able to get there. When Elsie had to spend considerable time in hospital he wrote her exquisite letters expressing his deepest affection for her. These she greatly treasured, for he was a gifted letter writer and often expressed in writing tender feelings and deep thoughts that he was unable express in other ways.

He was undaunted by difficulties and had great ingenuity in devising ways of solving them and at the same time making the pennies go as far as possible. He once bought at a bargain price two second-hand Rover 90 cars, which when new had been elegant, high quality and well-powered saloons. One he used for getting about, the other he kept parked outside to provide spare parts. In summer he grew tomato plants in the spare car and when they grew too big wound down the windows to let them climb upwards. Laborious work was no problem to him if it had a useful purpose. He came across an unused, out-of-date diary. Needing one and not wanting to waste money on a new one, he went through each day and changed the 365 dates by hand. His efforts did not always meet with the family's approval. The household needed a wheelbarrow at one time and he decided to make one. He did so from an extra, but never used, leaf belonging to the mahogany dining-room table and painted it green. He was indeed ingenious and had no hesitation in resorting to unorthodox or even comical measures. In fact, his sense of humour was one of his strongest assets; not least in that he was able to laugh at himself.

Jim's life had more than its share of sadness, and there were frequent periods of depression and distress. However, he kept in touch with his old friends, especially Vernon Carr and Andrew Bishop. By a strange irony of fate another old friend, Harry Smith, had now become the owner of Radbrook. He sold the house but retained the land as a dairy farm. Gloria meanwhile had developed a good business sense and was working as an executive in a large food company. After Elsie's death she realised that Jim needed looking after and she made a home for him from then onwards.

In the early 1980s Gloria married a chemical engineer, David Hudson, whom she had known for some time. He had made a friend of Jim and understood him. David and Gloria suggested the three of them should move into a new house and make a home together. They moved to a new housing development on the edge of the countryside. Jim took charge of growing the vegetables. He had his own study where he could use his old typewriter and work on his papers, for by now he had amassed a large collection of milling information – historic photographs, newspapers, magazine articles and the like – gathered over a period of forty years. For some time he had been a regular contributor to the correspondence columns of local newspapers. He had a neat turn of phrase and a pungent manner of expression, and wrote on a variety of local topics about which he was concerned. In these latter years, until his death, he was fortunate to have the

Gloria Hudson, daughter of Jim.

Jim Sisam in later years. 'He had a remarkable brain' and a 'heart of gold'.

companionship and support of his daughter and son-in-law. He needed their care at this time, for sometimes the dark shadow of past unhappiness would fall upon him. He had a remarkable brain, clever and creative, and had he been given the right opportunities there is no telling what it might have achieved. By nature he was warm-hearted. He had a heart of gold, with the capacity to show consideration towards others and to care deeply for those nearest to him, even in the minutest details of daily life.

❖ ❖ ❖

Frank Marshall Sisam, Jim's uncle who did his best to help and advise him when he inherited Radbrook, was a farmer by nature. He was a genial character, almost jovial, and broad of build. As a young man he was given the opportunity by his father, James Leonard Sisam, to run one of the farms leased by the family, Primrose Hill Farm, which Frank later bought. In the area surrounding Arrow there were, for many years, two families who were closely acquainted and who had become household names. One was the Sisam family at Arrow, the other the Bomford family who farmed at Exhall Court nearby. They were part of the large Bomford clan who had played a leading part in the development of the Vale of Evesham as one of the great market garden areas of England, famous especially for its asparagus and plums and all kinds of fruit and vegetables. The Sisams and Bomfords in the Arrow and Alcester district knew each other well. As far back as the 1860s, before he emigrated to New Zealand, Walter Sisam of Arrow Mill had been a close friend of Fred Bomford of Atch Lench. In 1904 Frank Sisam married Winifred Bomford, daughter of Henry Butler Bomford, of Exhall Court. Previously she had worked in London as a private secretary to the eminent musician Sydney Jones.

Frank Marshall Sisam.

As was natural, since the Bomfords of Exhall were Baptists, the wedding took place in the Baptist chapel at Dunnington. Frank Sisam, although he was a man who held strong views on many issues and had an independent nature, was generous hearted. By upbringing Winifred was chapel. Frank was anglican. But every Sunday he would drive with Winifred in the pony trap, taking his mother-in-law to Dunnington chapel when he really would have preferred to go to Arrow church. This he did for her week after week, and on into the years when the pony and trap gave way to the motor car, for she loved going to chapel. When the well-known Baptist preacher, Dr. Charles Browne, came down from London to preach in the district, he always stayed with the Sisams. Winifred had come to know him through attending his church when she was working in London.

She was a very private person and shunned anything public. Her needlework was exquisite but she was not a cook by nature. She would say, 'Now, I wonder what we're having for dinner today ?' for she was not a person who could plan ahead. Her time-keeping was 'dreadful', as her daughters used to say. Frank would say to her, 'The only thing you'll ever be in time for is your funeral'. Both she and Frank were kind to others. She would make puddings and other good things for the men working on the farm to take home. She would always feed the tramps who came begging at the door. One of them, an old man, lived in the barn for a very long time. She made him food every day. One day he disappeared and took with him a number of things that didn't belong to him.

At Primrose Hill Farm, their first family home, four children were born, two sons and two daughters. The family lived there for ten years, and then, in 1914, moved to Kingley Farm, a few miles away on the Ragley Estate, where they occupied what had been a dower house for the Marquis of Hertford's mother.

Kingley Farm, Ragley, the home of Frank and Winifred Sisam.

Frank Sisam was proving himself to be a competent farmer and businessman, and as such became well-known in that part of Warwickshire. In the course of time at Kingley he expanded his farming operations to include, in addition to Kingley, Moor Hall Farm and Dunnington Court Farm. The whole at one time totalled over 1,000 acres. He would ride across most of this each day on his horse. He employed 35 men and 4 women permanently. At Kingley he grew wheat and raised cattle and sheep. Moor Hall, which was about 300 acres of excellent soil, was primarily used for growing vegetables, especially potatoes, for the Birmingham and local markets. There were other specialised crops such as strawberries, raspberries, black currants, and mushrooms. The latter, after being cut at daybreak, were despatched on the earliest possible train from Wixford station at 8 a.m., in time to reach the morning market in Chesterfield, Derbyshire. The dealer who purchased them was Sir Ernest Shentall, who ran the market. One day the Kingley men cut over a ton of mushrooms. They sold for ninepence a pound.

Frank was successful and did well financially. He was recognised as a man of wide practical experience, and for many years served as governor of the Studley Agricultural College. This was a pioneer establishment, being one of the first colleges in Britain for women agriculturalists. However, as far as his own daughters were concerned, Frank Sisam had old-fashioned ideas and would not allow the girls to go near the farmyard or get involved in farmwork, probably because of the rough language they might hear. He was, at the same time, of an hospitable and generous nature and often entertained friends at shooting parties at Kingley. A photograph of one of these occasions shows Tom Rouse of Cold Comfort Farm, Frank Adkins of Broom Mill (who married the daughter of George Clarke the Arrow wagon-builder), Tom Hieatt of Quinton, Cornelius Corbett from the farm next to Primrose Hill, and Sir Ernest Canning who had Oversley Farm opposite Oversley Green Farm, home of Frank's sister, Marian, and her husband George Hunt.

Sir Ernest was a Birmingham businessman, who later became Lord Mayor. He was a close friend, to whom Frank often sent fresh mushrooms and strawberries. The shooting parties were a happy meeting together of friends and neighbours, drawn from the same community, and became a regular custom. At the end of the day the whole company adjourned to Kingley for a hot, roast goose supper, after which they spent the evening playing solo whist.

A few years after the family moved to Kingley a third daughter, Phyllis Marian, was born, named after her aunt Marian of Oversley. Arriving on the scene some years after her brothers and sisters, she was affectionately referred to by her mother, then in her forties, as 'a Michaelmas chicken'. Sadly, Marian was never very strong.

Frank Sisam's sons, Walter Leonard (Len) and Francis Henry (Harry), like their ancestors before them, went to Alcester Grammar School. They were known as Sisam I and II. Len was a good footballer. In 1923 the Grammar School beat Redditch Secondary School 11–1. Len scored five of the goals, and was the top scorer for the year. That same year his sister Winifred Mary (Molly), for the Grammar School was now co-educational, distinguished herself at hockey and in the summer reached the final in the Gold Medal Singles Tennis Championship. Harry, their younger brother, developed into a fine cricketer and used to open the batting for the school.

Len loved farming, but his father wanted him to be an auctioneer and paid for him to be apprenticed to the firm of E.G. Righton of Evesham. After two years Len felt that it was not the life for him and that he preferred farming. Frank was angry at what he felt was the waste of money, but nevertheless put Len in charge of Moor Hall Farm, where he did well.

Winifred Mary (Molly) Bunting, Walter Leonard (Len) and Phyllis Marian Sisam.

Harry, his younger brother, had a good brain. He not only did well at cricket while at the Grammar School but developed a flair for writing. He wanted to go to Oxford University and study English Literature, but his father was so annoyed at the money wasted on Len's training, that he refused to pay for Harry to go to Oxford, thinking he might waste his time playing cricket. His prowess at cricket was such that he might well have been awarded a blue at Oxford. In the end he left school and joined the *Evesham Journal*, a local newspaper, as a reporter and was later put in charge of the Moreton-in-Marsh branch.

In the meantime there were weddings in the family. Dorothy, the second daughter, married George Clarke, nephew of the renowned wagon and coach builder. The wedding was at Wixford, the parish in which Kingley farm was situated. George was a farmer and he and Dorothy settled at Sambourne Hall, near Inkberrow, not far from where Joseph Sisam, the founder of the Sisam line in America, had worked as a young man. Sambourne Hall became their permanent home. Dorothy's wedding was in the spring of 1934. It was a year of happy celebration at Kingley Farm. Molly, the talented tennis player, had fallen in love with Fred Bunting, a son of a well-known Alcester family who had a long-established grocery business in the High Street. They were married in the same church at Wixford as Dorothy. Fred at the time was working with a company in Birmingham learning the wholseale grocery trade. They went to live in Birmingham, and their first child, a daughter Jill, was born in August 1936.

Within a few years World War II broke out. In 1940, after the fall of France, Fred went into the Royal Corps of Signals. The following year Harry joined the Royal Navy. The year 1941 was one of continuing crisis, with a few gleams of hope. The cities of Bristol, Plymouth, Exeter and others had been subjected to mass bombing and in April Coventry, some twenty miles from Kingley, was devastated. A month later the House of Commons was

Dorothy Gertrude Clarke.

severely damaged. After the bombing of Coventry, Molly moved from Birmingham with her five year old daughter, Jill, and young son, David, to the safety of Kingley, which was already providing a home for children evacuated from Coventry. Harry meanwhile was serving as a lieutenant on the cruiser *Suffolk*, when it detected the German battleship *Bismark* off Denmark, and joined in the pursuit which ended with the sinking of the German battleship by the aircraft carrier *Ark Royal*, which itself was sunk the following November. The Japanese attacked Pearl Harbour in December and in the New Year began to infiltrate the supposedly impenetrable Malaysian jungle, moving south on bicycles and on foot towards Singapore.

Fred's Signals regiment was posted overseas. It was sent as a reinforcement to Singapore. On February 15, a week after they landed, the city fell and the thousands of British and Commonwealth troops captured there were marched up country to forced labour camps in the jungle. Molly did not know where Fred had gone when he was sent overseas. It was not until four months after the fall of Singapore that she heard officially that it was Singapore, and that he was now 'missing'. She was in hospital at the time, expecting another child. The news was a terrible shock to her and the child did not survive. Her brother Harry was home on naval leave; he was a tower of strength and very good to Molly, getting her home safely and looking after her.

Marian, Molly's youngest sister, was called up for war service. Because she was not very strong she was sent to work in a local NAAFI (Armed Forces) canteen at a Royal Engineers base near Long Marston. It was hard work, at all hours of day and night, and this was probably a contributary cause to her developing multiple sclerosis.

Like all farmers Frank Sisam and his eldest son Len worked extremely hard during World War II to increase food production, at a time when food was strictly rationed and

Francis Henry Sisam (Harry) at Kingley, on leave from the Royal Navy on 1942. With him are Molly's two children David and Jill.

there was an acute shortage of agricultural manpower. In the spring of 1943, during this war period, Frank broke his leg. He was driving round Dunnington Court Farm looking at the corn crop when he noticed wood pigeons were attacking it; so he stopped. Taking his gun he walked into the field, but in going through a gate it suddenly closed on him and he fell heavily. He managed to crawl the 150 yards to the car and drag himself into the driving seat. He drove slowly home to Kingley where he sat in the car outside the house, blowing the horn to attract the family's attention. He was carried off to Birmingham to hospital. He made good progress and was expecting to come home in about a week. However, just after a visit from Winifred, he coughed a little, lay back on his pillow and died. He was found to have unsuspected cancer of the lungs.

The family left at Kingley consisted of Len, who took charge of the farms, his mother, his youngest sister Marian when she wasn't on canteen duties, and Molly with her two children, Jill and David. Unfortunately, they were not able to remain long at Kingley. At that time the Ragley Estate was being administered by trustees who wished to let Kingley to other tenants, so the Sisams had to leave. Within a year they moved to a modest house in Arrow Road, Alcester. Len continued the family's lease of Moor Hall Farm at Wixford.

In 1946, a year and a half after the war ended, Molly heard officially that Fred had died in a Japanese Prisoner of War Camp on May 3, 1943, the same year in which Molly's father, Frank Sisam, had died. Fred had been nearly two years toiling on the construction of the Burma Railway. One of the Ragley farmworkers had been taken prisoner about the same time as Fred and was in a similar camp, but survived. He came to see Molly. He said that it was the extreme heat, the hard labour, and having practically no food, that carried off so many lives. Like many of his comrades, Fred was not used to manual labour. His grave lies with that of many others on the site of the prison camp up country at Changchek. It is beautifully laid out and carefully tended. Fred and Molly's two children, although having no father for most of their lives, experienced a happy childhood and fulfilment in adulthood. Fred would have been proud of his son David's sporting reputation, and his work to keep youngsters off the streets through the promotion of village cricket at Bromere in Shropshire. Likewise he would have been amused to see Jill's daughters, one teaching Latin at an American university, and the other travelling the world as a highly qualified and highly paid oceanographer.

Harry left the Navy in due course and came home. At one point during the war his naval service took him to Canada, where he had to wait to join a newly commissioned ship. This gave him a chance to see something of the country. He liked what he saw and in 1948, his hopes of marriage having unfortunately been dashed, he decided to emigrate to Canada. He went into business successfully in the fashion trade. In the course of his work he travelled widely in many areas, and visited every state in the USA. In England he was remembered with affection and respect in the *Evesham Journal* offices, especially by old colleagues who had been young reporters in his day. They had looked up to him as a kind of hero to be emulated, and would cast an appraising eye on his sporty red automobile, his journalistic skill, and his cricketing prowess. Years later the office disposed of an old chair which was found to have carved on it in rough letters the name 'Harry Sisam'. Hearing in a letter about this discovery, he modestly denied all responsibility. Perhaps it was the work of some admirer or wag, long after he had left.

Meanwhile, his sister Marian's duties in the NAAFI had ended and she looked round for some interesting job that was within her strength. She had a good farming background and some wartime catering experience. Because of this she went to work for one of the leading Cotswold farmers, John Bourne of Snowshill, and ran the hostel for his farm students. Marian remained a cheerful person despite having to live under the shadow of sclerosis. She had an old MG, open-top sports car, with a faithful dog as a companion, and enjoyed living high up in the hills under the boundless skies.

Dorothy and her husband, George Clarke, remained on their farm at Sambourne Hall until George retired. They had one daughter, Rachel, who married a research chemist. The young couple settled near Worcester. They also had a daughter.

Molly had taken over the running of the home in Arrow Road, Alcester which in addition to herself consisted of her elderly mother, her brother Len, and her own two children. Len continued to farm at Moor Hall with great proficiency, following the age-old principle of putting into the soil at least as much fertility as was taken out. In doing so he was going against the growing practice, especially with cereals, of maximum cropping at minimum cost and of quick returns regardless of the long term effects on the land. He was a familiar figure at the cattle markets and sales, and won prizes for his cattle. All in all he was much respected in the farming community. He never married, and sought consolation and companionship in the cosy, cheerful atmosphere of country inns. He died in 1960.

Winifred their mother died three years later. Marian, as her strength began to decline, left the Snowshill hostel and went as a companion to an elderly lady in the Cotswold village of Broad Campden. Marian died in 1968. She and her father, mother and brother Len are all buried near one another in Arrow churchyard, to the left of the church. On the right of the church lie the graves of the early Sisams of Arrow Mill: William who first occupied the mill, Henry and Caroline – the parents of those who went to New Zealand, and others.

24
Fresh Fields

BANKING IN THE COTSWOLDS – ADVENTURES IN FILM-MAKING

Frank Sisam was devoted to his younger brother, Walter. They had been at Alcester Grammar School together. Walter was slight of build, whereas Frank was tough and burly. In their early schooldays Frank stood up for his brother when there was bullying. In later years, when both were married and had their own families, Frank would visit Walter regularly, bringing produce from his farm and the two would spend the evening in heart-to-heart conversation. Both had done well at school. In 1892 Frank was joint top in Mathematics and top in Divinity. Later, in the senior school, in two successive years Walter carried off the High Burgess' Prize for Mathematics. He was the youngest son in the family and because of that seemed to have been specially cherished. To his widowed grandmother, Caroline Sisam, he became a favourite grandson. She was now living at Park Cottage in Arrow village, where he was regularly invited to Sunday afternoon tea, on which occasion the best silver would be used. That she was fond of her grandchildren there is no doubt, whether they were in England or distant New Zealand.

After leaving school Walter worked for a while as bailiff on a farm his father had bought when he retired from Arrow Mill. This was South Arrow Farm in Arrow Lane, a narrow roadway leading up towards the Ridgeway by way of a steep gradient known as Hanging Well Hill. When the Arrow Mill wagons climbed this slope with full loads they would take on an extra horse at South Arrow Farm. Unfortunately Walter was not a success as bailiff. He had had little farming experience and did not have the knack of handling animals. So he decided to follow his mathematical bent and went to work in the Capital and Counties Bank in Corporation Street, Birmingham, living at Arrow Mill and commuting each day by walking down the railway track to Alcester station to catch the Birmingham train. He did well in the Bank, having a good head for figures and gained experience in a number of other branches following his initiation in Birmingham.

In Birmingham there was the opportunity to mingle with a wider cross-section of his contemporaries. Here he could enjoy a more sophisticated society than he could in Alcester. He was a typical young man of the Edwardian era, slim and athletic, smartly dressed and debonair, a football enthusiast, and bubbling over with the jingles and popular songs of the day. Being bright and ebullient, he was a good mixer. It was not long before he became engaged to a likeable young lady but the family at Arrow Mill disapproved of her. She lived at Coughton which for generations had had a thriving Catholic population. His family's disapproval distressed him and he was torn by inner conflict. By now he was working in a branch of the bank at Shrewsbury, an important town on the Welsh borders. In desperation he turned for advice to the vicar of a church in the centre of the town. The vicar was an understanding man and a wise counsellor. His advice was simple, albeit old fashioned. He told Walter to go home and read the Bible, and indicated which passages. By his upbringing Walter was familiar with the Bible, but this was putting it in a new perspective, treating it almost as a practical guidebook in which might be found illumination about a particular situation.

During the time of quiet reading, something happened within Walter's inner consciousness. He saw his life in a new light. He knew that there had to be fundamental change. A theoretical knowledge of God, gleaned from books or other sources, was replaced by a sense of being in God's presence, and with it the clear thought and desire to give God first place in his life in every respect. This he saw did not mean withdrawing from the real world or becoming a priest, which he would have liked to do, but living his everyday life with different motives and different attitudes towards others. He felt that this was the way the Kingdom of Heaven could be built. At the same time, clarification came about his engagement. The couple met and talked over the situation frankly and both decided to break off their relationship.

On the surface his existence during the next years might have appeared humdrum. A bank clerk's life is not normally an adventurous one, but his was happy and fulfilled and also had its adventures. It took him into people's lives and, having a warm and generous heart, people responded to him. He became a friend and help to many. His income was never large, yet he gave generously to those in need. He made steady progress in the bank and in 1911 was appointed cashier at Shrewsbury. Two years later he was posted to a branch in the Cotswold market town of Moreton-in-Marsh. It had a broad High Street, tree-lined, with grass verges and a wide open space in front of the bank where he worked. Here, although of a retiring nature, he believed in making known the spiritual gifts that were available to all men and women. He held open-air meetings in the evenings in the main street for the men standing on street corners, and any passers by who cared to listen. This astonished some people, not least a Scottish doctor in the town, Dr. Clark Nicholson, who held decidedly agnostic views. Many years later this doctor, having survived the horrors of dealing with the war-wounded in France, said, recalling those open-air meetings, that what Walter Sisam did in Moreton in those early days was one of the bravest acts he had seen.

There was romance in Moreton-in-Marsh. Walter had retained the twinkle in his eye and had a smile for everyone he met. He also had a capacity for enjoyment of the simple pleasures of life. His lodgings were in a little house at the back of the town called Langates Lodge, behind which there was a footpath through the meadows and up into the hills. Here Walter would sometimes have small supper parties with bank clerks from both the two banks in the town, Lloyds and the Midland. (Lloyds had by now acquired the old Capital and Counties Bank.) To one of these parties the wife of the Midland Bank cashier brought her sister who had come on a visit. The sister was Catherine Fincher. She had striking auburn hair and was the daughter of a builder and engineer in Stratford-upon-Avon. She and her family lived within sight of Ann Hathaway's Cottage. Catherine's father, John Gazeley Fincher, was a gifted builder and also an architect with high standards of craftsmanship. For years he maintained and restored the historic buildings associated with Shakespeare, which visitors from all over the world were wont to visit.

The supper party was a success, not only because Walter's landlady was a good cook, but because much fun was had playing old-fashioned games. One was 'Up Jenkins' in which a sixpence was passed from hand to hand under the table, until the cry of 'Up

Jenkins' when hands came up, palms down; and a designated person had to guess in whose hands the sixpence was hidden. Walter was sitting next to Catherine Fincher, and this was the beginning of a romance which very soon became a happy marriage.

Walter was fortunate in spending the rest of his life living and working in this beautiful north-west corner of the Cotswold Hills. In 1913 after he and Catherine were married they set up home in the village of Blockley at Porch House, built in the 15th century. Walter by then was working some miles away in the hilltop town of Stow-on-the-Wold, where 'the wind blows cold'. He would cycle each day over the hills from Blockley, wet or shine. Then came the 1914 war, when their first child was on the way. Very soon after this he received his call-up papers for the armed forces. He said his farewells, perhaps his last, and reported for duty. The next day he was back home again, rejected because of a hammer toe. It was a genuine case, for his boots always had to be specially made. So it was back to the bank and the struggle to make do with locally recruited, untrained women staff, who replaced the men called-up.

In the latter part of the war the family moved to the other side of the hills, to the picture-postcard village of Lower Slaughter. They lived opposite the water mill, near which the village boys used to tickle trout in the stream that flowed through the centre of the street. By now there were two children, Peter and Lettice (Letty). In 1918 all the family were stricken by the serious influenza epidemic, known as the 'Asian 'flu'. Catherine was just able to crawl downstairs to let the doctor in. It was evening. He looked at three-year old Peter and said the child would be gone by morning. But by morning the boy was better and survived, as did the whole household.

Walter's daily journey by bicycle from Lower Slaughter to Lloyds Bank at Moreton-in-Marsh was a tiring one, and in both directions involved a long, steep hill-climb. It was a relief, therefore, when the family moved to the hill-side village of Bourton-on-the-Hill, which was much nearer the bank. They found a large house named The Firs near the top of the hill with lofty views over the valley. In front of the house was a stand of Scotch pines, rising tall and straight from the precipitously sloping grass running down to the wicket gate by the road. In stormy weather the sound of the wind in the topmost branches was like the roar from a distant sea shore. Being in an elevated spot the upper windows of the house caught all the sounds of the village below – the barn-owl calling in the night, the cockerel at daybreak, the hen clucking over a newlaid egg, the jingle of harness and the creak of wagons hauling huge tree-trunks up the steep incline; the squeal of the family pig meeting its destiny, or the sweet singing of children's voices in the village school across the road.

Bourton was a picturesque village where the steep road was lined with miniature 'hanging' gardens. It was also a closely-knit and friendly community, boasting a post office, two small shops, a bakery, a blacksmith, a pub, a school and a church. The villagers were mainly farmworkers, farmers and stonemasons, plus a few aristocratic eccentrics. Most of the village women had never been outside its confines. Walter's wife, Catherine, started a weekly sewing group which led to the foundation of a Women's Institute. This flourished and awoke hidden skills and theatrical talents. Perhaps the most exciting of their activities was the yearly outing. The first was to Gloucester where everyone made for the Bon Marché, the first department store they had ever seen. Some spent most of the day riding up and down in the elevator, just for the fun of it.

In 1925 Walter was made manager at Moreton-in-Marsh. An important factor in his

Walter Sisam of Moreton-in-Marsh, country bank manager and lay reader, youngest son of James Leonard Sisam.

promotion there, where he had been cashier for a number of years, was a public petition to Lloyds Bank's London headquarters by people in Moreton and the surrounding district. They asked that he be appointed as a man whom they trusted and respected. Walter's appointment meant another move for the family, this time to Lloyds Bank House in Moreton; an imposing, Georgian building in the High Street where there was accommodation for the manager and his family on the ground and upper floors, with the bank offices in part of the ground floor. Walter had already made many friends in the area, espcially in the farming community and among the families in the country houses, and also among the country clergy. Many of these, coming into town to bank and shop, would find their way at four o'clock to the Sisam fireside for a cup of tea and chat. The bank having been closed for business at 3 p.m., Walter would slip upstairs and join the family circle for tea. It was a welcome break for him, as he would usually return to his desk afterwards and work until eight o'clock supper time. The following morning, if the weather was fine, he set off at 6.30 for a brisk walk round the hills before breakfast. He always took the same route and kept the same time. He passed a group of isolated cottages, where a farmworker and his wife, Mr. and Mrs. Shadbolt lived. When the wife heard Walter's footsteps she would nudge her husband and say, 'Come on now. There goes Mr. Sisam. Time you got up and went to work.'

Walter worked hard. He had to, for the world economic depression of 1929 had led to the freezing of bank managers' salaries. A contributing factor was the fact that Lloyds, together with other banks, suffered heavy losses during the financial scandals of the 1920s surrounding the speculator, Clarence Hatry. He and his colleagues had liabilities totalling £29 million. They were tried at the Old Bailey in January 1930 and imprisoned for fraud.

From that time onwards Walter received no annual increase in salary. His income remained the same for the next eighteen years, until he retired, when his pension reflected the reduced salary level. But he continued to give privately from his own pocket to those in need in the neighbourhood. Some thought he was over-generous; others that he was a soft touch. Amongst the impecunious the word was, 'When things are tight, try the vicar. If that fails, try John Barkes the solicitor. If that doesn't work, try Mr. Sisam.' Against the advice of others, and at a time when he could not really afford it, he paid for his son, Peter, to go to Oxford University to study. This was in the days when there were no state grants to students, and few scholarships. But it was an opportunity to teach his son about economy. He sent him off with £5 in his pocket for incidental expenses such as books, and a penny cashbook, telling him to write down everything he spent and only when he reached his last ten shillings to write home for more. It was a salutary experience, which the young man remembered all his life.

In the midst of these events Walter undertook more rather than less spiritual work. With the blessing of the Bishops of Coventry and Gloucester, he became licensed as a lay reader, authorised to preach and take church services in those two dioceses. This enabled him to give help wherever it was needed in the Moreton area. On a Sunday morning or evening he would set off for some distant village to share with the people there the simple, eternal truths. His sermons were more of a quiet talk than an elaborate discourse, for he

The village church at Chastleton close to the early 17th century Jacobean mansion, Chastleton House.

was neither scholar nor public speaker. One Sunday morning he was in the village of Chastleton, where the village church nestled against the walls of the ancient manor house. The house had been built by Walter Jones, a wealthy woollen merchant. His descendant, Mrs. Whitmore Jones, was the lady of the manor in Walter Sisam's day. On the particular morning that he was to preach she was present in her front pew. She had with her a weekend guest, a distinguished looking older man. Walter gave a simple discourse, as was his custom, and afterwards was introduced to the guest, of whose identity he was quite unaware. The guest was in fact the chairman of Lloyds Bank.

With the coming of World War II, life became much harder for bank managers. Staff disappeared and, after a long days work, there were hours of fire-watching through the night as the turn for duty came round remorselessly on the rota. Walter had now reached his sixties and felt the need to take the early retirement that was available. He had longed for years for this moment and hoped to spend that retirement, perhaps twenty years or so, in the Cotswolds. His brother Frank, generous as ever, promised to build or buy him a cottage wherever he would like to be. So in 1942 Walter resigned from the bank. He and Catherine moved out of the Bank House, sold by auction most of the contents, and went into temporary lodgings in Moreton until their promised dream-house should materialise. Frank, meanwhile, had broken his leg and was in hospital in Birmingham. There, as already told, he suddenly and unexpectedly died. With him also died the possibility of a new home for Walter and Catherine, since nothing had been put in writing and Frank's own family needed whatever inheritance there was.

That September, Walter and Catherine borrowed a friend's caravan for a Cotswold holiday. It was an idyllic interlude, in balmy early autumn sunshine, but while there he began to feel unwell and they had to return home. The family doctor and friend – the Scottish agnostic – diagnosed cancer, too far advanced for treatment, and by mid-October Walter was gone. He had never fretted. His only concern had been for his family. He knew he had very little to bequeath to them. The children had already left home and were making their way in the world. But Catherine would have no home to live in, and her bank widow's pension would not amount to much more than two pounds a week. There was little he could do about it. In the will that he made then, he ended with these words: 'I do entreat them to keep united and loyal to each other and above all else 'Do justly and love mercy and walk humbly with their God', and I resign my soul into the hands of Almighty God.' At his funeral service in Moreton Parish Church practically every seat was taken, and nearly every shop in the town closed. The *Evesham Journal* wrote of him, 'Greatly respected, and held in the highest esteem by all with whom he came in contact, Mr. Sisam was very popular in the Moreton-in-Marsh district and his death has caused a most painful impression in the town. One who never sought the limelight, but was ever ready to do a kindness, such was the character he possessed, and he will be sorely missed.' He was buried at Arrow near his brother Frank.

❖ ❖ ❖

Walter Sisam's son, Peter James, was fortunate in his upbringing. He was born in the heart of the Cotswolds, and grew up surrounded by mellow, medieval stone cottages, barns and churches, dotted over a landscape of hills and valleys. Early childhood was followed by five years at Stratford-upon-Avon Grammar School as a boarder, where he was taught in the same schoolroom where Shakespeare is said to have been taught. It was a long, half-timbered room beneath which was the old Guildhall in which in Shakespeare's days visiting companies of players from Queen Elizabeth's court in Westminster would perform plays.

Initially he did well in his work at Stratford. At the age of sixteen in the Oxford School Certificate examinations, to everyone's surprise, he gained what was then known as First Class Honours. He stayed on in the sixth form, but here there were difficulties. Work in the sixth form was often unsupervised study. He was easily distracted and found it hard to concentrate. Yet he had ability, for in his last year he won both the English Literature and English Essay Prizes. However, in the final examinations for the Higher School Certificate, he failed in his best subject, English Literature. This was a hard blow, but fortunately it did not prevent his entrance to Oxford University. He entered St. Peter's Hall – later to become St. Peter's College – in October 1933.

Oxford was indeed unforgettable, but not only for its beauty and history. It opened new cultural horizons and also brought a sharp awareness of the state of the world. A wide range of newspapers and journals in the college commonroom told of National Socialism in Germany and Italy, of the Civil War in Spain and of unemployment in Britain. Welsh coal miners, during their hunger march on parliament at Westminster, passed through Oxford. Later, Oswald Mosley and his fascist blackshirts held a violent rally in the Oxford Town Hall. The Communists, though banned in the university, operated under the name of the October Club and were equally active. The younger generation, especially in Oxford, were restless and seeking an active role in solving the ills of society. In the midst of this turmoil a clear challenge was being proclaimed by what had become known as the Oxford Group. It was not an organisation, but a spontaneous coming together of committed individuals, many of them Oxford men and women, moved by the same spirit. Their approach to the problems of the time was that human nature was the fundamental cause, and they propounded a world scale initiative to tackle it by moral and spiritual means. Expressed in simple terms its message was: 'When man listens God speaks, and when man obeys God acts. When men change, nations change. When nations change, the world changes.'

Armed with convincing evidence from a recent coast-to-coast campaign in Canada, to which the Canadian prime minister paid strong tribute, the Group received considerable support in Oxford. This was true of both undergraduates and senior academics, among them the noted scholars Professor Streeter, Provost of Queens College, and Professor Grensted of Oriel College. There were some senior men who attacked the Oxford Group.

Notwithstanding this individual lives were changed in a revolutionary fashion at many levels, with salutary and constructive results. Peter was amongst many who experienced a complete turn-around in their lives. It came about through a talk he had with another undergraduate, Kenneth Prebble[15], who in later years lived in New Zealand. The practice of quiet meditation in the early hours of each day and following inner conviction was the key. That same year certain experiences riveted for him the effectiveness of this approach to life. During the summer he wrote to an old friend with whom he had had a quarrel, to clear the matter up. A reply came within days, not from the man's home but from an army barracks in Winchester. The man had had a bitter disagreement with his father, been thrown out of the house, lost the chance of a much sought-after job, and in desperation had joined the army. He was posted to the King's Royal Rifle Corps. Peter's letter had reached him the morning he had decided to commit suicide. He asked if they could meet one weekend. They did so. The man regained his confidence in life, continued in the army, seeing service in India and then in World War II. He later married and settled in South Africa.

The influence of the Oxford Group spread rapidly, not by persuasion or propaganda but by the fact that it generated an infectious quality of life that frequently had a knock-on effect. It influenced situations and often offered a key to apparently insoluble deadlocks. This happened in the Cotswold market town where Peter lived. He made friends with Stanley F. Barnes the manager of the milk processing plant, which was the main source of employment in the town. The manager's attitude to his workers and suppliers, the local farmers, changed completely. One result was that the area was prevented from becoming engulfed in a nation-wide farmers' strike. This meant that in the Moreton district essential milk supplies remained uninterrupted. This manager was later sent by the government to establish the first safe milk supply in the Island of Malta. Subsequently he took charge of the Royal Air Force's petrol supplies during the siege of Malta in World War II. Later he became a world expert on milk-products.

Involvement with the Oxford Group meant ever wider horizons and direct contact with situations beyond the academic world. In the Easter vacation of 1935 Peter went to Denmark with a group of Oxford graduates and undergraduates, selling his stamp collection to pay the fare. A postcard he wrote from Copenhagen to a friend in vivid 'telegraphese' describes the action: 'Over 25 of us here – newspapers all agog – meetings packed out – average of 35 flying squads going out every day to homes, factories, business lunches, schools, unemployed meetings – all of us busy from 6.30 a.m. to 12 midnight daily – tremendous fun – lives changing daily – in touch with all sections from workers to diplomats – Philips of Philips Electrical (Holland) with us – atheists demanding meetings – real revolution.' This campaign was part of a move by the Oxford Group through the Nordic countries requested by Carl Hambro, President of the Norwegian Parliament, that had international repercussions. The media reported it widely and it was watched with great care by the Nazi leaders in Germany. The work of the Oxford Group in these Nordic countries did much to strengthen their spirit and moral fibre, which stood them in good stead in the dark years of enemy invasion and occupation from 1940 to 1945.

In addition to his studies at Oxford, there were other extra-curricular activities. Through spending many leisure hours in cinemas, Peter became a serious student of the art of film and its potential for the presentation of ideas. When the Oxford Group produced *Bridgebuilders*, an artistic interpretation of its impact on Denmark, he felt Oxford should see it. The Scala Cinema in the town booked it into the normal programmes and posters went up on every college notice board. The film was well received in Britain and overseas. The British Film Institute in reviewing it wrote: 'An excellent production, making fine use of quickening tempo, and all the technical fireworks associated with some docucmentary and propagandist films. . . . The commentary is clear and pungent, and the final scene where the nations are marching with their flags singing 'Bridgebuilders' is thrilling.'

While at Oxford, Peter also wrote film reviews for the weekly under-graduate magazine *Isis*. His academic studies, on the other hand, were not as satisfactory as he would have wished. He was still beset with the difficulty of concentration on his books, of which there were a vast number to be read, his main subject again being English Literature. His concentration had greatly improved since his association with the Oxford Group but his

Senior Tutor, who was a somewhat fearful man, did not feel the improvement was sufficient to ensure that his pupil would do well in the Final Honours Degree Examination. He therefore insisted that Peter abandon his two-year's study of English and take an easier Pass Degree in a selection of subjects that included English and History. When the time came Peter romped through these, subsequently obtaining his BA and MA degrees. But not being allowed to sit for an Honours Degree was a hard blow to bear, because he knew the sacrifice his father had made in order to send him to Oxford. Many years later he was at a College reunion and found himself sitting at High Table next to his old tutor. Soon after this the tutor suggested a walk over the Berkshire Downs during which they had a long talk. His old tutor inquired as to how he had fared on leaving Oxford and showed great interest in all that he had been doing. In the course of the walk he apologised for having forced Peter to take a Pass Degree, and said he hoped it had not injured his career.

On leaving Oxford Peter set about finding a way into the film industry. At the time there was no recognised route by which practical experience or training could be obtained, and without experience or influence entry was almost impossible. Oxford University's career advisory department had had no advice to give on such an unorthodox profession. Then came an invitation from the producer of *Bridgebuilders*, Eric Parfit, to join him in the making of further films. There was one proviso. There would be no salary, for those who gave their whole time to the work of the Oxford Group, soon to be known as Moral Re-Armament (MRA), were expected to live by faith. Crazy perhaps but Biblical, though not all Christians are called to practise their faith to that extent. These two adventurers made a number of short films. In 1937 they completed *Youth Marches On*, a short documentary filmed in Canada and England, portraying a new motivation and purpose for youth. It received record-breaking commercial distribution throughout Britan, and ran in five of London's West End cinemas simultaneously. It was also linked with current nationwide mayoral youth campaigns. At the time few people realised the importance of that distribution, but the timing of it proved significant.

It was immediately prior to the outbreak of World War II. The film made its mark with the thousands of young men and women who filled the cinemas of those days. Within a very short space of time most of them were manning vital factories and farms, tanks, warships, and combat aircraft in the desperate battle to free Europe from an evil tyranny.

Peter was rejected from military service on medical grounds and instead served in London's Civil Defence Force. The duties involved were to warn of air raids, control bomb incidents and care for the civilian population. There were also training courses, which included the detection of unexploded bombs. One day he was examining a building that had been partially destroyed in an earlier raid sometime before he entered the service. He noticed the tell-tale signs of an unexploded bomb. The tail fins were caught in the remains of the roof and a hollow in the earth indicated where the bomb had entered the ground. It had lain there unnoticed since the first air attacks three years previously. It was only a short distance from General Eisenhower's European Naval Headquarters in Grosvenor Square. Peter reported it and, in great secrecy, an army bomb disposal unit was called in; the bomb was defused and then whisked away for detonation at Wormwood Scrubbs. It was a 1,000 pounder.

Not far away was the Marble Arch intersection in Hyde Park. Part of it was known as Speakers' Corner, where various strange gentlemen on soapboxes would address and argue with crowds of spectators who gathered each day for the fun. At the time of the German

Peter James Sisam.

rocket attacks on London Peter raised the question of what would happen if a rocket hit this spot. The rockets travelled faster than the speed of sound. There could be no warning of their approach, and the sound of the explosion was only heard after they had impacted. Speakers' Corner was at the point where three different operational areas met. In the event of a rocket incident all three local Civil Defence organisations would converge there. Without a pre-arranged plan of co-ordination and mutual understanding there could be chaos and tragedy. He suggested visiting the other adjacent command posts so that personnel could get to know one another. This was done. A short time later a rocket actually hit Speakers' Corner in the early hours of a Sunday morning. All the Civil Defence services worked efficiently and cooperatively. There were fortunately no casualties, but a previously planned military parade to be reviewed by King George VI was due there later in the day. By the afternoon all repairs had been completed, the debris removed and the royal parade took place as scheduled. It so happened that Peter was away on sick-leave. Had he been on duty he would have been close to Speakers' Corner when the rocket struck.

During the war there were restrictions on film production, so in his off-duty hours Peter learnt to be a photographer. After the war he was made an Associate of the Institute of Incorporated Photographers, the national organisation of British professional photographers, and later still an Associate of the Royal Photographic Society. His pictures appeared regularly in annual exhibitions in London.

In the early 1950s he returned to film-making. This work took him to different countries. *Freedom*, made in Nigeria in 1956, was the first indigenous African feature film, and was Peter's first introduction to Africa. This film was shown at the Berlin Film

Festival. Other films on which he assisted included *The Crowning Experience*, a musical film made in the U.S. featuring Muriel Smith, who had played the title role in the Royal Covent Garden Opera production of *Carmen*. During the making of both these films highly skilled, professional technicians, hired to work on them, were profoundly moved by their quality and content. In the 1960s, Peter worked on films for the Foreign Office in London to further friendly relations with other countries. Then for four years he made educational films for the publishing house of Macmillan. Later he directed *One Word of Truth*, a visual interpretation of Alexander Solzhenitsyn's concept of the role of writers and artists in the world of today. This received a Bronze Award at the 1982 New York International Film & Television Festival.

His sister Letty had spent the early months of the war helping her father in the bank and then joined the diet department of the Radcliffe Infirmary in Oxford, one of Britain's main teaching hospitals. Because of the wartime shortage of manpower the workload was heavy. Often after a day's work she would be woken in the night to cook for night-duty surgeons, the part-time cooks from the town having failed to report for duty. It proved too arduous for her and she transferred to the medical records department. The hospital's labour force was supplemented by a number of Jewish refugee girls who had fled the Nazi menace. Some of these came from distinguished academic families. Letty befriended two of them who, when they arrived, had been put to scrubbing floors. She championed them and helped them find their feet and move to more appropriate work within the hospital. After the war she took over the record department of the Canadian Memorial Hospital at Taplow in Buckinghamshire. She lived with her mother in nearby Marlow until she died of cancer in 1968. A tree was planted in her memory at Taplow.

Peter had often considered the question of marriage, but found it difficult to come to a decision on the matter. Finally in 1976 he married Margaret Barnes, whom he had known and cared for over many years. This was a late marriage, which meant there were no children. However it proved to be happy and rewarding. He and Margaret settled in Marlow, Buckinghamshire and made a home for Peter's widowed mother Catherine, for the last few years of her life, until she died in 1980 at the age of 92.

By 1980 the line of Sisams descending from the family at Arrow Mill appeared to be coming to an end in Britain. There were no male descendants of William Henry Sisam of Harvington. Henry Leonard Sisam's only son, James Leonard (Jim) had married and had one daughter, Gloria. Neither of Frank Sisam's sons married, and Walter Sisam's son, Peter, had no children. Kenneth Sisam's son, Hugh, who like his sister Celia made Britain his home, did not marry. There was just one descendant of Frederick Francis Sisam, the John Sisam who had studied mathematics at Oxford, but he has not yet married. It looked as if New Zealand, Canada and the United States were the only countries that would carry forward the family name. There was, however, one unresolved mystery, and that was Thomas Marshall Sisam, the eldest of the three brothers who went out from Arrow Mill to New Zealand; the one who almost immediately returned home sick to England. What happened to him and did he have any descendants?

25
The Lost Branch

THE STORY OF THOMAS MARSHALL SISAM AND HIS FAMILY

Very little about Thomas Marshall Sisam has been handed down to later generations. In the 1920s and 1930s the family used to speak of two elderly Sisam relatives living in the Worcestershire village of Cleeve Prior, thought to have been the last descendants of Thomas Marshall, and that when they died there was no one left. If Cleeve Prior had been the last abode of his family then perhaps the churchyard would reveal some clues. This was the starting point of the search.

Cleeve Prior church is a old building near the village green, surrounded by cottages and houses. Over the entrance to the churchyard is is an old lantern arch and near the church door is an ancient yew tree, a reminder of the middle ages when every churchyard had a yew to supply wood for the archer's bows. On one of the buttresses of Cleeve Prior's church tower there are deep furrows in the stonework said to have been made by medieval bowmen sharpening their arrows. For those were the days when every village provided its quota of archers for the defence of the realm.

The churchyard has a great variety of gravestones spanning several hundred years of village life. Many of the older stones are still standing and some have legible inscriptions, such as the one near the church porch to Anne Stephens, who died in 1609. In the search for Thomas Marshall's family every tombstone was carefully examined, row by row, and no trace of Thomas Marshall or his descendants was found; until finally, behind the church and quite close to it, his stone was discovered. The inscription read: 'In loving memory of Thomas Marshall Sisam, who died October 17th, 1896, aged 55 years. "Here we have no enduring city".' Beneath his name was the inscription: 'also of Mary Jane the wife of the above who died May 11th 1924, aged 89 years.'

So Thomas Marshall not only survived his illness of 1862, but married and lived another thirty years or more. The question now was how to fill in the missing years. What did he do, where did he live, how did he make a living, what children did he have and what became of them? Were there any descendants still living ?

An obvious starting point was the village of Cleeve Prior, on the assumption that the family may have lived there for some time. But a search of the parish records, although they showed several Sisam burials, did not show any Sisams being born there. So where had Thomas Marshall and Mary Jane Sisam settled originally, and where had they lived until finally coming to Cleeve Prior?

The likelihood was that it was within the same area, since this was where Thomas grew up, and the area to which he probably returned from New Zealand in 1863. But where exactly ? The Public Record Office in London, which held weighty bound volumes of births, deaths and marriages in Britain from 1837 onwards, provided pointers, but only pointers. Under Births they listed the names of children born, but not their parents' full names, and also the districts in which the births were registered but not the actual places of birth. Likewise, marriages were listed under districts rather than actual places. It was a question then of matching the right children to the right parents, and the right families to the right places within a district.

Various scraps of information were helpful at this point. One such was provided by a distant Sisam relation in New Zealand, Ben Copedo. He was a descendant of one of Thomas Marshall Sisam's brothers, Walter Sisam, who had gone with him to New Zealand and looked after him when he was taken ill. Ben had in his possession letters written during the 1870s and 1880s by Caroline Sisam of Arrow Mill to her grandchildren in New Zealand. A study of her letters helped to clarify which children belonged to which parents. In one of them she wrote of Thomas Marshall's' son, Charlie, giving his age. This matched with a Charles Sisam listed in the London Records, and gave the district of his birth as Winchcombe.

Then it was remembered that family tradition related that James Leonard Sisam, youngest brother of Thomas Marshall (Tom), had at sometime helped him set up in corn-milling in the town of Winchcombe in Gloucestershire. A further resort was made to official records, this time to the Census Office. The Census in Britain had been taken every ten years, and showed individual names from 1841. Would the Census of April 1871, which listed every household and those living in it, show Tom and his family in Winchcombe? The answer was yes. The records showed that Thomas Marshall Sisam, aged 30, a miller employing three men, occupied a house in Alms Houses Lane, in the centre of Winchcombe, with his wife Mary Jane. No children were listed, for Charlie, their firstborn, did not arrive until later that year, as further searches revealed. Caroline Sisam's letters to New Zealand also gave a clue to as to where the couple's marriage had taken place. She mentioned that grandmother Davis, Mary Jane's, mother was living at Bourton (Bourton-on-the Hill). A copy of the marriage certificate obtained from London showed that the wedding was on May 29, 1869, in the parish church of Bourton-on-the-Hill. With the aid of such records, including Land Tax Returns, old county directories, poll books, together with family recollections, it was possible to piece together a reasonably coherent account of Tom's life after his return to England.

He came back from New Zealand in 1863, or perhaps 1864, about a year and a half after he had set out from his home at Arrow Mill, and it was most probably to his old home that he returned. His father and mother, Henry and Caroline Sisam, were getting on in years. Henry, in fact, only lived another 6 years, and much of the work of running the Mill had already devolved upon Tom's young brother, James Leonard, who was 19. Tom was 23. His most immediate need was to recover his health, find his feet again, and consider how to set about making a living. Everything points to the family having made a home for him at Arrow Mill; and it looks as if his two brothers, James Leonard at Arrow and William Henry at Harvington, did all they could to help him.

Like his brothers, he had worked with his father in the Mill as a young man before he went to New Zealand. Now that he had returned, unforseen though that was, it would be natural for him to go into the family corn-milling business, if there was a place for him and if his health and strength would permit. In addition to Arrow Mill, the family had held the lease of Harvington for over twenty years, and Tom's older brother, William Henry, was now in charge of it. Within a short time, Tom recovered sufficiently to join his brother at Harvington. This was notwithstanding the Auckland Hospital's report on him in New Zealand that he had 'heart disease'. Perhaps he consulted a doctor on returning home. Whether he did or not, medical knowledge in England at that time, especially amongst local doctors, was very limited. If a man looked fit and felt fit, he was deemed fit, especially if he was young. However, the work at Harvington did not appear to be beyond his strength, so much so that, after two years, he married and set up on his own as a cornmiller. In this he had the help and guidance of his brother James Leonard, with whom he jointly leased another mill. He himself was able to back the undertaking with £600 in capital which he had saved. The mill was in Winchcombe, in the centre of the town. The Sisams had close connections with Winchcombe. John Sisam, one of Tom's uncles, had milled there for some time, having taken the lease of Postlip Lower Mill on the outskirts of the town in 1847; and there had been Sisams living in the district as early as the 1680s.

These moves into different corn-mills were very much family events. A pattern had developed whereby Arrow Mill, being the family home, was usually occupied by a son of the Sisams who had lived there, whereas Harvington was sometimes manned by members of the wider family, dependent on circumstances. Under this system Harvington remained in the family for over fifty years. After Tom moved to Winchcombe in 1869 from Harvington, where he had been working under his brother William Henry, William Henry continued at Harvington for a short spell. He was succeded there by his uncle, John Sisam,

Winchcombe Mill.

who had now left Winchcombe. There continued to be a number of such family interchanges in the years that followed.

Tom's wife Mary Jane had been born on a farm in the hamlet of Idlicote in Warwickshire, near Shipston-on-Stour. Idlicote consisted of a church, a few farms and cottages, and a manor house which owned the village and surrounding land. Later the Davis family moved to the Downs Farm on the Cotswolds near Bourton-on-the Hill. Bourton is an attractive village built on a steep slope of the hills, with a main street winding upwards through it and cottages and gardens on either side, and a sturdy-looking church halfway up. This is the church where Tom and Mary Jane were married in May 1869. Tom's brother, William Henry, stood as a witness. Marriage was very much in the air in the Sisam family just then, for William Henry was married the following month in Winchcombe parish church to Helen New from Langley, a farm hamlet on the hills above the town.

Winchcombe Mill, where Tom and Mary Jane had their first home, was built on the River Isbourne. It stood at the bottom of a lane leading down from the main street and occupied a sizeable area. The miller's house at Winchcombe Mill was separate from the mill but close to it. Like most of the town's buildings, both house and mill were built of golden-coloured Cotswold stone, quarried locally. The couple's first child, Charles, was born here in 1871 and christened in the Parish Church near the top of the mill lane. It was a pleasant place in which to establish a home and family, yet Tom and Mary were only there about three years; possibly because it was on a short lease, perhaps the tail end of a longer lease which the previous occupier had not been able to complete. Whatever the reason, Tom's brother, James Leonard at Arrow, would have been involved, since he and Tom were joint tenants of the Winchcombe mill.

The departure from Winchcombe was the beginning of a series of moves for Tom. The absence of any diaries or letters makes it difficult to determine the exact circumstances surrounding these moves. The birth certificate, dated October 1872, of Tom and Mary Jane's second child, Thomas Jnr., records the family as living at Sandford Mill on the outskirts of Cheltenham. This was on the River Chelt in what was then a rural area, but now part of the suburb of Charlton Kings. The building still stands, on the edge of some parkland and is now a private house. The walls are the original ones, three-feet thick, made of brick, with solid oak beams, providing an attractive interior. Two of the old millstones stand outside the house.

As well as their second son, a daughter, Mary Edith, was born at Sandford in 1875, making a family of three children in all. The family stayed at Sandford about four years. They then moved on to Tom's old home ground, to the village of Atch Lench, not far from Harvington and Arrow. There were family friends at Atch Lench, for Fred Bomford lived there, an old colleague of Tom's brother Walter. When Tom and Walter were in New Zealand, Walter and Fred had kept up a regular correspondence.

It is uncertain whether Tom was milling at Atch Lench in the brief time the family were there, though there was a mill in the village. On the birth certificate of their second daughter, Katherine Helen, born there in December 1876, he is described as a miller of Atch Lench, but no specific mill is named. This may be because he was looking for another mill, or working temporarily for another miller whilst hoping to return to the family's mill at Harvington. At that time the situation at Harvington was uncertain. For the last six years John Sisam had run the Mill, William Henry having set up a corn-dealing business in Alcester. But by 1876 John was feeling his years and William Henry came back to help him. So there were now two experienced millers at Harvington. In 1877 William Henry died unexpectedly at the age of 39, John Sisam retired soon afterwards and James Leonard took charge of Harvington. Tom now went to work at Aldington Mill, near Evesham. The miller's wife and children still occupied the Mill House, so Tom and Mary Jane moved into adjacent premises towards the end of 1878. It was a combined mill and bakery at which Tom employed two men, but his pay was meagre.

Since they were living nearer to the rest of the family it was now easier to make visits. In March 1878, Mary Jane (or 'Polly' as she was known by in the family) took her two boys Charlie and Thomas Jnr., together with baby Kate, to see Tom's mother, Caroline Sisam, at The Priory in Alcester. Afterwards Mary Jane and Baby Kate went over to Grafton to visit Tom's sister Alice who was farming there with her husband, John Fisher. There Tom met them and drove them home. Charlie and Thomas Jnr. stayed with Grandma Caroline Sisam for a week. While they were there Helen Sisam, William Henry's wife, who also lived in Alcester, came in bringing her four children, Emily, Caroline, William and Baby Alfred. 'I had quite a party!' was Grandma Caroline's comment.

The following year another daughter, Mabel, was born to Tom and Mary Jane, but the child died within a year. Two years later, in 1881, a third son, Alexander, was born. During all these moves the family were not more than three or four years in any one place, presumably because there were no suitable long leases available. There was therefore little chance to develop any of these corn-mills into more flourishing businesses. At the same time there were more mouths to feed as the family increased. In 1883 the opportunity to return to Harvington materialised, and James Leonard installed Tom and his family in the mill where Tom had begun milling twenty years before.

Perhaps he felt he had come home, even though this time he was living in a cottage on the property as the Mill House was let. Certainly the familiar surroundings and the support of his brother James Leonard must have given him a sense of security. There were further additions to the family. Three more children were born there, all boys. They were John Francis born in 1883, Edmund Herbert 1885, and Arthur Gordon 1890. The local land tax returns record that Thomas Marshall Sisam was operating Harvington Mill for, or jointly with, James Leonard Sisam of Arrow Mill. This was the period when James Leonard had the lease of three corn-mills in the district, Harvington, Arrow and Oversley, and in 1887 Tom took charge of Oversley for a while and then returned to Harvington.

As so often happened in those days with large families, Tom and Mary Jane had difficulties with some of their children. Grandma Caroline Sisam, writing of the eldest boy Charlie in one of her family letters to New Zealand had, commented: 'He is a very aimiable, good natured boy but not very quick and does not get on very well at school, and he can't talk quite plain, which is against him.' Charlie it is true had a speech impediment and was retarded. A younger boy, Alexander (Alec), was also rather slow. On the other hand, Caroline had observed : 'Tom is much quicker and gets on very well.' Young Thomas in fact, while the family were at Oversley Mill, won prizes for history and geography at Alcester Grammar School. At the annual prize-giving in the summer of 1888, he, together with his cousin William and two other boys, was singled out as having done very well in the senior class.

Unfortunately, Tom's health had begun to deteriorate, to the extent that in 1894 he had to give up milling completely. The family left Harvington in that year and went to live at

Peacock House, Cleeve Prior.

Cleeve Prior, where he farmed a few acres and kept some dairy cows. It was a peaceful village on the other side of the River Avon from Harvington, about two miles distant. They lived quietly here at Peacock House by the village green. Their house took its name from the fine piece of topiary in the front garden, where part of the hedge had been shaped into a large peacock. It was a good place for the children, and the river just across the meadows provided plenty of interest. Tom, having lived and worked by rivers all his life, saw to it that they all learned to swim at an early age. Edmund, one of the youngest, used to recall that the method used was very simple. Their father would throw them in where the water was shallow, and they learned very quickly. These were happy interludes, reminiscent of his younger days when Tom was known for his cheerfulness and merry spirit.

We do not know for certain when Tom's health first began to decline seriously. Presumably it was due to a recurrence of the heart trouble originally diagnosed in New Zealand. We do not know what caused the constant moving from place to place; whether it was short leases, bad luck, or increasing ill-health or all these things. Whatever the causes, income decreased as the years went by and the family continued to increase. Large families were the custom of the time, for the infant mortality rate was still high and, as there were no old-age pensions, most people relied on their children to look after them when they became elderly and infirm.

The idyll at Cleeve was short-lived. Tom's health deteriorated further and within two years he died, on October 17, 1896, at the age of 55. When he died he had very little to leave to his family. It was a desperate situation for Mary Jane. Her eldest son, Charlie, was incapable of earning his living. Thomas, aged 24, had already left home and was working for the railways at Peterborough in Northamptonshire. The family who remained at Peacock House now consisted of Mary Jane and seven children: Charlie, the retarded son, aged 25, Mary Edith 21, Katherine 20, Alec 15, John Francis 13, Edmund Herbert 11, and Arthur Gordon 6.

When James Leonard at Arrow Mill, nine miles away, heard the sad news of Thomas Marshall's death, he realised that Mary Jane and her family were in deep financial need, and that swift action was necessary. He probably made sure that she had enough for her immediate needs; but, being a practical man, he knew that long-term help was also required. Accordingly, out of his own pocket he established an annuity that would provide her an assured, regular income for the rest of her life. In the meantime, there was the question of the welfare of the children still living at home. Charlie would always have to be cared for and provided for. The youngest boy, Arthur Gordon, being only aged 6 would need care for some years. The two girls would, of course, be of help in the house. However the younger, Katherine, married three years later and emigrated to South Africa, where she raised a family. Alec aged 15 who was rather slow and would not be able to make his way in life, but could earn modestly at farmwork, even though it were casual labour. John Francis (Jack) would soon be able to earn for himself; and within a few years he left home for Monmouthshire, South Wales, where he worked as a railway plate-layer and track-maintenance man. Edmund Herbert, aged 11, was a bright boy, but how was he to get an education that would equip him to go out and earn a living? The answer to this question, and the unfolding of the story of Tom's descendants, came from following yet another trail of exploration and research.

Someone had once mentioned having been told by another member of the family that they had come across the name Sisam in the Birmingham area. At the time no one paid much attention but now, in the search for Tom's family, this seemed a straw worth clutching at; particularly as Birmingham attracted many people from all over the Midlands who were seeking to improve their lot. The records of marriages and births revealed several names in the Birmingham area, and the telephone directory gave several addresses. At the same time a study of the map showed that Birmingham was but thirty miles or so from Cleeve Prior. So the search moved to Birmingham.

26
Phoenix Arising

CLEEVE PRIOR, BIRMINGHAM AND THE FUTURE

Today Birmingham continues its long record as one of Britain's major manufacturing centres. Its industrial roots go back to the sixteenth century, when John Leland the historian noted that a large number of iron-smiths were working there. Later it was at the heart of the Industrial Revolution. The inventors of the steam engine, James Watt and Matthew Boulton, were both Birmingham men. There is practically nothing that Birmingham has not manufactured at one time or other, and the world has been its market for bicycles, motor cycles, automobiles, steam engines, machine tools, glassware, nails, screws, safety pins, ball bearings, and the like. Some industries have declined, others have expanded. Some have moved elsewhere, others have moved in, but Birmingham still follows its historic role and will always be remembered for certain famous names such as Cadbury, Austin, Rover, BSA, Lucas, Guest Keen and Nettlefold, Boulton and Paul. Yet the clatter of industry is not the whole of Birmingham. It is a city of parks, and open spaces, and is close to some of the finest English countryside.

The search for Tom's descendants led finally to the south-western edge of the city, to Northfield and the home of Richard Sisam. Richard, it was discovered, was Tom's grandson. Richard never knew his grandfather Tom, nor his grandmother Mary Jane. They had both died before he was born. As children, he and his brother and sister thought that Thomas Marshall Sisam had spent his time travelling the world and that this was the reason the family had so little money. They had not heard of the emigration to New Zealand, or of their grandfather's illness and return to England, or of the close relationship he had with his brother, James Leonard Sisam of Arrow Mill. Richard was heartened to hear news of other Sisams in New Zealand, Canada, America and England. His father was none other than Edmund Herbert Sisam, Tom's younger son, about whom Mary Jane Sisam was so concerned when the boy's father died in 1896. Richard had a few family papers, and from them produced a small, neatly printed card dated 1897, from which the whole story of Tom's descendants gradually unfolded. The card read as follows:

BRITISH ORPHAN ASYLUM
January Election 1897
Your VOTES and INTEREST are earnestly solicited on behalf of
EDMUND HERBERT SISAM
of Cleeve Prior, Worcestershire, born Aug. 27, 1885,
Whose father, formerly a miller, died in October 1896, in very reduced circumstances, leaving a widow with eight children unprovided for; of these, four are wholly, and two more partially dependent upon their mother.
The father, a man of education and refinement, started in business in 1869, with a capital of

BRITISH ORPHAN ASYLUM.
JANUARY ELECTION, 1897.

Your VOTES and INTEREST are earnestly solicited on behalf of

EDMUND HERBERT SISAM,

Of Cleeve Prior, Worcestershire, born Aug. 27, 1885,

Whose father, formerly a miller, died in October, 1896, in very reduced circumstances, leaving a widow with eight children unprovided for; of these, four are wholly, and two more partially, dependent upon their mother.

The father, a man of education and refinement, started in business in 1869, with a capital of £600, which he lost, owing to ill-health and bad debts, after which he was obliged to work for low wages, hampered by constant ill-health. In 1894, he was compelled by increasing illness to give up this occupation, and has since farmed a few acres in Cleeve Prior, with very precarious results. It was thus impossible for him to make any provision for his family.

His widow hopes to pay the rent of her house and earn a livelihood by taking in boarders in the spring and summer, and by farming some allotments.

The eldest son, aged twenty-five, is unable, through general weakness of constitution, to leave home, or to take any responsible situation.

THIS CASE IS RECOMMENDED BY

The Rev. B. H. Sheppard, St. Stephens, Worcester;
John Corbett, Esq., Impney, Droitwich.

Votes will be thankfully received by the Rev. James D. Knipe, M.A., Cleeve Prior Vicarage,

The appeal issued to secure a place in a boarding school for Edmund Herbert Sisam, son of Thomas Marshall Sisam.

The impressive Royal Hotel at Slough, which became the school at which Edmund Herbert Sisam was educated.

£600, which he lost, owing to ill-health and bad debts, after which he was obliged to work for low wages, hampered by constant ill-health. In 1894, he was compelled by increasing illness to give up this occupation, and has since farmed a few acres in Cleeve Prior, with very precarious results. It was thus impossible for him to make any provision for his family.

His widow hopes to pay for the rent of her house and earn a livelihood by taking in boarders in the spring and summer, and by farming some allotments.

The eldest son, aged twenty-five, is unable, through general weakness of constitution, to leave home, or to take any responsible situation.

THIS CASE IS RECOMMENDED BY
The Rev. B.H.Sheppard St. Stephens, Worcester;
John Corbett Esq., Impney, Droitwich.
Votes will be thankfully received by the Rev. James D.Knipe, M.A., Cleeve Prior Vicarage, Evesham, and by the Widow, Mrs. Sisam, The Peacock House, Cleeve Prior, Evesham.

It is a sad story, but with a happy ending, for the success of the appeal provided Edmund Herbert with a good education, and board and lodging, until he could earn his own living. The answer to Mary Jane Sisam's need had come from the village of Cleeve Prior itself, through James Knipe, the vicar, who knew where practical assistance could be found. Today social security would care for these needs, but in those days such rescue operations were unusual and were made possible mainly by the selfless giving of individuals, who pioneered the social welfare we now take for granted.

There is no question that the school where Edmund Herbert was placed provided him with a sound education and good character training. It was founded to educate the orphans of those 'once in prosperity', especially the sons of professional men and tradesmen. It was in fact a highly reputable boarding school rather than an asylum or institution. There was nothing Dickensian about it. It originated in London and later moved to Slough in Buckinghamshire, which at the time was a small market town about two miles from Windsor. A large hotel in the centre of Slough had been bought by means of donations and effectively adapted. As *The West Surrey Gazette* reported, it was opened in 1863 by the Prince and Princess of Wales at a ceremony attended by the Lord Mayor of London, two bishops, and a large number of supporters and contributors. The bands of the 18th Hussars and the Commissionaires provided music, and there was a choir from the Royal College of Music.

It was thirty years after this event that Edmund Herbert was admitted to the school. The converted building was impressive. At the front, facing the street it had a series of terraces, and running the whole length of the facade was a portico, in the centre of which was the main entrance.

There were two towers, one at either end. Inside there were spacious dormitories, classrooms, a dining hall, and sick bays. Edmund seems to have enjoyed being there and always referred to it as 'my school'. Not many of his recollections of those days remain. He recalled having rheumatic fever, and that he had enjoyed the long convalescence. He remembered being pushed about by his schoolmates in a wicker-basket wheel-chair, and the exhiliration of being launched from the top of a hill and rushing all the way down to the bottom. Because of this illness he left the school earlier than planned. This was in the early 1900s, when he was apprenticed to the grocery trade in the Moseley district of Birmingham. His bout of rheumatic fever later kept him out of the 1914 War until near the end, when he was called into the Royal Flying Corps for ground staff duties.

After demobilisation Edmund returned to his old job in the grocery trade and continued to progress there. Later he moved to the George Mason chain of stores. In 1921 he married Emily Mabel Hawes. She had been in service in many large houses in different parts of England, and in World War I was a postwoman. Their wedding was in St. Paul's Church, Balsall Heath, just south of central Birmingham. They had a daughter and two sons, the younger of whom was Richard. In the George Mason company Edmund acted as manager at the King's Heath branch, then manager at a number of other branches, finally becoming a senior manager. His wife was a regular churchgoer and he went with her. He was a quiet man and did not say very much. She, on the other hand, was a great talker. When the children were growing up they lived at Billesley, a southern area of Birmingham.

❖ ❖ ❖

The home at Peacock House, Cleeve Prior remained in the family for some years. With Edmund Herbert safely launched in the world, Katherine married, Thomas working in Peterborough and Jack in Wales, Mary Jane made a home for Charlie, Alec and Arthur Gordon, with Edith to help her. It was a simple home, but the villagers noted that she kept it spick and span. Though poor, she did her best to maintain standards. In later years Edmund often recalled the fact that the house had a backstairs. It used to astonish him that they lived in a house with two staircases and, although Peacock House was a somewhat superior establishment, there were no servants to use the backstairs. Financially they managed with what little they had. There was the annuity, Mary Jane received an inheritance at some point from the Davis family, there were Arthur Gordon's earnings from farmwork, and Alec's occasional earnings, and probably Thomas, Jack and Edmund sent her something from time to time. She also had the comfort and assurance of knowing that Arrow Mill and the rest of the family were only nine miles away.

When World War I broke out Arthur Gordon was called up. He left his work on the land and joined the South Wales Borderers, but while still in the army succumbed to the influenza epidemic of 1918. His name is on a memorial plaque in Cleeve Prior church to those who lost their lives while serving. For the next six years or so the smaller family at Peacock House consisted of Mary Jane, her daughter Edith, and her two sons, Charlie and Alec; with Edith doing what she was told by her mother to keep the home running, as Mary Jane advanced in years. The villagers remembered how she used to sit in her window, wearing a lace cap, and watch the world go by, for she very rarely went out. A regular event of those days was the yearly visit of Mary Jane's young granddaughter, Edith May Sisam, from Peterborough. She was the daughter of Mary Jane's son Thomas. The child looked forward to these visits, though she found conversation with poor Charlie rather difficult.

Mary Jane lived to a good age. She died in 1924, aged 89. On her death the regular payments from James Leonard Sisam's annuity automatically came to an end. James Leonard himself had died three years previously, and there was now a new generation which did not have such a close touch with the Cleeve Prior situation as their forebears had. The family moved from Peacock House to a small cottage – later known as 'Sisams Cottage' – in Nightingale Lane, near the farm where Alec occasionally worked. The farmer, Joseph Smithin, let the family have it for a rent of five shillings a week. Edith, who was now 49, kept house as best she could but rarely if ever cleaned house as Mary Jane had once done. She was called Cissie by the family, this being a nickname meaning 'sister'. She shared the home with her two brothers, Charlie aged 53, who could not work, and Alec aged 43, who worked whenever he found jobs within his capabilities.

An unexpected train of events brought help. About the same time, a Miss Hoddinott from Lower Lemington, near Moreton-in-Marsh, was visiting Cleeve Prior when she met two of the Sisams in the street. She spoke to them and realised they were finding it hard to make ends meet. When she reached home she went to Lloyds Bank in Moreton-in-Marsh, where she knew the chief cashier, Walter Sisam, the youngest son of James Leonard Sisam of Arrow Mill. She told him how touched she had been by her meeting with the two Sisams in Cleeve Prior, and wondered if he knew of their need. He did not know and was deeply distressed by what she told him. He got in touch with his two farming brothers, Henry and Frank Sisam, and together they set up a fund which would provide a weekly income for the Cleeve Prior family. This continued for nearly twenty years.

In the early 1930s Jack came back from Monmouthshire where for thirty years, ever since he was a young man, he had worked on the railway. By now he had lost the sight of an eye and could no longer continue working. He had been based at a railway engineering works at Rogerstone, near Newport, from which repairwork and tracklaying over a wide area was undertaken. It had been a lonely life. His only home was a men's hostel where he lived along with his workmates. There was nothing to do in the evenings but to go down to the pub and meet whatever company he might find there. When he came home to Cleeve Prior and joined Cissie, Charlie and Alec in the cottage he was in his early fifties. It was not easy at his age and with his disability to find regular work. The kindly farmer, Joseph Smithin, had been good to the Sisam sons, especially to Alec, and had given them work on his farm whenever he could. Now he did the same for Jack.

Jack's nephew Richard Sisam, whom the family called Dick, when he left school had worked for two years in a wholesale warehouse and three years in a factory. In 1941 he was called up into the Oxford and Bucks Light Infantry (now part of the Green Jackets). He saw service in India, Malaya and Hong Kong, after being transferred to the Devonshire Regiment. After the War he spent three months helping his parents and then took a job with the Post Office. He worked his way up and eventually became a postal executive officer. In 1953 he married Patricia Irene Douglas (Pat), whose family were Irish. Dick's parents considered her 'a foreigner', and it was some years before they fully accepted her into the family.

Dick remembered regular summertime visits as a boy to the family at Cleeve Prior with his brother Arthur, sister Marian and their parents. They stayed in the cottage where his Aunt Edith (Cissie) kept house for her brothers Charlie, Alec, and Jack. The whole family slept in one room, the parents in the bed and three children on the floor. The cottage was sparsely furnished but clean. It was about a hundred years old and had a shingle roof. There was always a kettle on the range, and bacon and pork racks on the ceiling. The water tap was outside, and there were was no indoor toilet – just a shed in the back garden. But Cissie made the visiting children very welcome. She fed them well but never sat down with them. She said she preferred to eat by herself afterwards. The children seemed to think she made do with bread and water, in order to economise, which would explain why she ate alone. Yet there was always money in the home, for none of the children ever left without a silver coin in their hands. There were bookshelves in the cottage, and once the children found a pound note in one of the books, hidden away there by Cissie in case the men should spend it. She and her brothers had a small but regular income from the fund contributed to by the Arrow Sisams, as well as Alec's occasional earnings, and there were regular parcels of groceries from their younger brother in Birmingham; however Cissie tended to hoard these away. As a child she had grown up during years of family insecurity and no doubt this had made her anxious about money ever since. The children enjoyed their holidays in Cleeve. It was a welcome change from living in a city. They delighted in the river, which flowed close to the village, and in stories of how their grandfather had taught his children to swim. There was also the excitement when their brother, Arthur, managed to fall into the river wearing his best suit.

Charlie at this time, though handicapped, was a well-known figure in the village. In a small community, where everyone knew everyone, the handicapped were understood and cared for in a way that would be impossible in a large city. He used to go every morning to the farm to fetch the milk for the family, carrying a jug upside down very carefully in front of him, and very carefully the right way up on the way home. The people at the farm knew him and there was no need for explanations in words. For him fetching the milk was an important and fulfilling task, which he was performing for the family. Charlie died in 1936 and five years later the faithful and self-sacrificing Edith died. Her burial is recorded in the church register under the name of Cissie Sisam.

Jack and Alec lived on in the cottage doing for themselves. Frank Sisam at Arrow used to send them a cartload of logs every year for firewood. But in 1943 the weekly payments from the family fund ceased, as Frank Sisam and his brother Walter both died that year, and those left could not continue the contributions. However, Alec and Jack seemed to manage by occasional work and the groceries sent them from their brother Edmund.

The two men were quite different types. Jack, having roughed it with plate-layers and the like in Wales, loved company; and his greatest pleasure was to go down to the King's Head, the inn in the village, for his nightly pint of Mackie's ale and a tot of whisky. Alec had lived quietly all his life in Cleeve Prior, never able to make much of a living. He was an upright man and strict in his standards. He could not stand bad language. When the farm workers stopped for a midday bite, and all sat round to eat their lunch, Alec would turn his back on them because of their swearing. Yet he had a wry humour behind his apparent simplicity and had the reputation of being quite clever. The village was full of tales about him.

Alec sometimes helped at another farm owned by the Archer family. The men were building a rick one day and Alec was standing on top forking the hay into place as the others tossed it up. 'Where will you have it, Alec, in the corner, in the middle, at the side?' one of them said. Alec, who wasn't going to be hustled, replied simply, 'Up here.' On another occasion someone's heifer fell into the river. Alec and others were helping to get it out. Alec, who had a wisdom of his own, never worked harder than he had to. One of the other helpers noticed this and remarked afterwards, 'They tell me Alec hasn't got all his buttons on, but he's got more on his waistcoat than I have, because we was pulling this cow out and Alec was on the end of the rope, but he wasn't pulling. I turned round and said, 'Alec, you ain't pulling.' 'No,' said Alec, tapping his forehead, 'you men need it up here' '.

When the farmer one day set him to dig a hole in which to plant a tree, he didn't do it correctly. Either it was in the wrong place or it was too big. When the farmer saw it he said, 'O, you haven't got that right.' In exasperation Alec threw down his tools and went home. Two hours later he came back and apologised. He said, 'I know what was the matter.' The other farmworkers heard all this. They liked Alec because, as they said, 'He was a very human chap.'

He was over sixty when he decided to learn to ride a bicycle. It was a lady's bicycle, probably Cissie's old one, and he asked young Don Archer, the farmer's son, to teach him. They rode side by side down the lanes, but whenever a car passed them Alec went straight through the hedge. When he got off the bike he would never push it. He carried it carefully. He learnt eventually, though it took a long time.

Alec went to church regularly. Every Sunday morning he would be seen walking to church carrying his own prayer-book and wearing his one dark suit, albeit without a tie. Jack on the other hand would be at home cooking the Sunday dinner. When Alec died in 1963 Jack stayed on in the cottage. His niece and nephews who used to visit Cleeve Prior as children, kept in touch with him. Jack made regular visits to Birmingham, when Richard would fetch him in the family motor-cycle and sidecar (known as a 'combination'). Jack usually brought with him whatever vegetables were in season. On one occasion he came with a quantity of asparagus. It was an enormous quantity which lasted so long that no one wanted to see asparagus again. He never had to buy these gifts of vegetables. His friends in the village used to let him go and cut whatever he wanted from their patches. He travelled light and brought very few personal things with him. Once when he went to visit Marian and her family he arrived with a suitcase of vegetables and one clean collar. He had quite an appetite, no doubt because he rarely prepared a proper meal for himself. Once Dick and Pat had to go out while Jack was staying with them. They left food for him in the fridge. He ate it all and, being still hungry, devoured a whole rice pudding that had been prepared for another day.

Jack was very fortunate in the friends he had in Cleeve Prior. His closest friend was Reg Taylor, who had known him for over forty years. Reg and his wife were warm-hearted souls and were extremely kind to him. Knowing that Jack rarely made himself a square meal, they always had him to Sunday dinner at their little High Street house, Wellington Cottage. On Saturday afternoons he called in there to watch the football on television. He would sit in front of the screen enrapt in the game, and wouldn't allow anyone to talk. His other delight was to meet his cronies in the King's Head. The pub was kept by a retired army major and had a front parlour and a back room. The back room was where Jack liked to sit. It was a friendly place with a stone floor covered with sawdust and old fashioned spitoons here and there. On the way to the King's Head each evening he would always drop in on the Taylors for a chat. Then, by and by, he would say, 'Ah well, I must go now and get my feet in the sawdust.'

He had another good friend in the village, a neighbour named Dr. Mackenzie known as 'Doctor Mac'. She was retired, about his age, and understood him. One day Jack was visiting Dick in Birmingham and suddenly asked him, 'Would you bury me?' and said he had money saved that would cover the cost. When the time came it was just enough. He had also asked to be buried next to his brother Alec. Jack died in 1972 at the age of 89. When he went to look in Cleeve Prior churchyard Dick found that none of the family graves had headstones, with the exception of Thomas Marshall and Mary Jane. He could not find the spot where Alec had been buried, so in the end they buried Jack quite close to his good friend 'Doctor Mac', who had died a short while before.

It was the task of Dick and Pat to clear the old cottage. There was very little in it and it was in a sadly neglected state. Ironically, the larder was full of hoarded food parcels, most of them the legacy of poor Cissie's economy, and which Jack did not know what to do with. They were groceries sent regularly sent by Edmund. Needless to say much of it had perished. All the rubbish from the house had to be consigned to a large bonfire in the back garden.

There still remained the mystery of what happened to Jack's older brother Thomas, the first to leave Cleeve Prior and who was said to have gone to work on the railways at Peterborough, about the turn of the century. Did he marry and did he have any children?

Richard knew of him but that was all. The answer came by studying the list made at the General Records Office in London of all birth and marriage entries under the name Sisam. There were several entries for Peterborough, the dates of which were of the right period. The next step was to look in the Peterborough telephone directory. There was one entry for E. Sisam. The voice that answered the telephone was a young woman's. She said she was Estelle Sisam and gave the name and address of her parents, Clive and Victoria Sisam, also living in Peterborough. Arrangements were made to visit them. There was a warm welcome from this couple. Clive had strong Sisam resemblances and his wife, Victoria, instantly identified one of the visitors as a Sisam. Then the family photograph albums and papers were produced. Clive was the grandson of Tom and Mary Jane's son Thomas, who had done so well at Alcester Grammar School. When Thomas left school he first worked on the land at Cleeve Prior, this being the only opening locally for youngsters who had had no special training or resources. But he soon decided to seek his fortune elsewhere, and went to Peterborough in Northamptonshire. There he married Ann Johnson in 1906. Peterborough was an important railway centre and provided good opportunities for work. He took a job with the North Eastern Railway, and in the course of time received promotion, and finally was selected to be a train guard. When he retired he went into the shoe-repair business, with considerable success. It seems that he was much respected and was held in great affection by those who knew him well. He was known as 'Pop' Sisam. He had a Bible which he read assiduously, and a copy of Fox's 'Book of Martyrs'. His grandson, Clive Sisam, inherited both volumes and found the Bible well annotated.

This Thomas Sisam had three children, Edith May Sisam (b.1908), Frank Edmund Sisam (b.1910), and Gladys M. Sisam (b.1917). Edith May was named after Edith (Cissie) of Cleeve Prior, her aunt. Thomas' son, Frank Edmund, continued the family shoe-repair business in partnership with a Walter Pepper, trading under the name of Re-Nu Repairs. He married Beatrice Marion Pettican in 1938 and Clive was their only child. The family remembered Frank Edmund particularly because he had such perfect manners, was always well turned out, and in fact was 'a gentleman'. He was a kind man and, like his father, was devout. He wrote a great deal on all kinds of subjects, and when young compiled a piece on the evils of smoking. It is interesting that he made a profound impression on Victoria, the girl who became the wife of his son, Clive. She summed up her father-in-law in these words, 'He completely altered my view of men.' The character qualities of both Thomas Sisam and his son, Frank Edmund, stemmed apparently from Thomas' contact as a young man with the much-maligned Jehovah's Witnesses, through whom he found a genuine religious experience. His quality of living was the fruit of it.

Clive became a fitter-engineer with a company making printing machines for export. In his spare time he and his friends built a church, since the Jehovah's Witnesses in that area did not have one. Clive and Victoria had one daughter, Estelle, but no sons, so the male Sisam line in Peterborough comes to an end with Clive Sisam.

❖ ❖ ❖

Since the Peterborough line of Sisams ends with Clive Sisam, the only male descendants of Thomas Marshall Sisam likely to continue the Sisam name in England were the sons of Edmund Herbert. He, it will be remembered, was a younger son of Thomas Marshall Sisam, who had been educated in a Christian orphanage school, and had made his way successfully in

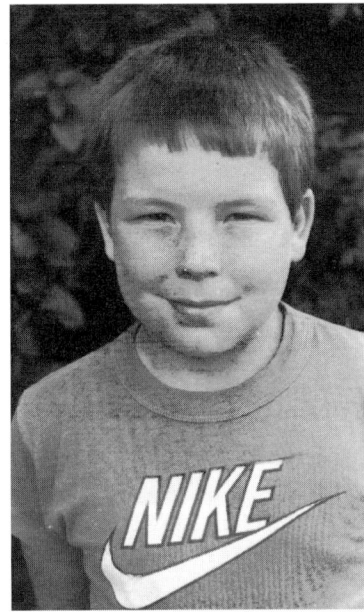

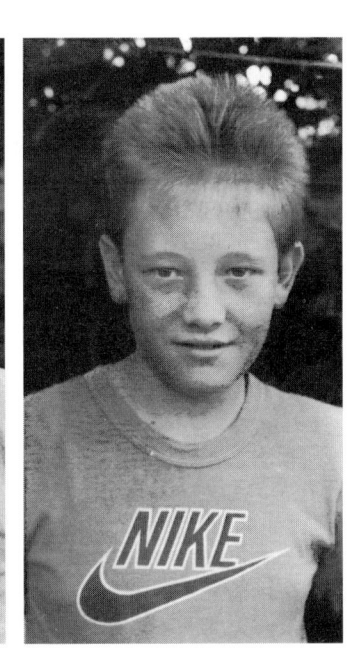

Edmund Herbert Sisam in World War I uniform, and his 5 great-grandchildren.

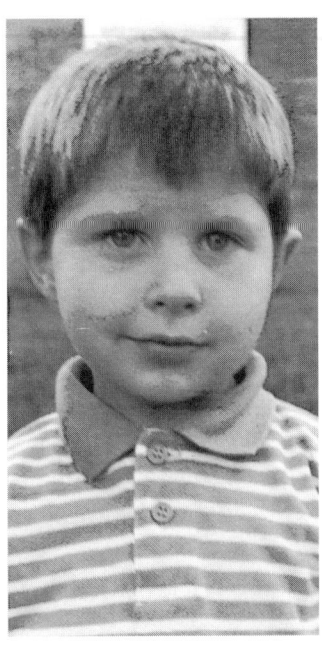

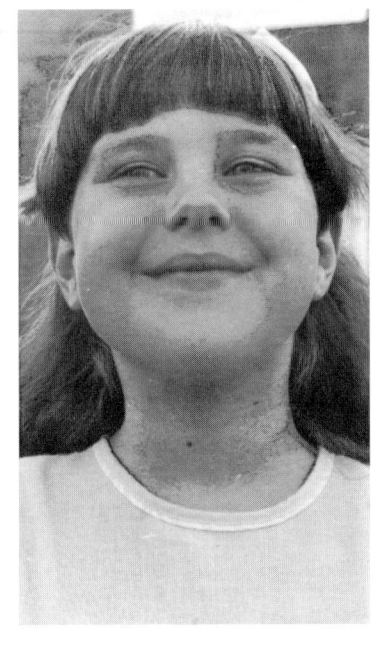

the Birmingham grocery trade. Of his two sons, the younger, Richard, had one daughter, Sheila; but the older one, Arthur Edmund, had two sons, Graham Arthur and Peter Edmund.

Arthur Edmund had also begun his adult life in the Birmingham grocery trade. He was appointed manager of a store in the Hall Green area of Birmingham, then was in the army during World War II, serving in North Africa, Sicily and mainland Italy. When he was demobilised his commanding officer wrote a recommendation and referred to his conduct as 'exemplary'. He was in fact, like his father, conscientious and a man of principle.

Arthur returned to the grocery business in Birmingham when World War II ended. He also moved to the George Mason company to manage one of their stores. He married Barbara Stewart in 1949 and they both lived above the store. About that time the British car industry began to boom. Arthur left the grocery business about 1951 and went to work at Morris Motors at Washwood Heath, producing Morris Minor cars. He became a skilled tool-setter. Barbara also went to work there, working at the giant press that turned out body panels. They were both involved in the production of the famous Mini. She was there from 1951 to 1982, and saw the last Mini come off the production line. She took a pride in her work and boasted in later years that the cars on which she worked were solidly built of metal. There was no plastic in them.

This entry into the car industry took the family into the mainstream of Midlands industry and the vast workforce of skilled engineers that manned it. After some years, Arthur's health broke down and he had to retire. He showed great courage throughout his illness. Barbara looked after him and their last days together, though numbered and sometimes sad, were a time of happiness and oneness. He died in 1981.

Of Arthur's two sons, Graham became a telecommunications engineer, and his younger brother, Peter, a machine-tool engineer in the Hardy-Spicer company, making differential gears and other components for car manufacturers. Graham and Peter were both married and had flourishing families. Graham had three sons, Andrew Graham, Stephen Paul and Christopher Charles; and Peter had a daughter, Kerry, and a son, Gary.

The story of Thomas Marshall Sisam and his family began full of youthful hope in the 1860s with the three brothers setting out for New Zealand. It continued through sudden illness, health regained and lost, marriage and children, and finally family impoverishment. Then, like the ancient phoenix rising out of the ashes, his younger son Edmund became father of a new branch of the family tree. So the tree goes on growing in England, as well as in America, Canada and New Zealand.

There are old-fashioned qualities which recur in this history of the Sisam family, such as integrity, independence, loyalty, uprightness, and adherence to principle; which have made for sound family life, stable relationships, and the readiness to help one another in difficult times. Individuals in the family were faced with distinctive personal decisions. History is made by personal decisions. They are the fabric of it and for good or ill they set the course and the tone of an age. It is for new generations, who will continue the story told in this book, to write the chapters of the future.

❖❖❖

Sources and Notes

In addition to Parish Records, Census Returns and Land Tax Assessments the sources listed below were consulted.

Chapter One:	*Portrait of the Cotswolds*, E. Brill
	Highways & Byways in Shakespeare's Country, W.H. Hutton
	Long Barrows of the Cotswolds, O.G.S. Crawford.
	Will of Nicholas Sysom, 1728
	Will of John Sysom, 1762 (Proved 1763). Original in the Gloucestershire Record Office. Reproduced by permission of the Bishop of Gloucester
	Note 1: Buckle Street, part of a Neolithic trackway leading to Salmonbury Camp, Bourton-on-the Water.
	Note 2: According to Kenneth Sisam, Anglo-Saxon scholar.
	Note 3: *Adderbury Award, 1768*. County Record Office, Oxford.
Chapter Two:	*English Social History*, G.M. Trevelyan
	English Farming, Past and Present, Lord Erle
	Will of John Sisam I, 1779. Hereford and Worcester Record Office.
	Will of John Sisam II, 1801
	Enclosure Award Map, Hill and Moor. Property of E. Righton of Hill, Fladbury.
	Will of David Sisam of Hill, 1865 (Proved 1869)
Chapter Three:	*Encyclopedia Britannica* 1911
	Will of William Sisam, 1834
	Letter from Peggy Rattigan to author, 1965.
	Records of the Ragley Estate, County Record Office, Warwick.
	Alcester, a History, G.E. Saville
	Records of the Walton Estate, 1848. Held by Elizabeth Hamilton of Walton
	Stratford-upon-Avon Herald, 1915.
	Reminiscences of Winchcombe, John Oakey
	Glossop Heritage (Glossop Heritage Committee).
	Marriage Certificate of Frederick Sisam. The design is Crown copyright and is reproduced with the permission of the Controller of HMSO.
	Note 4: Originally at Temple Tysoe, later recut near the Sunrising Inn, Edgehill.

Chapter Four:	*Alcester, a History*, G.E. Saville. *A History of Worcestershire Agriculture and Rural Evolution*, R.G. Gaut *English Social History*, G.M.Trevelyan. *Centennial of Albertland*, I.E. Farr & W.H. Marsh Recollections of W. Leonard Sisam told to Benjamin Copedo Jnr.
Chapter Five:	*Registrum Orielense* (Shadwell), Oriel College, Oxford. *Encyclopedia Britannica*, 1911. *Collins Encyclopedia*, 1986. Records of the Oxford Forestry Institute. Letter from J.W.B.Sisam to author, 1987. Dioscesan Archives, Fredericton, New Brunswick. *The Forestry Chronicle*, 1989. *Crockford's Clerical Directory* 1937 *Church of England Yearbook* 1887 Recollections of Peter Neill Sisam (Toronto) Recollections of Catherine N. Sisam.
Chapter Six:	*Rural Rides*, William Cobbett *Berrow's Worcester Journal*, 1830, 1831. Records of the Worcester Lent Assizes, 1831. Public Record Office, Kew. *Quarterly Prison Returns 1832–1847* (from Hobart). *Worcestershire in the Nineteenth Century*, T.C. Turberville.
Chapter Seven:	*Encyclopedia Britannica*, 1911 *Ship's Passenger Lists, JOHN BRIGHT*, 1866, 1868. Recollections of Ruth Moulton. *The American West*, D. Lavender. *The Mormons*, R. Mullen. *The World Rushed In*, J.S. Holliday. *Lost Towns of Carbon County*, W.W. Daley Archives, Wyoming Department of Commerce. *The Fetterman Massacre*, D. Brown. *A History of the United States*, R.B. Nye & J.E. Morpungo
Chapter Eight:	*History of the Jordan Area, West Jordan*, L. & A. Holt *Treasured Memories of West Jordan*, C.B. Richards. *Encyclopedic History of the Church of Jesus Christ of Latter Day Saints*, A. Jensen *The Mormons*, R. Mullen. *Records of Members*, Genealogical Library, Church of Jesus Christ of Latter Day Saints, Salt Lake City *To the Salt Lake Valley*, (Daughters of Utah Pioneers Museum) *The Deseret News*, 1895, 1896 *The Salt Lake Tribune*, 1895 *Life Behind Bars*, M.L. Bashore MSS. Recollections by Ruth Moulton, 1990 Note 5: Historical Department Records, Church of Jesus Christ of Latter Day Saints Headquarters, Salt Lake City.

Sources and Notes

Chapter Nine:
Recollections of Ruth Moulton and Laverne Greathouse told to author 1990.
A Pictorial History of the Automobile, P. Roberts.
Encyclopedia Britannica 1911

Note 6: Told to Ruth Moulton by Hannah Sisam.

Chapter Ten:
Encyclopedia Britannica, 1982
Idaho, Lane.
Recollections of Lorne Richard Sisam, Ruth Moulton, Laverne Greathouse & Violet Seal told to author 1990.

Chapter Eleven:
Encyclopedia Britannica 1911
The Times-News, Twin Falls, Idaho. 18 August 1985
Recollections of Richard J. Sisiam, Nelse Sisiam & Mary Goff Bateman told to author in Idaho, 1985

Note 7: Told to Ruth Moulton by Hannah Sisam
Note 8: Letter in the possession of Ruth Moulton

Chapter Twelve:
South Auckland, H. Wily
Centennial of Albertland, S. Farr & W.H. Marsh
The Albertlanders, Sir Henry Brett & Henry Hook
Charles Blomfield, his Life and Times, (Whakatane and District Museum)
G.F. Bomford. Papers. 1860–1864, 1944. MS-Papers-1813. Held by Alexander Turnbull Library, NLNZ, New Zealand
The City of Auckland, J. Bass
The New Zealand Wars, J. Belich
The Waikato War, John Featon
A History of New Zealand, K. Sinclair
Recollections about Alfred John Sisam by Walter John Sisam, Joan Stewart, Leonard A. Sisam, & Kenneth Sisam
Letters of A.J.Sisam to NZ Department of Defence, 1913 & 1917

Note 9: *The Times* London, 15 November 1862.
Note 10: Discharge from the Auckland Provincial Hospital 23.11.1863, signed by the Supervising Surgeon, J.H. Bond. Condition described as 'Heart Disease'.

Chapter Thirteen:
Early Life in New Zealand, G. Clarke
The Maori Wars, Tom Gibson
The Road to War – The Great South Road, Maurice Lennard (Whakatane & District Historical Society)
Te Kooti, W.H. Ross
The New Zealand Wars, J. Belich
A History of New Zealand, K. Sinclair
Recollections of Alfred John Sisam's descendants
Letters of A.J. Sisam to NZ Department of Defence, 1913 & 1917
Recollections of William M. Lamont & Marjorie Braae to author 1990

Note 11: *Waitakere East Assessment Roll 1867–8*, for Lot 86
Note 12: Some of these confiscated lands later formed part of properties acquired or purchased by the Sisam family.

Chapter Fourteen: Recollections of W. Leonard Sisam to Benjamin Copedo Jnr. and author, Pokeno 1985.

Chapter Fifteen: *Opotiki 100 Years*, (Opotiki County Council)
Letters of Caroline Sisam to Walter Henry and Mary Caroline in New Zealand 1876–1884, held by Benjamin Copedo Jnr.
MSS. Diary of Maria Sisam 1890–1894. Held by Joan Stewart
The Hieatt Centenary, Y. Lonsdale & B. Copedo Jnr.
Recollections of W.Leonard Sisam, & Wynne Eccles

Chapter Sixteen: MSS. Diary of Maria Sisam 1876–1884. Held by Joan Stewart
Bay of Plenty Mirror 1974.
Opotiki 100 Years, (Opotiki County Council)
Their Greatness, (Whakatane Women's Institute)
The Opouriao-Taneatua Settlement 1896, A.B. Heath (Whakatane & Distict Historical Society)
Whakatane Postal History, R. Craddock
Archives of the Whakatane Museum
Recollections of Kenneth Sisam & Walter H. Sisam
Recollections of W. Leonard Sisam, Ivy R. Christian, & Martha M. Copedo to Benjamin Copedo Jnr.

Chapter Seventeen: Recollections of Dulcie R.Ingley, Isabel M. Quick, Leonard A. Sisam & Walter J. Sisam.

Note 13: New Zealand Records of Births, Deaths and Marriages. Maori family oral tradition.

Chapter Eighteen: Recollections of W.Leonard Sisam to B. Copedo Jnr.

Chapter Nineteen: *The Oxford University Press*, P. Sutcliffe
Kenneth Sisam, N. Kerr
Archives Department, Oxford University Press
Recollections of Daniel Davin, Kenneth Sisam's assistant at the Oxford University Press, to author
Recollections of Celia Sisam to author

Chapter Twenty: Recollections of Harold Walter Sisam told to Wynne Eccles
Recollections of Eileen McCracken, Harold W. Sisam & Edna Sisam to author.
Recollections by Dulcie Ingley, Isabel Quick, Joan Stewart & Hazel Sisam to author
Recollections of Walter J. Sisam to author

Sources and Notes

Chapter Twenty-one:	Recollections of Walter J. Sisam, Hazel Sisam & Edna Sisam to author.
Chapter Twenty-two:	*Milling,* 1909 Armfield
	Alcester Grammar School Records
	Recollections of Marian Hunt to Peggy Rattigan
	Recollections of Peggy Rattigan to author 1965
	Recollections of James L. Sisam to author.
	Recollections of Gloria Hudson to author
	Recollections of Vernon Carr, Harry Smith & Andrew Bishop to author 1992

Note 14: Two pairs of steel rollers were used, set diagonally. These had graduated grooves becoming finer and finer, which removed the wheat bran. This fine grain then passed through two pairs of smooth rollers emerging as white flour. The process also removed the wheat germ, which, being oily, would otherwise have prevented the flour from keeping in good condition. Steel rollers were costly. Many millers could not afford them and continued with millstones, producing mainly coarse grain for animal feed.

Chapter Twenty-three:	Recollections of Molly Bunting to author
	Recollections of James L. Sisam to author
	Recollections of Peggy Rattigan to author 1965
	Recollections of Vernon Carr, Harry Smith, & Andrew Bishop to author 1992
	Recollections of Gloria Hudson to author
	Recollections of Catherine Sisam to author
Chapter Twenty-four:	*Wold Without End*, H.J. Massingham
	Frank Buchman – a Life, G.D. Lean
	Recollections of Catherine Sisam to author

Note 15: Kenneth Prebble became a Canon in the Anglican Church in New Zealand. One of his sons held cabinet posts in the Lange government.

Chapter Twenty-five:	Recollections of Richard J. Sisam, Marian Archer & Barbara Sisam to author
Chapter Twenty-six:	*West Surrey Gazette*, 27 June 1863
	Documents of Richard J. Sisam
	Recollections of Richard J. Sisam, Marian Archer, & Barbara Sisam to author
	Recollections of Clive Sisam to author
	Recollections of Donald Archer & Reginald Taylor to author

Genealogical Tables

Explanatory Notes:

Some people's names feature twice in these Tables, once in the Tree from which they descend and again at the head of the Branch of all their descendants. In each such case a reference to the other Table is given.

Abbreviations are: b.   =   born
　　　　　　　　　　bur. =   buried
　　　　　　　　　　Ch. =   Christened
　　　　　　　　　　d.   =   died, or burial date
　　　　　　　　　　m.   =   married

The Christened or Baptism Date (Ch.) is from the church Parish Registers. Sometimes Baptism was a few days after birth, but sometimes it was several months or a year later. Where these Ch. dates only are used there are no records of the actual date of Birth. The Death Date (d.) is in some cases the actual date of death, where this is known, but more often is the date of the Burial taken from church Parish Registers, which would have been within a day or two of the death.

Years before 1752 ended on 25th March, instead of on 31st December. All dates falling in January, February and part of March in those years are written 2 Feb. 1718/19 or 8 March 1725/6, etc. They would in those days have been known as the earlier date, but by our reckoning are at the start of the later year.

A, B, C, D, E, F, G, at the top of the Tables show the Generations descending from JOHN SISAM (1720–1786) and his wife ANN COLE.

For example, all those listed under a 'C' are of the same generation, and are the great-grandchildren of that John Sisam.

For more detail on the main characters of the Family, see 'Biographical Notes – Who is Who' following these Tables.

TABLE 1

The SISAM Family of GREET in the Parish of WINCHCOMBE, GLOUCESTERSHIRE (also spelt SISOM, SYSOM, SEISOM, etc.)

THOMAS SYSOM Ch. 9 Sept. 1712

SUSANNA SYSOM Ch. 5 May 1714
m. 1742 Thos. TOWNLEY

SARAH SISOM Ch. 3 Sept. 1716

JOHANIS (John) SYSOM Ch. 1 Feb. 1718/19
d. 1762 or 1763 (WILL 1763)
m. —
 ├─ a **daughter** ANN, who m. Henry SMITH

WILLIAM SISOM Ch. 30 May 1721

ELIZABETH SISOM Ch. 26 Dec. 1723
d. Feb. 1724/5
 ├─ **WILLIAM SEISOM** Ch. 24 April 1757
 ├─ **BENJAMIN SISOM** Ch. & d. 26 April 1760
 ├─ **ELIZABETH SISOM** Ch. 4 April 1761 d. 29 May 1761
 ├─ **MARY SISOM** Ch. May 1763
 └─ **JANE SISOM** Ch. 20 Oct. 1765

ELIZABETH SISUM Ch. 6 Feb. 1725/6
d. March 1726

JANE SYSUM Ch. 3 April 1727

JACOBUS (James) SEISOM Ch. 17 Sept. 1731
d. 5 Sept. 1773
m. Mary —, who d. 23 Dec 1781

MARY SEISOM Ch. 20 June 1736

NICHOLAS SYSOM Ch. 22 May 1682
d. 16 April 1771
m. 1 Nov. 1711 Sarah DAY
who d. 28 May 1747

A SON Ch. and d. 18 June 1711

MARIA SYSOME Ch. 10 Aug. 1712

SARAH SYSOM Ch. May 1714

JOSEPHUS (Joseph) SISOM Ch. 28 Dec. 1715
d. 29 May 1776
m. 21 Nov. 1742 Sarah GRANGER who d. 8 March 1754
 ├─ **HESTER SEISOM** Ch. 26 Feb. 1743/4 m.(?) 1776 Henry STURMEY
 ├─ **MARY SEISOM** Ch. 14 July 1745
 ├─ **SARAH SEISOM** Ch. 7 Dec. 1746
 ├─ **ELIZABETH SEISOM** Ch. 3 Jan. 1747/8
 ├─ **SARAH SEISOM** Ch. 12 Nov. 1749
 ├─ **ANN SOISOM** Ch. 28 Dec. 1751 m. 1774 Thos. LOVESAY
 └─ **WILLIAM SEISOM** Ch. 1 Feb. 1754(?)

HANNA SISOM Ch. 25 March 1718

JOHANIS (John) SYSOM Ch. 26 Dec. 1720
(See TABLE II)

WILLIAM SISOM Ch. 8 March 1723/4

NICHOLAS SYSUM Ch. 18 Dec. 1726

NICHOLAS SISOM b. —
d. 25 Oct. 1728 (WILL 1728)
m. 30 June 1681 Maria DIDCOAT who d. 1700

JOSEPH SYSOM Ch. 31 March 1684
d. 16 June 1731
m. 26 Nov. 1709 Sarah MINETT

MARGARITTA SYSOM Ch. 5 Sept. 1686
d.(?) 13 May 1777

RICHARD SYSOM Ch. and d. 15 Oct 1688

RICHARD SYSOM Ch. 23 Feb. 1689/90
m. 18 April 1715 Margaret DAY

JOHN SYSOM Ch. March 1693/4
d. 29 Nov. 1761 (?) or 1762 (?)
m.(?) Anna —, who d. 5 July 1767

A SON, stillborn 23 Aug. 1696

TABLE II

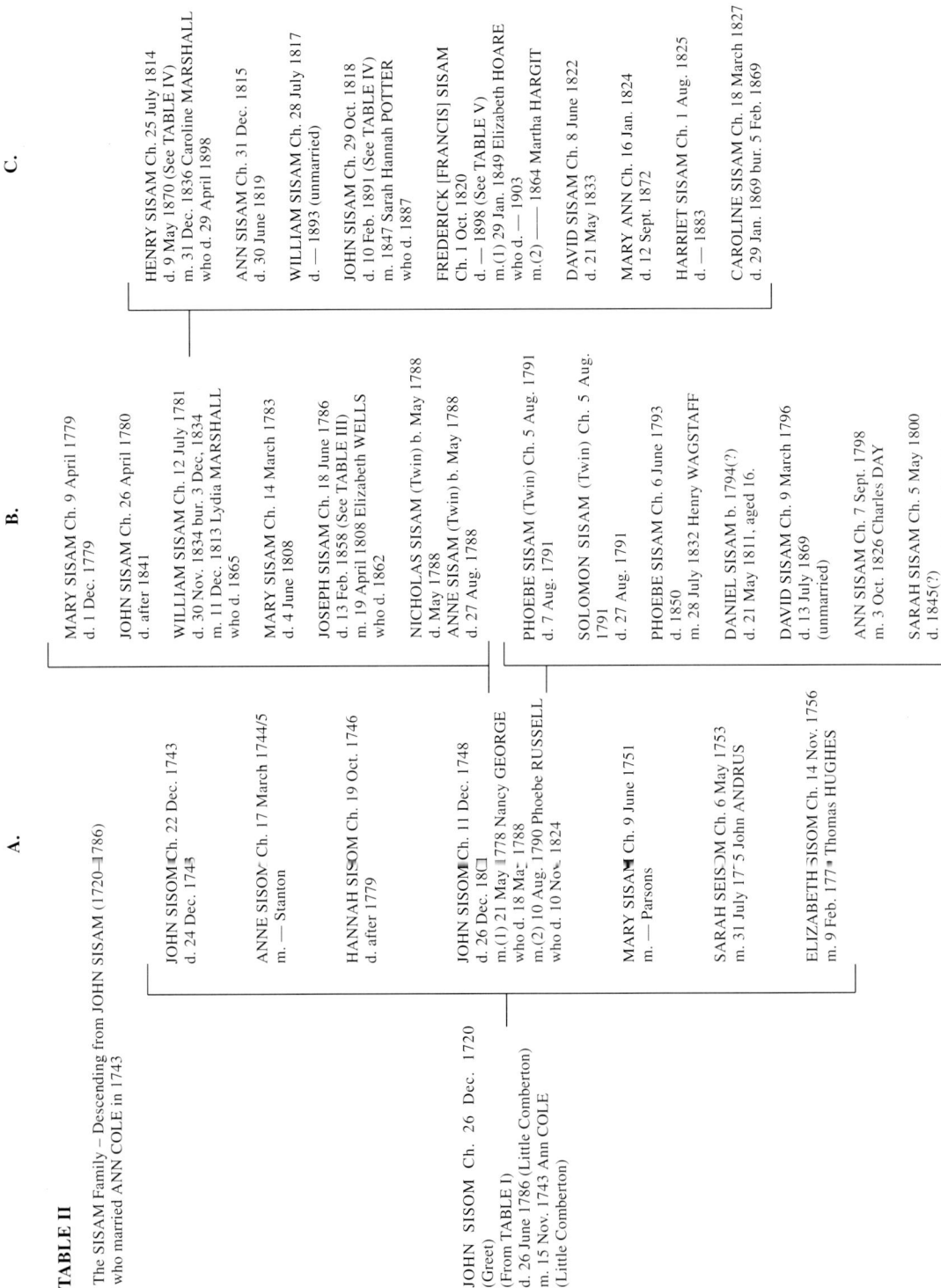

The SISAM Family – Descending from JOHN SISAM (1720–1786) who married ANN COLE in 1743

JOHN SISAM Ch. 26 Dec. 1720 (Greet) (From TABLE I) d. 26 June 1786 (Little Comberton) m. 15 Nov. 1743 Ann COLE (Little Comberton)

- **JOHN SISOM** Ch. 22 Dec. 1743 d. 24 Dec. 1743
- **ANNE SISOM** Ch. 17 March 1744/5 m. — Stanton
- **HANNAH SISOM** Ch. 19 Oct. 1746 d. after 1779
- **JOHN SISOM** Ch. 11 Dec. 1748 d. 26 Dec. 1801 m.(1) 21 May 1778 Nancy GEORGE who d. 18 May 1788 m.(2) 10 Aug. 1790 Phoebe RUSSELL who d. 10 Nov. 1824
  - **MARY SISAM** Ch. 9 April 1779 d. 1 Dec. 1779
  - **JOHN SISAM** Ch. 26 April 1780 d. after 1841
  - **WILLIAM SISAM** Ch. 12 July 1781 d. 30 Nov. 1834 bur. 3 Dec. 1834 m. 11 Dec. 1813 Lydia MARSHALL who d. 1865
    - **HENRY SISAM** Ch. 25 July 1814 d. 9 May 1870 (See TABLE IV) m. 31 Dec. 1836 Caroline MARSHALL who d. 29 April 1898
    - **ANN SISAM** Ch. 31 Dec. 1815 d. 30 June 1819
    - **WILLIAM SISAM** Ch. 28 July 1817 d. — 1893 (unmarried)
    - **JOHN SISAM** Ch. 29 Oct. 1818 d. 10 Feb. 1891 (See TABLE IV) m. 1847 Sarah Hannah POTTER who d. 1887
    - **FREDERICK [FRANCIS] SISAM** Ch. 1 Oct. 1820 d. — 1898 (See TABLE V) m.(1) 29 Jan. 1849 Elizabeth HOARE who d. — 1903 m.(2) — 1864 Martha HARGIT
    - **DAVID SISAM** Ch. 8 June 1822 d. 21 May 1833
    - **MARY ANN** Ch. 16 Jan. 1824 d. 12 Sept. 1872
    - **HARRIET SISAM** Ch. 1 Aug. 1825 d. — 1883
    - **CAROLINE SISAM** Ch. 18 March 1827 d. 29 Jan. 1869 bur. 5 Feb. 1869
  - **MARY SISAM** Ch. 14 March 1783 d. 4 June 1808
  - **JOSEPH SISAM** Ch. 18 June 1786 d. 13 Feb. 1858 (See TABLE III) m. 19 April 1808 Elizabeth WELLS who d. 1862
  - **NICHOLAS SISAM** (Twin) b. May 1788 d. May 1788
  - **ANNE SISAM** (Twin) b. May 1788 d. 27 Aug. 1788
  - **PHOEBE SISAM** (Twin) Ch. 5 Aug. 1791 d. 7 Aug. 1791
  - **SOLOMON SISAM** (Twin) Ch. 5 Aug. 1791 d. 27 Aug. 1791
  - **PHOEBE SISAM** Ch. 6 June 1793 d. 1850 m. 28 July 1832 Henry WAGSTAFF
  - **DANIEL SISAM** b. 1794(?) d. 21 May 1811, aged 16.
  - **DAVID SISAM** Ch. 9 March 1796 d. 13 July 1869 (unmarried)
  - **ANN SISAM** Ch. 7 Sept. 1798 m. 3 Oct. 1826 Charles DAY
  - **SARAH SISAM** Ch. 5 May 1800 d. 1845(?) m. 9 Nov. 1820 John SHERRARD
- **MARY SISAM** Ch. 9 June 1751 m. — Parsons
- **SARAH SEISOM** Ch. 6 May 1753 m. 31 July 1775 John ANDRUS
- **ELIZABETH SISOM** Ch. 14 Nov. 1756 m. 9 Feb. 1777 Thomas HUGHES

TABLE III

The Family of JOHN SISAM of HILL, FLADBURY and his first wife NANCY GEORGE

A.

JOHN SISOM Ch. 11 Dec. 1748
d. 26 Dec. 1801 (From TABLE II)
m.(1) 21 May 1778 Nancy GEORGE
who d. 18 May 1788

m.(2) 10 Aug. 1790 Phoebe RUSSELL
who d. 10 Nov. 1824
(See TABLE II for her children)

B.

MARY SISAM Ch. 9 April 1779
d. 1 Dec. 1779

JOHN SISAM Ch. 26 April 1780
d. After 1841

WILLIAM SISAM Ch. 12 July 1781
d. Nov. 1834, bur. 3 Dec. 1834
m. 11 Dec. 1813 Lydia MARSHALL
(See TABLE II)

MARY SISAM Ch. 14 March 1783
d. 4 June 1808

JOSEPH SISAM Ch. 18 June 1786
d. 13 Feb. 1858
m. 19 April 1808 Elizabeth WELLS
who d. 1862

NICHOLAS SISAM (Twin) Ch. May 1788
d. May 1788
ANNE SISAM (Twin) Ch. May 1788
d. 27 Aug. 1788

C.

SARAH SISAM b. 1809(?)
m. 5 June 1831 William FAIRFIELD

WILLIAM GEORGE SISAM Ch. 9 June 1811
d. 1874(?)
(Transported to Tasmania, 1831)

ANN SISAM Ch. 22 Aug. 1813
m. 24 Feb. 1847 Daniel BAYLISS

JOHN SISAM
Ch. 11 Feb. 1816 (Fladbury)
Ch. 21 July 1816 (Welford)
d. 6 Aug. 1821

PHOEBE SISAM b.(?) 1817
Ch. 19 July 1819
m. 4 Dec. 1837 Henry COWPER

JOSEPH SISAM b.(?) June 1820
Ch. 2 Sept.1821
d. 1899
m. 30 July 1843 Catherine PAYNE
who d. —
(Both to USA in 1868)

MARY SISAM Ch. 10 Oct. 1824
m. 9 March 1846 John ORCHARD

SUSANNAH SISAM Ch. 5 Nov. 1826
m. 19 Feb.1844 Thomas WILLOUGHBY

HARRIET ELIZABETH SISAM
Ch. 31 Jan. 1830
d. 1851

DANIEL SISAM Ch. 29 Jan 1833
d. 2 Feb. 1835

D.

HARRIET SISAM b. 1844
(To USA 1866)
m. 1867 William TIMMS

ANN SISAM b. 1847
(To USA 1866)
m. 1867 Isaac GOFF

EMMA SISAM b. 1849
(To USA 1868)
d. 1894

JOSEPH HENRY SISAM b. 1852
(To USA 1868)
d. 1917
m. (1) 1877 Hannah POULSON
who d. —
m. (2) 1878 Ingrid POULSON
(See TABLES VIII, IX, and X)

REBECCA SISAM b. 1855 d. 1859

TABLE IV

The Families of HENRY SISAM and JOHN SISAM, in England

HENRY SISAM who d. 1924
Ch. 25 July 1814
d. 14 May 1870
m. 31 Dec. 1836
Caroline MARSHALL
(From TABLE II)

- **THOMAS HENRY SISAM** Ch. 6 Jan. 1837 d. 31 May 1838
- **WILLIAM HENRY SISAM** Ch. 9 Aug. 1838 d. Dec.1877 bur. 1 Jan. 1878 m. 1869 Helen NEW
  - **HENRY CHARLES SISAM** Ch. 6 July 1870 d. 21 Sept. 1872
  - **EMILY MARY SISAM** Ch. 11 Oct. 1871 d. 1933
  - **CAROLINE HELEN SISAM** Ch. 24 Aug. 1873 m. 1902 John HOOK
  - **WILLIAM SISAM** Ch. 6 June 1875 d. 1947 m. 1910 Florence Louise HALL
  - **ALFRED JOHN MARSHALL SISAM** b. 1876 d. 1927 Ch. 6 May 1877
- **ANN EMILY SISAM** Ch. 22 Dec.1839 m.(1) 1871 William James BULLOCK m.(2) — DAVIS
- **THOMAS MARSHALL SISAM** Ch. 12 March 1841 d. 17 Oct. 1896 (See TABLE XI) m. 1869 Mary Jane DAVIS
- **WALTER SISAM** Ch. 18 June 1842 d. — 1910 (See TABLE VI) (To New Zealand 1862) m.(1) 1866 Mary Anne MASON m.(2) 1893 Nellie HEWITSON
- **ALFRED JOHN SISAM** Ch. 14 Feb. 1844 d. — 1928 (See TABLE VII) (To New Zealand 1862) m. 1870 Maria KNIGHTS
  - **MARIAN SISAM** b. 3 Feb. 1877 m. 1906 George HUNT
    - **JAMES LEONARD SISAM** Ch. 21 Sept. 1916 m. 1946 Elsie IRELAND
      - **GLORIA MARY SISAM** b. 1950 m. 1986 David L. HUDSON
    - **WALTER LEONARD SISAM** b. 1905 d. 1960 (unmarried)
    - **WINIFRED MARY SISAM** b. 1907 m. 1934 Frederick BUNTING
    - **DOROTHY GERTRUDE SISAM** b.1909 m. 1934 George CLARKE
    - **FRANCIS HENRY** b. 1910 (To Canada 1948)
    - **PHYLLIS MARIAN SISAM** b. 1918 d. 1968
  - **HENRY LEONARD SISAM** d. 1991 b. 26 Jan. 1879 d. 1935 m. 1910 Mary ROUSE
  - **FRANK MARSHALL SISAM** b. 14 Sept. 1880 d. 1943 m. 1904 Amy Winifred BOMFORD
  - **WALTER SISAM** b. 23 Sept. 1882 d. 1943 m. 1913 Catherine Nellie FINCHER
    - **PETER JAMES SISAM** b. 19 Dec. 1914 m. 1976 Margaret Honor BARNES
    - **LETTICE SISAM** b. 9 Oct. 1916 d. 1968
  - **JOHN WILLIAM BERNARD SISAM** b. May 1906 d. 1989 m. Oct. 1932 Elizabeth Stewart NEILL (Betty)
    - **CHRISTOPHER NEILL SISAM** b. 1960 m. Donna MOTTERSHEAD
    - **JOANNE MARY SISAM** b. 1962 m. Paul DAVENPORT
    - **PATRICK HAMILTON SISAM** b. 1965
    - **PETER NEILL SISAM** b. 1937 m. 1959 Mary Susan HAMILTON
      - **KATE SISAM**
      - **AMY SISAM**
      - **MATTHEW SISAM**
    - **JOHN DAVID SISAM** b. 1945 m. 1977 Elizabeth SZUBSKI
- **JAMES LEONARD SISAM** Ch. 9 Oct. 1845 d. — 1921 m. 1876 Letitia NEW
- **MARSHALL SISAM** Ch. 10 June 1847 d. March 1877 (unmarried)
- **ALICE JANE SISAM** Ch. 27 Dec. 1848 m. 1876 John FISHER

JOHN SISAM
Ch. 29 Oct. 1818
d. 1891
m. — 1847
Sarah Hannah POTTER
(From TABLE II)

- **ELIZABETH LYDIA SISAM** b. 1848 d. 1935
- **EDWARD GODFREY SISAM** b. 1851 d. 1855
- **WILLIAM BERNARD SISAM** b. 30 Dec. 1854 d. Feb. 1937 (To Canada) m. Sept. 1904 Emma Annie ANCIENT who d. 1962
- **MARY CATHERINE SISAM** Ch. 11 Oc 1857 d. 1895

TABLE V

The Families of FREDERICK [FRANCIS] SISAM

FREDERICK [FRANCIS] SISAM Ch. 1 Oct. 1820 d. 1898 (From TABLE II)

m.(1) 29 Jan. 1849 Elizabeth HOARE who d. 1903

- HENRIETTA PHOEBE SISAM b. 1849 d. 1917 Ch. 4 Jan. 1850
- ELIZABETH HOARE SISAM Ch. 16 July 1851 d. 1935
- MARIAN SISAM b. 1852 Ch. 3 Apr. 1853 m. 1890 Charles Hugh LEWIN
- HARRIET SISAM b. 5 June 1854 d. —

m.(2) 24 Oct. 1864 (bigamous) Martha HARGIT who d. 1904

- HECTOR MARSHALL SISAM b. 1865 d. 1943 m. 1890 Mary Ellen FITZGERALD
- GEORGE HARGIT SISAM b. 1867 d. 1902 (unmarried)
- HERBERT SISAM b. 1869 d. 1956 m. 1900 Sarah Ann JONES
- MARY ANN SISAM b. 1872 m. 1903 Dick LAYCOCK
- HARRIET SISAM b. 1874 d. 1887

FREDERICK FRANCIS SISAM b. 1892 (Father 'Gilbert') d. 1967

- GEORGE SISAM b. 1897 d. 1963 m. 1931 Annie BEELEY
  - JOHN SISAM b. 1934
- HARRIET SISAM b. 1900 m. 1923 — MEREDITH
- EVELYN SISAM b. 1902 m. 1946 James ANDERSON
- LILIAN SISAM b. 1904 m. 1947 — STEAD
- CLIFFORD SISAM b. 1908 d. 1981 m. 1943 Kathleen F. DOLAN
  - MARGARET SISAM b. and d. 1945
  - LORRAINE SISAM b. 1946 m. 1964 — DAWES

TABLE VI

The SISAM Family in New Zealand – Descendants of WALTER SISAM

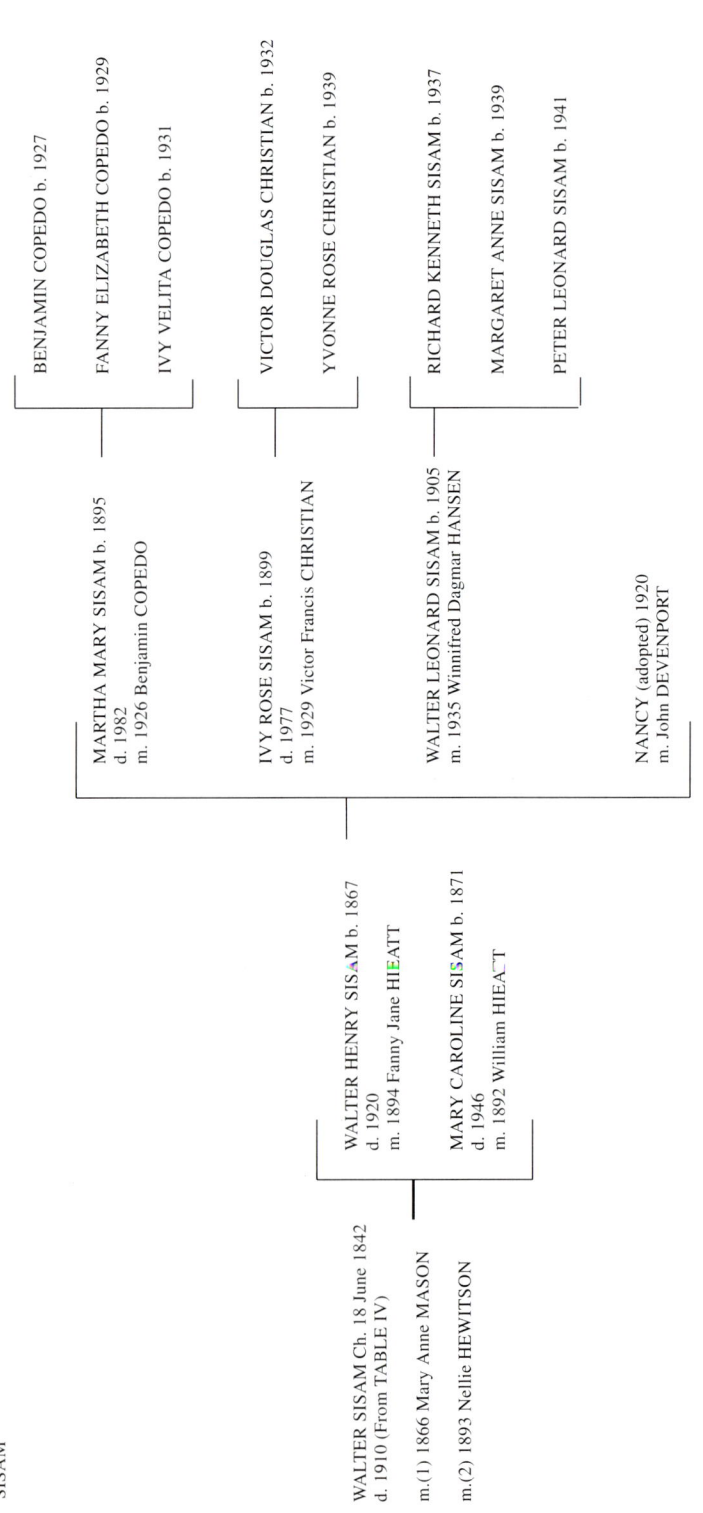

WALTER SISAM Ch. 18 June 1842
d. 1910 (From TABLE IV)

m.(1) 1866 Mary Anne MASON
m.(2) 1893 Nellie HEWITSON

- WALTER HENRY SISAM b. 1867
  d. 1920
  m. 1894 Fanny Jane HIEATT
  - MARTHA MARY SISAM b. 1895
    d. 1982
    m. 1926 Benjamin COPEDO
    - BENJAMIN COPEDO b. 1927
    - FANNY ELIZABETH COPEDO b. 1929
    - IVY VELITA COPEDO b. 1931
  - IVY ROSE SISAM b. 1899
    d. 1977
    m. 1929 Victor Francis CHRISTIAN
    - VICTOR DOUGLAS CHRISTIAN b. 1932
    - YVONNE ROSE CHRISTIAN b. 1939
  - WALTER LEONARD SISAM b. 1905
    m. 1935 Winnifred Dagmar HANSEN
    - RICHARD KENNETH SISAM b. 1937
    - MARGARET ANNE SISAM b. 1939
    - PETER LEONARD SISAM b. 1941
  - NANCY (adopted) 1920
    m. John DEVENPORT
- MARY CAROLINE SISAM b. 1871
  d. 1946
  m. 1892 William HIEATT

TABLE VII

The SISAM Family in New Zealand – Descendants of ALFRED JOHN SISAM

ALFRED JOHN SISAM
Ch. 14 Feb. 1844 (Arrow)
d. 1928
(To New Zealand 1862)
m. 1870 Maria KNIGHTS
who d. 1895
(From TABLE IV)

- **OLIVIA MARIE** b. 1866, dau. of Maria and adopted by Alfred John Sisam
  d. 1950
  m. 1887 John A.C. LAMONT
- **ALICE SISAM** b. 1871
  d. 1961
  m. 1891 William Parry BROWNE
- **ALFRED SISAM** b. 1872
  d. 1913
- **CAROLINE MARSHALL SISAM** b. 1875
  d. 1949
  m. 1906 Edward Von STURMER
- **MAY SISAM** b. 1877
  d. 1962
- **LEONARD WILFRID SISAM** b. 1879
  d. 1961
  m. 1905 Mabel Jane McGARVEY
  who d. 1956
  - **LEONARD ALFRED SISAM** b. 1906
    d. 1982
    m. 1933 Edna Carina LIST
    - **MARLENE SISAM** b. 1938 d. 1939
    - **ROSALIE SISAM** b. 1940
      m. 1965 Peter PRESTON
    - **PETER SISAM** b. 1942 d. 1987
      m. 1969 Carol WELLINGS
    - **MARGARET SISAM** b. 1945
      m.(1) 1968 Derek PHILPOTT
      m.(2) 1974 John Rhys COLLIE
  - **DORIS MABEL SISAM** b. 1908
    d. 1983
    m. 1927 George SYMMANS
  - **MONA SISAM** b. 1911
    d. 1958
    m. 1932 Guy FOWLER
  - **HAROLD WALTER SISAM** b. 1912
    d. 1988
    m. 1947 Adele NANKIVELL
    - **JILL SISAM** b. 1948
      m. 1972 Donald McLEOD
    - **MARILYN JANE SISAM** b. 1950
      m. 1980 Barry SHAW
    - **HAROLD ROBERT SISAM** b. 1952
      m. 1982 Elspeth BLAIR
  - **LORNA SISAM** b. 1916
    d. 1985
    m. 1939 Geoffrey FOGERTY
  - **EILEEN SISAM** b. 1918
    m. 1944 Frederick James Harold McCRACKEN
  - **KENNETH CHARLES SISAM** b. 1921
    d. 1968
    m. 1950 Joan BURNARD
    - **PAUL SISAM** b. 1952
      m. 1976 Anne STEVEN
    - **MARK SISAM** b. 1954
      m. 1979 Shellie ROGERS
    - **NICOLA SISAM** b. 1957
      m. 1978 Duncan HUMPHREY
- **WALTER HOLTOM SISAM** b. 1880
  d. 1931
  m. 1914 Rose Stansfield ALLEN
  - **DULCIE ROSE SISAM** b. 1915
    m. 1938 Percy INGLEY
  - **JOAN CECILY SISAM** b. 1917
    m. 1950 Alan STEWART
  - **WALTER JOHN SISAM** b. 1919
    m. 1946 Noeline OGDEN
    - **JOHN WALTER SISAM** b. 1947
      m. 1971 Margaret NEIGHT
    - **LYNNE PATRICIA SISAM** b. 1951
      m. 1972 David Owen ROBERTS
    - **WENDY GRACE SISAM** b. 1958
      m. 1980 Eric RUSSELL
  - **ALLEN LEONARD SISAM** b. 1921
    d. 1988
    m. 1947 Hazel CAVE
    - **GILBERT BRENT SISAM** b. 1948
      m. 1976 Kathleen RANUM
    - **RICHARD GRENVILLE SISAM** b. 1950
      m. 1974 Susan Janet BAYLY
    - **NEIL MILTON SISAM** b. 1953
      m. 1983 Janet Dawn ALLEY
  - **ISABEL MARIE SISAM** b. 1925
    m. 1950 Graham QUICK
    - **BRUCE ALLEN SISAM** (Twin) b. 1955
      m. 1977 Pauline MUDGE
    - **BRIAN WALTER SISAM** (Twin) b. 1955
      m. 1986 Jane Clare BARNSLEY
- **KENNETH SISAM** b. 1887
  d. 1971
  m. 1915 Naomi GIBBONS
  - **HUGH SISAM** b. 1923
    d. 1989
  - **CELIA SISAM** b. 1926
    - **CLIVE STANSFIELD** b. 1957

TABLE VIII

The SISAM Family of UTAH, U.S.A.

D.

JOSEPH HENRY SISAM b. 1852
(To USA 1868)
d. 1917 (From TABLE III)
m.(1) 1877 Hannah POULSON
who d. 1941

m.(2) 1878 Ingrid POULSON
who separated and m. Christian LILYA
(See TABLE X for her descendants
by Joseph Henry Sisam)

E.

ANNIE CATHERINE SISAM b. 1878
d. 1938
m. 1900 David BUTTERFIELD

GEORGE HENRY SISAM b. 1882
d. 1883

ALBERT ANDREW SISAM b. 1884
d. 1917
m. 1911 Margaret Louise GREEN

ALMA NEILS SISAM b. 1887
d. 1971
m. 1909 Edith Lilian BESS

WILFORD MARTIN SISAM b. 1889
d. 1970
m. 1910 Mary Elizabeth BUTTERFIELD

HAROLD JOHN SISAM b. and d. 1892

LAURA MAY SISAM b. 1893 d. 1984
m. 1912 Benjamin Franklin ATKINSON

AMIL ARTHUR S SAM b. 1896 d. 1974
m. 1920 Elesta Mae ROBERTSON
(See TABLE IX)

IRENE LEONE SISAM b. 1900 d. 1989
m. 1919 Leo TRIPP

LAVERNE SISAM b. 1903
m.(1) 1923 William A. SHEPPICK
m.(2) 1946 Marvin R. GREATHOUSE

F.

DELILAH MAY SISAM b. 1912
m. 1928 Arthur Julius CHARTER

VERA MARGARET SISAM b. 1914
m. 1937 Henry Louis McGILL

WILLIAM ALBERT SISAM b. 1916
m.(1) 1937 Belva Louise HAUGHT

m.(2) — Mabel Louise BALOSKI

RUTH LILIAN SISAM b. 1911
m. 1929 Carl Ernest MOULTON

ALMA LESLIE SISAM b. 1915
d. 1936
m. 1933 Marge HANSEN

HENRY WHITNEY SISAM b. 1918
d. 1933

LORNE RICHARD SISAM b. 1926
m. 1954 Colleen MOORE

MYRTLE LEONE SISAM b. 1911
m. 1930 Maurice JEX

VIOLET ELIZABETH SISAM b. 1913
m. 1939 Morrell SEAL

DONALD WILFORD SISAM b. 1922
m. 1941 Mildred BROWN

DARRELL HENRY SISAM b. 1924
d. 1944

ROBERT ARLON SISAM b. 1928
m. — Lavalee JOHANSEN

PATSY ELNA SISAM b. 1933
m. 1954 Angus YOUNG

G.

WILLIAM FLOYD SISAM

RON SISAM

GLEN WILLIAM SISAM

ALVIN SISAM

CLAUDIA GAY SISAM
b. 1934
m.(1) 1953 Varle REYNOLDS
m.(2) —

LORRIN RICHARD SISAM
b. 1956
m.(1) — Robyn Lynn SMITH
m.(2) 1986 Lawana Orton WITTKE

REBECCA ANN SISAM
b. 1958
m.(1) 1978 Hyram Fielding KOENIG
m.(2) — Michael HUBERT
m.(3) 1985 Darrell Don Van COTT

DAVID MICHAEL SISAM
b. 1961

SHANNON KAY SISAM
b. 1965
m. 1986 Jeffrey Allen WILDE

E.

TABLE IX

The SISAM Family of UTAH, U.S.A. (Continued)

AMIL ARTHUR SISAM b. 1896
d. 1974
m. 1920 Elesta Mae ROBERTSON
(From TABLE VIII)

F.

- MILDRED CONNIE SISAM b. 1921
  m.(1) Herman GREY (2) Dale McMUSTRY
  m.(3) Charles CROSSEN

- DONNA MAE SISAM b. 1923
  m. 1943 Richard MIX

- FAYE LEONE SISAM b. 1925
  m.(1) Joseph John LARENZINE
  m.(2) Jack PARRETT
  m.(3) Chet HIGGINBOTHAM

- ELVIN ARTHUR SISAM b. 1927
  d. 1987
  m.(1) 1960 Dorothy HARRIS
  m.(2) 1982 Faye Ann CROWLEY

- BETTY JEAN SISAM b. 1930 d.1932

- LORAINE SISAM b. 1932
  m.(1) Sherman WILKINSON
  m.(2) Bill MAYBERRY
  m.(3) Harold SANSLOW

- SHIRLEY ANN SISAM b. 1934
  m.(1) Harold NELSON
  m.(2) Lee THORNBURG

- RONALD SHERMAN SISAM b. 1936
  m. 1959 Donna PARKER

- CAROLYN LEE SISAM b. 1939
  m. 1964 Gilbert CARRASCO

- DENNIS LAVON SISAM b. 1942 d.1952

- JENNIS YVONNE SISAM b. 1942
  m.(1) Joel LITTLE (2) — GRAY

TABLE X

The SISIAM Family of IDAHO, U.S.A.

The spelling of the surname of her children was changed by Ingrid when she had to separate from Joseph Henry Sisam, in order to differentiate them from the children of her sister, Hannah, who remained Joseph Henry's wife.

JOSEPH HENRY SISAM b. 1852
d. 1917
m.(1) 1877 Hannah POULSON
(See TABLES VIII & IX for her family)

m(2) 1878 INGRID POULSON
(who later separated and re-married)

- **JOSEPH WILLARD SISAM** b. 1878
  d. 1950
  m. 1908 Ruth HURST
    - **RICHARD JOSEPH SISAM** b. 1910
      d. 1988
      m. 1935 Ruby Geraldine TURNER
        - WAYNE JOSEPH SISIAM b. 1936
        - GERALDINE MAY SISIAM b. 1943
    - **STELLA INA SISAM** b. 1912
      m. 1938 Rex JAMES
    - **RUTH HELEN SISAM** b. 1914
      m. — Phenoy FISCHER
    - **NELSE SISAM** b. 1917
      m.(1) 1940 Helen RICHARDSON
      m.(2) 1963 Carolyn BLACK
        - VIRGIL NELSE SISIAM b. 1945
        - JO ANNE SISIAM b. 1948
          m. — Samual TORREZ
    - **ROY ELMER SISAM** b. 1919
      m. 1941 Violet RICHARDSON
        - ROY VIRGIL SISIAM b. 1942
        - LARRY LENARD SISIAM b. 1948
        - DEBBRAH LEE SISIAM b. 1951
        - LESLIE JERRY SISIAM b. 1954
        - RUSSEL PAUL SISIAM b. 1956
        - TODD BRIAN SISIAM b. 1958
    - **WILFORD GALE SISAM** b. 1927
      m. 1947 Juanita JAMES
    - **VIRGINIA ROBERTA SISAM** b. 1930
      m.(1) 1948 John KNOWLES
      m.(2) 1965 Harold HARVEY
        - VICKI LYNN SISIAM b. 1956
          m. — Stephen Lloyd DICK
    - **HENRY WILLIAM SISIAM** b. and d. 1934
- **MIRANDA SISAM** b. 1881 d. 1882
- **ALICE ELLEN SISIAM** b. 1884
  d. 1971
  m.(1) 1903 James BROADHURST
  m.(2) 1920 Carl HURST

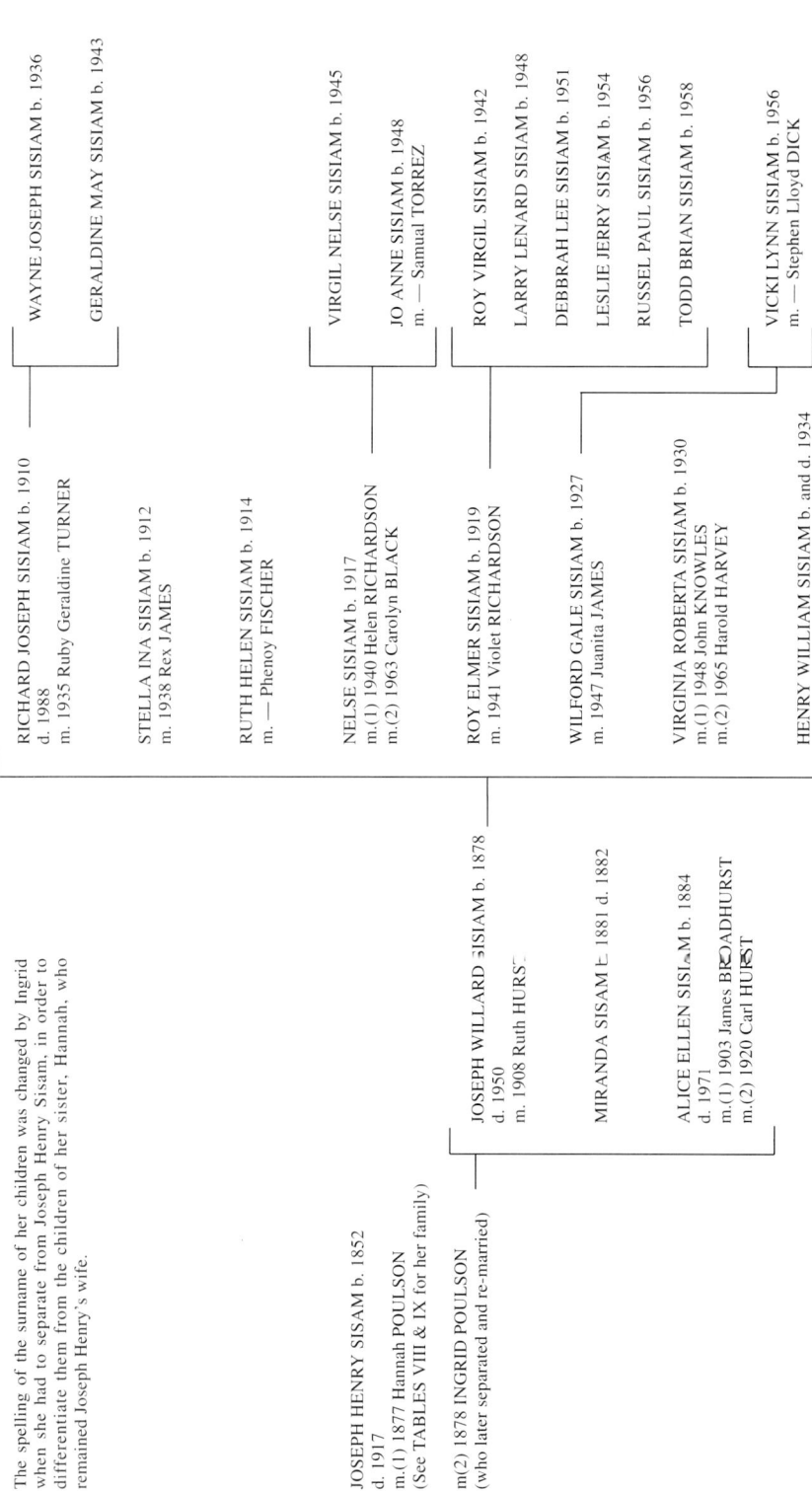

TABLE XI

The Family of THOMAS MARSHALL SISAM in England

THOMAS MARSHALL SISAM
Ch. 17 Oct. 1896 (From TABLE IV)
d. 12 March 1841
m. 1869 Mary Jane DAVIS
who d. 1924

- **CHARLES MARSHALL SISAM** b. 1871
  d. 1936
  - **EDITH MAY SISAM** b. 1908
    m.(1) 1932 Walter OFFIELD
    m.(2) 1940 Walter SMITH
  - **FRANK EDMUND SISAM** b. 1910
    d. 1981
    m. 1938 Beatrice Marion PETTICAN
    - **CLIVE A. SISAM** b. 1939
      m. 1963 Victoria ALLEN
  - **GLADYS M. SISAM** b. 1917
    m. 1942 Charles F. BEEBY

- **THOMAS SISAM** b. 1872
  d. 1950
  m. 1906 Ann JOHNSON
  (To Peterborough)

- **MARY EDITH SISAM** b. 1875
  d. 1941

- **KATHLEEN HELEN SISAM** b. Dec. 1876
  d. — Ch. 22 April 1877
  m. 1899 — SNOW (To S. Africa)

- **MABEL SISAM** b. 1879
  d. 1880 Ch. 8 Feb. 1880

- **ALEXANDER SISAM** Ch. 5 June 1881
  d. 1961 (unmarried)

- **JOHN FRANCIS SISAM** b. 1883
  d. 1972 (unmarried)

- **EDMUND HERBERT SISAM** b. 1885
  d. 1959
  m. 1921 Emily Mabel HAWES
  - **MARIAN J. SISAM** b. 1922
    m. 1946 Derrick ARCHER
  - **ARTHUR EDMUND SISAM** b. 1923
    d. 1980
    m. 1949 Barbara STEWART
    - **GRAHAM ARTHUR SISAM** b. 1950
      m. 1972 Elizabeth Anne WILLIAMS
    - **PETER EDMUND SISAM** b. 1955
      m. 1977 Jacqueline Rosina DAVEY
  - **RICHARD JOHN SISAM** b. 1924
    m. 1953 Patricia DOUGLAS
    - **SHEILA SISAM** b. 1954
      m. — Peter AXON

- **ARTHUR GORDON SISAM** b. 1890
  d. 1918

Biographical Notes

WHO IS WHO in the SISAM Family

(SISAM and SISIAM members, including women who married them)

List giving the Generation as on the Genealogical Tables (e.g. –C–) and also giving Chapter references.

ADELE SISAM (Del) [née NANKIVELL]   –F–   Chapters 20, 21
m. 1974 Harold Walter Sisam (Mannie).

ALBERT ANDREW SISAM (Berta)   –E–   Chapters 9, 10
Automobile Engineer.
   son of Joseph Henry Sisam and Hannah Poulson
b. 6 April 1884 West Jordan, Utah.   d. July 1917
m. 26 April 1911 Margaret Louise Green.

ALEXANDER SISAM (Alec)   Farm worker.   –E–   Chapters 25, 26
   son of Thomas Marshall Sisam and Mary Jane Davis
b. Aldington. ch. June 1881 Badsey.
d. Dec. 1961 Cleeve Prior, unmarried

ALFRED SISAM (Alfie)   –E–   Chapter 16
   son of Alfred John Sisam and Maria Knights
b. 1872 Opotiki, New Zealand.   d. 1913

ALFRED JOHN SISAM   Farmer and Landowner.   –D–   Chapters 4, 12, 13, 15,
In Maori Wars. Constable at Opotiki and Whakatane,   16, 17
Clerk of the Court.
   son of Henry Sisam and Caroline Marshall
ch. 14 Feb. 1844 Arrow, Warwickshire.
Emigrated to New Zealand 1862.
m. 1870 Maria Knights.   d. 1928

ALFRED JOHN MARSHALL SISAM   –E–   Chapters 4, 22
   son of William Henry Sisam and Helen New
b. 1876 ch. 6 May 1877 Harvington.
d. 1927, unmarried.

ALICE SISAM (Allie)   –E– Chapters 13, 15, 16
    dau. of Alfred John Sisam and Maria Knights
b. 1871 Opotiki, New Zealand.
m. 1891 William Parry Browne

ALICE ELLEN SISIAM   –E– Chapters 8, 11
    dau. of Joseph Henry Sisam and Ingrid Poulson
b. 1884 Bingham, Utah.
m. (1) 1903 James Broadhurst.
m. (2) 1920 Carl Hurst.   d. 1971

ALICE JANE SISAM   –D– Chapters 4, 25
    youngest dau. of Henry Sisam and Caroline Marshall
ch. 27 Dec. 1848 Arrow.
m. 19 April 1876 John Fisher.

ALLEN LEONARD SISAM   Farmer.   –F– Chapters 17, 20, 21
    son of Walter Holtom Sisam and Rose Stansfield Allen
b. 1921 Opotiki, New Zealand.   m. 1947 Hazel Cave.
d. 1988

ALMA LESLIE SISAM   –F– Chapter 10
    son of Alma Neils Sisam and Edith Lillian Bess
b. 8 April 1915 Salt Lake, Utah.
m. 9 Aug. 1933 Marge Hansen.   d. 28 April 1936

ALMA NEILS SISAM   Electrical Contractor.   –E– Chapters 9, 10
    son of Joseph Henry Sisam and Hannah Poulson
b. 21 Feb. 1887 West Jordan, Utah.
m. 27 Oct. 1909 Edith Lillian Bess.   d. 8 Jan. 1971

ALVIN SISAM   –G–
    youngest son of William Albert Sisam and Mabel
Louise Baloski.

AMIL ARTHUR SISAM   Smelter-worker and farmer.   –E– Chapter 10
    son of Joseph Henry Sisam and Hannah Poulson
b. March 1896 West Jordan, Utah.
m. 4 Dec. 1920 Elesta May Robertson.
d. 21 July 1974

AMY WINIFRED SISAM (Winifred) [née BOMFORD]   –E– Chapter 23
    dau. of Henry Butler Bomford of Exhall Court.
m. 1 Dec. 1904 Frank Marshall Sisam

ANN SISAM   –B–   Chapter 2
    dau. of John Sisam and Phoebe Russell
ch. 7 Sept. 1798 Hill, Fladbury.
m. 3 Oct. 1826 Charles Day.

ANN SISAM   –C–   Chapter 6
    dau. of Joseph Sisam and Elizabeth Wells
b. Marlcliff. ch. 22 Aug. 1813 Bidford.
m. 1847 Daniel Bayliss, Leamington Priors.

ANN SISAM   –C–   Chapter 2
    dau. of William Sisam and Lydia Marshall
b. North & Middle Littleton. ch. 31 Dec, 1815 Fladbury.
d. 30 June 1819, aged 3 years 6 months.
Tombstone in Bidford churchyard.

ANN SISAM   –D–   Chapters 6, 7, 9
    dau. of Joseph Sisam and Catherine Payne
b. 11 Oct. 1847 Inkberrow, Worcs. To U.S.A. 1866
m. 9 March 1867 Isaac Goff.
d. 29 Feb. 1916 at Sandy, Salt Lake, Utah.

ANN SISAM [née COLE]   Chapters 1, 2
    dau. of John Cole of Little Comberton.
b. 1716 (?)
m. 15 Nov. 1743 John Sisam at Little Comberton.
d. before 1779.

ANN SISAM [née JOHNSON]   –E–   Chapter 26
m. 1906 Thomas Sisam.

ANN EMILY SISAM   –D–   Chapters 3, 4
    dau. of Henry Sisam and Caroline Marshall
ch. 22 Dec. 1839 Arrow.
m.(1) 21 Jan. 1871 William James Bullock.
m.(2) — — Davis

ANNE SISAM   –A–
    dau. of John Sisam and Ann Cole
ch. 17 March 1744/5 Little Comberton.
m. — — Stanton

ANNE SISAM (Nancy)   –B–
    twin dau. of John Sisam and Nancy George
b. May 1788 Hill, Fladbury.
d. 27 Aug. 1788, an infant

ANNE SISAM [née STEVEN] –G–
m. 1976 Paul Sisam.

ANNIE SISAM [née ANCIENT] – see EMMA ANNIE SISAM

ANNIE SISAM [née BEELEY] –E– Chapter 3
m. 1931 George Sisam.

ANNIE CATHERINE SISAM –E– Chapters 9, 10
   dau. of Joseph Henry Sisam and Hannah Poulson
b. 23 Dec. 1878 West Jordan, Utah.
m. 17 Oct. 1900 David Ensign Butterfield.
d. 8 Jan. 1938

ARTHUR EDMUND SISAM –F– Chapter 26
   son of Edmund Herbert Sisam and Emily Mabel Hawes
b. 1923 Kings Norton, Birmingham.
m. 1949 Barbara Stewart.   d. 1980

ARTHUR GORDON SISAM –E– Chapters 25, 26
   son of Thomas Marshall Sisam and Mary Jane Davis
ch. 18 May 1890 Harvington.   d. 1918, unmarried.

BARBARA SISAM [née STEWART] –F– Chapter 26
m. 1949 Arthur Edmund Sisam.

BEATRICE MARION SISAM [née PETTICAN] –F– Chapter 26
m. 4 June 1938 Frank Edmund Sisam.

BELVA LOUISE SISAM [née HAUGHT] –F–
m. 1937 William Albert Sisam (1st wife).

BETTY JEAN SISAM –F–
   dau. of Amil Arthur Sisam and Elesta Mae Robertson
b. 1930   d. 1932, an infant

BRIAN WALTER SISAM   Farmer. –G–
   twin son of Allen Leonard Sisam and Hazel Cave
b. 1955 New Zealand.   m. 1986 Jane Clare Barnsley.

BRUCE ALLEN SISAM   Farmer. –G– Chapter 21
   twin son of Allen Leonard Sisam and Hazel Cave
b. 1955 New Zealand.   m. 1977 Pauline Mudge.

CAROL SISAM [née WELLINGS] –G–
m. 1969 Peter Sisam.

CAROLINE SISAM –C– Chapter 3
    dau. of William Sisam and Lydia Marshell
ch. 18 March 1827 Arrow.
Lived at Walton near Wellesbourne with her brother William.
d. 29 Jan. 1869, aged 41, buried at Arrow, 5 Feb. 1869.

CAROLINE SISAM [née MARSHALL] –C– Chapters 3, 4, 14, 25
m. 31 Dec. 1836 Henry Sisam.

CAROLINE HELEN SISAM –E– Chapters 4, 22
    dau. of William Henry Sisam and Helen New
ch. 24 Aug. 1873 Harvington.   m. 1902 John Hook.

CAROLINE MARSHALL SISAM (Lena) –E– Chapters 15, 16, 17, 19
    dau. of Alfred John Sisam and Maria Knights
b. 1875 Opotiki, New Zealand.
m. 1906 Edward von Sturmer.   d. 1949

CAROLYN SISIAM [née BLACK] –F– Chapter 11
m. 1963 Nelse Sisiam (2nd wife).

CAROLYN LEE SISAM –F–
    dau. of Amil Arthur Sisam and Elesta Mae Robertson
b. 28 Oct. 1939 Salt Lake City, Utah.
m. 10 Aug. 1964 Gilbert Carrasco.

CATHERINE SISAM [née PAYNE]   Glove-maker. –C– Chapters 6, 7, 8, 9
    dau. of Richard and Ann Payne of Inkberrow,
Worcestershire.
b. Oct. 1824   ch. 19 June 1825 Inkberrow.
m. 30 Dec. 1843 Joseph Sisam, at Alcester.
To USA 1868.   d. 28 Oct. 1907 Midvale, Utah.

CATHERINE NELLIE SISAM [née FINCHER] –E– Chapter 24
    dau. of John Gazeley Fincher of Stratford-upon-
Avon.
m. 8 May 1913 Walter Sisam.

CELIA SISAM –F– Chapters 19, 21
Fellow and Tutor in English at St. Hilda's College,
Oxford.
    dau. of Kenneth Sisam and Naomi Gibbons
b. 1926 Oxford.

CHARLES MARSHALL SISAM (Charlie)   –E– Chapters 25, 26
   son of Thomas Marshall Sisam and Mary Jane Davis
b. 1871 Winchcombe.
d. 1936 Cleeve Prior, unmarried.

CLAUDIA GAY SISAM   –G– Chapter 10
   dau. of Alma Leslie Sisam and Marge Hansen
b. 1934   m.(1) 1953 Varle Reynolds   m.(2) —

CLIFFORD SISAM   –E– Chapter 3
   son of Herbert Sisam and Sarah Ann Jones
b. 1908 Glossop, Derbyshire.
m. 1943 Kathleen F. Dolan.   d. 1981

CLIVE A. SISAM   Machinist.   –G– Chapter 26
   son of Frank Edmund Sisam and Beatrice Marion Pettican
b. 1939 Peterborough.   m. 1963 Victoria Allen

CLIVE STANSFIELD SISAM   –G–
   son of Allen Leonard Sisam and Hazel Cave
b. 1957 New Zealand.

COLLEEN SISAM [née MOORE]   –F– Chapter 10
m. 2 July 1954 Lorne Richard Sisam.

DANIEL SISAM   –B– Chapter 2
   son of John Sisam and Phoebe Russell
b. 1794(?)
d. 21 May 1811 aged 16 years. Tombstone at Fladbury

DANIEL SISAM   –C– Chapter 6
   son of Joseph Sisam and Elizabeth Wells
b. Marlcliff   ch. 29 Jan. 1833 Bidford.
d. 2 Feb. 1835 aged 2 years

DARRELL HENRY SISAM   –F– Chapter 10
   son of Wilford Martin Sisam and Mary Elizabeth Butterfield
b. 12 Jan. 1924 Midvale, Utah.
d. 28 Oct. 1944, killed in World War II

DAVID SISAM   Farmer at Hill, Fladbury.   –B–   Chapters 2, 6
   son of John Sisam and Phoebe Russell.
Inherited farm from his mother.
ch. 9 March 1796 Hill, Fladbury.
d. 13 July 1869 aged 73 yrs, unmarried.
Tombstone at Fladbury

DAVID SISAM   –C–   Chapters 3, 22
   son of William Sisam and Lydia Marshall
ch. 8 June 1822 Arrow.
d. 21 May 1833 aged 11 years, drowned in River Arrow.
Tombstone at Arrow

DAVID MICHAEL SISAM   –G–
Actor under the name of Michael Moore.
   son of Lorne Richard Sisam and Colleen Moore
b. 1961 Salt Lake, Utah.

DEBBRAH LEE SISIAM   –G–
   dau. of Roy Elmer Sisiam and Violet Richardson
b. 1951

DELILAH MAY SISAM   –F–   Chapter 10
   dau. of Albert Andrew Sisam and Margaret Louise
Green
b. 11 May 1912 Union, Utah.
m. 24 Nov. 1928 Arthur Julius Charter

DENNIS LAVON SISAM   –F–
   twin son of Amil Arthur Sisam and Elesta Mae
Robertson
b. 26 March 1942 Salt Lake City, Utah.
d. 5 July 1952

DONALD WILFORD SISAM   –F–   Chapter 10
   son of Wilford Martin Sisam and Mary Elizabeth
Butterfield
b. 29 April 1922 Midvale, Utah.
m. 12 Jan. 1941 Mildred Brown

DONNA SISAM [née PARKER]   –F–
m. 12 April 1959 Ronald Sherman Sisam.

DONNA MAE SISAM   –F–
   dau. of Amil Arthur Sisam and Elesta Mae Robertson
b. 4 Feb. 1923 Midvale, Utah.
m. 17 Feb. 1943 Richard Lee Mix

DORIS MABEL SISAM —F— Chapters 17, 20
    dau. of Leonard Wilfred Sisam and Mabel Jane McGarvey
b. 1908 Opouriao, New Zealand.
m. 1927 George Symmans   d. 1983

DOROTHY SISAM [née HARRIS] —F—
m. 1960 Elvin Arthur Sisam (1st wife).

DOROTHY GERTRUDE SISAM —F— Chapter 23
    dau. of Frank Marshall Sisam and Amy Winifred Bomford
b. 21 March 1909 Arrow.   m. 1934 George Clarke

DULCIE ROSE SISAM —F— Chapters 17, 20
    dau. of Walter Holtom Sisam and Rose Stansfield Allen
b. 1915 Opouriao, New Zealand.
m. 1938 Percy Ingley

EDITH LILIAN SISAM [née BESS] —E— Chapter 10
m. 27 Oct. 1909 Alma Neils Sisam.

EDITH MAY SISAM —F— Chapter 26
    dau. of Thomas Sisam and Ann Johnson
b. 1908 Peterborough.
m.(1) 1932 Walter Offield   m.(2) 1940 Walter Smith

EDMUND HERBERT SISAM   Retailer. —E— Chapters 25, 26
    son of Thomas Marshall Sisam and Mary Jane Davis
b. 1885 Harvington.
Educated at the British Orphan Asylum, Slough.
m. 1921 Emily Mabel Hawes.   d. 1957

EDNA CARINA SISAM [née LIST] —F— Chapters 20, 21
m. 1933 Leonard Alfred Sisam (Pete).

EDWARD GODFREY SISAM —D— Chapter 3
    son of John Sisam and Sarah Hannah Potter
b. 1851 Winchcombe.   d. 1855

EILEEN SISAM —F— Chapter 20
    dau. of Leonard Wilfrid Sisam and Mabel Jane McGarvey
b. 1918 Whakatane, New Zealand.
m. 1944 F. James Harold McCracken (Buster)

ELESTA MAE SISAM [née ROBERTSON]　　　　　–E–　Chapter 10
m. 4. Dec. 1920 Amil Arthur Sisam.

ELIZABETH SISAM　　　　　　　　　　　　　　–A–
　　dau. of John Sisam and Ann Cole
ch. 14 Nov. 1756 Little Comberton.
m. 9 Feb. 1779 Thomas Hughes, Fladbury

ELIZABETH SISAM [née WELLS]　　　　　　　–B–　Chapter 6
　　dau. of Samuel and Sarah Wells of Broad Marston,
Glos.
ch. 28 Feb. 1790
m. 19 April 1808 Joseph Sisam at Worcester,
St. Clements.　　d. 24 Dec. 1862 aged 72, at Warwick.

ELIZABETH SISAM [née HOARE]　　　　　　　–C–　Chapter 3
　　dau. of John Hoare of Radway.
m. 29 Jan. 1849 Frederick Sisam.
By 1861 he had abandoned her.
Lived at Warwick with her daughter.　　d. 1903

ELIZABETH ANNE SISAM [née WILLIAMS]　　　–G–
m. 1972 Graham Arthur Sisam.

ELIZABETH LYDIA SISAM (Lily)　Schoolteacher.　–D–　Chapters 3, 5
　　dau. of John Sisam and Sarah Hannah Potter
b. 1848 Winchcombe.　　d. 1935 Halford

ELIZABETH HOARE SISAM　　　　　　　　　　–D–　Chapter 3
　　dau. of Frederick Sisam and Elizabeth Hoare
ch. 16 July 1851 Harvington.　　d. 1935 Alcester

ELIZABETH STEWART SISAM (Betty) [née NEILL]　–E–　Chapter 5
m. Oct. 1932 John William Bernard Sisam.

ELSIE SISAM [née IRELAND]　　　　　　　　　–F–　Chapter 23
　　dau. of Leonard Clifford Ireland.
b. June 1921 at Little Woolford.
m. 1946 James Leonard Sisam (Jim)

ELSPETH SISAM [née BLAIR]　　　　　　　　　–G–
m. 1982 Harold Robert Sisam.

ELVIN ARTHUR SISAM –F–
son of Amil Arthur Sisam and Elesta Mae Robertson
b. 11 Nov. 1927 Midvale, Utah.
m. (1) 1960 Dorothy Harris   (2) Faye Ann Crowley.
Had issue: including Mark Sisam by Laura Ann Drake.
d. Nov. 1987

EMILY MABEL SISAM [née HAWES] –E– Chapter 26
m. 1921 Edmund Herbert Sisam.

EMILY MARY SISAM –E– Chapter 4
dau. of William Henry Sisam and Helen New
ch. 11 Oct. 1871 Alcester.
A governess in Brighton. Then a Salvation Army officer.
d. 1933 Birmingham

EMMA SISAM –D– Chapters 6, 7.8
dau. of Joseph Sisam and Catherine Payne
b. 6 Nov. 1849 Inkberrow, Worcs.
Crippled and could not walk.
To USA 1868 with her parents.   d. 9 Oct. 1894

EMMA ANNIE SISAM [née ANCIENT] –D– Chapter 5
dau. of a clergyman in Nova Scotia.
m. Sept. 1904 William Bernard Sisam.

ESTELLE SISAM Chapter 26
dau. of Clive A. Sisam and Victoria Allen
b. 1964 Peterborough.

EVELYN SISAM –E– Chapter 3
dau. of Herbert Sisam and Sarah Ann Jones
b. 1902 Glossop, Derbyshire.
m. 1946 James Anderson

FANNY JANE SISAM [née HIEATT] –E– Chapters 15, 16, 18
dau. of William Hooper Hieatt
m. 1894 Walter Henry Sisam.

FAYE ANN SISAM [née CROWLEY] –F–
m. — Elvin Arthur Sisam (2nd wife).

FAYE LEONE SISAM –F–
dau. of Amil Arthur Sisam and Elesta Mae Robertson
b. 26 Feb. 1925 Midvale, Utah.
m. (1) 1945 Joseph John Larenzine
(2) 1955 Jack Parrett   (3) — Chet Higginbotham

FLORENCE LOUISE SISAM [née HALL]   –E– Chapter 4
m. 1910 William Sisam.

FRANCIS HENRY SISAM (Harry)   Businessman.   –F– Chapters 5, 22, 23
   son of Frank Marshall Sisam & Amy Winifred Bomford
b. 1910 Arrow. To Canada 1948.

FRANK EDMUND SISAM   Businessman.   –F– Chapter 26
   son of Thomas Sisam and Ann Johnson
b. 1910 Peterborough.
m. 4 June 1938 Beatrice Marion Pettican   d. 1981

FRANK MARSHALL SISAM   Farmer.   –E– Chapters 22, 23, 24
   son of James Leonard Sisam and Letitia New
b. 14 Sept. 1880 ch. 10 Oct. 1880 Arrow.
m. 1 Dec. 1904 Amy Winifred Bomford at Dunnington Chapel.   d. 1943

FREDERICK [FRANCIS] SISAM   Miller.   –C– Chapters 2, 3
   son of William Sisam and Lydia Marshall.
ch. 1 Oct. 1820 Bidford.
m. (1) 29 Jan. 1849 Elizabeth Hoare, Radway.
m. (2)(bigamously) 24 Oct. 1864 Martha Hargit at Penistone, Yorks.
d. 1898

FREDERICK FRANCIS SISAM   –E– Chapter 3
'Father Gilbert', priest of a Franciscan order.
   son of Hector Marshall Sisam and Mary Ellen Fitz-Gerald.
b. 1892 Hayfield, Derbyshire.   d. 1967

GEORGE SISAM   Party Political Agent.   –E– Chapter 3
   son of Hector Marshall Sisam and Mary Ellen FitzGerald
b. Dec. 1897 Hayfield, Derbyshire.
m. 1931 Annie Beeley.   d. 1963

GEORGE HARGIT SISAM   Cotton twister.   –D– Chapter 3
   son of Frederick [Francis] Sisam and Martha Hargit
b. 1867 Wortley, Yorkshire.   d. 1902, unmarried.

GEORGE HENRY SISAM   –E–
   son of Joseph Henry Sisam and Hannah Poulson
b. 14 June 1882 West Jordan, Utah.
d. 1 April 1883, an infant.

GERALDINE MAY SISIAM   –G–   Chapter 11
    dau. of Richard Joseph Sisiam and Ruby Geraldine Turner
b. 1943

GILBERT BRENT SISAM   –G–
    son of Allen Leonard Sisam and Hazel Cave
b. 1948 New Zealand.   m. 1976 Kathleen Ranum

GLADYS M. SISAM   –F–   Chapter 26
    dau. of Thomas Sisam and Ann Johnson
b. 1917 Peterborough.   m. 1942 Charles F. Beeby

GLEN WILLIAM SISAM   –G–
    son of William Albert Sisam and Mabel Louise Baloski

GLORIA MARY SISAM   –G–   Chapter 23
    dau. of James Leonard Sisam (Jim) and Elsie Ireland
b. 1950   m. 1986 David Leslie Hudson

GRAHAM ARTHUR SISAM   –G–   Chapter 26
Telecommunications engineer.
    son of Arthur Edmund Sisam and Barbara Stewart
b. 1950 Birmingham.
m. 1972 Elizabeth Anne Williams.

HANNAH SISAM   –A–   Chapter 1
    dau. of John Sisam and Ann Cole
ch. 19 Oct. 1746 Little Comberton.   d. after 1779

HANNAH SISAM [née POULSON]   –D–   Chapters 8, 9, 10
m. 4 Feb. 1877 Joseph Henry Sisam (1st wife).

HAROLD JOHN SISAM   –E–
    son of Joseph Henry Sisam and Hannah Poulson
b. and d. 1892

HAROLD ROBERT SISAM   Accountant.   –G–   Chapter 21
    son of Harold Walter Sisam (Mannie) and Adele Nankivell
b. 1952 New Zealand.   m. 1982 Elspeth Blair

HAROLD WALTER SISAM (Mannie)   Farmer.   –F–   Chapters 17, 20, 21
    son of Leonard Wilfred Sisam & Mabel McGarvey
b. 1912 Opouriao, New Zealand.
m. 1947 Adele Nankivell   d. 1988

HARRIET SISAM –C– Chapter 3
   dau. of William Sisam and Lydia Marshall
ch. 1 Aug. 1825 Arrow. Lived at Walton, Wellesbourne.
d. 1883

HARRIET SISAM –D– Chapters 6, 7
   dau. of Joseph Sisam and Catherine Payne
b. 1 October 1844 Alcester. To USA 1866
m. April 1867 William John Avery Timms
d. 3 Aug. 1917

HARRIET SISAM –D– Chapter 3
   dau. of Frederick Sisam and Elizabeth Hoare
b. 5 June 1854 Sedgeberrow, Worcs.

HARRIET SISAM –D– Chapter 3
   dau. of Frederick [Francis] Sisam and Martha Hargit
b. 1874 Hayfield, Derbyshire.   d. 1887

HARRIET SISAM –E– Chapter 3
   dau. of Herbert Sisam and Sarah Ann Jones
b. 1900 Glossop, Derbyshire.   m. 1923 — Meredith

HARRIET ELIZABETH SISAM –C– Chapter 6
   dau. of Joseph Sisam and Elizabeth Wells
b. Marlcliff ch. 31 Jan. 1830 Bidford.
d. 12 Dec. 1851 Warwick

HARRY SISAM – see FRANCIS HENRY SISAM

HAZEL SISAM [née CAVE] –F– Chapter 21
m. 1947 Allen Leonard Sisam.

HECTOR MARSHALL SISAM   Cotton weaver. –D– Chapter 3
   son of Frederick [Francis] Sisam and Martha Hargit
b. 1865 Wortley, Yorkshire.
m. 1890 Mary Ellen FitzGerald   d. 1943

HELEN SISAM [née NEW] –D– Chapters 4, 22
   dau. of Charles Morris Marshall New
m. 24 June 1838 William Henry Sisam.

HELEN SISIAM [née RICHARDSON] –F– Chapter 11
m. 1940 Nelse Sisiam (1st wife).

HENRIETTA PHOEBE SISAM   Dressmaker.   –D– Chapter 3
   dau. of Frederick Sisam & Elizabeth Hoare
b. 21 Dec. 1849 Harvington. ch. 4 Jan. 1850
d. 1917 Warwick

HENRY SISAM   Miller of Arrow Mill.   –C– Chapters 2, 3, 4, 25
   eldest son of William Sisam and Lydia Marshall
ch. 25 July 1814 Welford-on-Avon.
m. 31 Dec. 1836 Caroline Marshall
d. 9 May 1870 Tombstone at Arrow.

HENRY CHARLES SISAM   –E– Chapter 4
   son of William Henry Sisam and Helen New
ch. 6 July 1870 Alcester.
d. 26 Sept. 1872, aged 2 years, Arrow.

HENRY LEONARD SISAM Miller and Farmer.   –E– Chapter 22
   son of James Leonard Sisam and Letitia New
b. 26 Jan. 1879 ch. 20 April 1879 Arrow.
m. 7 April 1910 Mary Westlake Rouse, at Par, Cornwall.
d. 1935

HENRY WHITNEY SISAM   –F– Chapter 10
   son of Alma Niels Sisam and Edith Lillian Bess
b. 1918 Salt Lake, Utah.   d. 1933

HENRY WILLIAM SISIAM   –F–
   son of Joseph Willard Sisiam and Ruth Hurst
b. and d. 1934

HERBERT SISAM   Cotton twister.   –D– Chapter 3
   son of Frederick [Francis] Sisam and Martha Hargit
b. 1869 Hayfield, Derbyshire.
m. 1900 Sarah Ann Jones   d. 1956

HUGH SISAM   Businessman.   –F– Chapter 19
   son of Kenneth Sisam and Naomi Gibbons
b. 1923 Oxford.   d. 1989, unmarried.

INGRID SISAM [née POULSON]   –D– Chapters 8, 11
m. 1878 (LDS polygamously) Joseph Henry Sisam.

IRENE LEONE SISAM   –E– Chapter 10
   dau. of Joseph Henry Sisam and Hannah Poulson
b. 24 March 1900 West Jordan, Utah.
m. Oct. 1919 Leo Tripp   d. 1989

ISABEL MARIE SISAM   –F– Chapters 17, 20, 21
  dau. of Walter Holtom Sisam and Rose Stansfield Allen
b. 1925 Whakatane, New Zealand.
m. 1950 Graham Quick

IVY ROSE SISAM   –F– Chapters 16, 18
  dau. of Walter Henry Sisam and Fanny Jane Hieatt
b. 1899 Auckland, New Zealand.
m. 1929 Victor Francis Christian.   d. 1977

JACQUELINE ROSINA SISAM [née DAVEY]   –G–
m. 1977 Peter Edmund Sisam.

JAMES SISAM   Chapter 1
  son of Nicholas Sysom and Sarah Day of Greet, Winchcombe.
ch. 17 Sept. 1731
Brother to John who d. 1763, witness to WILL.

JAMES LEONARD SISAM   –D– Chapters 4, 16, 17, 22, 25
Miller at Arrow and Farmer.
  son of Henry Sisam and Caroline Marshall
b. 10 Aug. 1845 ch. 9 Oct. 1845 Arrow.
m. 20 April 1876 Letitia New, Winchcombe.   d. 1921

JAMES LEONARD SISAM (Jim)   Farmer and Miller.   –F– Chapters 22, 23
  son of Henry Leonard Sisam and Mary Westlake Rouse
b. 19 Aug. 1916 ch. 21 Sept. 1916 Arrow.
m. 1946 Elsie Ireland   d. 1991

JANE CLARE SISAM [née BARNSLEY]   –G–
m. 1986 Brian Walter Sisam.

JANET DAWN SISAM [née ALLEY]   –G–
m. 1983 Neil Milton Sisam.

JENNIS YVONNE SISAM   –F–
  dau. of Amil Arthur Sisam and Elesta Mae Robertson
b. 26 March 1942 Salt Lake City, Utah.
m. (1) 1963 Joel Wallace Little
(2) — — Gray   (3) 1988 ——

JILL SISAM   –G–
  dau. of Harold Walter Sisam and Adele Nankivell
b. 1948 New Zealand.   m. 1972 Donald McLeod

JO ANNE SISIAM –G– Chapter 11
   dau. of Nelse Sisiam and Helen Richardson
b.1948   m. — Samuel Torrez

JOAN SISAM [née BURNARD] –F– Chapter 21
m. 1950 Kenneth Charles Sisam.

JOAN CECILY SISAM –F– Chapters 17, 20, 21
   dau. of Walter Holtom Sisam and Rose Stansfield Allen
b. 1917 Opouriao, New Zealand.
m. 1950 Alan Stewart

JOHN SISAM Chapter 1
   son of Nicholas Sysom and Sarah Day of Greet, Winchcombe.
ch. 1 Feb. 1718/19
d. 1763 (WILL proved Nov. 1763)

JOHN SISAM I   Yeoman. Chapters 1, 2
   assumed son of Joseph Sysom & Sarah Minett of Greet, Winchcombe
ch. 26 Dec. 1720 Winchcombe.
m. 15 Nov. 1743 Ann Cole, Little Comberton.
d. 26 June 1786

JOHN SISAM –A–
   first son of John Sisam and Ann Cole
ch. 22 Dec. 1743 Little Comberton.
bur. 24 Dec. 1743, an infant.

JOHN SISAM II   Farmer at Hill, Fladbury. –A– Chapter 2
   son of John Sisam and Ann Cole
ch. 11 Dec. 1748 Little Comberton.
m.(1) 21 May 1778 Nancy George
m. (2) 10 Aug. 1790 Phoebe Russell.
d. Dec. 1801

JOHN SISAM   Gardener. –B– Chapter 2
   eldest son of John Sisam and Nancy George
ch. 26 April 1780 Hill, Fladbury.
d. after 1841 census, unmarried.

JOHN SISAM   Miller. –C– Chapters 2, 3, 4, 5, 25
   son of William Sisam and Lydia Marshall
ch. 29 Oct. 1818 Bidford.
m. 30 Dec. 1847 Sarah Hannah Potter at Stretton-on-Fosse.
d. 10 Feb. 1891, Weston-super-Mare

JOHN SISAM −C− Chapter 6
   son of Joseph Sisam and Elizabeth Wells
ch. 21 July 1816 Welford-on-Avon.
d. 6 Aug. 1821 aged 5 years

JOHN SISAM   Computer programmer. −F− Chapter 3
   son of George Sisam and Annie Beeley
b. 1934 Altrincham.

JOHN DAVID SISAM (David)   Architect. −F− Chapter 5
   son of John William Bernard Sisam and Elizabeth
Stewart Neill (Betty) of Canada.
b. 1945 Oxford.   m. 1977 Elizabeth Szubski

JOHN FRANCIS SISAM (Jack)   Farmworker. −E− Chapters 25, 26
   son of Thomas Marshall Sisam and Mary Jane Davis
ch. 3 June 1883 Harvington.
d. 1972 Cleeve Prior, unmarried.

JOHN WALTER SISAM −G−
   son of Walter John Sisam and Noeline Ogden
b. 1947 New Zealand.   m. 1971 Margaret Neight

JOHN WILLIAM BERNARD SISAM −E− Chapter 5
Forester and Academic.
   son of William Bernard Sisam and Annie Ancient
b. May 1906 Canada.
m. Oct. 1932 Elizabeth Stewart Neill (Betty).
d. 1989

JOSEPH SISAM Chapter 1
   son of Nicholas Sisam and Maria Didcoat
ch. 31 March 1684 Winchcombe.
m. 26 Nov. 1709 Sarah Minett.   d. 1731
Father of John (Johanis) Sysom who was ch. 26 Dec.
1720, and is assumed to be the John who married
Ann Cole 15 Nov. 1743 from whom the family descend.

JOSEPH SISAM   Farmworker. −B− Chapters 2, 6
   son of John Sisam and Nancy George
ch. 18 June 1786 Hill, Fladbury.
m. 19 April 1808 Elizabeth Wells   d. 1858

Biographical Notes

JOSEPH SISAM   Farmer.   –C–   Chapters 6, 7, 8, 9
   son of Joseph Sisam and Elizabeth Wells
b. June 1820 ch. Sept. 1821 Bidford.
m. July 1843 Catherine Payne
Both to USA 1868, founder of US branch of family.
d. 1899

JOSEPH HENRY SISAM   Farmer.   –D–   Chapters 6, 7, 8, 9, 10
   son of Joseph Sisam and Catherine Payne
b. 22 July 1852
m.(1) 4 Feb. 1877 (Civil) & 1878 (LDS) Hannah Poulson
m.(2) 1878 (LDS polygamously) Ingrid Poulson.
d. 21 Sept. 1917 bur. Midvale

JOSEPH WILLARD SISIAM   Farmer.   –E–   Chapters 8, 9, 10, 11
   son of Joseph Henry Sisam and Ingrid Poulson
b. 1878 West Jordan, Utah.
m. 1908 Ruth Hurst.   d. 1950

JUANITA SISIAM [JAMES]   –F–   Chapter 11
m. 1947 Wilford Gale Sisiam

KATHERINE HELEN SISAM (Kate)   –E–   Chapter 25
   dau. of Thomas Marshall Sisam and Mary Jane Davis
b. 28 Dec. 1876 Atch Lench, Worcs.
m. 1899 — Snow. Went to S. Africa

KATHLEEN SISAM [née RANUM]   –G–
m. 1976 Gilbert Brent Sisam.

KATHLEEN F. SISAM [née DOLAN]   –E–   Chapter 3
m. 1943 Clifford Sisam.

KENNETH SISAM   Academic and Publisher, Oxford.   –E–   Chapters 16, 19, 20
   son of Alfred John Sisam and Maria Knights
b. 1887 Opotiki, New Zealand. Rhodes Scholar.
m. 1915 Naomi Gibbons.
Retired to Isles of Scilly.   d. 1971

KENNETH CHARLES SISAM   Businessman.   –F–   Chapters 20, 21
   son of Leonard Wilfred Sisam and Mabel McGarvey
b. 1921 Whakatane, New Zealand.
m. 1950 Joan Burnard   d. 1968

LARRY LENARD SISIAM   –G–
   son of Roy Elmer Sisiam and Violet Richardson
b. 1948

LAURA MAY SISAM   –E–   Chapter 10
    dau. of Joseph Henry Sisam and Hannah Poulson
b. 4 June 1893 West Jordan, Utah.
m. 1912 Benjamin Franklin Atkinson
d. 27 Nov. 1984

LAVALEE SISAM [née JOHANSEN]   –F–
m. — Robert Arlon Sisam.

LAVERNE SISAM   –E–   Chapters 9, 10
    dau. of Joseph Henry Sisam and Hannah Poulson
b. 11 July 1903 West Jordan, Utah.
m.(1) 20 Oct. 1923 William Adelbert Sheppick
m.(2) 6 Aug. 1946 Marvin Robert Greathouse

LAWANA SISAM [ORTON / WITTKE]   –G–
m. 1986 Lorrin Richard Sisam.

LEONARD ALFRED SISAM (Pete)   –F–   Chapters 17, 20, 21
Agriculturalist and Business executive.
    son of Leonard Wilfred Sisam and Mabel McGarvey
b. 1906 Opouriao, New Zealand.
m. 1933 Edna Carina List   d. 1982

LEONARD WILFRID SISAM   Farmer.   –E–   Chapters 15–17, 20, 21
    son of Alfred John Sisam and Maria Knights
b. 1879 Opotiki, New Zealand.
m. 1905 Mabel McGarvey   d. 1961

LESLIE JERRY SISIAM   –G–
    son of Roy Elmer Sisiam and Violet Richardson
b.1954

LETITIA SISAM [née NEW]   –D–   Chapters 3, 4, 16, 22
    dau. of Charles Morris Marshall New
m. 20 April 1876 James Leonard Sisam.

LETTICE SISAM   Archivist.   –F–   Chapters 5, 24
    dau. of Walter Sisam and Catherine Nellie Fincher
b. 9 Oct. 1916 Blockley, Glos.
d. 1968 Marlow, Bucks.

LILIAN SISAM   –E–   Chapter 3
    dau. of Herbert Sisam and Sarah Ann Jones
b. 1904 Glossop, Derbyshire.   m. 1947 — Stead

LORAINE RUTH SISAM –F–
    dau. of Amil Arthur Sisam and Elesta Mae Robertson
b. 13 July 1932 Midvale, Utah.
m.(1) 1953 Sherman Wilkinson
m.(2) — Bill Mayberry
m.(3) — Harold Sanslow   d. March 1984

LORNA SISAM –F– Chapters 20, 21
    dau. of Leonard Wilfrid Sisam and Mabel McGarvey
b. 1916 Whakatane, New Zealand.
m. 1939 Geoffrey Fogerty   d. 1985

LORNE RICHARD SISAM (Richard) –F– Chapter 10
Electrical engineer.
    son of Alma Neils Sisam and Edith Lilian Bess
b. 11 Sept. 1926 Salt Lake, Utah.
m. 2 July 1954 Colleen Moore

LORRAINE M. SISAM –F–
    dau. of Clifford Sisam and Kathleen F. Dolan
b. 1946 Glossop, Derbyshire.   m. 1964 — Dawes

LORRIN RICHARD SISAM   Electrical engineer. –G–
    son of Lorne Richard Sisam and Colleen Moore
b. 1956 Salt Lake, Utah.
m.(1) — Robyn Lynn Smith
m.(2) 1986 Lawana Orton Wittke

LYDIA SISAM [née MARSHALL] –B– Chapters 2, 3
m. 11 Dec. 1813 William Sisam.

LYNNE PATRICIA SISAM –G–
    dau. of Walter John Sisam and Noeline Ogden
b. 1951 New Zealand.
m. 1972 David Owen Roberts

MABEL SISAM –E– Chapter 25
    dau. of Thomas Marshall Sisam and Mary Jane Davis
b. 1879 Aldington ch. 8 Feb. 1880 Badsey, Worcs.
d. 1880, an infant

MABEL JANE SISAM [née McGARVEY] –E– Chapters 17, 20, 21
m. 1905 Leonard Wilfrid Sisam.

MABEL LOUISE SISAM [née BALOSKI] –F–
m. — William Albert Sisam (2nd wife).

MARGARET SISAM –G– Chapters 20, 21
   dau. of Leonard Alfred (Pete) Sisam and Edna Carina List
b. 1945 New Zealand.
m.(1) 1968 Derek Philpott
m.(2) 1974 John R. Collie

MARGARET SISAM –F–
   dau. of Clifford Sisam and Kathleen F. Dolan
b. 1945 Glossop, Derbyshire.   d. 1945, an infant

MARGARET SISAM [née NEIGHT] –G–
m. 1971 John Walter Sisam.

MARGARET ANNE SISAM –G– Chapter 18
   dau. of Walter Leonard Sisam and Winnifred D. Hansen
b. 1939 Auckland, New Zealand.
m. 1960 Kenneth W. Allan

MARGARET HONOR SISAM [née BARNES] –F– Chapter 24
   dau. of Anthony Charles Barnes.
b.1921   m. 1976 Peter James Sisam.

MARGARET LOUISE SISAM [née GREEN] –E– Chapter 10
m. 26 April 1911 Albert Andrew Sisam.

MARGE SISAM [née HANSEN] –F– Chapter 10
m. 1933 Alma Leslie Sisam

MARIA SISAM [née DIDCOAT] Chapter 1
m. 30 June 1681 Nicholas Sisam.

MARIA SISAM [née KNIGHTS] –D– Chapters 13, 15, 16
   dau. of Henry Knights
m. 1870 Alfred John Sisam.

MARIAN SISAM –D– Chapter 3
   dau. of Frederick Sisam and Elizabeth Hoare
b. 1852 ch. April 1853 Harvington.
m. 1890 Charles H. Lewin

MARIAN SISAM –E– Chapter 23
   dau. of James Leonard Sisam and Letitia New
b. 3 Feb. 1877. ch. 29 April 1877 Arrow.
m. 14 June 1906 George Hunt

MARIAN J. SISAM –F– Chapter 26
dau. of Edmund Herbert Sisam and Emily Mary Hawes
b. 1922 Kings Norton, Birmingham.
m. 1946 Derrick Archer

MARILYN JANE SISAM –G–
dau. of Harold Walter Sisam (Mannie) and Adele Nankivell
b. 1950 New Zealand.   m. 1980 Barry Shaw

MARK SISAM   Lawyer. –G–
son of Kenneth Charles Sisam and Joan Burnard
b. 1954 New Zealand.   m. 1979 Shellie Rogers

MARLENE SISAM –G– Chapter 20
dau. of Leonard Alfred Sisam (Pete) and Edna Carina List
b. 1938 New Zealand.   d. 1939 an infant

MARSHALL SISAM –D– Chapter 4
son of Henry Sisam and Caroline Marshall
ch. 10 June 1874 Arrow.   Clerk in Alcester.
d. March 1877 unmarried

MARTHA SISAM [née HARGIT] –C– Chapter 3
m. 24 Oct. 1864 (bigamously) Frederick [Francis] Sisam.

MARTHA MARY SISAM –F– Chapters 16, 18
dau. of Walter Henry Sisam and Fanny Jane Hieatt
b. 1895 Auckland, New Zealand.
m. 1926 Benjamin Copedo   d. 1982

MARY SISAM –A– Chapter 2
dau. of John Sisam and Ann Cole
ch. 9 June 1751 Little Comberton.   m. — — Parsons

MARY SISAM –B–
1st dau. of John Sisam and Nancy George
ch. 9 April 1779 Hill, Fladbury.
d. 1 Dec. 1779 an infant

MARY SISAM –B– Chapter 2
2nd dau. of John Sisam and Nancy George
ch. 14 March 1783 Hill, Fladbury. Lived in S. Littleton.
d. June 1808

MARY SISAM –C– Chapter 6
    dau. of Joseph Sisam and Elizabeth Wells
ch. 10 Oct. 1824 Bidford.   m. 1846 John Orchard

MARY ANN SISAM –C– Chapter 3
    dau. of William Sisam and Lydia Marshall
ch. 16 Jan. 1824 Arrow. Lived at Walton near
Wellesbourne with her brother William.
d. 12 Sept. 1872, aged 48, buried at Arrow

MARY ANN SISAM –D– Chapter 3
    dau. of Frederick [Francis] Sisam and Martha Hargit
b. 1872 Hayfield, Derbyshire.
m. 14 April 1903 Dick Laycock

MARY ANNE SISAM [née MASON] –D– Chapters 13, 14
m. 1866 Walter Sisam (1st wife).

MARY CATHERINE SISAM –D– Chapter 3
    dau. of John Sisam and Sarah Hannah Potter
ch. 11 Oct. 1857 Stretton-on-Fosse.
d. 1895 Weston-super-Mare

MARY CAROLINE SISAM (Carrie) –E– Chapters 14, 15
    dau. of Walter Sisam and Mary Anne Mason
b. 1871 Thames, New Zealand.
m. 1892 William Hieatt   d. 1946

MARY EDITH SISAM (Cissie) –E– Chapters 25, 26
    dau. of Thomas Marshall Sisam and Mary Jane Davis
b. 1875 Cheltenham.   Lived at Cleeve Prior
d. Sept. 1941

MARY ELIZABETH SISAM [née BUTTERFIELD] –E– Chapter 10
m. 12 Oct. 1910 Wilford Martin Sisam.

MARY ELLEN SISAM [née FITZGERALD] –D– Chapter 3
m. 1890 Hector Marshall Sisam.

MARY JANE SISAM [née DAVIS] –D– Chapters 25, 26
m. 29 May 1869 Thomas Marshall Sisam.

MARY SUSAN SISAM [née HAMILTON] –F– Chapter 5
m. 1960 Peter Neill Sisam.

MARY WESTLAKE SISAM [née ROUSE] –E– Chapters 22, 23
m. 7 April 1910 Henry Leonard Sisam

MAY SISAM –E– Chapters 15, 16, 17, 20,
    dau. of Alfred John Sisam and Maria Knights   21
b. 1877 Opotiki, New Zealand.   d. 1962

MILDRED SISAM [née BROWN] –F–
m. 12 Jan. 1941 Donald Wilford Sisam.

MILDRED CONNIE SISAM –F–
    dau. of Amil Arthur Sisam and Elesta Mae Robertson
b. 1921 Midvale, Utah.
m.(1) 1939 Herman Grey   (2) — Dale McMustry
m.(3) 1969 Charles Crossen

MIRANDA SISAM –E– Chapter 8
    dau. of Joseph Henry Sisam and Ingrid Poulson
b. 1881 d. 1882, an infant

MONA SISAM –F– Chapters 17, 20
    dau. of Leonard Wilfrid Sisam and Mabel Jane
McGarvey
b. 1911 Opouriao, New Zealand.
m. 1932 Morley Guy Fowler   d. 1958

MYRTLE LEONE SISAM –F– Chapter 10
    dau. of Wilford Martin Sisam and Mary Elizabeth
Butterfield
b. 9 July 1911 Midvale, Utah.
m. 20 Feb. 1930 Maurice Jex

NANCY SISAM –F– Chapter 18
    adopted daughter of Walter Henry Sisam and Fanny
Jane Hieatt
b. 1921   m. — John Devenport

NANCY SISAM [née GEORGE] –A– Chapter 2
m. 21 May 1778 John Sisam, farmer at Hill, Fladbury.

NAOMI SISAM [née GIBBONS] –E– Chapter 19
    dau. of Robert Pearce Gibbons
m. 1915 Kenneth Sisam.

NEIL MILTON SISAM –G–
    son of Allen Leonard Sisam and Hazel Cave
b. 1953 New Zealand.   m. 1983 Janet Dawn Alley

NELLIE SISAM [née HEWITSON] –D– Chapters 15, 16
m. 1893 Walter Sisam (2nd wife).

NELSE SISIAM   Rancher.   –F–   Chapter 11
   son of Willard Joseph Sisiam and Ruth Hurst
b. 1917 Bellevue, Idaho.
m.(1) 1940 Helen Richardson
m.(2) 1963 Carolyn Black

NICHOLAS SISAM   Chapter 1
   First known ancestor of Sisams of Greet near
Winchcombe
b. — ?
m. 30 June 1681 Maria Didcoat at Winchcombe.
d. 25 Oct. 1728 (WILL 1728)

NICHOLAS SISAM   Chapter 1
   eldest son of Nicholas Sisam and Maria Didcoat, of
Greet
ch. 22 May 1682 Winchcombe.
m. 1 Nov. 1711 Sarah Day   d. Ap. 1771

NICHOLAS SISAM   –B–
   twin son of John Sisam and Nancy George
ch. May 1788 Hill, Fladbury.
d.(bur.) 18 May 1788 an infant

NICOLA SISAM   –G–
   dau. of Kenneth Charles Sisam and Joan Burnard
b. 1957 New Zealand.   m. 1978 Duncan Humphrey

NOELINE SISAM [née OGDEN]   –F–   Chapters 20, 21
m. 1946 Walter John Sisam.

OLIVIA MARIE SISAM (Tottie)   –E–   Chapters 13, 15, 16
   dau. of Maria Knights wife of Alfred John Sisam
b. 27 June 1866 Tauranga, New Zealand.
m. 1887 John A.C. Lamont

PATRICIA SISAM [née DOUGLAS]   –F–   Chapter 26
m. 1953 Richard John Sisam (Dick).

PATSY ELNA SISAM   –F–   Chapter 10
   dau. of Wilford Martin Sisam and Mary Elizabeth
Butterfield
b. 14 March 1933 Midvale, Utah.
m. 25 June 1954 Angus Young

PAUL SISAM   Property dealer.   –G–
   son of Kenneth Charles Sisam and Joan Burnard
b. 1952 New Zealand.   m. 1976 Anne Steven

PAULINE SISAM [née MUDGE]   –G–
m. 1977 Bruce Allen Sisam.

PETER SISAM   Accountant.   –G–   Chapters 20, 21
   son of Leonard Alfred Sisam (Pete) and Edna Carina List
b. 1942 New Zealand.   m. 1969 Carol Wellings
d. 1987

PETER EDMUND SISAM   Machine-tool operative.   –G–   Chapter 26
   son of Arthur Edmund Sisam and Barbara Stewart
b. 1955 Meriden, Warwicks.
m. 1977 Jacqueline Rosina Davey

PETER JAMES SISAM   Film-maker.   –F–   Chapter 24
   son of Walter Sisam and Catherine Fincher
b. 19 Dec.1914 Blockley, Glos.
m. 1976 Margaret Honor Barnes

PETER LEONARD SISAM   Shepherd.   –G–   Chapter 18
   son of Walter Leonard Sisam and Winnifred Hansen
b. 1941 Auckland, New Zealand.

PETER NEILL SISAM   Television executive.   –F–   Chapter 5
   son of John William Bernard Sisam and Elizabeth Stewart Neill (Betty) of Canada.
b. 1937 New Haven, USA.
m. 1960 Mary Susan Hamilton

PHOEBE SISAM   –B–
   twin dau. of John Sisam and Phoebe Russell
ch. 5 Aug. 1791 Hill, Fladbury.
d.(bur.) 7 Aug. 1791 an infant

PHOEBE SISAM   –B–   Chapter 2
   2nd dau. of John Sisam and Phoebe Russell
ch. 6 June 1793 Hill, Fladbury.
m. 28 July 1832 Henry Wagstaff.   d. 1850

PHOEBE SISAM   –C–   Chapter 6
   dau. of Joseph Sisam and Elizabeth Wells
b. 1817 ch. 19 July 1819 Welford-on-Avon.
m. 4 Dec. 1837 Henry Cowper

PHOEBE SISAM [née RUSSELL]   –A–   Chapter 2
m. 10 Aug.1790 John Sisam (2nd wife).

PHYLLIS MARIAN SISAM   –F–   Chapter 23
   dau. of Frank Marshall Sisam and Amy Winifred
Bomford.
b. 30 Aug. 1918 Arrow.   d. 1968

REBECCA SISAM   –D–   Chapter 6
   dau. of Joseph Sisam and Catherine Payne
b. 12 April 1855 Inkberrow, Worcs.   d. 19 July 1859

REBECCA ANN SISAM   –G–
   dau. of Lorne Richard Sisam and Colleen Moore
b. 1958 Salt Lake, Utah.
m.(1) 1978 Hyram Fielding Koenig
m.(2) — Michael Hubert
m.(3) 1985 Darrell Don Van Cott

RICHARD GRENVILLE SISAM   –G–
   son of Allen Leonard Sisam and Hazel Cave
b. 1950 New Zealand.   m. 1974 Susan Janet Bayly

RICHARD JOHN SISAM (Dick)   –F–   Chapter 26
Telecommunications engineer.
   son of Edmund Herbert Sisam and Emily Mabel Hawes
b. 1924 Birmingham North.   m. 1953 Patricia Douglas

RICHARD JOSEPH SISIAM   Rancher and Miner.   –F–   Chapter 11
   son of Willard Joseph Sisiam and Ruth Hurst
b. 1910 Silver Creek, Idaho.
m. 1935 Ruby Geraldine Turner.   d. 1988

RICHARD KENNETH SISAM   Builder.   –G–   Chapter 18
   son of Walter Leonard Sisam and Winnifred Dagmar
Hansen
b. 1937 Auckland, New Zealand.

RICHARD LORNE SISAM or RICHARD LORRIN SISAM:
   see LORNE RICHARD SISAM b. 1926 or
   LORRIN RICHARD SISAM b. 1956

ROBERT ARLON SISAM   –F–   Chapter 10
   son of Wilford Martin Sisam and Mary Elizabeth
Butterfield
b. 11 June 1928 Midvale, Utah.
m. — Lalavee Johansen

Biographical Notes

ROBYN LYNN SISAM [née SMITH] –G–
   m. — Lorrin Richard Sisam (1st wife).

RON SISAM –G–
   son of William Albert Sisam and Mabel Louise Haught

RONALD SHERMAN SISAM –F–
   son of Amil Arthur Sisam and Elesta Mae Robertson
   b. 18 May 1936 Midvale, Utah.
   m. 12 April 1959 Donna Packer

ROSALIE SISAM –G– Chapters 20, 21
   dau. of Leonard Alfred Sisam (Pete) and Edna Carina List
   b. 1940 New Zealand.   m. 1965 Peter Preston

ROSE STANSFIELD SISAM [née ALLEN] –E– Chapters 17, 20, 21
   m. 1914 Walter Holtom Sisam.

ROY ELMER SISIAM   Railroad engineer. –F– Chapter 11
   son of Willard Joseph Sisiam and Ruth Hurst
   b. 1919 Idaho.   m. 1941 Violet Richardson

ROY VIRGIL SISIAM –G–
   son of Roy Elmer Sisiam and Violet Richardson
   b. 1942

RUBY GERALDINE SISIAM [née TURNER] –F– Chapter 11
   m. 1935 Richard Joseph Sisiam.

RUSSEL PAUL SISIAM –G–
   son of Roy Elmer Sisiam and Violet Richardson
   b. 1956

RUTH SISIAM [née HURST] –E– Chapter 11
   dau. of Jack and Nancy Jane Hurst
   m. 1908 Joseph Willard Sisiam.

RUTH HELEN SISIAM –F– Chapter 11
   dau. of Willard Joseph Sisiam and Ruth Hurst
   b. 1914 Silver Creek, Idaho.
   m.(1) — Phenoy Fischer   m.(2) — Skipp

RUTH LILLIAN SISAM –F– Chapter 10
   dau. of Alma Neils Sisam and Edith Lillian Bess
   b. 11 Jan. 1911 Salt Lake, Utah.
   m. 29 May 1929 Carl Ernest Moulton

SARAH SISAM   –A–
   dau. of John Sisam and Ann Cole
ch. 6 May 1753 Little Comberton.
m. 31 July 1775 John Andrus, Fladbury

SARAH SISAM   –B–   Chapter 2
   dau. of John Sisam and Phoebe Russell
ch. 5 May 1800 Hill, Fladbury.
m. 9 Nov. 1820 John Sherrard

SARAH SISAM   –C–   Chapter 6
   eldest dau. of Joseph Sisam and Elizabeth Wells
b. about 1809 at Long Marston.
m. 1831 William Fairfield.   Lived at Warwick

SARAH SISAM [née DAY]   Chapter 1
m. 1 Nov. 1711 Nicholas Sisam.

SARAH ANN SISAM [née JONES]   –D–   Chapter 3
m. 1900 Herbert Sisam.

SARAH HANNAH SISAM [née POTTER]   –C–   Chapters 3, 4
   dau. of William Potter of Lark Stoke, Ilmington.
m. 30 Dec. 1847 John Sisam.

SHANNON KAY SISAM   –G–
   dau. of Lorne Richard Sisam and Colleen Moore
b. 1965 Salt Lake, Utah.   m. 1986 Jeffrey Allen Wilde

SHEILA SISAM   G   Chapter 26
   dau. of Richard John Sisam and Patricia Douglas
b. 1954   m. — Peter Axon

SHELLIE SISAM [née ROGERS]   –G–
m. 1979 Mark Sisam.

SHIRLEY ANN SISAM   –F–
   dau. of Amil Arthur Sisam and Elesta Mae Robertson
b. 4 Dec. 1934 Midvale, Utah.
m.(1) 1955 Harold Nelson
m.(2) 1963 Lee Thornburg   m.(3) 1967 Dennis Barker

SOLOMON SISAM   –B–
   twin son of John Sisam and Phoebe Russell
ch. 5 Aug. 1791 Hill, Fladbury.
d.(burial) 22 Aug. 1791, an infant

STELLA INA SISIAM –F– Chapter 11
   dau. of Willard Joseph Sisiam and Ruth Hurst
b. 1912 Silver Creek, Idaho.   m. 1938 Rex James

SUSAN JANET SISIAM [née BAYLY] –G–
m. 1974 Richard Grenville Sisam.

SUSANNAH SISAM –C– Chapter 6
   dau. of Joseph Sisam and Elizabeth Wells
ch. 5 Nov. 1826 Bidford.
m. 19 Feb. 1844 Thomas Willoughby, Warwick

THOMAS SISAM   Railway guard. –E– Chapters 25, 26
   son of Thomas Marshall Sisam and Mary Jane Davis
b. 19 Oct. 1872 Cheltenham.
m. 1906 Ann Johnson.   d. 1950

THOMAS HENRY SISAM –D– Chapter 3
   son of Henry Sisam and Caroline Marshall
ch. 6 Jan. 1837 Arrow.
d. 28 May 1838, aged 11 months

THOMAS MARSHALL SISAM (Tom)   Miller. –D– Chapters 4, 12, 25, 26
   son of Henry Sisam and Caroline Marshall
ch. 12 March 1841 Arrow.
To New Zealand 1862 and returned to England.
m. 29 May 1869 Mary Jane Davis
d. 17 Oct. 1896   Tombstone at Cleeve Prior.

TODD BRIAN SISIAM –G–
   son of Roy Elmer Sisiam and Violet Richardson
b. 1958

VERA MARGARET SISAM –F– Chapter 10
   dau. of Albert Andrew Sisam and Margaret Louise Green
b. 12 June 1914 Union, Utah.
m. 27 May 1937 Henry Louis McGill

VICKI LYNN SISIAM –G– Chapter 11
   dau. of Wilford Gale Sisiam and Juanita James
b. 1956   m. — Stephen Lloyd Dick

VICTORIA SISAM [née ALLEN] –G– Chapter 26
m. 1963 Clive A. Sisam.

VIOLET SISIAM [née RICHARDSON] –F–
   m. 1941 Roy Elmer Sisiam.

VIOLET ELIZABETH SISAM –F– Chapter 10
   dau. of Wilford Martin Sisam and Mary Elizabeth
Butterfield
b. 29 Oct. 1913 Midvale, Utah.
m. 9 Sept. 1939 Morrell Seal

VIRGIL NELSE SISIAM –G– Chapter 11
   son of Nelse Sisiam and Helen Richardson
b. 1945

VIRGINIA ROBERTA SISIAM –F– Chapter 11
   dau. of Willard Joseph Sisiam and Ruth Hurst
b. 1930 Idaho.   m.(1) 1948 John Knowles
m.(2) 1965 Harold Harvey

WALTER SISAM   Farmer in the Waitakeres. –D– Chapters 4, 12–16, 18
   son of Henry Sisam and Caroline Marshall
ch. 18 June 1842 Arrow. To New Zealand 1862
m.(1) 1866 Mary Anne Mason
m.(2) 1893 Nellie Hewitson   d. 1910

WALTER SISAM   Bank Manager. –E– Chapters 22, 24
   son of James Leonard Sisam and Letitia New
b. 23 Sept. 1882 Arrow.
m. 8 May 1913 Catherine Nellie Fincher.   d. 1943

WALTER HENRY SISAM   Farmer. –E– Chapters 14–18
   son of Walter Sisam and Mary Anne Mason
b. 1867 Thames, New Zealand.
m. 1894 Fanny Jane Hieatt.   d. 1920

WALTER HOLTOM SISAM   Farmer. –E– Chapters 16, 17, 20
   son of Alfred John Sisam and Maria Knights
b. 1880 Opotiki, New Zealand.
m. 1914 Rose Stansfield Allen.   d. 1931

WALTER JOHN SISAM   Bank Executive. –F– Chapters 17, 20, 21
   son of Walter Holtom Sisam and Rose Stansfield Allen
b. 1919 Whakatane, New Zealand.
m. 1946 Noeline Ogden

WALTER LEONARD SISAM (Len) Farmer. –F– Chapter 23
  son of Frank Marshall Sisam and Amy Winifred Bomford
b. 27 Sept. 1905 Primrose Hill, Arrow.
d. 1960 unmarried

WALTER LEONARD SISAM Forest Ranger. –F– Chapters 16, 17, 18
  son of Walter Henry Sisam and Fanny Jane Hieatt
b. 1905 Thames, New Zealand.
m. 1935 Winnifred Dagmar Hansen

WAYNE JOSEPH SISIAM –G– Chapter 11
  son of Richard Joseph Sisiam and Ruby Geraldine Turner
b. 1936 Idaho.

WENDY GRACE SISAM –G–
  dau. of Walter John Sisam and Noeline Ogden
b. 1958 New Zealand. m. 1980 Eric Russell

WILFORD GALE SISIAM Businessman. –F– Chapter 11
  son of Willard Joseph Sisiam and Ruth Hurst
b. 1927 Idaho. m. 1948 Juanita James

WILFORD MARTIN SISAM Automobile engineer. –E– Chapter 10
  son of Joseph Henry Sisam and Hannah Poulson
b. 28 Oct. 1889 West Jordan, Utah.
m. 12 Oct. 1910 Mary Elizabeth Butterfield
d. 27 Dec. 1970

WILLIAM SISAM Maltster and Miller. –B– Chapters 1, 2, 3, 6
  son of John Sisam and Nancy George
ch. 12 July 1781 Hill, Fladbury.
m. 11 Dec. 1813 Lydia Marshall
First Sisam tenant of Arrow Mill.
d. 30 Nov. 1834 Tombstone at Arrow

WILLIAM SISAM Farmer at Walton. –C– Chapters 2, 3
  2nd son of William Sisam and Lydia Marshall
ch. 28 July 1817 Bidford. d. 1893, unmarried

WILLIAM SISAM Medical Practitioner. –E– Chapter 4
  son of William Henry Sisam and Helen New
ch. 6 June 1875 Harvington.
m. 1910 Florence Louise Hall d. 1947

WILLIAM ALBERT SISAM   Truck Driver.   –F–   Chapter 10
   son of Albert Andrew Sisam and Margaret Louise Green
b. 19 Sept. 1916 Union, Utah.
m.(1) 1937 Belva Louise Haught
m.(2) — Mabel Louise Baloski

WILLIAM BERNARD SISAM   –D–   Chapters 3, 5
Church of England clergyman.
   son of John Sisam and Sarah Hannah Potter
b. 30 Dec. 1855 Winchcombe.   Settled in Canada.
m. Sept. 1904 Emma Annie Ancient   d. Feb. 1937

WILLIAM FLOYD SISAM   –G–
   son of William Albert Sisam and Belva Louise Haught

WILLIAM GEORGE SISAM   Ploughman.   –C–   Chapter 6
   Eldest son of Joseph Sisam and Elizabeth Wells
ch. 9 June 1811 Bidford.
Transported to Penal Colony in Tasmania 1831.
d. 1874 (?) unmarried

WILLIAM HENRY SISAM   –D–   Chapters 3, 4, 25
Miller at Harvington Mill and Corn-dealer.
   son of Henry Sisam and Caroline Marshall
b. 8 Aug. 1838 Arrow.   m. 24 June 1869 Helen New
d. 23 Dec. 1877, bur. 1 Jan 1878 Arrow

WINIFRED SISAM [née BOMFORD] – See AMY WINIFRED SISAM.

WINIFRED MARY SISAM (Molly)   –F–   Chapter 23
   dau. of Frank Marshall Sisam and Amy Winifred Bomford.
b. 9 March 1907 Arrow.   m. 1934 Frederick Bunting

WINNIFRED DAGMAR SISAM [née HANSEN]   –F–   Chapter 18
m. 1935 Walter Leonard Sisam.

Index

PLACES ETC. & PEOPLE OTHER THAN SISAMS

Aberdeen High School, Moncton, NB Canada 51
Adkins, Frank (Broom Mill) 245
Albany, New York USA 93
Albertland, NZ 39, 113–117, 122, 125
Alcester 3, 21, 24, 35, 36, 39–41, 43, 44, 63, 65, 66, 231, 233, 250, 265
Alcester, Arrow Road 248, 249
Alcester Chronicle 40–41
Alcester Corn Exchange 36, 37, 40, 43
Alcester Grammar School 36, 229–231, 245, 246, 250, 265
Alcester High Street 36, 37, 40–43, 137, 246
Alcester Warren 63
Alcester Warren Farm 63, 64
Aldington Mill 265
Alexander Turnbull Library, NZ 118
Alms Houses Lane, Winchcombe 262
Alscot Park, Preston–on–Stour 235, 240
Altrincham 34
America (see also USA) 39, 65, 67–69, 71, 277
American Indians 68, 69, 72, 76, 78, 80, 85
American War of Independence 50
Anglican Church (see Church of England) 37
Arab and cross–bred Arab horses 217, 220, 221
Archer family (Cleeve Prior) 273
Arden, Phillip (Auckland NZ) 168
Armed Constabulary, NZ 126–128, 134, 147, 148
Arrow 21, 24, 36, 39, 43, 44, 63, 229
Arrow Churchyard and Church 24, 28, 37, 43, 233, 249, 255
Arrow Farm, Waitakere NZ 138–141, 143, 144, 154–156, 163, 165, 166, 168, 174, 180, 181, 183
Arrow Mill 2, 21–25, 27, 28, 36–40, 43, 44, 65–66, 113, 135, 137, 139, 226–229, 231, 233–235, 237, 243, 250, 262, 263, 265
Arrow Parish Council 232
Arrow River 21, 28, 63, 64, 233, 234,
Ashchurch 41
Aston Magna 239, 240
Atch Lench 36, 37, 264
Atlantic, SS 49
Auckland NZ 39, 113–116, 118, 120–127, 132, 139, 148, 153, 156, 162, 163, 168, 173, 177, 178, 188
Auckland Agricultural Show, NZ 162
Auckland City Council, NZ 180, 181, 183
Auckland Grammar School, NZ 162, 168, 173, 188, 200, 209, 213
Auckland Hospital, NZ 263
Auckland Public Library, NZ 163
Auckland, University College, NZ 168, 186, 188
Australia 49, 115, 116, 132, 138
Australia & New Zealand Bank 204, 215

Australian Mutual Provident Society 205
Avondale, NZ 155
Avonmouth Docks, Bristol 233, 240
Avon River 1, 10, 18, 25, 56, 62, 266
Aylett, Bishop John (Midvale USA) 99

Bacon, George (Waitakere NZ) 125
Bald Hill, Mauku NZ 120
Ballarat, Australia 132
Balliol College, Oxford 186, 192
Baptists 37, 123, 244
Barkes, John (Moreton–in–Marsh) 254
Barnes, Stanley F. (Moreton–in–Marsh) 257
Bates, Fred (Opotiki NZ) 151
Bates, S. (Opotiki NZ)) 149, 151
Baton Broadcasting, Toronto, Canada 55
Baxter's Store, (Fred) Waitakere NZ 137
Bay of Plenty, NZ 125, 130, 131, 199, 200
Beckford 41
Belas Knap, Winchcombe 29
Bellevue, Idaho USA 107, 108, 112
Benford & Company, Leamington Spa 241
Benton, Wyoming USA 76
Berrow's Worcester Journal 60
Bevington 24
Bidford–on–Avon 1–3, 18–20, 24, 56, 57
Bidford Bridge 1, 2, 24
Big Elk, Chief (Omaha USA) 78
Big Wood River, Idaho USA 86, 96, 106–109
Birmingham 39, 65, 229, 234, 245, 246, 248, 250, 255, 267, 268, 270, 271, 273, 277
Bishampton 13
Bishop, Andrew (Preston–on–Stour) 236, 242
Bishop, Edmund (Downside) 188
Bishops Cleeve 41
Bismark 247
Black Hills, South Dakota USA 74
Bledisloe, Lord 183
Blenheim, NZ 209, 210
Blockley 252
Boar's Hill, Oxford 189, 190, 191, 193
Bockett, C.F. (Opotiki NZ) 149
Bodleian Library, Oxford 188
Bombay, India 44
Bomford family 36, 37, 243, 244
Bomford, Fred (Atch Lench) 36, 37, 116, 118, 121–124
Bomford, Henry Butler (Exhall) 243
Bordighera, Italy 34
Bosanquet, Sir John Bernard 59
Boucher, Mr. (Tasmania) 61
Bourke, Australia 49

Bourne, John (Snowshill) 249
Bourton–on–the–Hill 252, 262, 264
Bradley, Professor Henry (Oxford) 189
Brailes 240
Brame, William Rawson (Birmingham) 39
Brannigan, Colonel 127
Bredon Hill 9, 41
Brenta River, Italy 214
Bridges, Robert (Oxford) 190, 191
Briscoe, Rev.William (Shipston–on–Stour) 45
British Academy 198
British Orphan Asylum 268, 269
Broad Campden 249
Broad Marston 56
Broom 19, 57
Browne, Dr.Charles (London) 244
Browne, William Parry (Whakatane NZ) 152, 154, 163
Buckle Street 1
Buckworth, Mrs. (Whakatane NZ) 151, 152, 157
Buddhists 47, 48
Buick, David (Detroit USA) 93
Bullock family (Harvington) 27, 41
Bullock, William James (Harvington) 27, 41
Bunting, Frederick J. (Alcester) 246, 248
Burley, Idaho USA 86
Burma 47–49
Burma Railway 248
Burmington 31
Bush, Mr. (Opotiki NZ) 145, 148
Butterfield, David (Salt Lake City USA) 94, 99

Cambridge 34
Camden Town, London 47
Cameron, General (NZ) 118, 120, 133
Canada 49, 51, 190, 249, 256, 277
Canadian Memorial Hospital, Taplow 260
Canning, Sir Ernest (Birmingham) 245
Cannock Chase 40, 41
Cape of Good Hope, S. Africa 114
Capital & Counties Bank 250, 251
Carr, Vernon 237, 242
Cascades, Waitakere NZ 124, 135, 181
Cassino, Italy 214
Cassio County, Idaho USA 96
Castle Farm, Arrow. 228, 229
Catholics 34, 171, 250
Center Street house, Salt Lake City USA 97, 101
Central Pacific Railroad, USA 77
Chalmers, Mrs. (Whakatane NZ) 151
Changchek, Thailand 249
Charlett, Richard Bourne 10, 11, 14
Charman, Henry 133
Chastleton 254, 255
Chatham Islands, NZ 127
Chatham Prison Hulks 60, 61
Cheltenham 16, 29, 41, 237, 264
Cheltenham Ladies' College 31
Chelt River, Sandford 264
Cheyenne, Wyoming USA 76
Chesterfield 245
Christchurch, NZ 133, 215
Christian, Victor 181

Church of England 45
Church of Jesus Christ of Latter Day Saints (LDS)
  (see also Mormons) 65, 84
Church Street, Opotiki 134, 145
'City of Rocks', Idaho USA 85, 86
Cladswell Lane, Cookhill 63
Clarendon Press 189, 190–193, 198
Clarke, George (Arrow) 232, 234
Clarke, George (Sambourne) 238, 246, 249
Clark's Mills, Banbury 240
Cleeve Prior 261, 266–268, 270–275
Cleeve Prior, King's Head 273, 274
Clevedon, Somerset 34
Clydesdale horses 172, 176
Cold Comfort Farm, Arrow 232
Cole, John the Elder (Little Comberton) 10
Cole, John the Younger (Little Comberton) 10
Colonial Defence Force, NZ 118, 120, 122, 125,
  133, 148, 159
Commonwealth Forestry Bureau, Oxford (formerly
  Imperial Forestry Bureau) 52
Compton Verney 32
Connors, Mr. (Opotiki NZ) 149
Continental Divide, Wyoming USA 75
Coombs, Joseph (Castlemaine, Australia) 116
Copedo, Benjamin (Waitakere town) 181, 183, 185
Copedo, Benjamin (Auckland) 262
Corbett, Cornelius (Arrow) 245
Corbett, John (Impney) 270
Coromandel Coast, NZ 201, 211
Cotswold Hills 1, 3, 5, 29, 229, 252, 255
Cottle, Fred (Waitakere NZ) 141
Cotton, William (Little Comberton) 14
Cottonwood Canyon, Utah USA 93, 104
Coughton 250
Coventry, Bishop of 254
Cowper, Henry (Marlcliff) 62
Cranwell, Lucy (Auckland NZ) 183
Craycombe, Fladbury 10
Creek, Mrs. (Whakatane NZ) 157
CTV Television Network, Toronto, Canada 55
Cullins Workshops, West Jordan USA 96, 97
Cundic, Francis (West Jordan USA) 82
Custer, General (US Cavalry) 74

Dalgety (New Zealand) 220, 223
Darling River, Australia 49
Davin, Daniel (NZ & Oxford) 193, 194, 198
Davis, Thomas (Hill) 11
Day, Elizabeth 'Betsy' (Hill) 16
Day, Charles Jnr. (Hill) 16
Dean Close School, Cheltenham 237
Denmark 257
Deseret News 85
Devenport, John (Waitakere NZ) 181
Devil's Gate, Wyoming USA 75
Dominion Forestry Service, Canada 51, 52
Downs Farm, Bourton-on-the-Hill 264
Drury, NZ 120
Dunnington 37, 244
Dunnington Court Farm 245, 248
Durya, Charles & Frank (USA) 93

Index

East India Company 10, 21
East India Dock, London 39, 113
Ebrington 229
Echo Canyon, Utah USA 75
Edison, Thomas (USA) 93
Edwards (Airedale) Street, Auckland NZ 124
Egerton, Professor (Auckland NZ) 168
Egypt 214
Enas, Mrs. (Whakatane NZ) 151
Epsom, Auckland NZ 123
Evesham 36, 41
Evesham Journal 41, 246, 249, 255
Evesham, Vale of 3, 9, 18, 243
Exeter College, Oxford 34
Exhall 19
Exhall Court 243

Fairfield, William (Warwick) 61–63
Fairfield, William Jnr. 63
Fairview House, Shipston–on–Stour 31
Falloon, Lt. James (NZ) 125, 126
FAO (Food & Agriculture Organisation UN) 55
Farquhar family (Auckland NZ) 163, 188
Ferguson, Bernard (NZ) 181, 182, 185
Fetterman, Captain (US Cavalry) 73
Fetterman Massacre, USA 73
Field, John & Mrs. D. (Little Comberton) 14
Fiji 173
Fincher, John Gazeley (Stratford–upon–Avon) 251
Firkins, William (Hill) 16
Fisher, John (Grafton) 43, 265
Fisher, Richard (Alcester) 36
Fladbury 3, 10
Fladbury Churchyard 15
Florence, Nebraska USA 69
Fogerty, Geoffrey (NZ) 209
Ford, Henry (Detroit USA) 93
Forest Gate, London 34
Forest Rangers (Flying Column) NZ 120
Forsyth, James (Ohiwa) 159
Fort Bridger, Wyoming USA 75
Fort Galatea, Urewera NZ 128, 131
Fort Kearney, Nebraska USA 72, 76
Fort Laramie, Wyoming USA 72, 73, 74, 76
Fowler, Guy (NZ) 209, 211, 215
Franciscan Order 34
Fraser, Major (NZ) 127
Fredericton, New Brunswick, Canada 51

Galena Summit, Idaho USA 109
Gannett, Idaho USA 86, 106–108
Gate Pa, Tauranga NZ 133, 170
Gee, Tommy (Owhakatoro NZ) 202, 205
George, John & Eleanor (Moor) 11
George Mason Company, Birmingham 270, 277
Ghana 34
Gibbons, Robert & family (Auckland NZ) 188
Gibson, Roland (Isles of Scilly) 196
Gilbert Ash Company (M1 Motorway) 241
Gillespie, Capt. John (US Overland Trail) 76
Gillett, Capt. C.M. (John Bright) 68
Gisborne (Turanganui) NZ 161, 172, 183, 200

Glenafton, Huntly NZ 124
Glossop 33, 34
Gloucester 252
Gloucester, Bishop of 254
Goff family (West Jordan USA) 87, 89
Goff, Hyrum (West Jordan USA) 87
Goff, Isaac Jnr. (West Jordan USA) 75, 87
Gorton, Manchester 34
Grafton, 19, 265
Greathouse, Marvin Robert (Salt Lake USA) 100
Great Plains, USA 67–69, 73
Green River, Wyoming USA 75
Greet, Winchcombe 5–7
Grensted, Professor L.W. (Oxford) 256
Grosvenor Place, London 35

Hailey, Idaho USA 106, 108, 109
Haines, Robert (Little Comberton) 10
Halford 31, 50
Halifax, Nova Scotia, Canada 49
Hamilton, NZ 127, 201, 213
Harvey, George (Winchcombe) 42
Harvington 27, 40
Harvington Mill 25–27, 31, 32, 36, 39, 41, 43–45, 113, 231, 262–265
Hatapere, Opouriao NZ 170–173
Hatry, Clarence (London) 253
'Hau Hau' 125–127
Hawthorne, Salt Lake City USA 94, 101
Heapham 159
Henare Taratoa (Gate Pa NZ) 133
Hertford, Marquis of 21, 36, 232, 235
Hewa, Jack (Whakatane NZ) 208
Hieatt, Fred (Waitakere NZ) 180
Hieatt, Tom (Quinton) 245
Hieatt, William (Swanson NZ) 154, 155
Hieatt, William Hooper (Souldern) 155
Hill, Fladbury 10, 11, 13–16, 58
Hill & Moor 10, 13, 56, 57
Hillary, Edmund (NZ) 181
Hillsborough Cemetery, Auckland NZ 179
Hlaing River, Burma 47
Hobart General Hospital, Tasmania 61
Hobart Penitentiary, Tasmania, 61
Hoddinot, Miss (Lower Lemimgton) 272
Hong Kong 272
Hook, John 44
Hovis Mills, Northampton 241
Howard family (Glossop) 34
Hudson, David 242
Hunt, Emily 'Peggy' (Alcester) 44, 231
Hunt, Ernest 'Josh' (Alcester) 44
Hunt, George (Oversley) 245
Hunt, Helen Diana (Alcester) 44
Hunt, William (Alcester) 44
Huntress Creek, Opotiki NZ 131

Icknield House, Bidford 18, 19
Idaho USA 85, 96, 106, 112
Idlicote 264
Ilmington 28, 29
Independence Rock, Wyoming USA 75

India 10, 47, 132, 272
Ingley, Percy 211
Inkberrow 32, 63
Insein, Burma 48
Intercolonial Railway, Canada 49
Irrawaddy River, Burma 47, 48
Isbourne River, Winchcombe 29, 30, 32, 264
Italy 34, 181, 211, 214, 277

Jackson, Samuel (Bevington) 24, 25
Jackson, Capt. William (Forest Rangers) NZ 120
Japan 215
Jehovah's Witnesses 275
Jenkins, Alfred (Isles of Scilly) 198
Jenson, Charles (West Jordan USA) 82
Jewish refugees 191, 192, 260
John Bright SS 68, 75
Jones, Sydney (London) 243
Jordan River, Salt Lake City USA 78, 80
Jordan Street, Glossop. 34

Kansas, USA 68
Kansas City, USA 96
Katikati, NZ 209
Kauri Park, Waitakere NZ 181, 185
Kauri Timber Company NZ 181
Kelly, W. (Opotiki NZ) 147
Kentucky, USA 104
Kereopa Te Rau, Chief (NZ) 125
Keri Keri, NZ 118, 119, 120
Kerr, Cecily 174
Kingley Farm, Arrow 244–248
King Street, Opotiki NZ 145
King Street home, Whakatane NZ 199, 201, 205–207, 215, 218
Kirkee, India 132
Knight, George (Arrow Mill) 39
Knights, Ellen (NZ) 131–133
Knights, Emma (NZ) 132, 133
Knights family (NZ) 131–134
Knights, Henry (1st Waikato Regt. NZ) 131–133, 147, 151
Knights, Mary Ann (NZ) 132, 151
Knipe, Rev.J.D. (Cleeve Prior) 270
Korean War 109

Lady Margaret Hall, Oxford 198
Lake Lugano, Switzerland 186
Lake Utah, USA 78
Lake Waiakaremona, NZ 128
Lamont, John Alexander Campbell (NZ) 148, 157, 158
Langates Lodge, Moreton–in–Marsh 251
Langley Farm, Winchcombe 41, 42, 264
Laramie River, Wyoming USA 72
Larkins prison ship 61
Lark Stoke, Ilmington 28, 29
Latter Day Saints (see Mormons)
Laycock, Dick (Glossop) 34
Leamington Priors/Leaminton 35
Leamington Spa 241
Leeston, NZ 49
Lewin, Charles Hugh (London) 35

Lichfield, UK 133
Lilya, Christian (Idaho USA) 84–87, 107
Lilya family 86, 107, 112
Lilya, Ingrid (Idaho USA) 84–86, 96, 107, 112
Lincoln, Abraham 69
Little Bighorn River, South Dakota USA 74
Little Comberton 5, 7, 9, 10, 13, 14, 16
Little River, NZ 49
Little Wood River, Idaho USA 86, 107
Liverpool 68, 75
Lloyds Bank 251–253, 255, 272
Locke family 68, 69, 74
Locke, Elizabeth 'Eliza', née Payne 68, 80
Locke, Joseph (Arrow & USA) 68, 75, 87
London University 44, 198
Long Buckby 240, 241
Longdon Farm, Ilmington 29, 31, 45
Long Marston 19, 56, 57, 247
Louisiana Purchase 68
Lower Lemington 272
Lower Farm, Preston–on–Stour 235
Lower Hutt, Wellington NZ 217
Lower Slaughter 252
Lucy's Mill, Stratford–upon–Avon 240

Maas, Paul (Germany & Oxford) 192
Mackenzie, Dr. (Cleeve Prior) 274
Mack trucks 104
Malaya 247, 272
Malmohus, Sweden 82
Malmstrom family 99
Malta 257
Mangawai, NZ 115, 116
Mangere, NZ 118
Manitoba, Canada 51
Maori farmworkers 217
Maori people 114, 116, 119, 126, 128, 147, 174
Maori War 114, 115, 118, 120, 122, 125, 126, 132, 139, 147, 170, 173
Maraetara Stream, Opotiki NZ 147, 148
Marble Arch, London 258
Marfurlong Farm, Pudlicote 229
Marlborough College, Blenheim NZ 210
Marlcliff 56–58, 61.62
Marlow 260
Maro (Opotiki NZ) 147
Marshall family (Harvington) 25
Marshall family (Whatcote) 16, 25
Marston 19
Martin's Farm, Drury NZ 120
Masefield, John (Oxford) 191
Mason, William (Derbyshire) 124
Massasoit, (USA) 79
Massey College & University, NZ 213
Matakohi, NZ 116
Matatua War Canoe 170, 171
Matilda Wattenbach 39, 113, 114, 124
McAllister, Mrs. (Whakatane NZ) 151
McCoogan, Barney (Owhakatoro NZ) 205
McCracken, Frederick J.H. (NZ) 210
McDonnell, Colonel (NZ) 127
McGarvey, Daniel (Whakatane NZ) 152, 170, 171, 173

McGarvey, Mrs. Daniel (Whakatane NZ) 151–153,
McGarvey's Store, (Whakatane NZ) 149
McGraw, Capt. James (John Bright) 75
Meikle, Mrs. (Waitakere NZ) 168
Meikle, Ned (Waitakere NZ) 168
Melbourne, Australia 115, 116, 121, 122, 132
Merton College, Oxford 186, 187, 198
Methodists 241
Mickleton 29
Middle Carn, St.Mary's, Isles of Scilly 195, 196
Midvale, Salt Lake City USA 99 (see also West Jordan)
Midway Island, USA 104
Minchinhampton 3, 5
Ministry of Food, London 190
Ministry of Pensions, London 190
Missippi River, USA 68, 69
Missouri River, USA 67, 68, 71, 74–76
Molesworth, Hannah (Arrow Mill) 39
Moncton, New Brunswick, Canada 49–51, 53
Monmouth, South Wales 267, 272
Moor, Fladbury 10, 11, 13, 14, 16
Moor Hall Farm, Wixford 245, 248, 249
Moral Re-Armament (MRA) 258,
Mordaunt family (Walton) 27
Moreton–in–Marsh 53, 239, 246, 251–253, 255, 257, 272
Mormons (Latter Day Saints) 63, 65–69, 77, 78, 80, 82–87, 93, 105
Mormon Temple, Salt Lake City USA 94, 95
Mormon Trail 71, 72, 75
Morris Motors, Birmingham 277
Mosley, Oswald 256
Moule, Colonel (Hamilton NZ) 127
Moulton, Carl Ernest (Salt Lake City USA) 101, 102, 104
Mounted Constabulary (Police) 148, 163
Mount Edgecumbe, NZ 125
Mount Pleasant Farm, Walton 27, 28, 36
Mount Tarawera, NZ 149, 162
Mulgan, John (NZ & Oxford) 192
Murray, Professor Gilbert (Oxford) 191, 192
Murray, Utah USA 102

Napier earthquake, NZ 209
Napier, Professor A.S. (Oxford) 186, 188–190
Napoleonic Wars 13, 36
Nebraska, USA 68, 71, 72, 78
Nelson, NZ 209
New Brunswick, Canada 49, 50, 53, 55
New Brunswick University, Canada 51
New, Charles Morris Marshall (Winchcombe) 41
New family (Winchcombe) 41, 42
New College, Oxford 196
New College School, Oxford 53
New Haven, Connecticut USA 51, 52
Newport, James Wakeman 14
New South Wales, Australia 49
Newton–le–Willows 46, 47
New York, USA 68, 69, 75
New Zealand 39, 40, 49, 67, 113, 114, 132, 161, 190, 191, 199, 204, 213, 223, 256

New Zealand Loan & Mercantile Company 201, 205, 206, 210, 211, 215, 218, 220, 223, 277
Ngatapa, NZ 127
Ngta–Te–Rangi tribe, NZ 170
Niagara Falls, USA 93
Nicholson, Dr.Clark (Moreton–in–Marsh) 251, 255
Nigeria 34, 259
Nightingale Lane, Cleeve Prior 271
Nixon, Col.M. (Colonial Defence Force NZ) 118–120, 122, 148
'Nixon's Cavalry' (NZ) 118–120, 125
Norrington, A.L.P. (Oxford) 192
North Eastern Railway, Peterborough 275
North Littleton 18
North Platte River, Wyoming USA 72
Nottingham 113
Nova Scotia, Canada 51

Oakey, John (Winchcombe) 29
Ogden River, Utah USA 93
Ohiwa, NZ 125–127, 159
Ohope, NZ 161, 200, 217, 223
Old, Charlie, (Opouriao NZ) 175
Olds, Random Ellis 93
Old Town, Isles of Scilly 196
Omaha Indians, USA 69, 78
Omaha, Nebraska USA 75, 76
Onehunga, NZ 132, 133
Ontario, Canada 51, 52, 55
Opotiki, NZ 125, 127, 128, 131, 133, 134, 143, 145, 147–149, 151, 152, 159, 161
Opotiki Garrison, NZ 128
Opotiki School, NZ 145, 147, 151
Opouriao farm, NZ 160, 163, 172–174, 199,
Opouriao School, Taneatua NZ 162
Opouriao Valley, NZ 159–162, 170, 171, 176, 199
Oquirrh Mountains, Utah USA 78, 81, 83, 99, 105
Orakau, Battle of, NZ 122
Oregon Short Line, Idaho USA 108
Oregon Trail, USA 73–75, 85, 86
Oriel College, Oxford 31, 45
Oruawharo, NZ 116, 122
Osler, Sir William (Oxford) 188
Otahuhu, NZ 118
Ottawa River, Canada 52
Oversley Green Farm 245
Oversley Mill, Alcester 39, 228, 231, 234, 265
Owhakatoro Farm, Taneatua NZ 172–174, 176, 199, 201, 202, 204, 206, 211, 215, 218
Oxford 45, 50, 52, 53, 169, 186, 188, 189
Oxford Group (see also Moral Re-Armament) 256–258
Oxford University 45, 186, 188, 190, 196, 199, 254, 256–258
Oxford University, Dept. of Forestry 52
Oxford University Press 189, 192, 193, 198
Oxspring 32, 34

Padua, Italy 214
'Pae Marire' 125
Paewiwi, Ohiwa NZ 147
Palmerston North, NZ 215

Papakura, NZ 118, 119, 121, 122
Paparoa, NZ 116
Par, Cornwall 232, 233
Parfit, Eric 258
Park Cottage, Arrow 44, 250
Parkinson, Arthur & family (Opotiki NZ) 149, 152
Parson's Hill, Waitakere NZ 139
Partridge, Clare (Arrow Mill) 39
Peacock House, Cleeve Prior 266, 267, 271
Pebworth 19, 56
Pekatahi, NZ 175
Penistone 32, 33
Pepper, Walter (Peterborough) 275
Perrott family (Craycombe, Fladbury) 10, 14
Perrott, George W. (Craycombe, Fladbury) 10
Petawawa Forest, Ontario, Canada 52
Peterborough 267, 275
Phillips, Hubert (Oxford & London) 186
Pimlico, London 35
Pizzini, Equilio 'Jo' (Arrow Farm NZ) 141
Platte River, Nebraska USA 71, 72, 74–76
Pohaturoa Rock, Whakatane NZ 170
Pokeno, NZ 120, 183, 185
Pokoroko, Thames NZ 120
Pomona, Waitakere NZ 139, 156
Poor Rate Tax 14, 58
Porch House, Bockley 252
Po River, Italy 214
Port Albert, NZ 116
Port Jackson, NZ 211
Postlip Lower Mill, Winchcombe 29, 30, 36, 263
Potter, Frederick Scarlett (Ilmington) 29, 31
Potter, William & Elizabeth (Ilmington) 28, 31, 45, 50
Poulson family (Sandy, Utah USA) 82, 83
Poverty Bay, NZ 127
Prebble, Kenneth (Oxford & NZ) 256
President Roosevelt's WPA program 109
Preston–on–Stour 236, 240
Primrose Hill, Arrow 21, 228, 243, 244
Prince Edward Island, Canada 49
Priory, Alcester 44, 139, 169, 231, 265
Prome, Burma 47–49
Pudlicote Mill, Ebrington 229
Puihi Ruawahine, Princess (NZ) 170
Pukekohe, NZ 118, 120, 211
Pukematakoe Hill, Waitakere NZ 141
Pumpkin Center School, Idaho USA 108
Pye, Captain (Colonial Defence Force NZ) 120

Quebec Province, Canada 51
Queen Mary College, London 198
Queen's Mine, Bellevue, Idaho USA 109
Queen's Redoubt, Pokeno NZ 120
Quick, Graham (Waikato NZ) 213

Radbrook, Preston–on–Stour 235–240, 242
Radcliffe Infirmary, Oxford 53, 260
Radclive 46, 47
Radway 27, 32, 35
Raft River, Idaho USA 85
Rangiaowhia, Waikato NZ 122

Rangitaiki River, NZ 128
Rangoon, Burma 47, 48
Rattigan, Clive 44
Rattigan, Emily 'Peggy' née Hunt 44
Rattigan, Terence 44
Rawiri Puhirake, Chief (NZ) 133
Reading, UK 44
Reading University 198
Red Cloud, Chief (Sioux Indians USA) 73, 74
Redhill, Waitakere NZ 168
Red Horse, Vale of 3, 27
Re–Nu Repairs, Peterborough 275
Reunion of Sisam Family, NZ 223–225
Rhodes Scholarships 168, 186, 189, 213
Righton, E.G. (Evesham) 245
'Ringatu' 127
Rivat House, Halford 31
Riverton, Utah USA 104
Rock Meeting House, W.Jordan, Utah USA 88, 89
Rocky Mountains, USA 67, 68, 72–75 77
Rogerstone Railway Workshops, Newport 272
Rolling, Henry (Oxspring) 32
Rotorua, NZ 161, 162, 200
Rouse family (Cold Comfort Farm, Arrow) 232, 233, 238
Rouse, Tom (Cold Comfort Farm, Arrow) 232, 245
Ruakituri River, NZ 127
Ruatoki, NZ 174, 217
Rushton, J.R. (Opotiki NZ) 147
Russell, near Greenup, Kantucky USA 104
Rutherford, James (Mangere NZ) 118

Salt Lake City, Utah USA 67, 75, 78, 82, 85, 87, 90, 91, 93, 94, 112
Salt Lake City State Penitentiary 84
Salt Lake Tribune 85
Salt Lake Valley, Utah USA 68, 69, 75, 76, 78, 80, 81, 105
Salvation Army 44
Sambourne 63, 246, 249
Sandford Mill, Cheltenham 264
Sandy, Utah USA 83
Sansun (Sisam?), George (Tasmania) 61
San Vito Chietimo, Italy 181
Sawtooth Mountains, Idaho USA 86, 96, 106, 109
Scala Cinema, Oxford 257
Scannel, Major (Armed Constabulary, Taupo) 148
Scilly, Isles of 195, 196, 198
Scott's Bluff, Wyoming USA 72
Sedgeberrow 32, 36
Selby's Farm, Pokeno NZ 120
Selwyn, Bishop, NZ 120, 133
Shadbolt, Mr.& Mrs. (Bourton–on–the–Hill) 253
Shakespeare, William 19, 251, 256
Shayler, Thomas (Arrow) 24, 25
Sheen Hill, South Littleton 1, 18
Sheenhill Farm, South Littleton 18, 25, 57
Shentall, Sir Ernest (Chesterfield) 245
Shepherd, Rev.B.H. (Worcester) 270
Sherris, Mrs.Arthur (Isles of Scilly) 198
Shipston–on–Stour 28, 31, 45, 46
Shoshone, Idaho USA 109

Index

Shrewsbury 250, 251
Shwe Dagon Pagoda, Rangoon, Burma 48
Silver Creek, Idaho USA 86, 87, 107
Singapore, 247
Sioux Indians, USA 68, 72–74, 76
'Sisam & Sons' 172, 174, 199, 205, 220, 221, 223
'Sisam Country' 3, 8
'Sisam Electrical', Salt Lake City, USA 101, 102, 104, 105
Sisam Place, Whakatane NZ 207
Sisam's Cottage, Cleeve Prior 271,
Sisam's Crossing, Taneatua NZ 175
Sisam's (Siseham's) Meadow, Adderbury 3, 4
Sisam Valley, NZ 219
Slough 269, 270
Smith, Harry, (Preston–on–Stour) 239, 242
Smith, Harvey (Preston–on–Stour) 235, 236, 238, 239
Smithin, Joseph (Cleeve Prior) 2712, 272
Snake River, Idaho USA 86
Snowshill 249
Souldern 155
Soutar, Rev.A.C. (Opotiki NZ) 145
South Africa 267
South Arrow Farm 228, 229, 231, 250
South Littleton 16, 18, 21
South Pass, Wyoming USA 75
South Road (from Auckland) 118, 120
Speakers' Corner, Marble Arch, London 258, 259
Spring Hill, Nova Scotia, Canada 49
Squire, Thomas (1st. Waikato Regt. NZ) 133
Stanford, Leland (San Francisco USA) 77
Starr's Crossing, Idaho USA 86
State Road homestead (see State Street)
State Street homestead, Salt Lake USA 82, 83, 88, 89, 91, 97, 99
Stewart, Sir Alan (NZ) 213
St.Clement's Church, Worcester 56
St.George's Church, Moncton, NB Canada 49, 51
St.Hilda's College, Oxford 198
St.Joseph, Missouri USA 68, 69
St.Luke's Church, Halifax, NS Canada 49
St.Mark's Church, Prome, Burma 48
St.Martin's Church, Birmingham 16
St.Mary's Church, Warwick 62
St.Paul's Church, Camden Square, London 47
St.Peter's Hall (College), Oxford 256
St.Philip's Church, East Rangoon, Burma 48
St.Stephen's Church, Opotiki NZ 125, 126, 134
Stocker Creek, Idaho USA 107
Stoneman, Rev. Mr. (Longborough) 231
Stour River 45
Stow–on–the–Wold 252
Stratford–upon–Avon 25, 27, 237, 240, 251
Stratford–upon–Avon Grammar School 237, 255
Streeter, Professor B.H. (Oxford) 256
Stretton–on–Fosse 28
Studley Agricultural College 245
Sublette's Cutoff, Wyoming USA 75
Suffolk, HMS 247
Summerside, Prince Edward Island, Canada 49
Sun Valley, Idaho USA 107

Suva Cathedral, Fiji 173, 175
Swain, William 75
Swanson, NZ 156, 165, 167, 168, 183
Sweden 139, 141
Sweet's Candy Company, W.Jordan USA 100
Sweetwater River, Wyoming USA 75
Swindly, Major (Whakatane NZ) 152
Swindly, Mrs. (Whakatane NZ) 151, 152
Switzerland 186, 189
Symmans, George (Whakatane NZ) 205, 206, 209
Syresham 2, 3, 47

Taneatua, NZ 171, 174, 175, 202, 204, 210, 213
Taneatua School, NZ 174, 202, 215
Taplow 260
Taranaki, NZ 118
Tasman Forestry Limited, NZ 223
Tasman Maid 114
Taupaki, NZ 139,
Taupo, NZ 148
Tauranga, NZ 127, 131, 133, 147, 170, 206
Tavistock 34
Taylor, Reg (Cleeve Prior) 274
Te Kooti (NZ) 127, 128, 130, 131, 147–149, 154, 161
Tempsky, Capt. Gustavus (Forest Rangers NZ) 120
Te Papa Camp, Tauranga NZ 133
Thames Barrage, London 241
Thames Ditton 213
Thames, NZ 124, 125, 135, 165, 200, 213
Thames Tunnel peepshow 132
Tharrawaddy, Burma 48
Throckmorton family 36, 228, 229
Thunder Mountain, Idaho USA 106
Tidmington 45
Timms, William John Avery 68, 75
Tinker's Close, Broom 57
Tokomaru, NZ 202
Tokyo Olympics 220
Tolkien, J.R.R. 189, 191, 198
Toroa, Chief of the Matatua 170
Toronto, Bishop of, (Canada) 53
Toronto, Canada 53, 55
Toronto University, Canada 53, 55
Trafalgar, Battle of 135
Tripp, Albert Walter (Utah USA) 112
Tripp, Leo (Utah USA) 99
Triumph Silver Mine, Bellevue, Idaho USA 109
Tryphena, near Auckland NZ 148
Tuck, Mr. (Mangere NZ) 118
Tuhoe tribe (NZ) 127, 159, 173, 208
Turanganui (later Gisborne) NZ 127

Unicorn Inn, Warwick 62, 63
Union Bank of Australia 204, 211
Union Pacific Railroad, USA 75, 77, 108, 109
United States Smelting Company, W.Jordan 94, 95
Upton, Mr. (Waitakere NZ) 166
Urewera Forest, Whakatane NZ 127, 128, 130, 131, 173, 217
USA (see also America) 249
US Cavalry 72–74

Utah, USA 67, 68, 79, 80
Utah River, USA 78
Utah University, USA 102, 104
Ute Indians, USA 80

Van Dieman's Land, Tasmania, Australia 61
Venice, Italy 214
Vinaver, Professor Eugene 194, 198
Volkener, Rev.Carl (Opotiki NZ) 125, 126
Von Sturmer, Edward (Auckland NZ) 159, 163
Von Sturmer, Maude and May (NZ) 163, 178

Wagstaff family (Hill) 14
Wagstaff, Henry (Hill) 14, 16
Waikato Regiment, 1st (NZ) 125, 126, 131, 133
Waikato River and region, NZ 118–120, 122, 125, 131, 213
Waikumete, Auckland NZ 141
Waimana East, NZ 133, 147
Waimana River, NZ 125, 131, 133, 171
Waioeka Gorge, Urewera Forest, NZ 161
Waiotahi, NZ 131
Wairoa, NZ 118
Waitakere area, NZ 124, 125, 127, 137, 139
Waitakere East, NZ 139
Waitakere Ranges NZ 124, 136, 140, 183
Waitakere River NZ 124, 136, 138, 170, 181
Waitakere Township, NZ 181, 183
Waitangi, Treaty of, NZ 114
Waitemata District Council, NZ 139
Wakara, Ute Chief, Utah USA 80
Walmsley, Major (NZ) 119, 120
Walton, near Wellesbourne 27, 32
Wandermere Park, Salt Lake City USA 91
Warm Springs, Wyoming USA 74
Warwick 61–63
Wasatch Range, Utah USA 67, 78, 105
Weil, Professor Arnold (Christchurch NZ) 181
Welford–on–Avon 17, 18, 57
Wellington, NZ 149, 215, 217, 218, 223
Wentworth, NSW Australia 49
West African Examinations Council 34
West Jordan Milling Company, USA 88
West Jordan, Salt Lake City USA 78, 80, 82, 84, 87, 88, 91, 94, 105
West, Mrs.(Alscot Park, Preston–on–Stour) 240
Weston–super–Mare 31
Whakatane, NZ 125–128, 131, 149–152, 154, 157, 159, 161, 163, 170, 171, 173, 199, 201, 202, 204–207, 209, 215, 217

Whakatane Cemetery, NZ 157, 158
Whakatane Freezing Works, NZ 176, 200
Whakatane High School, NZ 209, 210, 213
Whakatane Hospital, NZ 213
Whakatane River, NZ 130, 170–172, 174, 199, 204, 213
Whakatane saleyards, NZ 205
Whakatane School, NZ 161, 170, 200, 201
Whakatohea pa, NZ 127, 147
Whatcote 16, 25
White, Bennett (NZ) 126, 131
White, David (Opotiki NZ) 147
Whitelock, Professor Dorothy (Cambridge) 198
Whitmore, Colonel (NZ) 127, 128, 131
Whitmore–Jones, Mrs.(Chastleton) 255
Whyte, R.O. (Oxford) 52, 53
Wickham, Mary Ann 131, 132
Wilkins, Mrs. (Whakatane NZ) 151
Will, F. (Auckland NZ) 143, 144
William IV, King 59
Willicote 240
Wills, Rev.Mr. (Opotiki NZ) 149, 151
Winchcombe 3, 5, 7, 27, 29, 31, 41, 43, 226, 262–264
Winchcombe Mill 263, 264
Winchester College 196
Wincott, George 58–60
Winnett family (Inkberrow) 32
Wi Popata (NZ) 126
Wixford 19, 41, 245, 246
Woodford, Edward 132, 133, 145, 147, 152, 159
Woodford, Emma 145, 159
Woodford family (Opotiki NZ) 147, 161, 162
Worcester 56, 59, 63
Worcester Cathedral 45
Worcester County Assizes 59–61
Worcester Gaol 59, 60
Woodside Road, Auckland NZ 163, 178, 200, 209, 213
World War I 99, 100, 189, 190, 234, 252, 271
World War II 104, 191, 192, 194, 196, 211, 213, 238, 239, 246, 247, 255, 258, 272, 277
Wounded Knee, South Dakota USA 74
Wright, E.W. (Alcester) 41, 137
Wyatt, Thomas (Opotiki NZ) 151

Yale University, USA 51
"Yatsden", Boars Hill, Oxford 190–192, 196
Yeats, William Butler 192
Young, Brigham (USA) 67, 69, 75, 78, 80